BASEBALL
PLAY
AMERICA

Don Weiskopf

Play America Press
El Dorado Hills, California

Library of Congress Cataloging in Publication Data

Weiskopf, Don, 1928-
  Baseball Play America

1st ed.

ISBN 0-9674773-0-1

Published by Play America Press, a Subsidiary of Weiskopf Enterprises, P.O. Box 4182, El Dorado Hills, CA 95762

Printed by Publishers Press, P.O. Box 27408, Salt Lake City, UT 84127

Cover provided by TURFACE®Pro League, Profile Products, Buffalo Grove, Illinois. Game Scene at Coors Field, Denver, 1998 Major League All-Star Game.

Printed in the United States of America

To my loving wife, Annegrete,
without her much needed assistance
and strong support, this book would
never have been written

Contents

Chapter 1   Baseball Is Back! - - Or Is It?   2

Chapter 2   Still The National Pastime!   29

Chapter 3   A Plan For Baseball   61

Chapter 4   Major Leagues   189

Chapter 5   Minor Leagues   230

Chapter 6   USA Baseball/International   262

Chapter 7   Colleges/Universities   284

Chapter 8   Non-Pro/Semi-Pro/Adult   327

Chapter 9   High Schools   364

Chapter 10   Youth Baseball   396

Introduction

This book is about Baseball Play in America. When I retired from teaching I asked myself, "What did I want to do most of all?" Rather than teach another five years, I wanted to help the game of baseball, which has been so good to me since my days as a young pitcher in northern Illinois. Not happy with the direction baseball was moving, I wanted to make the game better, so I decided to do something about it.

My initial goal was to provide a status report on the overall quality of play and the fundamental abuses at the major league level, such as poor cutoff throws, failed attempts to sacrifice, mindless baserunning, and excessive one-handed fielding. However, as I delved deeper into my studies, it became quite apparent that many of baseball's problems and issues off the diamond were having a strong impact not only on how the game was played, but they had a direct bearing on the popularity and image of the game. The traditions and the continuity of baseball were being threatened, TV ratings were declining, over half of the major league clubs were losing money. Critics were taking shots at the game, yet no one was providing realistic solutions.

At this point, I saw the need to develop a plan for baseball, to upgrade the quality of play and help restore the greatness of the game. I felt strongly there was a need for a book that would provide solutions to these problems, realistic approaches to controversial issues, with the primary goal to revitalize the game and help it get back on track. What process did I take in forming conclusions and recommending solutions to the many problems and needs of baseball? Essentially, I followed the same basic principles and approach that I took in my post-graduate studies while preparing master's theses and doctoral dissertations: Review related literature, formulate conclusions, and make recommendations.

Six years ago, I wasn't sure what baseball should do relative to its problems and needs. I lacked in-depth knowledge, a large number of viewpoints of those involved in the game. Today, following an exhausting amount of study and research, the overall picture has become much clearer as to baseball's needs and how to go about solving its problems, largely because we have gathered an extensive amount of data.

Without a doubt, the most important chapter in Baseball Play America is "A Plan for Baseball", which includes an in-depth description of problems, issues, and needs on all levels of organized baseball. Conclusions and summations were then formulated from the opinions of over 2,000 respondents, and from this data, recommendations were made.

Having developed "A Plan for Baseball" (Chapter 3), including several I have become very committed to, there is an urgent need to implement the recommendations. As to how this can best be achieved, Annegrete and I will devote much of our work time on the Internet, operating our new Web Site she has designed. Baseball Play America is an organization established to promote and protect the best interests of baseball and upgrade the quality of play. Our mission is to offer critique and advice relative to the game's problems and needs and support worthwhile concepts and programs. Essentially, we will be assuming an advocacy role to assist organized baseball on all levels. I urge you to read pages 455-456 for more details on the movement and to visit our Web Site: www.baseballplayamerica.com.

Acknowledgments

Numerous people have contributed to the making of Baseball Play America whom I wish to acknowledge and express my thanks to.

First and foremost is my wife, Annegrete, for giving me the freedom to carry out this long and often times exhausting project. Even more significant to the book's overall look, she and I formed an effective production team, with me doing the writing and her excellent computer skills. Throughout the six years I spent working on the book, Annegrete gave me continual inspirational support and feedback, particularly the most difficult issues and areas of concern I had to deal with. During the late stages of production when confronting both a deadline and fatigue, she was the driving force and motivation, which meant so much to me.

I would like to extend my sincere thanks and appreciation to my family, for their understanding and having had to accept the sacrifices as a result of my strong commitment to achieve a goal. Daughter Christine contributed by typing several chapters, and daughter Lisa flew down from Washington to help out.

This book could not have been done without the input and knowledge of the people involved in organized baseball, coaches and administrators on all levels and the writers, columnists and broadcasters who cover the game, representing daily newspapers, periodicals, and the television-radio industry. Over 2,000 of the most respected and authoritative coaches and officials, from Major League Baseball on down to the youth leagues, responded by filling out my detailed questionnaires and provided invaluable commentary and critique.

Baseball Play America is my first attempt at self-publishing a book. The previous 13 books I have authored were published by major publishing companies. Therefore, it was a new ball game for this writer, and Annegrete and I are indebted to the self-publishing tips and advice found in the books authored by Avery Cardoza, Dan Poynter, Tom and Marilyn Ross, in particular.

As for being able to keep the project moving for six years, I should acknowledge the strong benefits, which helped prevent boredom and enabled me to withstand long periods at my writing desk. My workouts three times a week at 24-Hour Fitness were invaluable to me physically and mentally. And what would I have done without the beautiful music of such great composers as Mozart, Chopin and Beethoven! Their enduring classics kept words and thoughts flowing through my mind as I wrote.

Finally, I want to thank Lyle Mumford, John Newman, John Gallacher and staff at Publishers Press in Salt Lake City for the professional advice they gave us in preparing the files and materials for printing.

Don Weiskopf
El Dorado Hills, California

A Season for the Ages

Pastime catches on again

Has the thrill returned for baseball fans?

Are home runs getting ho-hum?

The Sporting News

What a season!

Euphoria of 1998 obscures ongoing revenue problems

The poor get poorer and the rich win pennants!

Economics of Game must change

Salaries still skyrocketing

Disparity in team payrolls alarming

1 Baseball Is Back!
- - Or is it?

The popularity of Major League Baseball has made an impressive comeback, and the impact has been felt at the lower levels of play. Despite the lack of competitive balance, out-of-control spending and huge payroll disparity, the 1998 season was one of the most exciting and dramatic in recent decades.

"Some called 1998 a dream season, while others called it a season of discovery," said Joe Buck, in his post-season summary following the Yankees' championship year. "Many fans who had left the game came back. A whole new generation may have been introduced to the game of baseball in 1998. Fans will be talking for years about the great home run race."

No one would have predicted Mark McGwire's unbelievable total of 70 home runs, breaking the revered single-season record held by Roger Maris. Big Mac and Sammy Sosa took their race into the final weekend, with Sosa finishing at 65 homers. Then, in 1999, the two sluggers amazed the baseball world once again. The game, indeed, is basking in the glory of a remarkable and unique regular season. "The summer of 1998 lifted people's emotions a little higher than before," wrote Bruce Jenkins in the San Francisco Chronicle. "For the first time since before the strike, baseball has got that old Hot Stove League feel, carrying the spirit right through winter and anxiously awaiting the next meaningful pitch."

For the first time in history, four players hit 50 or more home runs in 1998, with Albert Belle at 49. Certainly, no one would have predicted the total of 70 by McGwire, including many 500-foot shots. Evidence that baseball is enjoying renewed popularity came in a USA TODAY/CNN/Gallup Poll in mid-September in which 63% of the respondents identified themselves as a fan or somewhat of a fan. The turnaround started in 1995 with Cal Ripken's extraordinary record for consecutive games played, the beginning of inter-league play in 1997, and many brilliant individual and team performances the past two years.

Baseball attendance, sparked by the home run races in 1998 and 1999, has drawn closer to its average before the 1994-95 strike. In 1999, major league teams drew an average of 45,981 fans their 30 opening days. Baseball also enjoyed record television ratings in the 199 season. Fox's Saturday Game of the Week rose 15% over 1997, and ESPN p ted record ratings with its baseball coverage in September. But in the 1998 World Series, the Yankees' four-game sweep of the San Diego Padres produced the worst Series ratings in history.

Then, What's Wrong in Baseball?

From a popularity and interest standpoint, baseball appears to have recovered from the damaging strike of 1994. The facts and evidence, however, are very clear that the problems and needs of Major League Baseball are too many and much too disturbing to ignore. There is strong concern among owners and those in the Commissioner's office about the direction of the game's economy. The home run derby, itself, continues to undermine the best interests of the game. "Basically, the name of the game now is home runs," said Sammy Sosa. "All the people come to the park to see us hit them." If Sammy is correct, the game is really in trouble.

Economic Woes Have Hurt the Game   The economic stability of Major League Baseball has been shaken by a collective bargaining system, which has caused operating costs and ticket prices to soar. Steadily rising salaries cast a dark shadow on the game's economic health. Initiated by free agency and the arbitration process, the high salaries can be attributed to the greed of players and their agents, and owners who have been foolish enough over the years to pay such huge salaries and bonuses. In doing so, the game's salary structure has been thrown into disarray, causing widespread resentment and disgust among fans.

"While the game enjoyed a renaissance season in 1998, the euphoria masked structural problems in baseball's unbalanced economy," wrote Hal Bodley and Erik Brady. "The gap between the richest and poorest teams is widening at an astonishing clip. Ten years ago, the highest payroll in baseball was three times larger than the lowest, now it is nine times larger."

Baseball's average salary in 1999 jumped to $1,724,310, while the total team payroll for the 30 teams increased to an astonishing $1,420,831,174. Even more shocking is that MLB clubs have committed $934 million to just 275 players for 1999. According to USA TODAY's Survey of Salaries, clubs have guaranteed billions of dollars to 493 players --a staggering $2,186,417,091 through 2003. The Yankees' No. 1 payroll of $85,034,692 is nearly $70 million greater than Montreal's $16,175,000 -- lowest in the majors.

Baseball fans are paying the price of higher salaries. Many teams have raised ticket prices in order to maintain high payrolls. The Boston Red Sox are still the most expensive team to see, raising its tickets 16.6 percent to an average of $24.05. Teams are adding premium seats selling from $100 to $200 per game. World Series prices have doubled to $150. "It's impacting the affordability of baseball to the fans," said San Diego president Larry Lucchino. "It's impacting families and the competitive balance that's at the heart of baseball."

Fans Not Part of Economic Equation

Must baseball fans continue to accept the status quo of skyrocketing player salaries? The owners feel they deserve more income because they assume most of the risk, and the players believe they should have more and more because they put fans in the seats. These selfish attitudes have prevented owners and players from recognizing who truly deserves to participate in the profit-sharing: the FANS. There will come a time when fans will decide it's not worth buying overpriced tickets and excessive costs at big league ball parks to see marginally talented players make millions of dollars.

Fans have never been given any consideration in the bargaining talks between ownership and the Players Association. Higher and higher salaries and payrolls serve only the players' best interests. Likewise, the billion-dollar TV-rights revenue benefit only the players and the owners. These and other reasons is why increasing numbers of sports fans have grown tired of getting the cold shoulders of owners and players. Frustrated fans across the country who want their collective voice heard are uniting in groups, with a central theme: "We do not have to take this anymore."

The time will come when owners and players will eventually stop their selfishness and acknowledge the fact that the fans have put them in the position

Offensive Explosions of the 1990s

In the early 1990s, Major League Baseball set out to create more offense. They designed the current home run era. They have succeeded far beyond one's wildest imagination.

The offensive explosions of the '90s have now gotten out of hand. Nobody seems to remember the bunt, hit-and-run or putting one in play to the right side.

In 1999, Cincinnati set a National League record with 9 homers in a game! The Reds set a Major League record with 14 homers in two games.

The incredible hitting statistics today are inflated primarily because the ball was "juiced up" early in the 1990s.

In 1998, Mark McGwire hit a phenomenal 70 home runs.

Baseball's history is our inheritance, but if we cheapen the home run and make it routine, we will destroy what makes baseball special.

Baseball's standards and records, once cherished and revered, are becoming meaningless. Baseball needs to swing back toward the other direction.

to carve up billions of dollars. In chapters 2 and 3, I will provide organizational details on the growing movement of fans.

Offensive Records Are Hollow

Records set by today's hitters are ringing hollow, and baseball continues to do nothing about it. The offensive explosion that helped draw fans back to ball parks following the 1994 labor strike has now gotten out of hand. In the 15 games played on one Friday in 1999, 148 runs were scored, an average of 9.9 a game. Four teams scored in double figures, and 40 homers were hit. Six teams scored 20 runs in a game, like the April 19 slugfest in Texas: Rangers 26, and Orioles 7. Fifteen men hit three homers in a game; a total of 30 homers traveled more than 460 feet. As Ken Rosenthal wrote in the Baltimore Sun, "It's not baseball, it's bashball -- painful to watch and bad for the game. Attendance might be up 2 percent, but check out the empty seats at the end of the slugfests. Do fans want to see all these nightly marathons?"

Early in the 1990s, the goal of Major League Baseball was to create more offense, but as Rosenthal said, "They have succeeded only in numbing the senses. The question is not simply one of entertainment value. At stake is the game's legacy. One of baseball's most appealing qualities is the consistency of its statistics. The enduring values of a .300 batting average, 50 homers and 100 RBI. Such achievements once were considered remarkable. No more."

Most definitely, fans want to see home runs and offense, an occasional 8-7 slugfest, but as Sports Illustrated's Inside Baseball reported, "Few fans have the stomach to sit through massacres like the Giants' 17-1 bashing of the Cardinals. If baseball is serious in its search for ways to shorten games, curbing runaway offense is a logical place to start."

The Game Is Out Of Wack

On the playing field, the balance of baseball has swung much too far to the offense. The home run barrage of the 1990s has jolted the game. Runs are being scored at a record pace. With so many homers, the excitement and drama of the home run has diminished, the long ball devalued. The imbalance between hitting and pitching is turning off a growing number of fans.

Baseball's standards and records, once cherished and revered, have become meaningless with these much too often explosions. Twenty and thirty home runs once meant something. Now they mean something else – the game has been tinkered with, in the interest of Home Run Highlights. There are, of course, two different viewpoints. "Spectators enjoy the game more when hits and runs are made," said George Vass in Baseball Digest, "and plenty of chances for fielding and base running." Then, there are many who believe a well-pitched game is a thing of beauty. They like to see a good pitching duel. With equal balance, the two kinds of games can do a lot of good for baseball, to have both in a limited number.

Exciting Pennant Races Are Lacking
The excitement of pennant races has been made almost nonexistent by a wild-card system that has produced unfair match-ups in the post-season. The combination of the wild-card, mini-divisions and the balanced schedule has produced one travesty after another. As a result, the game is lacking today in exciting pennant races, the drama of stirring comebacks that electrified millions of baseball fans in the past. While the increase in playoff series and teams have pumped up interest, regular season interest and importance has suffered. Teams with the most revenue are making the playoffs while the rest do not have a chance.

As Bob Costas of NBC so eloquently wrote, "The ebb and flow of a true pennant race for the league championship or a division title was once one of the unique pleasures of baseball." By adding wild-cards, more divisions, and more playoffs, the postseason, even the World Series, is no longer special. Likewise, the season doesn't mean as much anymore either." As Costas pointed out, "The postseason is taking on the feeling of a protracted tournament in which the World Series is becoming nothing more than the baseball finals. The fewer post-season games there are, the more special and meaningful each of them feels."

Interleague Play Is Losing Support
Many thought interleague play was here to stay, but now players, managers and the news media are saying, "Should it be? Fans support is down from the first year, when the concept became a hotly debated issue. Proponents said the plan would take the sport into the future, while critics claimed it would wreck more than 100 years of tradition.

The cost for interleague has been ragged scheduling, a lack of quality time spent with league rivals and sometimes unfairness. "Any interleague format dilutes the rivalries within league divisions," said Tal Smith, president of the Houston Astros. The general feeling among players is that interleague play is more of a detriment and a distraction. "There is too much of it," said Tony Gwynn, while J.T. Snow would rather play more games against teams within the division. Henry Schulman wrote, "Baseball should scrap geography for variety and quality."

History and Traditions In Jeopardy
Baseball's great history and continuity are being threatened by interleague play and realignment. The traditions and uniqueness of baseball could be taken away by an ownership-oriented commissioner and pressured by owners who are more concerned in boosting the ratings of television networks who pay multi-millions to keep the salaries soaring.

In 1997, the owners yielded to an outpouring of criticisms and adopted a conservative realignment plan that did not seriously impact the integrity of the league structure. If then-acting Commissioner Selig's grandiose realignment scheme to reshape baseball had succeeded, fifteen teams would have switched leagues. Only one existing franchise, the Milwaukee Brewers, changed leagues and Detroit changed divisions.

Selig's failure to have his radical realignment scheme approved can be attributed largely to the fact that fan input became part of the process. And fan input will be even more important in the future. Still, Selig calls the Brewers' move to the National League "the initial stage" of major league realignment. He believes that more is to come. However, a poll conducted by Baseball America revealed that readers were adamantly against realignment, that teams should be kept in their respective leagues. More than 56 percent agreed that "realignment is inherently evil", and they questioned the owners' motive.

Quality of Play Has Declined
Quality of play, or lack of it, is still a major problem of baseball, having declined largely because of continual expansion. While expansion hasn't changed the competitive balance in the two leagues, it has diluted the quality of pitching. With the addition of two more teams, the problem has become even worse.

Rather than be overly concerned with the length and pace of the game, big league clubs should be more concerned with the quality of play. Baseball needs better games, not shorter ones, yet there appears to be little concern expressed by ownership. A large majority of big league players are executing the basics the fundamental way, but those who do not have increased over the past decade. Prospects are simply not spending enough time working on the basic skills in the minors. The strength of throwing arms has diminished at all positions, the result of excessive weight work on the upper body and not throwing enough.

Basic fundamental play has lost its importance to an increasing number of players. Ball players today are too concerned with home runs and do not give enough attention to base running and other basics. The stolen base, as a result, has become an endangered species. There is too much emphasis on the long ball.

Umpires' Threat To Resign Backfires
Responding to what they thought would be mass firings, big league umpires announced during the summer of 1999 that they would quit, effective September 2. Not waiting for the umpires to resign, baseball's front office took advantage of the lapse and dismissed 22 of their 68 umpires. Commissioner Bud Selig hired Triple-A replacements, those who had been working as vacation fill-ins. Then "Just two days after voting to resign, a crack began to develop in the umpires' union," wrote Hal Bodley. "Twelve umpires refused to resign and a growing list of those who did began asking that their letters be withdrawn."

Many grievances had created a large gap between management and its umpires. Commissioner Selig had talked about centralizing umpires by eliminating separate NL and AL staffs. Then, in February, new MLB vice president Sandy Alderson issued a memo demanding the rulebook's strike zone be enforced. Umpires union chief Richie Phillips complained bitterly.

Selig wants fundamental changes in the umpiring system beginning with Alderson assuming operational control from the two league presidents. The unwise action by Phillips provided owners the opportunity to start over. Umpire supervision will be centralized and an evaluation system will be installed that more easily allows for demotions and firings. Furthermore, the strike zone will be enforced that more closely resembles the one in the rulebook. These are measures which umpires have resisted.

In his column "Umpires playing into Selig's hands," Bodley said, "I've always had respect for umpires, have defended them when others were quick to criticize. But now the umpires must take a step back and open lines of communication with baseball."

Home Run Explosion - - How Did It Happen?

The home run explosion of the 1990s, climaxed by the season-long race by McGwire and Sosa, was so incredible that one has to wonder how it all began. Never before have so many hitters cleared or challenged the 50-homer plateau. McGwire's home run record of 70 is a number so amazing in its excessiveness that you have to wonder. Has the game changed? Can a reasonable explanation be made for the evolution of this record and the home run derby itself? The answer is yes. The game has changed dramatically. It all began in the early 1990s.

Baseball's Home Run Derby happened by design! From the very beginning, from the 1993 season on, Major League Baseball designed the current home run era. Major differences in the game created the annual chase for the home run record. For the past six seasons, the chase for 61 home runs has been the year's top baseball story.

The owners wanted more offense, more home runs. The Titleist Era emerged. In 1993, Major League Baseball introduced a new livelier ball and the juiced ball era of the '90s had begun. As Ray Ratto wrote in the San Francisco Examiner, "Major League Baseball spent year upon year supervising the development of the titanium kryptonite alloy added to the baseballs to make them scream." Glenn Dickey wrote in his column, "The ball that McGwire and other power hitters of this era are hitting is more like a golf ball than a baseball."

"There's no question about it," says Yankees pitching coach Mel Stottlemyre. "The ball's a lot harder than it used to be." In addition to a tighter wound and seamed livelier ball, bats are lighter and more lethal, hitters are bigger and stronger, the result of body building supplements, steroids and other drugs. Performance-enhancing drugs and substances have contributed bulging biceps and forearms and a much stronger hitter, and baseball, without a drug policy and testing and little concern for the health of the players (and the kids who worship them) has allowed these potent and dangerous chemicals to be used.

While some say the home run surge has restored the game, those who are responsible for creating the home run derby charade and allowing players to use performance-enhancing drugs will sooner or later have to answer for their actions. If baseball doesn't start setting controls, the game will continue to change even more, but not for the better.

Baseball's Darkest Secret

Baseball players, even team trainers and executives, talk about steroids and other drugs in hushed tones. "The taboo subject is anabolic steroids," wrote Bob Nightengale in USA TODAY Baseball Weekly. "It just might be baseball's deep, dark, sinister secret."

"We all know there's steroid use, and it could be as high as 30% among position players," says Detroit Tigers' general manager Randy Smith. "You just don't put on 30 to 40 pounds of muscle overnight and hit balls out of stadiums," said another top official. "I'm seeing guys now who were washed up five years ago and now they've got bat speed they've never had before."

"No question, there are guys on steroids," said Padres' manager Bruce Bochy. "You can look at their bodies and see the difference. You're also seeing some injuries that raise eyebrows, injuries now that you never heard of before." Many of baseball's top sluggers have been under suspicion for years because of their strength, weight gain or other conditions. But as Nightengale said, "Since there is no testing, no one knows for certain who is taking steroids, and who is clean."

No Longer A Mystery

Late in the 1998 season with the home run derby heating up, the steroids controversy became less of a mystery. Mark McGwire, the game's most productive home run hitter, confirmed to the Associated Press that he uses androstendione, an over-the-counter, testosterone-producing strength enhancer that is legal in baseball but banned by the NFL, the Olympics and NCAA. McGwire responded angrily to the story, stating that "Everybody that I know in the game uses the same stuff I use." (And much more!)

Reliable sources from inside the baseball establishment have revealed that in addition to androstendione, Creatine, and countless other chemical substances, most of baseball's power hitters, and others, begin their strength programs with anabolic steroids and rigorous weightlifting workout regimens during the off-season. For Creatine and andro to really work, an athlete has to receive a jump-start by the use of steroids. Many players start taking Creatine when they get off their steroid cycles. Then, during the playing season, players will depend on Creatine and numerous "nutritional" supplements.

Was androstendione and other chemicals responsible for McGwire's muscle-building success? Recent studies suggest andro use boosts testosterone by no more than 15 percent. Then, how did McGwire and others develop so much power? Pumping a lot of iron, combined with steroids and other performance-enhancing drug substances. But what the use of andro and other steroids did provide McGwire and others was significantly greater bat speed. Steroids not only build muscle mass but increases "twitch response". John Birch explained, "By getting onto a fastball just a tenth of a second faster, makes all the difference."

Drugs help players become stronger and faster, and strength and quicker bat reflexes have changed the game. Unquestionably, the use of androstendione (and what else?) by McGwire, and others, is performance enhancing. Combined with remarkable reaction time, he now has a shorter, more explosive swing than ever, powered by hulking thighs and Popeye arms. Once a lean 215-pounder, he has bulked up to 250 pounds. With significant benefits from Creatine and andro, McGwire is now able to train harder and recover more quickly from intensive exercise and withstand fatigue. Is all of this really fair?

Strong Influence on Youth   Having been thrilled by the

amazing success of McGwire and Sosa, numerous young players now have their minds on trying to emulate their heroes. The Associated Press reported that "Some boys and girls as young as 10 are taking andro and illegal steroids to do better in sports, according to the first survey to look at use of the body building drugs as early as fifth grade."

Many sports medicine doctors say androstendione and other chemical substances constitute a serious threat to McGwire, and others. Even more worrisome is that based on the huge sales of andro since he acknowledged its use, thousands of teenage athletes have followed his example. McGwire could have clarified his use of andro, that he in no way was encouraging anyone else to do the same. Actually, he should have brushed away public doubts by giving up the chemical, which he finally did the following season but the damage had been done.

Is McGwire's Record Tainted?

Now that the ancient record, first set by Babe Ruth and then Roger Maris, has been broken, there is a question in the air: Has Mark McGwire's remarkable record of 70 home runs been tainted by his use of muscle-building chemicals? Should the amazing feat be given an asterisk in the record books?

First, we need to review the performance-enhancing, body-building advantages that McGwire, Sosa, and many other players have benefitted from in the power-offensive-oriented era of the 1990s:

- Although androstendione was not illegal, it should have been.
- Since Major League Baseball has no drug-testing policy, the use of anabolic steroids cannot be detected.
- Androstendione hasn't been investigated fully because the Food and Drug Administration lacks authority to do so.
- Without andro and Creatine, McGwire would not have been able to lift as much, recovered so quickly, and would not have been able to withstand the always, grueling 162-game schedule.

Thus, McGwire and other big leaguers took advantage of everything baseball and the federal government provided -- a legal over-the-counter steroid and performance-enhancing, muscle-building chemicals, baseball's failure to initiate a drug-testing policy, juiced balls, home run-friendly ball parks and many mediocre pitchers.

Therefore, McGwire's extraordinary achievement will be tainted in the minds of a large number of baseball fans, with the ultimate (but deserved) asterisk placed next to his record. However, the people responsible for the blemish are the leaders of Major League Baseball. Fans should feel cheated that baseball refuses to participate in drug tests.

McGwire's use of androstendione and baseball's failure to ban the substance is shamefully irresponsible. The problem will continue until both Major League Baseball and the Players Association take a more responsible approach to a very serious problem by banning steroids, including andro, and finally initiate a mandatory testing program. It appears that baseball doesn't want to know about the drug problem. But, what would happen if the rest of the sports world followed along?

Who's To Blame For Baseball's Problems?

The complaints are many as to what is wrong with baseball and other professional sports. Yet, no one wants to do anything about excessive ticket prices, unbelievable salaries, unscrupulous and greedy agents, athletes behaving poorly, etc. but really, who is to blame? In his article "Choice of the Fan", Shaun Powell of The Sporting News wrote, "Those who complain the loudest are actually at the core of the problem, the fans, those who consider themselves the victims." I must say that I concur with Powell.

The message that Powell gave to fans was, "You're the creator and condoner of almost all that is evil or annoying about sports. You took a treasured segment of society and disfigured it, stripped away the innocence and allowed a seedy side to grow. You made it less about fun and more about business." In chiding fans themselves, Powell said, "Don't blame the athletes, the owners or the agents for what is wrong. Try looking in the mirror instead."

"The problem is that you, the fan, will tolerate just about anything," said Powell. "You allow yourself to be ripped off and stomped upon and do absolutely nothing to discourage it." What Powell is referring to, an average family of four cannot afford the cost of attending a professional sporting event. Yet, the prices keep rising. Owners raise prices every couple of years, but fans keep buying. Cities are being held hostage by owners to get a new stadium costing $300 million, which is usually paid for by taxpayers. Even if you don't buy a ticket, you're guilty because you watch on TV, which puts millions more in the kitty, which justifies paying the athlete in a proportion drastically out of wack to his worth in society.

"The athlete knows his place in society," said Powell. "It's near the top. Athletes don't save lives or educate children, yet society, driven by the fan, makes him believe he's above the law and beyond reproach. Athletes develop a sense of entitlement, which they usually receive, all because of the fan. Drug-abusers, steroid-takers, wife-beaters, they're all given multiple chances because you, the fan, demand to see them on the playing field."

You, the fans, should unite, stand firm, stop making owners rich and quit spoiling ridiculously paid athletes. But as Powell concludes, "You're a fan and can't help yourself." He asks, "So why should anyone help you?"

Other Levels of Baseball

Resurgence Of Interest In Minors   The minor
leagues continue to draw big crowds, while offering funful, inexpensive family
entertainment. For many fans, experiencing the small town atmosphere of a
minor league game is more fun than going to a big league game. A major reason
baseball is still the national pastime in the minors is because they still care about
the fans. In contrast to the majors, keeping all aspects of the game affordable
with fair pricing is how the minors are doing it.

Minor league baseball is experiencing one of its most prosperous periods in
history, with many new stadiums, more sophisticated marketing, and a fans-first
policy. "Attendance and revenue continues to grow," said Will Lingo in Baseball
America. "In the 1997 fiscal year, gross revenue for all NA clubs grew by nearly
$16 million to $300 million, a jump of more than 5 percent. The problem is that
its getting more and more expensive for minor league teams to do business.
Even with the phenomenal growth of recent years, 36 percent of minor league
clubs had operating losses. The minors' fiscal losses are most serious with
smaller market clubs, in that nearly three-fourths of the money-losing teams
were at Class A or below.

Status of Play in Minors   Based on our survey, although
fundamentals are stressed, minor league players are advancing without
perfecting or improving their skills. Expansion definitely has rushed the process,
and as a result, seasoning and time does not permit skills to be taught and
practiced as in the past. While the skills of today's players are as good or better,
the application of these skills continue to decline. Minor league coaches and
instructors believe there has been a general decline in play at the minor league
level. Players are better overall athletes, but they are not as fundamentally sound
as those of a decade or two ago.

Fielding fundamentals have given way to offensive output. Players are not as
well-rounded in all phases. There are few good bunters. Rundown plays are
botched, and cut-off men are missed. Players do not know how to run bases.
Sliding techniques leave much to be desired. Team play and winning are
stressed to a much lesser extent. "Each year there seems to be more and more

players who come out of the college programs, but can't properly do the fundamental aspects of baseball very well," wrote Butch Wynegar, former outstanding catcher and now a manager in the Texas Rangers farm system.

Independent Leagues   "The independent league boom is over," says Will Lingo of Baseball America. "The failures have equaled the success stories. Over a half-dozen leagues have become extinct. Now, the survivors of indy baseball must get on with the business of making what is left of an industry that could be on par with National Association leagues." But Lingo said, "That's not to say these leagues should seek to become developmental leagues like the affiliated minors. The success of independent baseball grew from its old-time approach, giving teams back to cities rather than major league organizations. The focus should be taking the success that independent leagues have enjoyed so far and building on it."

A full alliance could be in the best interests of independent baseball, but starting with the Northeast and Northern leagues. Once the alliance got started, other independent leagues would be welcomed. The alliance can be compared not to the National Association but to the NCAA. Leagues would have similar rules, ownership standards, standard contracts, and a standardized method of dealing with Major League Baseball.

Lingo believes, "The alliance would bring uniformity to a business that currently has almost none. It also could give a stamp of legitimacy to good independent leagues, giving them more credibility with Organized Baseball and with governmental and business entities."

The Northern League continues to be the great showcase for independent baseball. Following their initial success in 1993, the St. Paul Saints are attracting capacity crowds. The Northeast League, modeled after the Northern League, are drawing its players from the ranks of undrafted players, unsigned players, and former major and minor league veterans.

Baseball For Women Growing   Female baseball players in the United States are getting more opportunities to play, following several decades of inactivity. With World War II thinning the ranks of major league players, Chicago Cubs owner Philip K. Wrigley in 1943 came up with the idea of

women playing pro baseball. He created the All-American Girls Professional Baseball League, with teams in small Midwestern cities.

But it was not until 1994, a half century later, when the Colorado Silver Bullets began play as a barnstorming all-women baseball team, playing against professional male ballplayers in minor league cities. Although the Bullets folded in 1997 after losing their sponsor, Adolph Coors Brewery, they achieved a creditable .500 record in their final season.

In 1995, the All-American Women's Baseball League was established in the Midwest, with teams in South Bend, Fort Wayne, and Kane County, Illinois. According to Alan Levin, owner of the Class A team in South Bend, the league is a business venture and represents "an opportunity to give women a fair shot at playing baseball. Then in 1997, Ladies Professional Baseball began play with nine former Silver Bullets on the team rosters of the six-team league. Instead of playing against male teams, LPB teams play each other in a 56-game schedule that culminates with a best-of-five World Series. Each team has 18 players, making from $850 to $1,500 a month, about the same for a Class A men's player. However, players on the Bullets made as much as $30,000 a year.

Two women have distinguished themselves by pitching in the minor leagues, and in doing so, have inspired girls across the nation. In 1996, Pamela Davis became the first woman to play for a major league farm club. Davis, a 21-year old right-hander with the Silver Bullets, pitched a scoreless fifth inning and got the win in the Jacksonville Suns' 7-2 exhibition victory.

On July 9, 1998, Ila Borders, a 23-year old left-hander with the Duluth-Superior Dukes, became the first female pitcher to start and win a men's professional baseball game. The Sioux Falls Canaries failed to score in the five innings she pitched. Borders has been pursuing her dreams since she was 10 years old. She has also been a role model for girls everywhere, who typically play softball.

Pro's Now Represent USA Baseball
Professionals are now part of the landscape in international baseball. Major leaguers, however, will not represent the United States, or any other country, in the 2000 Olympics in Sydney, Australia. The USA team that competed in the 1999 Pan American Games was comprised of the first professional baseball players to represent their country in international competition.

A quickly assembled group of top minor league prospects not on 40-man major league rosters qualified the U.S. for Sydney by defeating Mexico 2-1, despite losing 5-1 to Cuba in the gold medal game. Earlier in the round-robin, however, USA's 10-5 victory over Cuba was their first against the Cubans since southpaw Jim Abbott beat them in the 1987 Pan Am games.

Actually, USA Baseball fielded two major teams during the 1999 summer, a national team of collegiate players and the Pan American Games team of professionals. In a tour of Japan, the national team dropped all five games to the Japanese, the first time the Japanese have swept the United States, which has not won a series in Japan since 1979.

Olympic Controversy Over Pro's Entry

As baseball grows internationally, USA's participation in the Olympics continues to intensify around the very controversial issue of professionals vs. amateurs. Americans are divided on whether professional athletes should compete in the Olympic Games. Numerous baseball coaches, officials, and fans have expressed strong opposition to the dilution of Olympic spirit by the invasion of pro athletes.

The movement to professionalism began when Juan Antonio Samaranch became president of the International Olympic Committee. He wanted the best athletes in the Games, so he initiated the crusade to eliminate amateurism and proceeded to professionalize Olympic sports. On September 21, 1996, the International Baseball Association voted to allow professionals to participate, after strong pressure was placed on IBA nations by the International Olympic Committee. The ruling removed the world "amateur" from the IBA's Constitution and By-Laws and allows professional athletes to represent their respective countries in international baseball competition, including the Olympic Games.

The growing movement toward professionals and dream teams is disturbing to those who understand the true meaning and spirit of the Olympic Games. Since the first Olympiad in 1896, the primary purpose has been to conduct "a universal celebration of sport and sportsmanship involving amateur athletes." Recent Olympic Games have been excessively commercialized, hyped by television and corporate advertising and now has moved blatantly toward professionalism. A strong public backlash has resulted from USA's Dream Team in basketball, and a growing number of baseball fans and officials are expressing similar sentiments relative to a Dream Team of American baseball stars.

Those who support the move to professionalize Olympic sports cite Cuba's strong advantage of a highly regimented government sponsorship. Since Olympic rules prohibited the use of professional players, only Communist Cuba was allowed to use their best players. Cuba has taken the gold medal at every world championship it has played since 1952, a total of 22 titles. While there have been various opinions expressed, the most overriding viewpoint relative to the controversy is what is best for USA's participation in international play, as well as baseball as a sport and our national pride.

Drug Use Threatens Athletic Ideals

Among the many benefits of athletic participation are the values that can be nurtured by a sport. Confidence, character and skills are some of the virtues an athlete gains in sports that can be applied to various other walks of life. These ideals, however, are being seriously threatened by the prevalence of illegal drug use within the athletic world.

"The virtues of athletics find the highest expression in the Olympics," wrote Barry R. McCaffrey, director of the Office of National Drug Control Policy. "These efforts embody the vision of Pierre de Coubertin, father of the Modern Olympics, of an ethos, linking the development of character and values with the struggle to excel athletically." George Will, the nationally-syndicated columnist and a baseball enthusiast, wrote, "Athletes who seek a comprehensive edge through chemical advantage do not just overvalue winning; they misunderstand why winning is properly valued."

The Olympics are not alone in its struggle with drug use. Baseball maintains rules that allowed pitcher Steve Howe to test positive for drugs seven times and still play. What message does baseball give when Mark McGwire and others are allowed to use androstendione and other performance-enhancing drugs and various other chemicals and supplements? Major League Baseball and other professional sports organizations are undermining the global fight against doping by failing to test for performance-enhancing drugs. Baseball is one of many sports bodies which has taken no measures to combat them.

"Baseball must set the score straight on drugs and sports," says McCaffrey. "Baseball must put in place league rules that provide for drug-testing programs and tough sanctions, accompanied by treatment for those who test positive".

Crucial Period for Collegiate Baseball As the 20th

century comes to a close, college baseball is in a crucial period. It has the potential to achieve unprecedented popularity and a higher level of play. The college game is capable of maximizing its potential, providing the NCAA would allow programs to do so. A closer relationship between Major League Baseball and the colleges would be in the best interests of both. If the colleges would do a better job of development, like correcting its developmental deficiencies, I believe the majors would look for ways to support college programs financially.

There appears to be a growing movement by Major League Baseball to utilize colleges to a greater extent in player development. Most of the great players in baseball today were produced by college programs. In fact, the success rate to make the majors is nearly double for a college athlete. According to player agent Scott Boras, "College players selected in the first round have a 60 percent rate while a high school player has only 35 percent."

Great Disparity Exists Between Programs A

longtime problem among northern teams could soon shake the stability of college baseball and bring about dramatic change. Major disparities exist between programs in warmer climates and those in cold weather areas. There is not a level playing field, and cold-weather teams need a major change. Because of the warmer weather, southern and far western schools are not only dominating play in the NCAA Division I but host nearly all the regional tournaments.

College baseball's potential to become a major sport would be significantly enhanced by a change-of-season. It would contribute much to the stability and popularity of the game. While the proposed change-of-season plan would have pushed the College World Series back two or three weeks, schools may want to push it back even further. Despite nine years of hard work by the American Baseball Coaches Association, the NCAA Management Council rejected even a "one-week" change.

Although Dave Keilitz, ABCA's executive director, plans to take the proposal back to the committee, the Big Ten and other northern conferences could take a different course of action. Minnesota baseball coach John Anderson stated that "There's clearly only one choice – we need to create an alternative -- probably a dramatic alternative. If we don't move the season, I think you'll see the Big Ten and other people break away and form our own season. We don't have a chance to go to Omaha in the current system."

Colleges Struggle With Bat Problem
Like the pro leagues, collegiate baseball has become much too offensively oriented, having to endure a decade of out-of-control scoring, produced by power-laden bats. Concerned about the explosive power of high-performance aluminum bats, the NCAA Executive Council voted to impose new standards on aluminum bats to reduce the speeds at which balls are struck. College teams switched to a slightly heavier and less powerful bat during the 1999 season. New bat standards are now being set relative to length-to-weight ratio and the barrel size.

But many coaches, like Texas A&M coach Mark Johnson, say the new standards do not go far enough. "The ball is still coming off a lot faster than it does with a wood bat," said Johnson. Safety remains a serious concern. The light weight of aluminum bats can produce a batted ball velocity of 103-110 mph, about 15 to 20 mph faster than a well-hit ball off a wooden bat.

Non-Pro Ball Enjoying A Revival
Non-pro baseball, or semi-pro as it used to be referred to, continues to be a "player's game". They play because they love it, without the need for fan support. In local baseball, players are rediscovering the thrill of playing America's game for fun, enjoyment and self-satisfaction. Many collegiate players provide a large source of talent in NBC's program, and this has contributed significantly to non-pro baseball. NBC's World Series in Wichita, Kansas is "the premier summer baseball tournament in the world."

Semi-pro baseball, in various forms, appears to be making a comeback. There is increasing interest in more local and town teams. While the number of teams just hanging on are many, the success stories, those in operation for many decades, continue to be the driving force of traditional semi-pro ball. The majority of NBC commissioners who responded to our survey believe the status of non-pro baseball is good, but sponsors and their coaches expressed strong concern for their team's financial stability. Financial burdens continue to have a major impact on travel, insurance, etc.

The survival of "semi-pro" type leagues has become dependent on sponsorships, but large sponsors are not easy to find. Non-pro ball would receive a big boost if a sufficient number of colleges and universities would host summer leagues. By bringing semi-pro ball back into prominence, the player development needs of the major leagues would be served. Student-athletes of the colleges would receive valuable playing experience, as well as receiving leadership and coaching training at morning youth camps and playground leagues.

Senior Leagues Enjoy Strong Growth

In recent years, the non-pro area of play has seen a remarkable growth of leagues involving older ball players continuing or returning to ball diamonds, with the desire for something more than softball. Among the thousands of senior league players are many former big league players, including Jerry Reuss, Jim Barr, and Bob Oliver. Senior leagues locally follow more of a recreational format, in that players actually pay to play. Age brackets and drafts keep teams competitive.

The most popular recreational leagues are the Men's Senior Baseball League (MSBL) and the National Adult Baseball Association (NABA). According to Steve Sigler, the founder and president of the MSBL, the league's growth has been phenomenal. During the fall, over 4,000 players ages 30-70 from 44 states and a growing number of foreign countries travel to Arizona and Florida to compete in the annual MSBL World Series.

Founded on Long Island with four teams a decade ago, the Men's Senior Baseball League now includes about 37,000 players in 260 leagues in 42 states and three Canadian provinces. Another 8,000 players are involved in the Men's Amateur Baseball League, a feeder circuit for players 18-30. Still another program, in the Los Angeles area, 28 teams compete in the "Thirty-Plus League", from March to September. They have their own World Series in October in Palmdale, with teams entering from all over the world. "World Series" rings go to the players who win the tournament.

While the traditional semi-pro leagues need to be boosted, adult and senior leagues comprised of over 30,000 players, is also deserving of community assistance, especially in the area of playing facilities. Such a cooperative relationship will contribute much to the comeback of the hometown baseball movement and Sunday afternoon baseball.

Baseball's Future Exists in Our H.S.'s

High school baseball is the center-piece in the development of highly skilled players in America. This is the opinion of a growing number of big league scouts, like Dale McReynolds of the Los Angeles Dodgers, who says, "The future of our game exists in the nation's high schools. The development of strong prep programs is not only the key to improved jaycee and collegiate baseball but the overall quality of high school players moving directly into professional ball will be at a higher level. Yet, high school programs are not receiving sufficient financial assistance to maximize their potential.

Cutbacks, however, continue to hold back the potential of high school programs. By cutting back on the number of games and practice time allowed, school and governing officials are seriously impeding high school players and programs. Schools have been squeezed drastically by economic deficits. The main complaints of high school coaches are the lack of enough playing dates and the amount of practice. Practice time prior to the first game is not adequate, particularly in Northern areas. There is an urgent need for more funding, promotion, and marketing.

The overall talent in H.S. programs appears to be declining, although viewpoints are mixed. Coaches in the warmer regions, like California and Florida, reported fundamental skills have generally been upgraded. From a national standpoint, however, our survey revealed that fundamental skills are being abused. Throwing technique, arm strength, and catching the ball are chief weaknesses. Like the big leagues, the trend has been directed to offensive skills and the long ball. This, of course, is because high school play is influenced significantly by how the game is played in the major leagues. The conditioning and nutritional habits of major league stars are also emulated by H.S. athletes, such as the use of performance-enhancing supplements and drugs, which have serious health implications.

High school age players, like those on other levels, are bigger and stronger, but there has been a decline in executing the basic skills. With less baseball being played at the pick-up and sandlot levels, the number of quality players coming out of the younger leagues are fewer today, largely due to a lack of quality instruction and repetitions at the lower levels of play.

Competition from other sports for the talented athlete is a major reason why "top-drawer" high school baseball players are getting scarce. Even the number of boys playing high school ball has dropped, due to various reasons such as finding other things to do and other sports to participate in. Competition for athletes is at an all-time high, and there are fewer multi-sport athletes.

High Schools' Urgent Need For Funding

Financial cutbacks have impeded high school programs, and there is a serious need for increased financial assistance. I share the feelings of concern and disappointment of many coaches and scouts as to why H.S. programs aren't supported more, even subsidized in part by Major League Baseball. Considering that the majors are throwing millions of dollars at H.S. draft prospects, there are many who believe that some of their money should be given to the programs that developed them. Yet, through the years, prep programs have received minimal support from the majors, other than the scouts who come out looking for talent.

If the future of baseball is dependent on strong high school programs, as scouts have stated, it would appear that major steps should be taken to upgrade and popularize them. From all the data I have gathered, I share the opinion of big league ivory-hunters that the high school game represents the key to baseball's career ladder and the success of its players.

As to how high school baseball can realize its potential, a plan of action will be presented in chapter three, including the organization of a national high school baseball tournament, similar to Japan's enormously successful event. In chapter nine, specific steps will be described in detail as to how to maximize the high school game.

Little League And Other Organized Youth Leagues Grow Despite Problems

Despite the unprecedented popularity of Little League and other organized youth baseball leagues, the most serious problems and weaknesses in America's player development system are in youth baseball. The excesses and abuses of Little League and other programs are impeding the growth and development of young players.

From the standpoint of participation and competition, youth league baseball has seen remarkable growth. The Sporting Goods Manufacturers Association reported that "The combined enrollment of children who were 18 years or younger in amateur leagues grew from 1.8 million players in 1985 to 4.6 million in 1996, an impressive 156% growth over 12 years."

Despite the impressive numbers of youth participating in organized leagues, however, young children and teenagers are not spending the time necessary to learn how to play baseball and develop their skills. Society has placed such an emphasis on organized play, and the result has been a drastic decrease of children playing the game, pick-up games, where repetition really occurs. In past decades, kids grew up playing baseball, but today they are pulled in multiple direction, from other sports to video games.

The failure of young players to learn the basic skills early continues to impact the quality of baseball play in America. Youth league coaches are failing to properly teach the basic skills, and kids are not playing enough on their own. Summer ball interest has declined because of too much emphasis on play-offs and all-star teams. As a result, the majority of kids are not playing, nor are they improving, during the summer months.

No wonder the Far East continues to dominate the Little League World Series. U.S. teams have won only six of the last 20 Series. The reasons are obvious. Japanese youth practice much more, are more dedicated, and receive better coaching.

An overwhelming number of H.S. coaches believe Little League programs are not adequately teaching the basic fundamentals. A large majority of youth league coaches are untrained, just supervising and not instructing. Little League's failure to improve the problem continues to undermine organized baseball's efforts to upgrade the quality of play in high schools and colleges. Fewer fundamentally sound players today are coming out of the youth leagues.

In greater numbers, kids are quitting organized baseball far too early. A major reason: too much emphasis is placed on winning the game. Many medical and child psychology authorities have expressed strong concerns about Little League's excessive emphasis on winning, competitive pressure, and the resulting anxiety. The excesses of Little League never end, another all-star team, another tournament, and more curve balls.

Renaissance Needed In Youth Baseball   A long, overdue renaissance is needed in America, involving not only the youth leagues but would re-open parks and playgrounds to baseball. The nationwide reform would be highlighted by a return of sandlot baseball and a revival of pick-up games.

If Little League truly desires to serve the social, physical and psychological well being of young children, it must make changes in its organizational structure, in addition to formulating a new philosophy, which would more effectively meet the basic needs of youth. Little League must take a serious look at their excessive approach to play-offs and all-star teams. Youth baseball continues to be excessively geared toward national championships. There is too much pressure to win.

The Return of Playground Baseball   Children today do not play enough playground baseball, and the concept should be revived and a movement promoted. Greater opportunities to play baseball in parks and playgrounds need to be provided by local park and recreation agencies, and school districts.

Young children need an alternative to the highly competitive pressure and atmosphere, which exists in Little League and other youth organizations. They need opportunities in a game more to their liking. Alternative programs are the key, to give them a choice, to play baseball without the highly competitive pressure and atmosphere which prevails in Little League today. Two examples of summer playground programs are the Wildcat Baseball League in Fort

Wayne, Indiana and Playground Baseball of America, both of which are described in detail in chapters 3 and 10.

Playground Baseball of America

A national organizational structure is now being developed, with the goal of locating playground baseball programs in cities and towns throughout the country. Playground Baseball will re-open playfields and parks to sandlot baseball, a mixture of informal, casual types of play activities, pick-up games and leagues, combined with instruction. League play will be organized by the local park and recreation department, with emphasis on drop-in participation.

For a playground baseball program to be successful nationwide, however, it must have the support and sponsorship of recreation and park agencies, schools, and parent-teacher organizations. For Playground Baseball of America to succeed as a national movement, it will be most urgent to obtain sponsorship and funding.

If successful, Playground Baseball will force Little League and other youth leagues to make changes. Youth baseball will also benefit by giving kids a much-needed alternative to Little League. Even more importantly, the program will contribute immeasurably to the revival of sandlot ball and the pick-up games concept, helping return the national pastime to America's parks and playgrounds.

Following its birth at Elysian Fields, baseball soon became regarded as America's national pastime.

Today, throughout the United States, baseball is still the national pastime.

2 Still the National Pastime!

As early as the late 1860s, baseball was widely recognized as America's national pastime. Even before the Civil War, amateur baseball clubs were springing up, as a growing number of men were playing baseball during their spare time. For the most part, they were seeking camaraderie, relaxation, and physical activity, as life in the United States was becoming increasingly industrialized and urban. Baseball was regarded as a pastime, a relief from the daily strains of work.

Following the Civil War, baseball experienced an explosion of popularity. Returning soldiers quickly spread the game's popularity and helped inspire a major baseball boom. Historians referred to the national pastime as "a great repository of national ideals," a game that "symbolized all that was good in American life." They lauded baseball for being a model for competition, fair play, civic pride, role models, and hero worship. With Americans losing their traditional ties, in an increasingly urban society, the game of baseball gave many the feeling of belonging. As increasing numbers of people moved from farms to large cities, rooting for a baseball team gave many a sense of community pride and satisfaction. Business leaders even urged their employees to learn the national game if they wanted to become "true Americans". They said, "If you want to know the heart and mind of America, you should learn the rules and realities of the game of baseball."

In the United States, baseball's rules and traditions, as well as the people who play the game, have become part of the fabric of our society. The reason baseball has endured for so long is because its rules and traditions endure. Americans love traditions and rituals, and baseball has many of them. Baseball has statistics that are meaningful and easily grasped. Winning twenty games or hitting .300 is still the same measure of excellence that it was a century ago. Memorabilia such as uniforms, caps, autographs and game paraphernalia still stir the emotions of people and provide ample evidence of baseball's enduring appeal.

The influence of baseball on the American English language is remarkably strong. There is a never ending list of terms and phrases that originated in baseball and have remained in our daily conversations, from Red Barber's "Ducks on the pond", Russ Hodges' "Bye-bye baby", Mel Allen's "How about that?", Vin Scully's "It's gone!", and Harry Caray's "Holy Cow!" With the loud crack of the bat, Caray's familiar voice would come to life, "It's a long drive, way back, WAAAY back. It could be! It is! A HOME RUN! HOOOOLY COWWWW!!" Behind the P.A. microphone, Rex Barney's trademark line was "Give that fan a contract!" when someone caught a ball in the stands.

The revival of the baseball short story has accompanied a wave of nostalgia for the game. In his book, "Baseball's Best Short Stories", Paul D. Staudohar compiled a very interesting and humorous collection of stories, like "Alibi Ike" by Ring Lardner, "The Rookie" by Eliot Asinof, and "What Did We Do Wrong" by Garrison Keillor. "Casey at the Bat", written by Ernest L. Thayer, tells about a player who strikes out at the crucial moment in the game.

Baseball's unofficial anthem is "Take Me Out to the Ballgame," written by Jack Norworth in 1908. Although he had never attended a major league game, Norworth penned the most famous baseball song ever written. Other popular songs are "It's a Beautiful Day for a Ball Game", "Joltin Joe DiMaggio", Frank Sinatra singing "There Used to Be a Ballpark", and the Broadway production "Damn Yankees". In 1999, Kenny Rogers recorded "The Greatest", about "a little boy in a baseball cap who stands in the field with his ball and bat and says 'I am the greatest.' The game is on the line, he gives his all one last time."

Hollywood's infatuation with baseball is quite evident in the production of many movies. "Pride of the Yankees" and "The Natural" portrayed the game superbly. And the documentary series, BASEBALL by Ken Burns, was a top television show in 1994. Kevin Costner's first two movies, "Bull Durham" and "Field of Dreams", are considered among the greatest baseball movies ever made. Mel Antonen of USA TODAY wrote, "To millions of fans, they were reminders to look beyond the modern sport's dollar signs and return to the childhood game, where first base was a tree and second base a dirt patch."

In Costner's third baseball movie, "For Love of the Game", Kevin stars as an aging pitcher who throws a perfect game in his final outing. In his review, Antonen said, "After 20 seasons with the Detroit Tigers, pitcher Billy Chapel is pitching the game of his life while confronting the confusing emotions that go with getting traded and the loss of love."

The key to Costner's success is that he has never outgrown the movies he makes. He grew up in the 1960s and early '70s, when Sandy Koufax and Harmon Killebrew were superstars. As Antonen stated, "Costner never stops asking questions about the game and when it comes to his movies, he's a stickler for detail."

As author Tristram Potter Coffin wrote in "The Old Ball Game", "Those in other sports who have hopes that their game can replace baseball as America's national pastime have two strikes on them before they come to bat." The great American historian and educator Jacques Barzun said it best, "Whoever wants to know the heart and mind of America had better learn baseball".

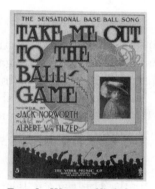

Baseball's unofficial anthem, written by Jack Norworth in 1908.

Field of Dreams and Bull Durham are among the greatest baseball movies ever made.

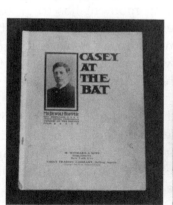

"Casey at the Bat" is a poem by Ernest L. Thayer that gives epic quality to a single strikeout.

What is Baseball?

Baseball has always been an elemental game---pitch, hit, catch, throw, like it's early ancestor games of ball. Branch Rickey said, "To play baseball, it's necessary only to have a ball, a bat, a glove, and the imagination of a young boy." As the manager in "Bull Durham" says, "This is a simple game. You throw the ball, you hit the ball, and you catch the ball." It is a game of fields and fences, 90-foot base paths, nine innings, nine men on the field, three outs to an inning, and three strikes." "Baseball is the smell of the glove, the crack of the bat, the white chalk running down the lines," wrote Commissioner Bud Selig in Sport magazine. "It's a high, hard one, the fresh hope of spring and the great potential of a raw rookie."

Baseball play involves many different qualities, such as power, speed, accuracy, timing and coordination, and mental instincts. Ernie Harwell, one of the game's top announcers, wrote "Baseball is continuity, pitch to pitch, inning to inning, game to game, series to series, season to season." It is a science in that is emphasizes repetitious precision in the execution of the various skill techniques. Baseball is not only a game of skills but of strange bounces. Anything can happen and usually does."

Baseball is low-key, in contrast to basketball and football. The pace is leisurely. Fans have time to sit and talk. But baseball is a thinking-man's game, a chess match, if you will. Fans try to figure out what move or pitch is going to be made next. It is a game of anticipation. The most exciting moment has to be bases loaded, two out, 3-and-2 on the batter, just before the pitcher throws the ball. "There is an old adage that says, 'Baseball is a game of firsts', explained former catcher Tim McCarver. "Getting the first one is very important. You get the first strike on the batter, the first out in the inning, and the first run of the game."

"The spirit of community is exemplified by baseball better than most institutions in American society," said Mario Cuoma, former New York governor, appearing on Ken Burns' BASEBALL documentary. "You can't win it alone. You can be the best pitcher in baseball, but somebody has to get you a run to win the game. It is a community activity. You need all nine people helping one another." What aspect of baseball appeals most to Cuoma? "I love the bunt. I love the idea of the sacrifice, giving yourself up for the good of the whole. Baseball has taught us that."

"There is nothing like baseball in the spring," wrote Larry King in his popular USA TODAY column. "It is a reaffirmation of our youth. It is fathers and sons, mothers and daughters. It's about life. It is grand."

What makes baseball so popular? A major reason is because baseball's records of accomplishments are the most extensive, historic, and oft-cited of any sport. A huge industry has sprung up on their collection and analysis, and the feats of past heroes are still as popular as ever. "Today, a baseball without records if inconceivable," wrote John Thorn. "They are what keeps the great performers – Babe Ruth, Ty Cobb, Henry Aaron and others – alive in our minds."

"The beauty of baseball is that it can be enjoyed at all levels," said Tim McCarver, one of baseball's top analysts. "The more you learn about it and the more exposed you are to its many subtleties, the more fascinating it will become." Jon Miller, who with Joe Morgan form the game's finest announcing team, said, "Baseball is the best arguing game. If you're passionate about the game, you argue. Everything is a potential argument in baseball. The topics and issues are endless."

Joan Ryan of the San Francisco Chronicle wrote: "Baseball brings a new tale of triumph in the most unlikely ways and the most unlikely moments — not merely once a week like football, but nearly every day." In her vivid description of baseball, Ryan explained "Baseball teams are the marrying kind. They're in it for the long haul. Just as you're ready to write a team off, it wriggles out of a bases-loaded inning. It lays a perfect bunt up the first base line, makes a catch against the wall, and nails a runner at the plate."

America's National Pastime? Baseball by a landslide! As Peter Gammons wrote, "Baseball is the only sport that is truly the American dream". Baseball players do look like human beings you see daily on the streets. "To play pro or college basketball today," said one fan, "you have to be 7'6". To play football, you have to be the same width". As the late Bill Veeck once said, "Baseball is the only game left for people". It doesn't matter whether you have a hearing deficiency, the loss of hand or arm, 5-feet four, or what country you are from. This is a game that has brought people in from all walks of life and diverse backgrounds. It made Ernie Banks exult with joy and gladness, "What a great day for baseball. LET'S PLAY TWO!!"

Early Origin of Baseball

The most direct ancestors of baseball were two British games, rounders, a children's sport brought to New England by the earliest colonists, and cricket. At the time of the Revolution in the 1770s, there were many variations but townball was the most popular. In this game, the pitcher, or feeder, was the least important player. It was his job to lob the ball to the striker, who could wait for the pitch he wanted. The runner was out if the ball was caught on the fly, or if he was "soaked", hit with the ball while running between bases.

By the 1840s, various forms of baseball were vying for acceptance, including the popular Massachusetts and New York versions of the game. Early in the 1840s, two clubs in New York City were playing a version of townball that would soon evolve into baseball. They were the Knickerbocker Club led by Alexander Cartwright and the New York Base Ball Club organized by Daniel Lucius Adams, known as "Doc". In September of 1845, Cartwright, a bank clerk and volunteer fireman, invited a group of friends, including Dr. Adams, to Elysian Fields in Hoboken, for the purpose of forming a new Knickerbocker Baseball Club. In laying out the regulation playing field, Cartwright developed new rules that would "change the game forever".

On October 21, 1845, the New York Club played a match against a team from Brooklyn at Elysian Fields. Many historians believe this was the first recorded interclub baseball game. The earliest game on record under the Cartwright rules, however, according to the Guinness Sports Record Book, was on June 19, 1846, at Elysian Fields. The New York Nine defeated the Knickerbockers 23 to 1 in 4 innings. The Knickerbockers standardized the number of men who could play on a side at nine and set the bases at 90 feet apart. As John Chancellor said, "90 feet was a pick from heaven. If it was 88 feet, there surely would have been fewer double plays."

During the Civil War years, soldiers played and watched games at camp sites and took the game home with them, and it grew. After the war ended, a baseball mania swept across the land. When the 1860s ended, baseball was widely acclaimed as America's "national game". As Walt Whitman wrote, "It has the snap, go, and swing of the American atmosphere."

ORIGINAL KNICKERBOCKER PLAY allowed for the batter to be retired on a ball caught on the first bounce as well as one caught on the fly. In 1864, the Association (NABBP) ruled that a ball hit into fair territory must be caught on the fly to retire the batter. The infield would be a four-base diamond. Foul lines were established, and the batter got three swings before he was called out. A batter could also be put out by a fielder catching a batted ball in the air or on the first bounce, or by throwing a fielded ball to the first baseman before the runner arrived. Most important, runners would now be tagged and thrown out, not thrown at. As John Thorn said, "It was now a more challenging game, faster-paced. American."

The pitching distance was set at forty-five feet from home base. Originally, the pitcher was required to toss the ball underhand, letting it leave the hand below the level of the hip, from a distance of 45 feet. The idea was to have the batter hit the ball to begin play, not to overpower him. Gradually, pitchers kept lifting their arms in the act of throwing. In 1884, the restriction was raised to "shoulder high", and in effect, straight overhand pitching was possible.

WHO INVENTED BASEBALL? Contrary to the popular belief that the game was invented by Abner Doubleday, baseball was not invented. Rather, it evolved from various other games, such as rounders, town ball and, in some respects, cricket. Three individuals played strong roles in the founding and development of the game. They are Alexander Cartwright, Daniel Lucius Adams, and Henry Chadwick. As leaders during the development, all three played key roles in forming the rules. While there were others who made important contributions, these three men truly were the "Fathers of Baseball".

One day in the spring of 1845, Cartwright proposed to his ball playing friends that they form a new club, the Knickerbocker Baseball Club. The Knickerbocker rules of 1845 did not represent "a brand new version of baseball", according to Frederick Ivor-Campbell. In writing down the playing rules, Cartwright and others quite likely firmed up rules that the founders had developed over the three or four years they had played the game before organizing as a club.

During his second term as president of the Knickerbockers from 1856 to 1858, Doc Adams prepared and presented the first thorough rewriting of the rules. Adams chaired the rules committee over a five-year period that shaped the game being played today. He added the shortstop position, in fact as a player, he was

The first official game of baseball was played in June 19, 1846 at Elysian Fields in Hoboken.

Alexander J. Cartwright, Jr., "Father of Modern Base Ball"; founder of American baseball rules.

Henry Chadwick shaped rules changes throughout the 19th century; author of the first rule book in 1858.

the game's first short fielder. He urged the adoption of the fly game, the elimination of the rule permitting outs on first-bound catches.

Chadwick not only reported and promoted the game, but for over half a century, helped shape baseball through his long-time service on official rules committees. He wrote, "It was not long before I was struck with the idea that baseball was just the game for a national sport for America." Chadwick developed and compiled the game's first detailed statistics and developed his own scoring system. "Through his pioneering work on baseball's statistics, Chadwick invented the game's historical essence," wrote Jules Tygiel.

ABNER DOUBLEDAY MYTH   For most of the 20th century, General Abner Doubleday was regarded as the man who invented baseball in 1839. Legend has it that "one day in Cooperstown, New York, Doubleday had scratched the shape of a diamond in the dirt and told the players where to position themselves." Historians, however, believe Doubleday, in his youth, was playing town ball, a version of the game that had been played for decades.

"The Doubleday myth is as much a part of our culture as George Washington's chopped-down cherry tree," wrote Bill Tammeus in the Kansas City Star. In fairness to the general, he never did claim to have invented the game. Historians point out Doubleday was a plebe at West Point in 1839. Following his death, credit was given to him by A.G. Spalding and a commission formed around the year 1900 to prove that baseball was a purely American creation.

REVOLT OF THE SERVER   In the early 1850's, the most significant change ever to affect baseball occurred. A pitcher chose to defy the Knickerbocker way of serving the ball. Originally, the pitcher was assigned the task of understanding the "softest and most hittable offerings possible". His sole function was to "serve the bat". Under the rules, the batter was privileged to stand at the plate for as long as it took to find a pitch "perfectly suited to his liking". On this day, the "rebel server" began to whistle the ball toward the plate with all the speed he could muster. William Curran wrote, "We don't know who first used his strength and dexterity to fog a pitch by a flailing batter." Of greater significance, however, the revolt of the feeder made possible the survival and remarkable growth of baseball, introducing the thrill of close competition and focusing the attention not only of the players but the spectators. That moment was born the basic duel between the pitcher and batter that remains the bedrock of baseball.

FIELDING WOES OF EARLY FIELDERS   Fielders during the early years of baseball did not have a glove to protect their hands and, as a result, numerous errors were committed. Some fielders tried catching fly balls in their caps to spare their hands. By 1857, however, that technique was outlawed. Infielders of that era often let drives go by in the interest of their safety. Actually, errors were not kept track of systematically until the National League was established in 1876. At which time, there was an appalling number of errors afield: 3,950 for the eight teams, or an average of 8.83 per game! Even in the 1880s, games were commonly lost to poor fielding. Some infielders even continued not to use gloves, that it was unmanly.

In the early 1870s, the ball was deliberately deadened in an effort to keep the scoring down and, perhaps, protect the lives of third basemen. However, most balls used by amateurs remained lively. One was nicknamed "The bounding rock!" Also, the batter was allowed to overrun first base. Catchers' masks did not appear until 1877, chest protectors not until 1886, which makes one wonder how catchers survived in that era. Gloves for catchers experienced a slow evolution. Not until 1890 did the Phillies' Harry Decker perfect the heavily padded target-like catchers' mitt. Until then, pitchers could not really cut loose with their pitches.

DECADES OF CHANGES: THE 1880'S   Professional baseball's growth and development as a sport was speeded by numerous rule changes between 1880 and 1889. Constant changes in playing rules resulted from practical experiments by major league rules committees, whose constant tinkering kept the game in continual change. Even into the 1880s, for example, batters ordered their pitches, and runners interfered with fielders trying to make plays. But the evolving game improved and advanced.

In 1876, if an umpire was unable to see whether a catch had been fairly made, he could confer with spectators and players. But in 1882, it was ruled that umpires could not confer with spectators or players. Furthermore, they may not reverse decisions on matters of judgment. In the 1870s, there was usually only one umpire per game and he called everything from behind the plate. In the 1880s, however, the umpire was mobile, moving behind the pitcher when there was a runner on base.

In 1880, the rules committee reduced the number of balls required for a walk from nine to eight, then six, five and finally in 1889 to four. The most promising concession made to hitters in the 1880s was the decision in 1881 to increase the pitching distance from forty-five to fifty feet. In 1887, the batter was no longer allowed to request a low pitch. A foul ball caught on the bounce ceased to be an out. It must be caught before touching the ground. The sacrifice was not recognized in the statistics until 1889. Then in 1893, the batter credited with a sacrifice would not be charged with a time at bat.

The most far-reaching change of the decade in pitching was adopted in 1884 to remove all restrictions on the pitcher's delivery. As late as 1882, pitchers were still required to deliver the ball underhand or, at least, from below the belt. Now able to throw from all angles, pitchers slowly shut down the hitters until averages dropped to alarmingly low levels. In the period from 1884-86, uneasy hitters were trying to adjust to the look of overhand pitching, and strikeouts increased by more than 50 percent. The invention of the curveball in the 1860s was also having a revolutionary impact on the game. The owners felt they had to do something or pitchers would continue to dominate the hitters.

PITCHING DISTANCE INCREASED In 1893, a major change in playing rules fixed the pitching distance at 60'6" from home plate. Why not just 60 feet? Actually, the rules committee did specify "60 feet, 0 inches", but the surveyor misread the "0" as a "6" and the mistake was never corrected! Unbelievable, but true. The rules committee also replaced the pitching box with a rubber slab atop a mound. By establishing the pitching rubber, it eliminated the practice of running up or stepping to deliver the ball. This permanent change was introduced in 1893 to correct "the pitching-batting imbalance", a goal which to this day remains elusive. The immediate effect of the lengthened pitching distance sent batting averages soaring. In 1894, the Phillies posted a .349 batting average. Their outfield had a combined .400-plus batting average! It took pitchers several years to adapt to the increased distance, but they did so by developing curves, changeups, and "ball-doctoring" trick deliveries to go with their fastballs.

WHAT BASEBALL WAS LIKE IN THE 1880s Fundamentally, it was very similar to the game being played today, but with important modifications still to come. Now catchers had to learn how to position themselves under the bat, grab the third one on the fly for it to be an out. Walks were something else. At one time the batter drew a walk on nine balls. Then it was eight, seven, six. Finally, an agreement was reached in 1889 that four balls constituted a walk.

Defensively, the biggest difference between then and now probably was in the mobility of the players. Infielders were more inclined to anchor themselves to their bases, and there was less movement that what we see today. Infielders were learning to back up bases, play shallow or deep, depending on the game situation and align themselves to turn double plays. Outfielders coordinated their play by using backups, cutoffs, and relays.

Freed from all restrictions as to the angle of delivery, pitchers were perfecting the art of overhand pitching. While it was more effective, it was harder on the arm. The modern strike zone was implemented in 1887 and to help offset this, hitters were granted a fourth strike. This rule change, however, caused ERA's to soar, and in 1888, the fourth strike was removed from the game. In 1895, a foul tip was finally made a strike.

Offensively, the home run was relatively unimportant in the 1880s, since the fences were too far to reach and the balls were dead. With pitchers in full control and the lack of home runs, the game featured such dead-ball strategies as bunting, base stealing, and the hit-and-run. The sacrifice bunt was known but scorned by many as a "sissy hit"! The art of stealing was practiced, especially the flourish of the slide, for which sliding pads already were in use. Among the famous innovations of the era, the Baltimore Orioles were known for performing such dirty tricks as hiding extra baseballs in the outfield grass or "giving passing baserunners a hip." Early in the 1890s, the slugging style of offense had feasted on pitchers, but the "scientific style" mastered by the Baltimore and Boston teams became the dominant offensive style of the next twenty years. Bunting, stealing, sacrificing and the hit-and-run were familiar tactics.

By 1884, crowds numbering into the thousands came to see the pros play. A.D. Suehsdorf wrote, "Professional baseball was first played on an exhibition, roadshow basis, then with organized clubs and seasonal schedules. General admission was fifty cents. Tickets would soon include rain checks. Ladies Day already was an institution, and the doubleheader soon found its way into the schedule. Turnstiles counted the crowds, and ballplayers, by contract, could be pressed into service as ticket-takers. Players also had to furnish their own uniforms and pay for cleaning and repair."

AGE OF PITCHING: 1900-1919   The age of pitching began in 1903 during the "deadball style" period and extended through 1919, to the Ruthian era. Pitching still had the edge over hitting. As the 20ᵗʰ Century began, a major rule change was adopted. A foul ball was counted as a strike, and ERAs decreased drastically.

Factors most responsible for the dominance of the pitcher were:

- The ball was dead; it had no resilience and carry
- Power hitters were few and so were the balls
- The rules and game conditions favored the pitchers

THE EARLY 1900s   Runs were down in both leagues. While batting averages and slugging percentages had declined, interest in the game increased. Fans were thrilled with the newly created World Series. Even after a livelier ball was used in 1911, the game did not change very much, as the pitchers continued to dominate. Now throwing overhand, pitchers found the 15-inch high mound easier on their pitching arm and to their advantage. Rapid advances in fielding were made in the 1900s. As a result of larger gloves, better maintained playing fields and improved catcher's equipment defense improved significantly. The great hitters continued to hit for average but homers were few. It was a short-range game of bunts, steal, sacrifices, strategic singles, hit-and-run, scoring flies, squeeze plays, plus a few extra-base hits.

The early years of the new century were an era of the stolen base, highlighted by such great base stealers as Ty Cobb and Honus Wagner. Teams employed the deadball style of play that resembled the "scientific game" of the 1890s. One run often made the difference in a game where home runs were few. While every team had more than one hundred steals per season, the faster, more ingenious teams had more than two hundred. Umpires were enforcing the balk rule more strictly, helping runners get better jumps. Between 1911 and 1920, the sixteen major league clubs stole 26,734 bases. Cobb's longtime record of 96 steals was achieved in 1915. New balls were seldom introduced into games, as pitchers took command, using a variety of deliveries, including spit-balls and defacing balls with other foreign substances.

By 1910, a decade before the dawn of the home run era, the bunt was widely used. The offense could do very little other than hit singles, bunt and steal bases. The success ratio of basestealing was about 67 percent, but many baserunners were less successful. Napoleon Lajoie once beat out six bunts in a doubleheader. Even Cobb and George Sisler bunted often in their .400 batting years. When the infield was playing in, looking for a bunt, they swung away. With the defense back, they bunted. When the lively cork-center baseball was adopted in 1911, a somewhat moderate explosion of the offense occurred. But, pitchers were still able to retain their control of the game. During the decade of the 1910s, baseball had survived a number of serious challenges, like dead-ball games, the Great War, and the shameful Black Sox Scandal of 1919.

MODERN ERA: 1920s OFFENSIVE BOOM   Babe Ruth, the Sultan of Swat, arrived in the major leagues at the right time. In 1920, baseball was struggling, having been hurt by the war, internal quarrels and tarnished by the Black Sox Scandal. Ruth's 59 homers as a Yankee in 1920 highlighted the incoming "big-bang" style of play that would characterize the decade of the 1920s. Batters, emulating Ruth's uppercut hitting swing began swinging for the fences of the new enclosed ballparks. The Babe's bat triggered an offensive explosion that not only brought back the fans but convinced most big league managers to play for "the big inning". Hitters switched to thick-barreled bats with thin handles that increased bat speed and generated more force. More hard hit balls led to more exciting fielding plays, reflected by a sharp rise in double plays in 1920.

The lively ball era had begun, largely attributed to Reach and Spalding, the ball manufacturers. Balls became more glossy and had countersunk seams. The cushioned cork-center introduced in 1926 really made the ball fly. Ruth hit an incredible total of 54, nearly twice as many as had ever been hit before. The Babe got 467 of his 714 career homers in this decade alone. After 1920, the lively ball era had players and fans believing the ball "had a rabbit in it". But, the explosion in hitting was what the owners wanted, and they did not hide the fact that they wanted a livelier ball. Outfielders began to play deeper and farther apart, thus widening the alleys where line drive hitters drove the ball.

When the Golden Twenties came to an end, a combination of factors had altered the balance of the game. The lively ball was introduced. Freak deliveries were banned, and no foreign substance, such as spit, could be used to tamper with the ball, except for "a few specified veterans". New balls were put into play so hitters could see them more clearly. The majority of the hitters concentrated on making contact rather than free-swinging. As a result, there was a huge increase in .300 hitters and home runs, while many of the weapons used in the previous

The early years of the 20th century was an era of the stolen base. The great base stealer Ty Cobb, above, slides into third base.

The lively ball era began in 1920 and Babe Ruth, "Sultan of Swat", took full advantage of a ball which had a "rabbit" in it.

The pitchers made a big comeback in 1930, as a result of an adjustment in the construction of the ball.

decade — the bunt, sacrifice, and the stolen base, were being used far less. More teams were using the hit-and-run, as the tendency toward stealing declined.

Infielders were making more double plays, as a result of quicker movement of the livelier ball on smooth infields, and improvement of gloves, as larger and better-padded gloves were being introduced. In 1919, Bill Doak, pitcher for the Cardinals, developed a new glove for the Rawlings Company, with a preformed pocket and webbing between the thumb and the index finger. This glove would set the pace and pattern for more than a quarter century. And the glove kept evolving, the round catcher's mitt with extra padding, and the first baseman's "Trapper" model. Indeed, gloves changed the style of play everywhere, especially the one-handed catch.

Fundamentally, it was Babe Ruth who changed the way the game was played. He made the home run the biggest play in baseball, and as a result of his prestigious slugging, other players began going for the long ball. Ballparks were now being built with "home run fences" that hitters were able to reach consistently. The construction of enclosed urban concrete-and-steel parks contributed significantly to the birth of the home run offense. While some insist "the modern game" began in 1921 with the introduction of the lively ball, others believe the turning point came in 1884 when overhand pitching was first allowed.

PITCHERS MAKE COMEBACK IN 1930s After being dominated by hitters in the 1920s and absorbing a devastating bombardment in 1930, pitchers made a big comeback in 1930, as a result of an adjustment in the construction of the ball. The owners allegedly had the ball "juiced up" to create more offense and action into the game and draw more fans to the parks. And their action worked, as hits and run totals were the highest in years, particularly in the NL which had a .303 league batting average. With home runs flying out of the parks at a record pace, owners now took action against the hitters to curb their lusty hitting. They had the seams on the ball raised so that the pitcher could get a better grip. Balls were wound more loosely. Even though the owners tried to curb hitting, home run totals held up well throughout the 1930s, despite a decline in batting averages.

The All-Star Game came into baseball in 1933, attracting a crowd of 49,000 at Comiskey Park. Conceived by sports editor Arch Ward of the Chicago Tribune, the game was introduced as a sidelight attraction for the Century of Progress Exposition in Chicago. The idea for baseball's Hall of Fame was proposed by

Ford Frick in 1935 soon after he became president of the National League. Both the museum and the Hall were established in 1939 as baseball's shrine in Cooperstown, N.Y. The museum is reserved for bronze plaques depicting and honoring the game's great players, with separate honor rolls for managers, owners, umpires and writers.

The first major league night game occurred on May 24, 1935, when the Cincinnati Reds defeated the Philadelphia Phillies, 2-1, before 20,422 spectators at Crosley Field. Night play was dubbed "MacPhail's Madness" after pioneering Cincinnati general manager Larry MacPhail. "There is no chance of night baseball ever becoming popular in the bigger cities," said owner Clark Griffith. "High-class baseball cannot be played under artificial light." The first baseball game was televised in New York by W2XBS in 1939. Princeton defeated Columbia 2-1 at Baker Field.

When the 1940 season ended, the two major leagues, consisting of sixteen clubs, had attracted over 35 million spectators. Almost 500 minor league teams were in action. More than ever, baseball was truly regarded as the national pastime.

EARLY 1940s WAR YEARS When 1941 came to a close, the nation went to war. Like every other sport, baseball lost many stars to the service. Those who remained behind made the best of it, responding to President Franklin D. Roosevelt's famous "green light" message. Robert Burnes wrote in the St. Louis Glove-Democrat that "Roosevelt asked that sports be allowed to continue for the relaxation and entertainment of war workers and worried families of the men overseas." But in 1946, baseball fans streamed back to the ballparks, eager to see for the first time in five years the game's greatest players.

POST-WAR YEARS LATE 1940s The closing years of the 1940s proved to be a roaring windup to the "Fifty Golden Years of Sports". Night games, televised games, and World War II had changed the way baseball was played during the 1940s. Following the war, everyone was swinging for the fences at the expense of their batting average. Increasingly, the threat of the long ball had managers lifting a tired pitcher before he gave up a three-run homer late in the game. Actually the relief specialists concept was slow in coming. It did not occur until after the war. Several factors appeared to be to the advantage of the pitcher. More pitchers were throwing the slider, referred by Ted Williams as "the greatest single detriment to hitting". Furthermore, night baseball was rapidly expanding, and pitching in the evening was less taxing. While night ball had done much to hike attendance, television sent the turnstiles spinning. Then, TV cut sharply into gate receipts of many major and minor league parks.

"The major leagues still represented only the sixteen cities that had participated in the National Agreement of 1903, none west of St. Louis, John Thorn wrote. "A handful of African-Americans were just entering the minor leagues after a half-century of exclusion and because television was not yet a staple of the American home, most baseball fans had never seen even a single big-league game."

No single event in this era could compare in significance to the day in 1947 when the racial barrier was broken. President Branch Rickey of the Brooklyn Dodgers signed Jackie Robinson, opening the doors for African-American players to begin entering Major League Baseball. "There were muttered threats in the dugouts of beanballs and spikings," wrote A.D. Suehsdorf. "One team even threatened not to take the field if the Dodgers played Robinson."

In responding to the crisis, National League President Ford Frick "did lasting honor to himself and to baseball", stated Suehsdorf. "Those who strike will encounter quick retribution. All will be suspended. I do not care if half the league strikes. This is the United States of America. One citizen has as much right to play as another." There was no strike, and following a shaky start, Robinson led the league in stolen bases, batted .296 and generally excelled. While opening the game to African-Americans was the right thing to do, it killed the Negro leagues, ruining owners, and ending many playing careers.

SECOND HALF OF TWENTIETH CENTURY   When the 1950s began, baseball was still dominated by the home run. As home run totals climbed, so did the attendance at ballparks. The home run or strikeout pattern was more dominant than ever. Whippier bats, protective helmets, and the strategy of platooning hitters strengthened offenses, but defenses were given a significant boost by more efficient gloves. Larger and more flexible gloves enabled fielders to become more proficient in making difficult one-handed catches but a growing number of players were developing bad habits in using one-hand too often.

Another major change which began in the '50s was the resurrection of the running game and base stealing. Few players had stole bases in large numbers in recent decades. In 1954, for example, NL teams averaged only 42 stolen bases. The offensive strategy in the 1950s was to play for the big inning and wait for a big swinger to hit one out. During the '50s, Casey Stengel of the Yankees had become the first manager to platoon his players. Casey relied heavily on relief pitching and pinch-hitting.

Another hitting explosion shook up the game in 1961. The New York Yankees, paced by Roger Maris and Mickey Mantle, hit an all-time record of 240 home runs. The 60 homers hit by Maris broke the game's most famous record, the 60 hit by Ruth in 1927. Expansion had thinned the quality of pitching, and the season was lengthened to 162 games. Alarmed by the big hitting, Commissioner Frick convinced team owners to enlarge the strike zone. He initiated a larger strike zone, bringing back its pre-1950 dimensions: top of the arm pits to the bottom of the knees. The larger strike zone gave pitchers much more room, high and low, to pitch to hitters. The pitcher's mound had to be 15 inches above the level of the baselines. The results were disastrous, decreasing home runs by 10 percent, increasing strikeouts, reducing walks, and shrinking batting averages by 12 points.

In 1968, pitchers dominated the game as never before. One out of every five games played was a shutout. Left-hander Sandy Koufax of the Los Angeles Dodgers became the most over-powering pitcher in the 1960s. Bob Gibson registered the lowest ERA in the history of the National League, 1.12. Denny McClain won 31 games and Don Drysdale threw 58 consecutive innings of scoreless ball. Carl Yastrzemski won the AL batting title with the lowest average ever at .301. Following the 1968 "Year of the Pitcher", the owners acted quickly again, returning the strike zone to the area between the arm pits and the top of the knees and cracking down on brush-back pitches. The pitcher's mound was lowered to 10 inches above home plate and the baselines, where it remains today.

Fielding in the 1960s was probably the finest ever, as teams averaged a remarkable one and a half errors per game. In 1964, Baltimore, paced by the great play of Brooks Robinson, committed only 95 errors in a 162 game season – a little more than half an error a game!

Speed returned to the game, as Maury Wills, Luis Aparicio, and Lou Brock initiated a base stealing revolution. The stolen base as an offensive weapon had been dormant since 1920. Stolen bases increased astronomically. The 741 steals in both leagues in 1958 had more than doubled to 1850 by 1969.

In 1958, following the movement of several big league franchises, The Dodgers and Giants left for the West Coast. Thorn wrote, "As distressing as it was for Brooklyn and Manhattan and roundly condemned by traditionalists, the placement of franchises in California may now be seen as the best thing to happen to the game. America's population had already begun the westward and southward shift and the move to Los Angeles and San Francisco brought baseball into step with America. Baseball could now call itself the national pastime without apology."

DECADE OF CHANGE IN THE 1970s   Change was a consistent factor in baseball during the 70s, with new stadiums, new teams, new rules, such as the designated hitter, new uniforms, and new legal decisions. The architectural design of stadiums dramatically affected the way the game was played. The new parks built between the years 1965 and 1977 had relatively the same dimensions – 330 feet down the foul lines, in contrast to the old stadiums which had varied distances and their own individual personalities. Fans were critical of the artificial turf in the new stadiums, insisting that baseball was meant to be played on grass. Hitters like Pete Rose and Rod Carew were very adept at punching, chopping and slicing the ball past the fielders. Balls that hit on the carpet would pick up speed as they traveled and would bounce extremely high. As a result, teams went after fleet-footed infielders and outfielders who could get a quick jump on the ball.

The use of pitchers began to change in the early 1970s, particularly after the designated hitter was introduced in the American League. Relief specialists, their recognition long delayed, has to be one of baseball's most significant changes after World War II. Relievers became specialists, rather than be the mop-up men. Managers began to focus on matchups, preferring one kind of pitcher to another in certain situations in the game. With the decline in starting pitching, middle-inning relievers became indispensable, called in to keep games close until the closer could come on for one inning to save the game. The modern closer, the one-inning man, came on the scene during the 1970s.

Baseball's boom in the '70s can be attributed to increased offense and exciting superstars. For the first time in many years, there were .350 hitters and 40-home run sluggers. Pitchers tried to cope with the batting resurgence. In the first year of the 1977 mini-expansion, American League sluggers slammed a record 2,013 home runs. Hitters in both leagues were now swinging at cowhide-covered balls. Along with the power game, the new emphasis on running saw such speedsters as Lou Brock and Davey Lopes challenging the game's top catchers, Johnny Bench, Carlton Fisk, and Thurman Munson.

Record home run explosions occurred in the 1980s. In 1987, home run records were set in both leagues, with 2,634 in the AL and the NL 1,824. Rulesmakers then came to the aid of shell-shocked moundsmen by widening the strike zone, and as a result, home run production declined in 1988 and 1989.

SOARING SALARIES IMPERIL BASEBALL'S FINANCIAL HEALTH The big numbers produced by the players meant rising salaries. By 1978, players drew salaries that averaged more than $100,000. More than any other aspect of the game, the 1970s will be known as the decade of intense legal battles, as players fought for their freedom. During the 1980s, the focus of the game shifted from the playing field to money and greed, on the part of both players and owners.

John Thorn wrote, "The game's financial health was imperiled by rising unrest over labor issues, centered on the reserve clause which bound a player to his team in perpetuity while denying him the opportunity to gauge his worth in the free market. It began with a momentous case brought against Organized Baseball by veteran outfielder Curt Flood in 1970, challenging the legality of the reserve clause. Then in 1975, arbitrator Peter Seitz ruled that a player could establish his right of free agency by playing out his option year without a signed contract. It was clear that free agency was the wave of the future."

Free agency, arbitration, collusion, even drugs, became as much a part of the game as hits, runs and errors. Still, the game's popularity was never greater. Annual attendance averaged more than 40 million, and average salaries increased to $300,000 by 1984, as thirty players joined the millionaire dollar ranks. The average-player salary soared past $1,000,000 during the 1990s. Free agency continued to break up teams. Although dynasties like the old Yankees are almost a thing of the past, the Jays and Braves proved that efficient management and a solid farm system could still produce perennial contenders.

Despite all of its troubles, the bitter feuding and numerous work stoppages, baseball in the 1980s and early '90s became more competitive than ever. In one ten-year period, ten different teams won the World Series, which had never happened before. The Mets and Twins, last place teams the year before, won the World Series the next. In the 1991 Series between Minnesota and Atlanta, five of seven games were settled by a single run, and four of those came with the last at bat! Three games went into extra innings, and two on spectacular players at the plate.

RECORD HOME RUN EXPLOSIONS   In the late 1980s and 90s, record home run explosions occurred. After records were set in 1987, "The Year of the Home Run" was in 1996 when the 28 teams combined for a season record 4,962 home runs, topping the previous high of 4,458 in 1987. The Orioles hit 257 to smash the AL team season record of 240 set by the Maris-Mantle Yankees of 1961. But the 1998 season proved to be one of the most unique and exciting years in baseball history. The drama of the home run race between Mark McGwire and Sammy Sosa made even casual fans pay attention. No player had ever hit more than 61 home runs in a season. Yet in 1998, both McGwire and Sosa surpassed that magical plateau.

SECOND HALF OF 20ᵀᴴ CENTURY   Until the 1990s, major league baseball had been successful in keeping the game competitive and interesting. However, the adjusted rules and changes have been designed mostly to help the hitter, other than the larger strike zone initiated briefly in the early 1960s. Today's strike zone is the smallest it has ever been. The controversial adoption of the Designated Hitter rule in 1973 gave hitters a further boost. While it has contributed to greater scoring, the D.H. rule has destroyed the traditional concept of baseball. Artificial turf has changed the way the game is played. In addition to excessively high bounces in the outfield, ground balls skip through the infield for undeserved hits. Playing fields with artificial surfaces take the bunt out of the game, changing defensive play significantly.

The balance of baseball swung strongly to the offense. A steady barrage of home runs dominated the game. Interleague play began with larger crowds and controversy. The wild-card system has marred pennant races, the long post-season has resulted in a World Series weather problem. The feud between baseball and the umpires continues and the need for drug testing became even more urgent.

Most of the changes and developments the past half-century have come off the field. Expansion continues to dilute pitching, and free agency has led to runaway salaries. Other major developments are night baseball, plane travel, television, integration, indoor and hitter-friendlier stadiums, relief specialists, expanded post-season play, and changes in player development and the minors.

Greatest Baseball in History

Next to a tight pennant race, what excites baseball fans the most is a debate about who are the game's greatest. While there have been numerous great players, managers, and teams in baseball over the years, the following are the greatest in my book.

GREATEST TEAM OF ALL-TIME The 1927 New York Yankees were known as the "Murderer's Row". Managed by Miller Huggins, the explosive "Bronx Bombers" were led by Babe Ruth, who hit a record 60 home runs, and Lou Gehrig, who batted in 175 runs. Combined with an outstanding pitching staff, the Yankees won 110 of 154 games, then swept the Pittsburg Pirates four straight in the World Series. Led by Waite Hoyt and Herb Pennock, Yankee pitchers compiled a 3.20 ERA, supported by rookie reliever Wilcy Moore who won 19 and lost only 7!

GREATEST PLAYER OF ALL-TIME   Babe Ruth, the Sultan of Swat, made the home run the most highly prized play in baseball. Prior to his slugging feats with the Yankees, Ruth was also an outstanding southpaw pitcher with the Boston Red Sox. During his illustrious career, Ruth hit a career total of 714 home runs, combined with a lifetime batting average of .342. His long ball prowess changed the way the game was played. He was perhaps the most popular figure in American sports history. Ruth was paid two million dollars for playing baseball 22 years – the biggest bargain the game ever had.

GREATEST PITCHER OF ALL-TIME   Walter Johnson, known as "The Big Train", was called the fastest who ever threw a baseball. Thrown with a whip-like sidearm motion, his pitches had a whooshing sound that exploded into the catcher's mitt with a boom. Pitching for a perennial second-division team, Johnson still won a total of 416 games, struck out 3,508. One year, he won 36 and walked only 38 men! In September of 1909, he performed the incredible feat of winning three consecutive games in four days, all of them shutouts. All that on a salary of $2,700 a year!

GREATEST MANAGER OF ALL-TIME   John J. McGraw, "The Little Napoleon", led the New York Giants for 33 years, winning ten pennants and three World Series. In 1916, he drove his team to a record 26 victories in a row. Among his many innovations, McGraw invented and developed the hit-and-run

Greatest Baseball in History

**Greatest Team - - - The 1927 New York Yankees,
known as the "Murderer's Row".**

**Greatest Player
- Babe Ruth**

**Baseball's Man of the
Century – Branch Rickey**

**Greatest Pitcher
- Walter Johnson**

**Greatest Umpire
- Bill Klem**

**Greatest Baseball
Announcer -
Vin Scully**

**Greatest Manager
- John McGraw**

play, made an attack weapon of the bunt, and was the first manager to pilot from the bench. He was the first to employ the science of psychological combative temperament. He said, "The only road to popularity is to win. The man who loses gracefully loses easily."

BASEBALL'S MAN OF THE CENTURY Branch Rickey was the most successful and innovative executive in the history of baseball. As general manager of the St. Louis Cardinals, Rickey invented the farm system. Later as president of the Brooklyn Dodgers, he was most instrumental in breaking the racial barrier by signing Jackie Robinson. Nobody in baseball history exercised as profound an influence on the game. His farm system revolutionized the recruitment and training of young talent in the minors. Rickey's systematic training laid the foundation of many pennant winners. "Make a man do it over and over again," he lectured. He originated Ladies Days, organized the Knot-Hole Gang program so school children could see Major League games, free or at a moderate price, and invented the sliding pit. Rickey's spirit and ideas live on through his many contributions.

GREATEST UMPIRE OF ALL-TIME Bill Klem umpired in the National League from 1905 through 1940 and officiated in a record 18 World Series. Mac Davis wrote, "His appearance, his walk, his manner of calling a play or waving a player to the showers, were all distinctive and characteristic." Klem's absolute integrity, his sense of authority, brought dignity to his job. "It ain't nothing till I call it," said the legendary umpire. Only Klem among all the umpires was ever honored by a special day in a big league park.

GREATEST BASEBALL ANNOUNCER With much respect to the late Mel Allen and Red Barber, and Bob Costas and Jon Miller today, Vin Scully is the master play-by-play announcer, and he has covered the Dodgers for 50 years! I can recall a poll conducted at Dodger Stadium when the fans were asked to name their most memorable Dodger. Scully won. Vin has a manager's knowledge of the game, and as Bob Keisser wrote, "He details the intimacies on the field in a language that fans on all levels can understand. Having worked in radio for so long, Scully has developed a keen sense of imagery and the art of the metaphor. Vin starts every game like a painter with a fresh, clean canvas in front of him."

Baseball's Hall of Fame

The National Baseball Hall of Fame and Museum is the oldest and most revered of all the sports Hall of Fame. In the beautifully written and illustrated book, "Players of Cooperstown", David Nemec, etc. wrote, "Enshrinement is the highest honor a major league player can receive." Dwight Chapin, Senior Editor of the San Francisco Examiner, said, "Baseball's Hall of Fame is a marvel, so filled with baseball treasures and memories that giving them the time they deserve would take a week."

The terms, Hall of Fame, embraces three branches of the sport's "Shrine": the gallery where the plaques of the Hall of Fame players hang, as well as the adjacent museum and library. The library has long been regarded as baseball heaven by writers, researchers and historians. The rules governing election to the Hall require that players be retired for five years and that the election is conducted by polling baseball writers by secret ballot. A candidate must receive a vote from 75 percent of those voting in order to be elected. Each year, a special exhibition game is played between two major league teams in conjunction with the annual induction ceremonies. The game is played on a Monday, usually the first Monday in August.

Baseball's Mid-Summer Classic

Major League Baseball's All-Star Game is today more than a game. When it first began in 1933, there was no Home Run Derby, nor an exhibition hall filled with baseball memorabilia and touring fans. "There really was little more to the first All-Star Game than the game itself," wrote Gregg Krupa in the Boston Globe. "Indeed, the game has endured and evolved into far more than just a game."

Today's All-Star Game is part of a five-day festival that celebrates the sport of baseball, beginning with the opening of the John Hancock All-Star Fan Fest. Baseball was the first sport to sponsor the Fan Fest, a huge, interactive exhibition that has received rave reviews. Over 80,000 fans attended 1998's event in Denver. "In the last five years, the All-Star Game has become a great spectacle," said Commissioner Bud Selig. "It's important in terms of what it does for us as a wonderful way of showing off all that is good about baseball in the middle of the season."

Baseball's Most Exciting Plays

Every baseball fan has his or her own favorite plays. Here are many of the most exciting:

- **HOME RUN**   A powerful swing that sends a ball soaring over the fences; the most exciting scene in baseball — the Grand Slam!!
- **STRIKE-OUT**   Striking out a hitter with the bases loaded, "blowing him away with the high, hard one!"
- **TRIPLE**   A runner speeding around the bases, a powerful throw from a fielder, with a close, "bang-bang" play at third base
- **OUTFIELDER**   Leaping high against the fence to rob the hitter of a sure home run; a spectacular circus catch

- **BEAUTIFUL SLIDE**   A sliding baserunner eludes the tag of a fielder

- **FAST BALL**   An explosive pitch with overpowering velocity and hop, one that rises or sinks
- **DOUBLE PLAY**   The artistry and deft footwork of infielders; the quick throws doubling up the runners
- **TRIPLE PLAY**   Though very rare, a situation in which there are three successive putouts on one play
- **SHORTSTOP**   Moving to his right in the hole, bracing on his right leg, making a strong and accurate throw to first base

- **OUTFIELDER**   A long, powerful throw to nail a sliding runner

- **RELAY PLAY**   An outfielder quickly hitting a well-positioned relay man who throws out a speeding base runner
- **HEAD-FIRST DIVING CATCH**   by a fielder to rob the hitter of a sure base hit
- **CATCHER'S STRONG AND ACCURATE THROW**   to cut down the runner
- **SQUEEZE PLAY**   The batter attempts to lay down a bunt to score the runner at third who is sprinting for the plate

Baseball Language

Baseball has its own jargon, its own language of describing plays, terms, events, etc. The more popular and colorful phrases include the following:

- **BANG-BANG PLAY** - When runner and ball arrive at the same time

- **BAZOOKA** (Or cannon) - A strong throwing arm

- **BRUSH BACK** - A pitcher throwing at or near the hitter

- **CAN OF CORN** - A high, easily caught fly ball

- **CUP OF COFFEE** - A brief trial with the parent club

- **DYING QUAIL** - Batted ball that drops suddenly, unexpectedly

- **FROZEN ROPE** - A hard-hit line drive, one with a rigid patch

- **HORSEHIDE** (Or apple, pill, etc.) - The ball

- **HOT CORNER** - Third base

- **HUMMER/SMOKE** - Whizzing speed, high velocity of a fastball

- **HUMP-BACK LINER** - A batted ball line drive, then sinks

- **LUMBER** (or stick, wood, war club, etc.) - The bat

- **ROUNDTRIPPER** (Or dinger, tater, homer) - Home run

- **SPLITTER** - Split-fingered fastball by the pitcher

- **STEP IN THE BUCKET** - To pull away from plate with front foot

- **TEXAS LEAGUER** - Poorly hit ball looping meekly over infield

- **TWIN KILLING** - A double play

Nicknames, A Baseball Tradition

Nicknames, for both players and teams, have always been a popular baseball tradition. Through the years, there have been numerous nicknames that have captivated the imagination and interest of fans and players alike. In recent years, nicknames have declined in number, other than David "Boomer" Wells and a few others. They need to make a comeback. True, ballpark nicknames are running wild, like "The Jake" in Cleveland, "Go to the Yard" in Baltimore, and "Bob", the new stadium in Phoenix. The appeal and image of players and the game itself could be enhanced if more players had nicknames.

SULTAN OF SWAT   George Herman "Babe" Ruth, as a result of his prodigious feats as a home run hitter

IRON HORSE   Lou Gehrig, the Yankees' durable slugger, who played in over 2,000 consecutive games

YANKEE CLIPPER   Joe DiMaggio, whose superlative play paced the Yankees to many world championships

THE BARBER   Sal Maglie would "shave" hitters with inside pitches

BIG BEAR   Fred Hutchinson was a big, burly pitcher in size

HOT POTATO   Luke Hamlin developed a juggling routine on the mound

THE PENGUIN   Ron Cey because of his walk or waddle

GABBY   Catcher Charles Leo Hartnett talked a lot

DAZZY   Pitcher Charles Arthur Vance dazzled hitters

RABBIT   Walter Maranville's size dictated the name

BOOM-BOOM   Walter Beck was a pitcher often battered by enemy hitters

OLD HOSS   Charles Radbourn, who won 60 games in 1884, because he was willing to work whenever asked

58

Top Baseball Web Sites

Exploring baseball Web pages on the Internet can be a most informative and often fascinating experience. There are thousands of Web sites that offer information about different aspects of baseball. In his book, Baseball on the Web, author Rob Edelman has done a superb job of simplifying the process of searching for baseball and selecting the best Web sites. From my own perspective, the following appear to be the most informative and meaningful.

Major League Baseball (MLB@BAT)
http://www.majorleaguebaseball.com/

This is the official site of Major League Baseball, attractively designed and filled with photos and visuals. One can even download video from "This Week in Baseball" clips to many classic baseball moments. The site provides numerous fact-filled links, team and league information, game highlights, player updates, statistics, a photo archive, trivia, and future events.

Minor League Baseball
http://www.minorleaguebaseball.com/

This is the official home page of Minor League Baseball, including information on teams, leagues, standings, commentary and line scores of games. This site features press releases and news items relating to the business of minor league baseball.

Total Baseball Online
http://www.totalbaseball.com/

This Web site is the online home of Total Baseball, the "Official Encyclopedia of Major League Baseball". It has many links, like "Total Baseball Daily", updated every day and includes extensive game reports, major and minor league news items, opinions, trivia questions, and events that happened 'today in history'. The site offers its own newsgroup and chat group in addition to a question and answer column called "Ask Total Baseball", in which visitors can submit baseball-related queries.

Baseball Play America
http://www.baseballplayamerica.com/

This is the Web site of Baseball Play America, an organization established to promote and protect the best interests of baseball and upgrade the quality of play. Our mission is to offer critique and evaluative analyses relative to the game's problems and needs and support worthwhile concepts and programs. BPA's site menu on the Internet is comprised of baseball's seven levels of play, including two movements we are strongly committed to: Baseball Fans Association of America and Playground Baseball of America. Membership information, benefits, etc. are provided in Chapter Three, A Plan for Baseball.

Serving Baseball's Research Needs

Formed in 1971 at Cooperstown, New York, the Society for American Baseball Research is now an organization of more than 7,000 members dedicated to promoting baseball as an institution and keeping accurate historical accounts of baseball events and issues. The founder and past president of SABR, Robert Davids, wrote: "One of the objectives in organizing SABR was to provide a forum for the exchange of historical and statistical information among members, as well as to disseminate this information to the public."

SABR is an open membership association of individuals interested in all aspects of baseball. Members receive the SABR newsletter and many other publications, including the Baseball Research Journal. They can exchange information and participate in research committees and regional groups. A national convention is held each summer in various cities, featuring research presentations, speakers and panels, trivia contests and professional ball games.

To learn more about SABR, its events and to find out how to join, write: Morris Eckhouse, Executive Director, SABR, P.O. Box 93183, Cleveland, OH 44101. Telephone: (216) 575-0500; Fax: (216) 575-0502. SABR's Web site is: http://www.sabr.org/.

Minor Leagues

Major Leagues

USA Baseball International

ORGANIZED BASEBALL

Colleges

Non-Pro/Semi- Pro/Adult

High Schools

Youth Leagues

Playground Baseball

3   A Plan for Baseball

As baseball moves into the next millennium with over 150 years of existence, there are positive signs of recovery from the damaging strike of 1994. In 1998, Major League Baseball enjoyed one of its most exciting seasons in recent years, highlighted by the "Great Home Run Race" between Mark McGwire and Sammy Sosa. Then in 1999, the two sluggers staged another dual.

Despite a "Season for the Ages", the game is in serious fiscal trouble at the major league level, with monumental problems which have disrupted the competitive balance of baseball. "No longer is the economic landscape haves and have-nots," wrote Tim Wendal in USA TODAY's Baseball Weekly. "In 1999, the gulf between payrolls of the richest and poorest teams surpassed $70 million. Over half the teams have no realistic chance of competing with the elite clubs. As for the fans, the costs of attending a big league game has gone beyond the reach of ordinary families." Although ownership complains about the widening payroll disparity, many clubs are still giving out excessively high salaries. Owners speak of cost containment and revenue sharing but continue to practice "doomsday economics." Baseball has become a corporate affair resulting in fewer kids and low-income families being able to afford to go to a big league game. Even Bobby Cox, manager of the Atlanta Braves, admits, "The game has become too costly for fans because high player salaries contribute to rising ticket and concession costs."

Baseball's failure to control the use of drugs, steroids and performance-enhancing substances is highly irresponsible. The lack of drug testing and other control measures has created an intolerable health problem not only for big league players but untold numbers of youths who have taken andro, a potentially dangerous supplement, simply because of McGwire's example.

Elsewhere in professional baseball, the problems and needs are less severe. The image and popularity of the minor leagues continues to attract family-oriented crowds and baseball admirers. Sparked by new ballparks, affordable fun and entertainment, with an intimate family atmosphere, attendance is at its greatest level since the late 1940s. Overemphasis on player development has turned off many local fans, as players come and go. Despite the boom in attendance and franchise value, the profit margins remain thin, as teams strive to cope with provisions of the Professional Baseball Agreement. Like in the major leagues, an increasing gap has developed between the haves and the have-nots.

At the international level, USA teams are striving to meet the challenge of stronger worldwide competition, as many nations have upgraded their national programs. At the 1999 Pan American Games, USA Baseball fielded a team of top minor league prospects in quest of an Olympic berth at the 2000 Sydney Games. And the Americans were successful in qualifying along with Cuba. For American teams to be more successful in the future, stronger and more efficient player development programs need to be implemented at all levels. Young players and teams need a more structured system of development and training.

USA's involvement in the Olympic Games has been rudely shaken, as the U.S. Olympic Committee and corporate sponsors struggle to deal with corruption and bribery by the IOC, creating huge repercussions for the Olympic movement. A most controversial issue for the IOC and its membership of over 100 countries deals with the questions, should professional athletes be allowed to compete in the Games? A growing number of Americans detest the dilution of the Olympic sprit by the invasion of pro athletes. Reversing the professional movement and allowing the true Olympic spirit to return to the Olympiad appears to be gaining increasing momentum, with a more practical and realistic code of rules, combined with financial guidelines and limits. As for how the major leagues fit into the international picture, the general thinking is that a World Cup of Baseball is much more appropriate for big league stars than sending "Dream Teams" to the Olympics.

While college baseball has the potential to achieve unprecedented popularity and a higher level of play, it remains to be seen whether the collegiate game has the program resources and administrative support to do so. For college baseball to achieve their goals, a significant structural change in the NCAA must be made, with less bureaucracy, with a willingness to be more receptive to change and reform. The NCAA, ruled tightly by college presidents and a maze of committees, have placed rigid restraints and controls on programs, preventing college baseball from maximizing its potential and optimum growth.

Challenged by the phenomenal growth of Men's Senior and Adult Baseball Leagues, non-pro leagues (better known as semi-pro) are beginning to show signs of recovery. The organization of more local teams and the return of hometown rivalries have stimulated both player and fan interest. Summer collegiate leagues are playing a major role in the revival of non-pro baseball. But a large number of managers and sponsors have expressed strong concern for their team's financial stability. The National Baseball Congress must take a more assertive stance in responding to the needs of its teams. For the non-professional game to realize its potential greater cooperation is needed between NBC leagues and the growing number of recreational programs for older adults and seniors.

Regarded by professional scouts as the key to baseball's career ladder, high school baseball continues its quest to elevate the game to a higher pedestal and greater profile. To become the centerpiece in the development of highly skilled players in the United States, high school baseball must receive funding from the community, corporate sponsors and Major League Baseball. There is an urgent need for prep programs to become revenue-producers themselves, using a Multi-funded Approach to Marketing. Later, I will describe what is needed to give high school baseball much needed visibility --- stage a national high school baseball championship!!

Despite the robust growth of Little League and other organized youth leagues, the most serious problems and weaknesses in America's player development system are in youth baseball. The many excesses and abuses of Little League Baseball continues to hinder the growth and development of young players. There is a disturbing absence of fundamental instruction at the younger age levels. Coaches lack coaching skills and knowledge of the game. The large majority of youth coaches are untrained, non-certified, mostly parents. Too much emphasis is placed on winning the game. Of even greater significance, society and our culture has had a profound influence on play. The need for reform in youth baseball is now greater than ever, highlighted by the return of sandlot baseball, unstructured play, a revival of pick-up games and a re-opening of parks and playground to baseball. Kids need to play on their own.

To learn baseball, you have to play it.
- Ted Williams

Restoring Baseball's Greatness

What baseball needs now is a true renaissance, a great revival of the sport, and every level of play must contribute. A major concern of baseball should be how the game can be restored to its old luster and glory and rebuild its popularity and credibility among the fans. It has to begin at the grass roots. While the greatest impetus has to come from the majors, the movement must have the active support and strong contribution from every level.

There were times many years ago when the phrase "for the good of the game" actually meant something in baseball. The game's commissioner, with the support of team owners and players, would do what was necessary for the good of the game. Much too often, however, these words have a hollow meaning today. The owners and players have been largely responsible for taking the glory out of the game. They must now work together to bring it back, re-energizing the fans. Both must realize how important the fans are. After ignoring them for so long, owners must make every effort to make the fans a part of baseball's equation.

What is needed now is a game plan for the entire sport, from the big leagues on down to youth baseball. Major emphasis in this chapter is given to what each of the seven levels of play must do to help restore the greatness of baseball. For a true renaissance to occur, all levels must become involved and make important contributions. Above all, decisions must be made and action taken for "the good of the game."

Everyone has a role in restoring the greatness of baseball. Owners must look beyond their own self-interests and do what is best for the game as a whole. Likewise, the players have a responsibility to those who pay their salaries, the fans.

Major League Baseball

Baseball continues to ride its revival, sparked by the home run derby of 1998 and the emergence of a new generation of exciting young stars. In a most remarkable offensive year, a total of 5,064 homers were hit. From a popularity point of view, baseball has recovered quite well from the strike of 1994. In the minds of those who read only the front page and the nightly home run highlights, the game is back. However, the facts are quite clear that some very serious problems and vital needs exist, no matter how many home run races are orchestrated by big league baseball.

Owner Peter Magowan of the Giants warned "People shouldn't get too giddy over baseball's comeback." He cited such problems as competitive imbalance, excessive salaries, payroll disparity, and rising ticket prices. "I'm very concerned about the pricing of tickets. Baseball is family entertainment, but ticket prices are going up substantially."

The chasm between small and large-market teams has widened significantly since only a decade ago. The disparity has grown both in terms of gross revenue and payroll. As Bruce Jenkins explained in the San Francisco Chronicle, "Baseball has become a prisoner of its own economic system. It is all big market vs. small market, teams that can win and the teams that have no chance."

While fan apathy and bitterness from the strike has diminished, a wide range of fan resentments still exist. The lack of responsible leadership by both ownership and the players' union and the lack of a strong and independent commissioner have hurt the image and integrity of the sport. An increasing number of fans do not believe the best interest of the game is given enough consideration when agreements and policies are being made. Furthermore, Major League Baseball and all professional sports for that matter have failed to make fans a part of the equation.

Perhaps there is a glimmer of hope on the horizon. The mindboggling $105 million contract of Kevin Brown could have some good for baseball. As Padres owner John Moores explained, "There is a theory that before you can affect change, you must have a crisis. The 1999 season could be that crisis." Paul Hagen wrote in Baseball America, "The Brown contract could be the 2-by-4 upside the head that the owners need to realize that they must compete and cooperate at the same time, that it isn't in their best interest to have only a handful of clubs with a realistic chance at winning in any given year."

The players, for the most part, are performing well, but many are arriving in the majors not knowing how to slide, bunt or run the bases properly. Nor are there very many strong throwing arms. Still, the quality of play does no appear to be as much a problem as it was early in the 1990s. Coaches and managers have done a good job in stressing the basic fundamental skills.

Top minor league prospects are being rushed too quickly to the majors. They are not maximizing their potential. In sharp contrast to the many Super-Stars of earlier decades, like the 1950s, being moved up too quickly has stunted the growth of young prospects. Big league clubs are not allowing their most talented farmhands to be fully developed. The attention to detail is not emphasized enough in either league. Many prospects are skipping the class AAA level entirely or just make a brief stop before being rushed up to the majors. Those who have an additional year in the minors and play more at AAA are better prepared when they reach the big leagues.

"When a player is rushed through the system and into the majors, he usually doesn't start to appreciate the total game," said Tony LaRussa of the Cardinals. "Outfielders miss the cutoff man, and infielders aren't in the right position. Base running is poor, like getting a good jump, making tighter turns and reading situations.

The complete player can impact a team greatly. But what usually is the case, one player can hit but not field. Another player is fast but doesn't know how to use his speed. One player can bunt, while another is the only one with a strong arm. The player who can do it all has inestimable value and importance to a team.

The game has swung too far to the offense. As a result of the power surge of the '90s, the excitement of home runs have diminished simply because there have been so many hit. A dilution of pitchers is quite apparent, young hurlers trying to cope with a greatly reduced strike zone, the tightest-wound ball ever, with shorter fences, and hitters with strong, bulging muscles. With so much emphasis on hitting, the rest of the game has been neglected. Many of the game's much admired subtleties have been lost. While kids don't play baseball on corner lots, they are swinging the bat a lot, at batting tees and in hitting tunnels.

How the Majors Can Help Restore Baseball

- Preserve baseball's connection to the past, traditions and continuity

- Solve baseball's economic problems – reducing competitive imbalance and correcting the game's fiscal imbalance

- Make fans a greater part of baseball's economic equation and more affordable for lower income families and children

- A strong, independent commissioner who will serve the best interests of the game

- A more responsible ownership which will exercise greater restraint in handing out excessive salaries

- A players' union which will consider not only the players' interests but the best interests of the game

- Upgrade the quality of umpiring, make umpires more accountable, and adopt one set of standards and a code of conduct with players

- Improve the game's television coverage, greater control of media empires

- Revitalize baseball's marketing; stronger efforts in winning kids back

- Take a moderate approach to realignment; reduce interleague play, limiting games to the first half of the season.

- Provide more balance to a game which has swung too far to the long ball; bring back some of the "lost arts of baseball"

- Correct baseball's biggest mistakes: the designated hitter, artificial turf and the low pitching mound

- Ban steroids, initiate mandatory drug testing.

Competitive Disparity is Widening

Revenue disparities pose an unprecedented threat to baseball's competitive balance. "Sports leagues have rules to contrive competitive balance," wrote George Will. "The aim is not to guarantee teams equal revenues, but revenues sufficient to give each team periodic chances of winning if each uses its revenues intelligently. Baseball's rules no longer suffice."

Revenue disparities have widened to the point that two-thirds of big league teams were virtually excluded from the 1999 winter market for top free agents." Will believes that "When fans of 20 or the 30 teams come to realize that under the current arrangements, their teams have no realistic hope of contending, ever, no matter how intelligently their teams use their resources, the spell of baseball will be broken in those cities."

What has changed the economic structure of big league baseball? Local broadcast revenues have become more important and more unequal. The Yankees, for example, receive $55 million, while the Royals get only $5 million. New ballparks with a variety of new revenue streams, including luxury boxes, are increasingly important. New corporate owners have new motives for ownership, such as the media giants who buy programming when purchasing a team.

Small-Market Teams Are Sinking Fast

Not long ago, many teams had a shot at winning the World Series. Today, however, small-market, small-payroll teams don't have a chance. As baseball heads into another century, the disparity between the haves and the have-nots is the No. 1 issue facing the game. Without change, the number of franchises could shrink.

"Baseball's deep-pocketed owners continue to throw cash around like it's Monopoly money," wrote Jim Van Vliet of the Sacramento Bee. Ten players now make $10 million or more a year, more than what the Montreal Expos paid their entire roster in 1998. There are many teams right now that just cannot afford to compete. As a result of widening disparity, more and more fans have the feeling their team has no chance to win. Andy MacPhail, chief executive of the Chicago Cubs, believes "The game has evolved beyond anybody's capacity under the current framework to be both profitable and competitive."

The chasm between rich and poor teams has widened greatly. Most recent estimates have the top-earning club with $170 million in revenue in 1998, and the bottom team taking in only $35 million. Many baseball people believe a solution to the economic problem has to start and stop with the owners. "We need a system similar to the National Football League, where they have equal revenue-sharing," said Oakland A's general manager Billy Beane. Baseball owners have looked with envy at the National Basketball Association, which got its players to agree to salary maximums: $9 million for those with one to five years of experience, $11 million for players with six to nine years and $14 million for players with 10 years or more.

The players' union has continually rejected a salary cap and has voiced their opposition to any additional luxury taxes and revenue sharing that, while promoting more equal team assets could exert a drag in the growth of their salaries. As a result, when the current collective bargaining agreement ends after the 2001 season, baseball could be faced with another work stoppage. "It's obvious," said Giants executive vice president Larry Baer, "that what's in place is not having a deterrent effect."

For baseball to achieve financial stability, the players must help to close the economic gap. "Otherwise," wrote Henry Schulman, "players and owners could be spoiling for a doozy of a fight." Players, though, if not their union leaders, are slowly beginning to recognize there needs to be a change. As Brian Giles of the Pirates explained, "A player doesn't think about it when he's on a contending team, but when traded to a smaller market, it really sinks in. It seems that each year there are six or seven teams contending and the others are not in the picture."

Tony Gwynn had a similar view, stating that "At spring training every year, you tell the media, 'If this goes right and that goes right, we can contend', but deep down inside, you know you don't have a shot."

Pittsburgh Pirates owner Kevin McClatchy expressed the viewpoint that "We have an obligation to put this sport in a position to be the best sport in America again. Only by increasing the level of sharing, can we have competitive franchises."

Has the Home Run Saved the Game?

Despite the fact that 1998 was one of the most exciting and dramatic seasons in many years, the home run is not saving the game. In fact, as Tim Keown aptly stated, "It has cheapened baseball, eroding legitimacy ever so slowly."

Juiced Ball Era

Today's ball carries 10-15 percent farther than it did 25 years ago. The 350-foot fly ball out in 1975 is today's 385-390-foot home run. Tests have proved this conclusively. Opposite-field home runs, traditionally the work of baseball's strong men, have risen dramatically in the 1990s.

The game has been tinkered with to increase scoring and attract more fans. Ordering livelier balls has been a century long practice of major league owners in the cloak of secrecy. But everyone, including the ball manufacturers, continually denies that it had been done. But, there is no question that since 1993, balls used in Major League Baseball have been "juiced". Based on all the data I have examined and reviewed, the "Juiced Ball Theory" is as valid as it can be. In 1987, the first rabbit-ball season in the modern era, Commissioner Peter Ueberroth stated that baseball needed more offense. As if by magic, balls left the park at a record rate of 2.12 per game that season.

During the winter of 1993, the owners' Executive Council approved specifications for "a new ball" to prop up sagging TV ratings. Rawlings Sporting Goods Company, who make baseballs used in the major leagues, shipped large quantities of flubber, the core of the new ball, to its plant in Costa Rica, replacing the old cork and rubber core. Baseball now has a jackrabbit of a ball.

How are baseballs made livelier? Juiced balls are harder and tighter. Winding better yarn tighter gives it greater resilience. The tightly stitched seams add to the rotation and the ball stays in the air longer. The higher, coarser seams reduce the ball's aerodynamic "drag", which increases its range.

There is a long overdue need for balls, even bats, to be uniformly consistent. The integrity of the game is not served when they are tampered with and changed, without respect to the rules. Baseball records are the most cherished and valued in sports, and the home run glut in the 1990s has made a mockery of records. Baseball must stop tampering with the ball. Those who manufacture the ball should be directed to reduce the liveliness of balls by 10 percent.

The theories that explain the Home Run Phenomenon do not begin and end with livelier balls. Along with diluted pitching staffs, there are various other factors, such as the following:

Bigger and Stronger Hitters

Many of today's hitters have powerful hitting swings capable of driving balls to all fields. They arrive in spring training with 10-15 more pounds of solid muscle. Can their muscular physiques be attributed just to pumping iron and consuming "food" substances such as Creatine? Perhaps for the majority of players, this is probably true, but based on extensive research and investigation, there has been alarming increases in the consumption of illegal growth hormones, anabolic steroids, in addition to androstendione and Creatine.

Lighter and More Explosive Bats

Bats used today are more resilient and explosive than ever. Hitters are now swinging lighter and smaller bats, with thinner handles. Hitters, as a result, can whip them faster for added propulsion. Bats are now being doctored with "long distance" lacquer. The theory is that bat speed, rather then bat mass, determines the force at the point of impact. For example, former Red sox outfielder Dwight Evans switched from a 37-ounce bat in 1986 to a 32-ounce bat in 1987, producing 34 homers, his career high at age 35.

The Shrunken Strike Zone

Around the mid-80s, for some unknown reason, the umpires arbitrarily decided to cut off the top of the strike zone to about the belt buckle. There are no more high strikes, resulting in too many hitters counts. By laying off the high fastball, hitters either draw walks or wait for a fat pitch at the belt. The official strike zone must be restored as prescribed in the rulebook. Calling the high strike would be an effective tool to speed up the game. If the umpires would call more strikes, there would be fewer walks and a better game because hitters will be swinging and putting the ball in play.

Small, Hitter-friendly Parks

Compared to old-time ballparks, many stadiums are now bandboxes, a major reason for the home run explosions of the '90s. With a few exceptions, the outfield fences of 50 years ago were much farther from home plate. A home run was once special but today it is often a cheap shot. While fans like to see high-scoring games and plenty of action, many like to see a pitching battle with outfielders given ample running room to go for a ball. I have to believe most fans want home runs to be legitimate. The time has come for baseball architects to move the fences back to realistic distances, allowing for livelier balls, powerful bats and stronger athletes.

The Threat of Radical Change   There is still the threat of major, even radical, realignment, which Acting commissioner Bud Selig tried to get approval in 1997. But he was rebuffed by owners and an overpowering outcry from fans and baseball's foremost writers and broadcasters who rose up to defend the preservation of the great traditions, history, and continuity of the game. Selig and Boston Red Sox CEO John Harrington are still after complete geographic alignment, even if "We must do it in bite-size chunks."

However, Bob Costas believes realignment could undo a century of tradition. "The most radical plans would essentially destroy the leagues as we know them," said Costas. "Many statistics, the heart and soul of the game for die-hard fans, would be rendered meaningless. Comparisons to past records would end. And league records in homers or strikeouts would have to start from scratch, because the teams comprising each league would be different."

From 1903, the rules and overall structure of baseball have been rooted in bedrock. They have resisted any number of gimmicks and fads, radical changes and the like. The game has prospered by its ongoing stability. The fact that the rules have stood for over a century makes one believe the early developers of the game got it right the first time. The expressions of change invariably come from people who either do not know or refuse to want to know what the game is all about, what it stands for, how the game evolved, its history and many traditions. Radical, extreme changes would only serve to erode the solid foundations of the game.

There is, however, the need to correct mistakes of the past, such as the designated hitter, artificial turf and the wild-card system. Among the positive changes off the field would be lower ticket and concession prices, the players' attitudes toward fans, more realistic salaries, a slow-down in players changing teams. But there is nothing wrong with the game. The rules are just as fine for modern day players as they were for the old-timers early in the century. But what baseball needs today is less tinkering, particularly with the ball and bat and to enforce the strike zone specified in the rulebook.

The interleague concept has the potential to be good for baseball, if not overdone. As Jon Miller pointed out, "We won't know for several years whether those games will be just as appealing to fans when the novelty wears off. The best thing about interleague play is evident when it accentuates intra-city and other geographic rivalries, for these match-ups excite the fans."

Baseball's Low TV Ratings

The declining ratings of both the World Series and League championships continues to be a serious concern to network executives and for baseball. Television ratings for baseball games have been in a slump for years. Despite a strong finish in Game 7, the 1997 classic was one of the lowest-rated since records began in 1959. But Fox Network finished the '98 season with an average rating of 3.1, 15 percent higher than the two previous years, the biggest jump in baseball's national Game of the Week package since 1966.

Among the many reasons for the low ratings of the 1990s:

- Baseball's expanded play-offs have diluted the impact of the LCS and the World Series.

- Baseball is still trying to recover from player strikes.

- Television starting times are too late for the Eastern half of the United States.

- The games are too long; the slow pace turns off viewers.

- Cold weather, almost unplayable, hurts the level of play.

- Failure to market effectively to young viewers.

- Lack of good story line, marquee teams, compelling match-ups.

Most importantly, the game is losing the youth of America who are being shut out from watching World Series games. Baseball and the TV networks share the blame for scheduling the Series in the evening, with 8:20 p.m. EDT starting times.

As manager Jim Leyland explained, "Most youths are sleeping at 9 o'clock and so is the guy who works from 7 a.m. to 4 or 5 in the afternoon. By the sixth inning, he is dozing off or asleep."

Major League baseball has to make a stronger effort to get the youth back involved, playing the game, coming out to the ballparks, and watching games on TV. Baseball has to be promoted and marketed as a kid-friendly game. It must keep ticket prices low enough so that families can afford to go to the games. In addition to reduced-price packages for families, baseball should re-institute the highly popular Knot-hole Gang program of the 1960s, with millions of free and reduced price tickets given to park and recreation agencies for organized trips to professional games.

Expand Baseball World-wide

Baseball on a worldwide scale is a sleeping giant, about ready to explode relative to competitive play, spectator entertainment and televised coverage. Until only recently, it has been underdeveloped by Major League Baseball. Now, Commissioner Bud Selig says, "Baseball must do more internationally, in terms of marketing as well as play." There is optimism that a World Cup of Baseball can be organized in the near future.

Baseball, meantime, is becoming increasingly involved in global competition. During the spring of 1999, the Baltimore Orioles played a home and away, two-game exhibition series with Cuba. The Padres-Rockies 1999 regular season opener was played in Monterrey, Mexico, and the Chicago Cubs and New York Mets will open the 2000 season in Japan.

World Cup of Baseball

The time has come for baseball competition to be expanded among the nations and continents of the world, on all levels of play with the most skilled professional players competing in a World Cup of Baseball. For international baseball to really take off, it needs more exposure and greater promotion, to make people sit up and take notice. A World Cup is the way to go!

A World Cup-type tournament will widen the sport's appeal on the international level. It would produce additional revenue for both players and owners. Such an event every 2 or 4 years would do more for the sport of baseball than have professionals compete in the Olympics or staging a World Series event.

A tournament format similar to soccer's World Cup could precede the MLB season, like March 24-April 1, or in early November, with games played in warm-weather areas. Since the World Cup of Hockey precedes the National Hockey League season, perhaps baseball's event could be scheduled prior to the MLB season. A double elimination tournament of one week would involve from 4 to 8 teams.

The best players representing the top baseball countries from around the globe should meet in the World Cup, matching national all-star teams. Major league players would return to their nation of origin. A committee of Professional Baseball Leagues should have jurisdiction over the event. Major League Baseball must have the close cooperation of the Commissioner's office, club owners, Players Association, and the Umpires Association.

Roles of Responsibility

Guided by the basic premise that everyone in Major League Baseball has a role to play, I believe the game can be upgraded significantly if the following would occur:

Commissioner's Role in Restoration
More than ever, baseball urgently needs strong and effective leadership. It needs a qualified, objective individual who has no ties to the owners or the players and will have the power to serve the overall best interests of the game. He should have the authority to govern, rule and discipline when situations arise. The commissioner must have the authority to make decisions final and absolute in all matters affecting the integrity and well being of baseball.

"A true baseball commissioner would represent owners, players, and umpires," said Jon Miller, "but also would look out for paying customers, the citizens of baseball. Fans are the reason professional baseball exists. Baseball's next commissioner should possess clear-eyed, far-reaching vision to take baseball into the next century."

More than ever, the game needs someone with strong leadership, a neutral voice, speaking for the best interests of all of baseball. To be truly effective, he has to be able to gain the trust of both sides. It is also essential for the commissioner to stay in touch and serve the concerns and needs of all levels of play.

Without a commissioner who oversees all of the sport, the baseball institution is crumbling, in need of support and direction. When the owners appointed one of their own to run the game, they abolished the office of the commissioner. "Baseball is still paying for that mistake," said Miller, "because for over five years, there was no central authority in the game."

Presently, Bud Selig is more the CEO of Major League Baseball, not a genuine commissioner. However, by adding Paul Beeston and Sandy Alderson, two outstanding baseball administrators, to the commissioner's office, Selig can now do what he does best, forming consensus and a united policy among the owners. With Alderson overseeing crucial projects, baseball's administration is moving in the right direction.

Ownership's Role in Restoring the Game

Of all those involved in baseball today, the people who could give the game the greatest boost are the major league owners, guided by the commissioner and the two league presidents. As baseball struggles to regain its appeal with fans, ownership has within its means the authority to get the game back on track, if only they would use their influence and power in a constructive and sensible manner. For the game to recover and regain its status as the national pastime, the owners should make a strong effort to correct mistakes of the past. How they respond to the serious problems and controversial issues confronting baseball will determine its future greatness. In coping with baseball's biggest problem, if they would exercise more restraint in handing out highly excessive salaries and multi-year contracts, baseball would be taking a major step in getting back on track.

For baseball to recover and truly prosper, each and every owner must look beyond their own self-interests and try to do what is best for the game as a whole. Baseball must listen more to the fans and consider their best interests more often, their sentimentality, even their ideas and opinions on the future direction of the game. Without fans, there would be no professional ball.

The perspective of the fans has never really been taken into account when determining the best interests of the game. Through the years, Major League Baseball has given minimal consideration to the best interests of the fans. Only in rare occasions have fans been given the opportunity to voice their opinions and concerns. As evidenced by the negotiations and settlements of the most recent pro sports strike or lockouts, the fans have never been a part of the economic equation.

Here are some ways owners can help restore baseball's greatness:

- Achieve greater parity between large and small market teams.

- Control spending, reverse increases in player salaries.

- Develop a more equitable system of revenue sharing.

- Sell the game to kids; direct promotions to families.

- Uphold baseball's reputation as the most economical buy.

- Develop closer, more friendly relations with players.

- Promote and market their skills more effectively.

- Protect the health and well being of the players by implementing stronger efforts to combat drugs.

- Slow down player movement, enhancing their identity with fans.

- Depend more on player development and the farm system.

- Increase your support of the amateur levels of play.

Players Union's Role in Restoration

Since it was established, the Players Association and the owners have not been able to work together for the good of the game. The union has become as arrogant today as the owners were two decades ago. Donald Fehr has never expressed concern for the overall economic health of baseball, other than getting an ever-increasing portion of the pie for the players, regardless of the impact on the sport. As Bob Costas said "Baseball's union find no merit in any idea that doesn't enrich its membership."

I like to think Fehr does care but I have never heard nor read where he articulated an empathy and concern for the game's stability and well being. He states that "Baseball should market itself to the fans", but he has yet to propose or support any plan or change that would serve the fans' best interest. What has the players' union done to help remedy baseball's economic problems? During the eight work stoppages since 1972, the players have made few concessions. Hopefully, the player reps on the thirty clubs will urge their union to start demonstrating more concern for the current health and future direction of the game.

Players Role in Restoring Baseball
Players, as well as the owners, need to portray a more positive image. The image of the game is vital to baseball's future and prosperity. In the best interests of the game, it is most essential for the players and owners to work closely together. Players should serve on committees and participate in the decision-making process. They should be willing to share fairly with the owners in the risks, as well as the revenues and opportunities.

Will players get behind measures intended to increase competitive balance if they result in a drag on salaries? Player agent Larry Reynolds expressed the feeling that "Many players probably would sacrifice some money as long as they're being well-paid." Pittsburgh outfielder Brian Giles believes "Players must work with owners to maintain baseball's fast-eroding competitive balance. The alternative is for only a few elite Super teams to compete each season for pennants and star free agents, a situation even the best-paid players don't want."

For baseball to recover its appeal, the players must realize they do have a public relations responsibility to those who pay their salaries, the fans. Players should make a stronger effort to communicate and show a greater concern for the fans, young and old alike, and their best interests.

Major league ballplayers have a responsibility to the people who pay their salary and to this game that provides them with a nice living," wrote Jon Miller. "That responsibility is to promote the game and to nurture it." Miller believes the solution to the problem is education. "Each club should launch an informational program for its players," he explained. "The curriculum would play up the history of Major League Baseball and the history of that particular team. And players can invest a little time learning why a team's fans --- who ultimately pay their salaries --- care so much about the uniform you're wearing."

The keys to this program are to create a connection and instill a sense of responsibility. "When a player is out in public," said Miller, "he should think about his responsibility as a public figure representing his team and baseball, and that awareness should be reflected in his actions. He shouldn't always blow off fans seeking autographs."

Umpires Role in Restoring Baseball

The on-going feud between Major League Baseball and the Umpires Association has gone far too long, and the negative relationship does not serve the best interests of the game. While we strongly support the need for an agreed upon Code of Conduct for managers and their players, as well as for umpires, we firmly believe a "zero-tolerance" policy is not in the best interests of baseball. Unquestionably, baseball, in their support of umpires, must not tolerate any physical abuse directed against them. Quicker and tougher penalties for bad behavior are essential.

Still, it should be said that umpires and managers engaging in "jaw-to-jaw" arguments has been a fixture in baseball for more than a century, providing fans with entertaining fun and excitement. Some umpires have become too confrontational and seem to be too willing to toss players from the game. Certainly, the game would be better served if umpires would allow a little showmanship and crowd-pleasing antics from the managers, provided of course, they do not go beyond the provisions of an agreed Code of Conduct.

Umpires should be held accountable and baseball should institute a process that increases the accountability of umpires. Jurisdiction should be shifted from the two leagues to the office of the Commissioner and have the game train its own umpires. A system that rewards merit should be implemented, one which will remove those who are incompetent. The very best umpires should survive, just like the players.

Umpiring is not an easy job, especially when close borderline calls need to be made. Umpires are just as human as ball players. This means that they do make mistakes occasionally. Too often, they receive an excessive amount of verbal abuse from players and managers, which is why they have been seeking stronger and swifter punishment meted out for misconduct. They want and deserve more support from baseball's leadership. Many people believe the umpires' aptitude is less a problem than their attitude, which often becomes arrogant, too confrontational. They say big league umpires need an attitude adjustment. Some are too hotheaded, lean too heavily toward ejecting and try to take over the game. They should remember: No fan pays to see umpires.

The Fans Role in Restoring the Game   The time is
long overdue for the fans to be added to the overall economic equation of baseball. But, how can they get baseball to listen? They need a stronger, unified voice in telling the major leagues how they should operate and have greater input in determining the direction of the game. The players have the skills and the multi-million dollar contracts, backed by a powerful union. The corporate owners have the ballparks and the team franchises, but without the fans, there would be no professional baseball.

If they would organize and take a more activist role, the fans could become a powerful force in baseball. They have the power and the means to do so – if they will only use it. "The caretakers of baseball's popularity are not the owners, or the players, but the fans," wrote Alan Schwarz. "They are the ones ultimately responsible for cradling the game's meaning and importance."

An increasing number of fans today are voicing strong objections over the high costs of attending a major league ball game. They refuse to support the self-centered greed of players and owners in professional sports. Until more fans take that stand, they will continue to be left out of the equation, despite having to assume the excessive salaries and ever rising ticket prices. As one fan said, "It's ridiculous to spend $150 to go watch a game when the players are making as much in one game as the average person makes in a year."

In strikes and lockouts, only the concerns of players and owners are being expressed, with no attention given to the feelings of the fans. When interviewed, some players say they don't care what the fans think. It is all about how much money they can make. Fans have yet to benefit from collective bargaining. Well, the sports fans of America are beginning to wake up and realize that they are paying the exorbitant salaries to athletes. They need to say, "Enough is enough! We're not going to stand for this."

The only way fans will be able to negotiate a better deal is to unite and organize. As the longtime consumer advocate Ralph Nader stated, "It's time to make the sports powers answer to those who make professional sports possible – the fans." Nader has organized a non-profit group to demand accountability from the business of sports. "Everything today is worse: taxes, personal seat licenses, price gouging." Like most grassroots political efforts, his group wants to give their constituents a voice. They get their message across with newsletters, organizational teams, etc. Funding comes primarily from members. For more information contact Nader and his staff at: Fans/Taxpayers' Group, P.O. Box 19367, Washington, D.C. 20036. Organized fan clubs can become a driving force of public opinion that can serve the best interests of baseball and other pro sports.

Do fans have any power? Why should sports and entertainment executives listen to the fans? Because if they don't, fans will do what they learned from the players and owners. They will boycott or even strike! It's time for a fans' union.

Voice of the Grandstand

In making baseball sit up and take notice, fans need to organize and demand that Major League Baseball add them to the overall equation. If organized, they could become a powerful force in baseball, even organizing boycotts if necessary (No strikes!). To achieve this goal, they need to get organized on the national level, such as the BASEBALL FANS ASSOCIATION OF AMERICA (BFAA).

The clout and stature of fans needs to be strengthened. Fans should have the opportunity to speak their minds relative to the problems, issues, needs and concerns of baseball. Chapters should be organized in every MLB city. Somebody has to serve as "watchdogs " of baseball. Why not the fans? (with support from dedicated writers, columnists, announcers). Such an organization would force MLB to listen more attentively to those who pay the bills.

Baseball Fans Association of America

BFAA, a subsidiary of BASEBALL PLAY AMERICA, will represent baseball fans on every level of play, giving them a stronger voice and input as to how organized baseball operates and the direction of the game. Organized on a national level, BFAA, in particular, will strive to promote interest in Major League Baseball and make their leaders listen more attentively to fans' concerns. Indeed, the organization will serve as a "sounding board" for the voices of baseball fans who want to be heard, become a part of the economic equation and play a greater role in baseball's policy-making decisions, such key issues as collective bargaining negotiations and new stadium projects.

Rather than assume the role of confrontist or adversary, however, the underlying purpose and intent of the BFAA, preferably, is to build and promote interest in baseball. A major attempt will be made to help America recapture the "Hot Stove League" spirit and to contribute to "Baseball Fever' nationwide. Until recent years, it was a tradition for fans to get together over a cup of coffee or a beer and talk about their favorite teams, the players, major issues of the present and coming seasons, who's going to win, the chances of our team, etc. A small group of baseball fans in the winter and during the season gather at a store or restaurant and talk-it-up, gossip about whatever comes to mind. They reminisce, going back over the season, talking "what –ifs", "shoulda beens", etc. They wonder about trades and those that might be coming up, the chances of their favorite teams and players.

Yes, that was the typical spirit and tradition of the "Hot Stove League" and those who love the game of baseball can bring back these "Glory Years". For fans to really get caught up with the spirit, the following scenes and atmosphere need to occur:

Restaurants, book stores, sports bars, coffee shops, and other businesses should be encouraged to support the movement by providing meeting places. A nostalgic atmosphere can be created by displaying framed photographs, some autographed by the stars, baseball scenes, along with pennants, banners, or a slogan or two, to stimulate interest; with an occasional visit by speakers, such as ex-pros, writers, broadcasters, front office personnel, etc. to answer questions and keep the discussions going.

Fans have longed for the off-season "Hot Stove League" that got rolling at the winter meetings in December. But as Paul White wrote, "Today, it has become 'Wait for spring and say: Just tell me who's playing on what teams in what cities.'" Fans have missed the cozy baseball gossip, and this spirit and tradition must be rekindled and brought back.

Baseball Play America

Baseball Play America was established to promote and protect the best interests of baseball. It was formed to help implement and support the goals and objectives of the Plan for Baseball which is designed to Restore Baseball's Greatness. The primary goal of BPA is to upgrade the quality of play on all levels. Our mission is to provide critique and evaluative analyses as to the game's problems, needs and concerns, clarify and explain major issues, and support worthwhile causes, concepts and programs. In addition to fans and families, members of BPA include coaches, players and administrators.

BPA's web-site menu on the Internet is comprised of eight areas of interest:

Major Leagues	Non-pro/semi-pro/adult/senior
Minor Leagues	High Schools
USA Baseball/International	Youth Baseball/Playground Baseball
Colleges and universities	Baseball Fans of America

For BASEBALL PLAY AMERICA and its subsidiary, BASEBALL FANS ASSOCIATION OF AMERICA, to achieve our goals and objectives, we will need financial support through membership dues, donations, and contributions from corporate sponsors and organizations that share our dedication and commitment. This revenue will help pay for operational expenses, such as publishing, printing, mailing charges, papers, and to operate our new web-site.

Members of BPA will receive the following:
- Quarterly newsletter consisting of BPA concerns
- Official report of the Plan for Baseball
- Membership card
- Access to BPA's web-site (news releases, surveys, forum, files, photos, etc.)
- Discounts, such as for books, memorabilia, tapes, etc.

Annual dues of $36.00 will provide membership in BPA. This can be paid by check or charged to your credit card. To learn more about Baseball Play America, visit the organization's web-site: www.baseballplayamerica.com. The e-mail address is: baplam@worldnet.att.net. Or, write: Baseball Play America, P.O. Box 4182, El Dorado Hills, CA 95762-0014. Telephone: (916) 933-7459   Fax No.: (916) 933-7447.

Economic Plan for Baseball

The economic problems of Major League Baseball have shaken the overall stability of the sport. Salaries have skyrocketed overwhelmingly out of control. There is great concern about the direction of the game's economy. Over half of the clubs have reported substantial budget deficits, forcing them to boost the prices to tickets even higher. Since 1991, prices have increased, on average, 39%!

Runaway spending continues to hurt the game, as the financial chasm widens between baseball's richest and poorer teams. There is little hope of bridging it without substantial market reforms. Small-market franchises cannot compete, forcing them to unload their high-priced talent. Furthermore, they are having difficulty obtaining financing for new ballparks.

The growing disparities between baseball's haves and have-nots have destroyed competitive balance, the game's lifeblood. Payrolls range from the Dodgers $85 million to the A's $12.6 million. To be competitive in the market, a club has to spend a minimum of $60 million. "Cash totally dominates a fun game," said an editorial in the Charleston (W.Va.) Gazette. "The richer a team is, the more it can hire millionaire star players, who draw fans paying outrageous ticket prices, making the team still richer." Revenue sharing and the luxury-tax system, which was designed to provide a balance, are not working.

For baseball to achieve economic stability, the fiscal imbalance must be corrected or significantly lessened. With greater self-control and holding back their spending, the owners have it in their power to take control of their costs. Innovative solutions need to be implemented that would control operating costs of the franchises. Both large and small-market teams must use greater restraint in giving out excessive salaries. For teams to remain stable and competitive, there has to be a significant increase in revenue sharing, which along with stiffer payroll luxury taxes, will result in a more equitable salary structure. The sharing of local and national TV and radio contracts and tighter ownership control of powerful media empires and Super stations will contribute to greater parity to the clubs.

The following measures will significantly help stabilize the marketplace and assure the long-term health and competitiveness of the game:

Cap Player Salaries
Major League Baseball must follow the example of the NBA by capping individual salaries. The NBA system lessens payroll disparity between large-market and small-market clubs. By doing so, baseball will achieve the cost certainty they have been seeking, while at the same time, player salaries will climb at a slow, controlled pace.

A major economic problem with baseball is that it does not have any kind of salary cap, like the NBA and NFL. Consequently, teams can spend as much money as they want to sign the best players. As a result of the widening gap between the haves and have-nots, at least 70% of the teams begin the season without a chance of getting into post-season play.

New restrictions would provide those clubs that don't generate huge revenue with a better chance to compete. Salary restrictions such as these would give smaller-market teams an opportunity to compete, to re-sign their own players and not get outbid by teams in other markets. They could actually tilt the field slightly in their favor by allowing them to:

1. Offer larger yearly raises (12.5 percent to 10 percent).
2. Longer contracts (seven years, as opposed to six).

While a cap appears to be the only way some small-market teams can survive, Sean McAdam of ESPN Sports believes a cap has two major drawbacks:

1. While it would limit the amount superpowers could pay their players, it would do nothing to increase revenues for small-market teams.

2. Many teams with extra revenues could find ways to circumvent the cap, such as offering large signing bonuses.

The players, of course, will continue to object to a salary cap. They have everything going their way and will make every attempt to resist it. However, they should look more closely at the provisions of the NBA's cap. NBA players work under a salary ceiling but their allotment is enhanced by a cut of money from parking, luxury suites, concessions, TV rights and advertising signs.

Substantial Increase in Revenue Sharing

Baseball needs a more effective form of revenue sharing that will keep teams from dealing away their best players. Small-market teams need more help to be competitive. To achieve these goals, the share of total revenues among clubs must increase significantly. Teams with big profits must share a larger portion of their income with the struggling teams. The NBA, NFL and NHL have all implemented revenue sharing, in addition to salary caps. The NFL has succeeded with its salary cap because it already had significant revenue sharing in place.

The contrasting local television contracts continue to be the most serious problem with small-market teams trying to compete with large-market clubs. Teams split up the revenue from national TV and radio contracts but are allowed to keep all monies from local broadcast rights. The Yankees, for example, receive more than $70 million annually in local TV revenue, while the Royals take in less than $5 million.

A new system should be implemented whereby clubs will split not only the revenue from national TV and radio contracts but monies from local broadcast rights as well. Baseball must follow the lead of the NFL, NBA and NHL by placing all radio and television money into a league fund and given out in equal proportions.

The industry growth fund that was created in baseball's last labor settlement should be given greater emphasis. Peter Schmuck wrote in The Sporting News, "The players and owners created the fund in an attempt to form a partnership to "grow the game", but the concept fell short of the revolutionary plan envisioned by Peter Angelos, owner of the Baltimore Orioles. Angelos proposed that all of the revenue-sharing money go into a fund to build new state-of-the-art stadiums for financially strapped clubs. He said, "A stadium with great revenue potential can change the economic profile of a franchise." Angelos predicted that municipalities would be more amenable to the public/private partnership concept than the "build it or we will go" approach that has been employed in the past.

Eliminate the Arbitration Process

Salary arbitration is more costly to teams than free agency. It has been the players' strongest vehicle, with mediocre players making far more than they would without the process. Nomar Garciaparra, with little more than two years in the majors, signed a contract worth $44 million over seven years.

Arbitration, which was initiated to protect players who fall short of six years of big league service needed for free agency, eliminates the possibility of a team clamping on a young player's earnings. The process enables players to request a certain salary, and management counters with its offer. An arbitrator then chooses the player's demand or the club's offer. However, in the process, it has devastated the economic structure of baseball. Average salary for the 80 players who filed for arbitration in 1997 increased 152.8%, a jump that more than doubled the increase of 73.1% in 1996. In 406 cases decided over the past quarter century, just five players have had their pay cut.

"The arbitration system is ludicrous," said Arizona Diamondbacks' owner Jerry Colangelo. "The sooner it can go, the better. What it does is divide – management, ownership, player agent." As a result, teams often avoid the sometimes damaging effects of a hearing by settling with the player. In hearings, representatives of teams tell the panel the player is not worth what he's asking for, not exactly a confidence builder. To avoid arbitration, teams have been signing young players, some with only one year in the majors to long-term deals.

Average raises for the 38 players who exchanged salary arbitration figures in 1999 nearly doubled compared to 1998 raises. USA TODAY's study reported that "Average increase for these players was $1,257,405. In 1998, when 60 players exchanged numbers, their average raise was $477,370. Hal Bodley wrote "The owners won the final two cases, giving management a 9-2 record against the players. Since the process began in 1974, owners lead 236-181."

"Baseball will not survive under the present system," said former Giants' general manager Al Rosen. "No industry in the history of our country has survived with final-offer arbitration. It's sheer lunacy."

Strengthen the Luxury-Tax System

Baseball's existing revenue sharing and luxury-taxes were designed to provide a balance between the large and small markets, but they are not working. The current luxury-tax system has done very little to deter spending because it affects so few ball clubs and those of little importance. It levied a toll on five teams that spent over $70 million on player salaries in 1998. Those teams paid less than $700,000 each, including the Dodgers who paid as little as $39,000. The richer teams will give a higher percentage of income to the poorer teams in 1999, and even more in 2000.

Some owners thought the luxury-tax would slow down the George Steinbrenners and Peter Angeloses, but it hasn't worked that way. As Henry Schulman reported, "Steinbrenner was forced to pay a $4.4 million luxury-tax and another $11 million in revenue sharing in 1998, but that did not stop him from re-signing star outfielder Bernie Williams to a seven year, $87.5 million contract."

Slash Club Payrolls

With the realization that a middle range payroll of $40 million will not suffice to contend with rich franchises, an increasing number of clubs have substantially reduced their payrolls. The new ownership of the Kansas City Royals has slashed their $35.6 million payroll by almost half. Montreal has done that for years, and Minnesota and other teams are moving in that direction.

"We've lost quite a bit of money at the range we've been in," said a Kansas City spokesman. "We're going to try to break even." Royals' general manager Herk Robinson said, "We're going with our kids," using a refrain gaining wider use all the time.

Many clubs believe a middle-range payroll of $35-$45 million will not suffice to contend with the richest franchises. As Rod Beaton wrote, "They figure, even with drastic payroll cuts, the results can't be much worse and at least they'll break even."

Enforce 60-40 Rule to Restrain Payrolls

Ownership must adhere to a guideline adopted by baseball in 1982, but rarely enforced. The 60-40 rule requires all franchises to maintain at least a 60-to-40 ratio of assets to liabilities. As defined, assets are a club's appraised value, while liabilities include total player salaries and all deferred money.

Approximately 10 teams are currently in violation of the 60-40 rule. If the violators do not fall in line within three years, the Commissioner has broad powers to get a team into compliance. An obvious course for a team attempting to comply would be to reduce its payroll. A team could conform to the rule by increasing its value, building a new stadium or negotiating a richer TV contract, while maintaining, or even increasing its payroll.

"The rule is meant to help ensure that we continue to have thirty healthy teams, without directly affecting players' compensation," said Bob DuPuy, baseball's chief legal officer. Gene Orza of the players union, however, states that "If it could be proved that a team didn't pursue a player because of 60-40, it could be grounds for a grievance. But in 1985, a union grievance against the edict was denied when an arbitrator ruled that the 60-40 rule does not necessarily limit what a team can spend.

NFL's Free-Agency Plan

With the free agency and arbitration processes pushing salaries to unbelievable heights, the year 2000 could see an even deeper free agent pool. In sharp contrast to baseball, pro football is stronger then ever. "Everyone in the National Football League is getting rich now," wrote Ira Miller in the San Francisco Chronicle. "Football's labor peace was essentially guaranteed in 1993 when the Players accepted a salary cap along with the NFL's first true free-agency plan."

For many years, excessive player movement has been a big problem in pro sports, diminishing competition and the quality of play. But NFL's free-agency plan, combined with salary cap provisions, has enabled the Minnesota Vikings to re-sign and keep their key free agents. "It's been good for everyone," admits Gene Upshaw, head of the Players Association. Miller wrote, "Competition has been enhanced. In 1998, six different teams other then the '97 league winner took division titles."

More Effective Compensation

For baseball to truly achieve economic parity and competitive balance, compensation is needed. Teams that lose a players to another team should be compensated, and not be a draft choice. Jim Wagner of Kalida, Ohio, explained that, "If Team A signs a free agent from Team B, then Team B is entitled to select anyone player from Team A's 40-man roster who makes less money than the free agent who was just signed. If this plan were used today, teams couldn't load up on free-agent players to buy a pennant."

The signing of three free agents by the Dodgers, including the $100 million deal for pitcher Kevin Brown, could have an adverse effect on the team's efforts to rebuild its farm system. Jorge Valencia said that "As compensation to the teams who lost those players, the Dodgers had to give up their picks in the first and second round of the June draft, a tough blow at a time when their system is devoid of top prospects."

Implement the Bob Costas Plan

When the time is right and conditions are favorable, Major League Baseball should expand to 32 teams, a workable number in terms of markets, divisions, and scheduling. In his excellent essay in The Sporting News, Bob Costas recommended that the owners and the commissioner's office should present to the players their plan for expansion to 32 teams, selling the plan as "Baseball's Vision in the 21st Century."

Costas wrote, "In a few years, we will have 32 teams, but we are not going there without cooperation and concessions from you. We will offer over 100 new jobs, double the minimum salary, and make all players free agents after four years, instead of six. In return, we ask that salary arbitration be abolished, elimination of the designated hitter rule, and some truly significant form of salary restraint, which when coupled with substantial revenue sharing, will help stabilize the market-place and assure the long-term health and competitiveness of the industry, while still handsomely compensating the players."

Control Media Empires/Super Stations

Media and entertainment empires and Super stations owned by big league clubs constitute a major problem, jeopardizing baseball's fiscal balance and the game's best interests. They need to be curbed. Baseball's worst fears about Rupert Murdoch are coming true. An editorial in USA TODAY said, "Murdoch has been buying teams and sports television rights worldwide, a parlay that could make billions in the entertainment world." Major League Baseball must implement controls on clubs owned by huge media, entertainment and Super station empires.

For many years, Super stations, like those owned by the Atlanta Braves and Chicago Cubs, have contributed to baseball's fiscal imbalance. They have overloaded television with baseball, undercutting the value of everybody else's TV rights. In cities with weak teams, a hot Super station club can overshadow the hometown team. They must be controlled by tight legislative rules.

Adopt a More Equitable Amateur Draft

Signing bonuses have increased to such a level that small-revenue clubs have been priced out of the market for the best amateurs. Baseball must find ways in which young players can be distributed among clubs in a way that ultimately makes all teams more competitive. Sandy Alderson emphasized that, "Baseball has to make sure money is not the common denominator that allows clubs to dominate every aspect of the game."

Teams should be allowed to trade their draft picks. Major League Baseball teams are currently forbidden from dealing draft picks, a situation that does not exist in any of the three other major sports. Being able to trade draft picks would give teams some flexibility, another option. If a small-market team could not afford the No. 1 pick, it could trade that pick and land a prospect or big league player in return.

With foreign players making a major impact, the problem is that the international market prices out small-market teams the same way the free-agent market does. By making every amateur player eligible for the draft, each team would have the same chance at the best players.

Revitalize Baseball's Marketing

Even though the heralded Home Run Race between Mark McGwire and Sammy Sosa did much to boost the popularity of the game, there is still an urgent need for Major League Baseball to re-focus and expand its marketing approach. Far too much emphasis has been placed on Corporate America, luxury boxes, season tickets, etc., and not enough consideration for lower income families, selling the game to the kids, and adding the best interests of the fans to baseball's economic equation.

Major League Baseball Enterprises, baseball's new marketing arm, appears to have been successful in developing marketing partnerships with many world-class companies, but the game needs far more promotion and development sponsors. The great marketing success of the NBA and NFL is because they get their marketing partners to promote the game along with the partner's product. However, as Bob Costas wrote, "Baseball must know and appreciate what is distinct about the game and market it. As baseball continues to try to win back fans, it must be careful what direction its marketing takes. The game cannot be something it's not."

The key to baseball's prosperity and greatness is that unique bond the game has with its fans. "Baseball fans are unique", said Dave Kindred, "in that they have a passion, an appreciation for the game's traditions and rich history and these cherished traditions need to be preserved."

Consider the Fans' Best Interests   Listen more to
the fans. Without them, there would be no professional baseball. The owners and players are not listening to the fans enough. A stronger effort must be made to win them back.

- Reduce prices of tickets, concessions and parking so every fan can afford to see a game. This would mean reducing salaries.

- Make the game a family outing again, like Saturday afternoon games and a few doubleheaders.

- Bring back both Ladies Day and Kids Day, with special pricing and free admissions.

- Find out what the fans want. Fans need and deserve the opportunity to voice their opinions, concerns and grievances.

- Hold a weeklong Fanfest during the winter for ticket buyers.

- Institute nostalgia night. Have current and former stars work the crowd. Set up autograph booths.

Selling the Game to Kids   To spark a true revival of the
game, there is an urgent need to market the game again to children. Baseball must get a better hold, a feel, on the imagination of young people. Kids need to

be turned on. They need to be convinced that baseball is contemporary, in addition to having great tradition and heritage. But more important, baseball should enlighten young fans as to what the game is, help them develop a greater understanding of the game, the subtleties and unique qualities.

Educate the kids on the great traditions and heritage of baseball but point out that the game is also contemporary and hip. Get them to appreciate the nuances of the game. So much of the enjoyment in baseball is the tactical strategy, tension, and drama, and our youth like these aspects. Baseball must do a more effective job of turning the kids on to playing and watching the game more. Help them develop an appreciation and greater understanding for the game and its unique qualities.

- Get youngsters into the ballparks, like baseball marketed the game in 1969. Make available free tickets and reduce rates.

- Bring back the Knot Hole Gang Club. MLB has already begun its Kids club, a national promotion that will help children attend games, learn more about baseball, compete in skill/trivia games.

- Do some other innovative things to make the game more appealing to younger people. The length of games needs to be shortened, considering our culture's ever decreasing attention span.

- Encourage more youth to get into the game. To really appreciate baseball, one has to play the game, whether in a league or playground play.

- Baseball should expand its RBI program to more inner cities.

- Television networks should give more consideration to the needs and availability of young children, such as the following:

    * Televise more day games, especially during postseason playoffs

    * Schedule some of the World Series during the day and the night games at earlier hours.

    * Game announcers should emphasize strategy more; focus on the tense interplay between pitcher and batter, defense and runners.

* Use greater discretion in the between-inning promo's of upcoming programs, those containing violent and sex scenes, etc.

* During interviews, ask players to tell how they first started playing baseball, to give tips for kids how to join fan clubs.

* A made-for-TV banquet during the annual winter meetings would create interest in the off-season, with present and past major league greats speaking.

* TV Game of the Week. As part of its contract with ESPN, MLB should negotiate a package deal that would provide for a minor league, college, etc. "Game of the Week".

* A weekly half-hour highlight show devoted to colleges, minors, etc., relative to the promotion, development of up-coming players.

How Baseball Can Boost TV Ratings

The following are ways baseball can strengthen its appeal while at the same time boost World Series television ratings:

• Market the game more effectively to young viewers.

• Make the game more accessible to most potential viewers, those who have to get up early on weekdays.

• Return half the World Series game to the daytime and start the weekend games at 4 p.m.

• Reduce the length of the season, so that postseason play will end by mid-October, thus eliminating some chilly nights.

• Shorten the time of games and keep the pace and tempo moving.

• Take steps to crack down on delaying tactics.

• Enforce the 2:05 to 2:25 minute time period between innings that TV must complete their commercials.

Baseball's Imbalance

For the past century, baseball has tried to perpetuate the intricate balance between hitting and pitching. Other than the juiced ball years, it has been successful, until the Home Run Barrage of the 1990s when the balance was rudely shaken. In recent years, it has swung alarmingly to the offense. The game now appears to have lost its special rhythm.

More and more, we hear the game reports of baseball dramatizing the home run to the neglect of everything else. With so many hit, the excitement and drama of the home run has diminished. The long ball has lost appeal and interest. Baseball's long revered and sought after standards and records become meaningless with these periodic "explosions". Twenty and 30 home runs once meant something. Now they mean something else. While today's fast-paced society enjoy seeing plenty of scoring, they want the additional offense to a point where it doesn't become too commonplace.

High-scoring games can provide much excitement for the fans but many fans also enjoy tight pitching duels. With equal balance, they can do a lot of good for baseball. A well-pitched game is a thing of beauty, and a high scoring game, now and then, can also be something to behold.

How Baseball Can Achieve Better Balance

In addition to the excitement of the home run, baseball should give fans other appealing aspects of the game, such as the plotting and counterplotting of one-run strategy, hit-and-run, bunt plays, the steal and the thrilling squeeze play. Such action also stimulates the fans.

Better balance can be achieved by implementing the following:

- Restore the official strike zone. Call a higher strike.

- Return the ball to "normal" and official specifications.

- Bats, likewise, should adhere to stricter specifications.
- Raise the pitching mound to 13 inches, primarily to ease the stress and strain of the violent pitching action.

- Move fences back a reasonable distance and stop building so many hitter-friendly ballparks.

- Umpires should not be so quick to protect hitters who crowd, even lean over, the plate.

- Pitchers need to reclaim the inner half of the plate and brush hitters off the plate.

- Umpires should stop throwing a baseball out of the game when it has picked up a few specks of dust.

- Eliminate the Designated Hitter rule.

- Place stronger emphasis on the basic fundamental skills.

- Pitchers can improve their effectiveness by:

  - Develop greater velocity; more emphasis on the fast ball.

  - The pitcher's best weapon is a fastball up and in.

  - Greater movement of pitches, in and out, up and down.

  - Strive for good location; change speed of pitches.

  - Come inside to neutralize hitters lunging out over plate, while concentrating on going way.

  - Reclaim the inner half of the plate and brush more hitters off the plate.

  - Mix the fast ball and change-ups with breaking stuff, sharp breaking curves, cut-fastball and hard-biting slider.

Creating a Better Game

While the game can be made better, the basic rules of baseball must be left alone. Indeed, the early rule makers got things right the first time, as history reveals that the rules have remained the same for nearly a century, until 1973 when the American league adopted the designated hitter. The D.H. is one of the few "wrongs of baseball" and must be eliminated.

Leave the rules alone, but follow them. Call the strike zone as written in the rulebook. Forget about gimmicks and stop tampering with the game. When changes are considered, so should the continuity of baseball and the need to uphold the cherished traditions of the game.

For some time baseball has been losing appeal among the younger generation, many of whom want games to be faster, more violent, characteristics of sports kids find attractive in today's modern culture. There are those who believe the game is out of step with the "in-your-face" video-game sensibilities of the age. Should baseball utilize characteristics of other sports? Certainly not! For baseball to reinvent the game would seriously damage the distinctive uniqueness of the sport. Instead, baseball should accentuate its history and charm, traits not shared by younger sports such as football and basketball. Baseball relies on its tradition, history and nostalgia more than any other sport.

Has the game changed? A half-century ago, Bill Veeck, the late owner whose promotional wizardry gave the game much needed entertainment and excitement, stated that, "Dugout to dugout, the game happily remains unchanged in our changing world." More recently, however, George Will's response to this question was: "Yes and no. Yes, the structure of the game is essentially what it has been since the turn of the century. But for many reasons, hitting and pitching and fielding and managing have changed enough over the years that it is not easy to make comparisons between the achievements of today and yesterday."

How to Achieve a Better Game

- Give the game better balance between hitting and pitching

- Keep the pace and tempo of the game moving

- Adopt a uniform strike zone, rather than for every umpire to have their own

- Correct the wrongs of baseball:
  - Eliminate the designated hitter
  - Raise the pitching mound
  - Get rid of artificial turf

- Bring about the return of the:
  - Stolen base
  - Little Ball
  - Feet first sliding
  - The bunting game

- Expand the strike zone to that specified in rule book and have umpires call the high strike

- Put all umpires under one umbrella group to increase consistency

- Stop tampering with the game, such as juiced balls and explosive bats

- Promote a "Get Back to the Basics" movement

- The comeback of two-hand catching in the field

- Strengthen the throwing arms of fielder with more daily throwing, stretching out their arms with long tossing

- Establish better balance in the game by having pitchers:
  - Bring back the good fastball, combining a riding four-seamer with the two-seamer that sinks and runs away

- Throw the quick, hard cutter in on the hands which will open up the outer half of the plate

• Prevent ugly brawls by making the pitcher bat -- no more designated hitter!

• Implement a drug policy that calls for mandatory testing and ban steroids, including androstendione

Get the Strike Zone in Line

Baseball has directed umpires to enforce the official strike zone in 1999. The move was especially designed to get umpires to call "high strikes." As Larry King noted in his USA TODAY column, "The strike zone used to be clearly defined and was easy to learn by simply reading the rule book." In recent years, however, umpires have rarely called any pitch above the belt a strike. Gene Orza of the Players Union, in rare support of the owners, stated that, "Players should not have to adjust to 32 different strike zones. Yankees' manager Joe Torre said, "If they're going to do anything with the strike zone, they should pull it in a little and push it up. At least hitters can reach that pitch."

Umpires have had individual interpretations of what the strike zone should be. Glenn Dickey wrote, "Managers say repeatedly that the first thing they have to establish in every game is what the umpire's strike zone is that day."

According to the rules, the strike zone goes from "a horizontal line at the midpoint between the top of the shoulders and the top of the uniform pants" to "a line at the hollow beneath the kneecap." In a memo to teams and umpires, Sandy Alderson said, "While the top of the strike zone is difficult to define, the upper limit of the zone will extend two inches above the top of the uniform pants." But, that still leaves a discrepancy of about 8-10 inches between what will be called and what the rulebook says.

Dump the Designated Hitter

For a number of reasons, the D.H. rule appears to be on the way out, a rule, which never should have been approved. Eliminating the D.H. not only will make the American League better but also baseball as a game. Rob Parker of Newsday wrote, "The D.H. was not a good idea in 1973 and it isn't one today. It takes away the best part of baseball -- the strategy." It also diminishes the ebb and flow, the rhythm of the game.

"You almost don't need a manager in the American League," said Sparky Anderson who managed in both leagues. "Other than pitching changes, there aren't many moves. You don't pinch hit much, nor bunt much. Basically, just wait for the three-run homer."

The only reason the Players Association opposes elimination of the designated hitter rules is because they are thinking of their pocketbooks. For years, Fehr and Orza have kept the D.H. afloat. Money aside, players and managers who have played and managed in both leagues prefer the National League.

Raise the Pitcher's Mound

In 1969, baseball was so desperate to help the hitters that they lowered the pitcher's mound from 15 to 10 inches. The lower mound gave hitters the boost owners were seeking, but in reducing the downward pitching plane, it contributed immeasurably to countless numbers of shoulder and arm injuries for pitchers. There is no doubt in my mind that the lower mound has been a major factor in ruining or shortening the careers of a great many pitchers.

If the owners had realized that a higher mound alleviates the stress and strain of the intensely violent pitching action, they would not have approved the flat mound. Consequently, the lower mound has cost owners multi-millions of dollars, in addition to the loss of a large number of stellar pitchers. A higher mound with a proper slope would diminish the force of a powerful overhand motion inflicted on the pitcher's vulnerable throwing arm and shoulder. The slope is just as important as its height.

Following the 1996 campaign, in an effort to help pitchers who had been clobbered in a barrage of home runs and scoring orgies, baseball's general managers suggested the major league rules committee consider raising the mound 3 inches for the 1997 season. Approval would have accomplished three things:

1. Help pitchers throw strikes
2. Speed up the time of the game, and in the long term,
3. Help medically in giving pitchers more longevity by alleviating the stress and force of a powerful throwing action.

Major league pitchers are still waiting for a higher mound. The rules committee was to have examined the proposal and the medical data. The last step would have been the required approval from the players union. The matter appears to be still in limbo.

Get Rid of Artificial Turf

From the standpoint of the game, artificial turf is one of the worst developments in baseball history. The hard, smooth surface distorts the basic skills of the game -- hitting, pitching and fielding. It ruins the rhythm of the game, especially in the outfield. A soft fly that falls in front of an incoming outfielder may well bounce over his head. A line drive, even a grounder into an outfield gap, which cannot be cut off, will skid or roll quickly to the fence.

To compensate, outfielders must play deeper and come in more cautiously, making the gaps even wider. Because of artificial turf, games have more "undeserved" hits, many of them for extra bases. It becomes a much less attractive game. Artificial turf diminishes the possibility of one of the most beautiful plays in baseball, when fielders move laterally to intercept the ball and throw to a base for a close play.

Umpires Must be Held Accountable

Baseball should institute a process that increases accountability of the umpires, and it must provide consequences for those unable to meet the standards. The very best umpires should survive, just like the players. Without fear of progressive discipline and not incentive for improvement, it is not realistic to expect umpires to improve. Baseball needs a system that rewards merit, one that would remove those who are incompetent. Umpires now are virtually tenured once they put in six years. Older declining umpires are protected while young talent withers in the minors.

Umpiring has to become more standardized which has become doubly important with interleague play. Some umpires are twice as likely to ring up a hitter on a two-strike pitch than others are. For this process to be effectively implemented, jurisdiction over umpires should be shifted from the leagues to the commissioner's office and have the game train its own umpires. But Union chief Richie Phillips maintains that centralizing umpires must be negotiated. The collective bargaining agreement expires after the '99 season.

In the best interest of the game, a much better relationship is needed between players and umpires. I think the current umpiring controversy would subside if umpires would focus on doing their job, call the pitches and the plays in accordance with the rules. They should let the players play the game without creating interference. With stronger support from the league presidents, they will be more inclined to be tolerant and understanding of those who argue.

Protecting Health and Safety

With a huge investment in the safety and health of their players, it would appear major league owners would make every effort to protect the overall well being of their players. But judging from the high price tag of baseball's disabled list and the alarming injury rate, ownership should try to determine what is causing the injuries and why so many players are hurt. The epidemic of arm operations, for example, has cost clubs millions of dollars.

Alarming Injury Rate and Disabilities   While big league clubs spend money to hire fitness specialists to design and conduct their conditioning programs, the injury rate is alarming. Players today are bigger and stronger, but why do they get hurt so much? With player salaries averaging well over a million dollars, this is a question that those in baseball need to figure out. Baseball's disabled list has become a high price tag. As many as 94 players were on the D.L. on May 22, 1996. The eye-catching number is what those players earned: $134,683,153., or 15% of the total opening day payroll of $901,464.368.

In an attempt to determine the specific causes of baseball's high injury rate, the following factors appear most significant:

- Improper training and conditioning: lifting excessively heavy weights in the throwing arm and shoulder areas; tightened muscles

- Not throwing often enough to keep the arm strong and loose, as well as excessive overuse of weights by pitchers

- Insufficient stretching exercises before and after lifting

- Not enough running, particularly daily wind-sprints

- Poor pitching mechanics, lack of good pitching rhythm
- The low pitching mound causes significant stress and strain of the pitchers' vulnerable arm and shoulder, because the flat mound reduces the downward pitching plane

- Pitchers are throwing too many breaking-stress pitches, particularly the hard slider and splitter

- The use of steroids, growth hormones, Creatine, etc. have contributed to pulled hamstrings, back injuries, cramping, in addition to many potentially dangerous health problems.

Epidemic of Pitching Arm Surgeries

Baseball is experiencing a serious epidemic of arm operations, costing the clubs multi-millions of dollars, but not enough is being done to remedy the problem. With the financial value of pitchers soaring in a limited market, impacted by numerous arm injuries, one would think the teams would show greater concern for the pitcher's health and well being.

Many injuries can be attributed to poor pitching rhythm, since the arm and shoulder are less inclined to be hurt when the delivery is rhythmic, smooth and fluid. The stress pitches have taken their toll on pitchers, too. The slider has damaged more pitching arms than any other pitch, especially the elbow. Pitchers are not running and throwing often enough. They are spending too much time in the weight rooms lifting weights too heavy for vulnerable shoulder and arm muscles. Strength, not bulk, is the key.

I strongly believe the owners could save themselves millions of dollars by raising the pitching mound and allow pitchers to again throw more downhill. A higher mound with a proper slope will diminish the stress and strain of pitcher's injury prone overhand delivery, one of the most violent actions in sports.

Since it was drastically lowered from 15 to 10 inches in 1969, the low mound has contributed significantly to countless numbers of shoulder and arm injuries. It has ruined or shortened the careers of great many pitchers.

Line Drives Up the Middle

A livelier ball and more powerful bats have resulted in more line drives careening through the pitcher's box. Early in the 1998 season, a rash of line drives nearly destroyed Baltimore's pitching staff. Steve Marantz wrote in The Sporting News, "Hard smashes toward the mound are occurring with alarming frequency."

There are many factors as to why the pitcher's safety has become such a serious concern. While lighter, more powerful bats, livelier balls and stronger hitters are foremost, the explanation by Marantz was more comprehensive. He wrote "More pitchers are being hit because more hitters stride toward the plate, more pitchers throw on the outer half of the plate, stronger hitters swinging lighter and whippier bats, hitters are wearing protective pads, and blinding backgrounds behind the plate." In addition, most of today's pitchers sacrifice fielding position to make an effective pitch, landing off-balance and finishing awkwardly.

Hall of Fame pitcher Jim Palmer pointed out that "Pitchers don't pitch inside, so hitters are programmed on two strikes to look away." Making things still more difficult for pitchers, umpires discourage throwing inside by giving pitchers quick warnings, in part because hitters theatrically overreact to inside pitches.

Among ways baseball can help protect pitchers:

- Pitchers should be allowed to throw inside, particularly when hitters lean out all over the plate

- Padding used by hitters should be legislated against; otherwise, let pitchers have some padding, too

- More stringent controls on specifications on the liveliness of today's ball, as well as the bat

- Coaches should instruct pitchers to finish their delivery more on-balance and be better prepared to stop "line shots"
- Remove the pale visual background and up-close seating in the new parks; darken the screen with a green tint

Baseball's Drug Policy Needs Revamping

While there are many who believe baseball does not have a drug policy, Major League Baseball does have one, but it is greatly out-of-date and in need of a major overhaul. C.W. Nevius wrote in the San Francisco Chronicle, "Until now, baseball's muscle building drug policy was simple: Don't ask, don't tell!"

Considering their response to Mark McGwire's use of androstendione, baseball has shown a glaring lack of concern for fair play and the health of its players. Baseball's tolerance for Andro has hurt anti-doping programs in other sports. What baseball does not want to admit, though, is that McGwire's performance was enhanced by substances and drugs.

What will Major League Baseball do if the study conducted by two Harvard physicians determines that a slugger taking Andro has a competitive advantage? "Both management and labor will attempt to shoot down the study," wrote Rick Reilly in Sports Illustrated. "Or they will bite the bullet on the McGwire legacy and ban Andro hoping the public thinks the issue has disappeared. It won't have. Until baseball decides to test for drugs, the ban isn't worth the paper the news release is printed on."

McGwire states emphatically that "Weight training and nutrition transformed everything." But there are many prominent medical and health authorities who strongly question McGwire" regimen, like Dr. Charles Yesalis, a Penn State professor of health and human development and author of the book, The Steroid Game. "Androstendione is a steroid, an honest-to-goodness drug,"said Yesalis, who has watched the growth of muscles in baseball with suspicion.

Yesalis says the talk about supplements is a smoke screen, that 25 to 30 percent of major league ballplayers are using anabolic steroids. "Over the last decade, I've seen lean-mass increases in players that I frankly cannot attribute to changes in strength training alone. Forget about Creatine. To me, it's very obvious that anabolic steroids have taken a major foothold in baseball."

For baseball to control the use of steroids, drugs and performance enhancing substances, it must set a policy and then enforce it. Dr. Gary Wadler of Cornell University, who co-wrote the book Drug and the Athlete, said, "The only way to catch offenders is to conduct random testing, including the off-season. Baseball has to change its policy on drugs."

Androstendione Should be Banned
Baseball must follow the lead of the NFL, NCAA, IOC, and other organizations in banning androstendione. The Association of Professional Team Physicians, comprised of doctors from all the major sports, have recommended that Andro be taken off the consumer market. If baseball fails to ban Andro and continues to refuse to make drug testing mandatory, the future health of the players and their families will be in jeopardy.

Baseball, of course, doesn't want to take any action that would diminish McGwire's record-breaking 70 home runs. But it would be wrong and highly irresponsible for the majors not to take action because of a desire not to tarnish the record. By boosting McGwire's testosterone levels, Andro and Creatine increased the number and length of his lifting workouts, thus building up strength. He was able to train harder and recover more quickly, resulting in more muscle power for quick bursts.

Require Mandatory Drug Testing
The most effective way to avoid the steroid controversy is to require mandatory drug testing, but the Union prohibits random testing for any non-drug offender, that it would violate individual rights. Obviously, Fehr refuses to recognize that baseball's problem is far more serious that the use of Andro and Creatine. Players are using Androstendione and other supplements to mask strength gains from actual anabolic steroids. They are not bulking up with steroids during the actual season. It is happening during their workouts during the winter.

Minor Leagues

The strong resurgence of the minors, which began in the mid-1980s, is still a bright spot in baseball's fabric. An increasing number of fans have grown tired of the overly commercialized major league ballparks where high priced and self-centered players perform. They aspire a return to baseball's simple roots emulated at minor league parks.

Despite the success and popularity of the minors, a large majority of teams are not big profit enterprises. Many clubs, in fact, are having fiscal problems, the result of more operating costs, overhead, and more employees, while they try to keep their games affordable to families and children. The new Professional Baseball Agreement with the majors has made it more difficult for the minors to achieve fiscal stability. More financial burden has been placed on the minors, including the costs of umpire development. While the agreement has resulted in closer relations, the minors have lost a lot of control, with the majors calling the shots and the minors forced to react.

Still, unity between the majors and minors is in the best interests of both levels. The return of the winter meetings provides opportunities to communicate more effectively. It is essential, however, that minor league clubs be able to strive for a "balanced franchise". While player development is essential, too much big league control can be detrimental to minor league franchises.

From a marketing and promotion standpoint, the minors have taken the initiative to add more appeal to their leagues. The All-Star Futures Game is part of an All-Star Sunday Celebration, an event designed to spotlight the best prospects. This approach is different from that of all-star games which reward players who are having good seasons.

Post-season play continues to be a disappointment, and both the majors and minors are to be blamed for the lack of interest. Just prior to the play-offs, the majors call up the best players, and the minors are not promoting the games like they do for the regular season. The overall quality of umpires is another shortcoming of the minors. A more efficient umpire development system is a major necessity and should be a priority project.

Ways the Minors Can Help Restore the Game

- Control the widening disparities between big and small revenue teams

- Stop the exodus of small-town teams from the minor leagues

- Stabilize franchise and league movement, with greater concern for geographic alignment

- Continue to administer the policy of the fan as No. 1

- Minor league teams and their fans deserve a more balanced franchise and major league clubs should help them do so

- The minors need and deserve a greater commitment from the major leagues for their financial stability and survival

- The majors can help the minors' play-off attendance by allowing top prospects to participate before moving up

- Farm directors should make greater effort to provide replacements for those called up, particularly during pennant races

- Majors should control the proliferation of games on cable-TV

- Top prospects should fully develop their skills and have more seasoning at Triple-A before moving up

- Improve the employment conditions of minor league players but not to the extent the majors lose its farm system

- Players can bolster their image with fans by saving their big league "attitudes" until they actually reach The Show

- Strengthen the umpire development system by providing more supervision and guidance

- More professional women's leagues should be established

Big and Small Market Gap Growing

As the gap between big and small-revenue teams continues to grow in the majors, minor league officials have expressed the warning that the same phenomenon is threatening the health of the minors as well. While the minors are presently in reasonably strong financial health, vice president Pat O'Conner has expressed strong concern about the rising cost of doing business.

Yet, attendance and revenue continues to grow in the minors. In the 1997 fiscal year, gross revenue for all NA clubs grew by nearly $16 to $300 million, a jump of more than 5 percent. Even with the sharp growth of recent years, 36 percent of the clubs had operating losses. "Nearly three-fourth of the money losing teams were at Class A or below," stated Will Lingo.

Small-town Teams Must be Saved

As a result of the growing gap between large and small-money franchises, with mounting fiscal deficits inflicted by greater operating costs, smaller markets are slowly disappearing. Should this trend continue it would do serious harm to the overall image and popularity of minor league baseball. The tide of struggling small market teams need to be turned. "The National Association is in danger of outgrowing small and Middle America, something we cannot let happen," said O'Conner. "While baseball in this day and age is not for every community, we can't idly stand by and lose our smaller cities and towns."

There are still people who want to operate teams in small towns, but they're going to need help," said O'Conner. "We must close the gap between the financial haves and have-nots and ensure baseball in America's heartland and small cities. New and bigger markets alone will not sustain us. As we creep up the ladder of higher fan costs, we will threaten the very core of our business – the working class and family unit."

More Balanced Franchise Needed

The minor leagues are the training ground for the major leagues. They exist today for the primary purpose of developing talent for the majors. But a more balanced franchise should be the goal of all minor league clubs. Too much emphasis, however, is currently given to player development. As crucial as it is to their financial stability, overemphasis on development has disenchanted many fans. Too often, players come and go.

·If restrictions were made on the number of player moves the parent club could make each season, fans could better identify with players and more meaningful rosters would be established for the play-offs. But Alan Simpson thinks, "The minor's emphasis on developing their players is not going to change much. For most Baseball America readers, it doesn't matter." However, for a growing number of fans, it does matter. They wonder, "Why should the minors be the least competitive level of play in organized baseball? Shouldn't winning, league titles and play-offs mean something?

Likewise, entertaining the fans and fielding a competitive team has to be among the major priorities of minor league franchises. The minors' strong commitment to maintain affordable entertainment with in intimate family atmosphere should remain one of their big selling points. But minor league ball has to be more than just a show. Every club has a responsibility to its fans to field a team that plays hard and goes all out to win.

Prospects Are Not Maximizing Potential

There are fewer Superstars today in the big leagues than 3 or 4 decades ago. Why? Because the major leagues today are not allowing the minors enough time to fully develop prospects. Because of baseball's player development timetable, big league prospects are not maximizing their potential. In sharp contrast, consider the number of star players in earlier decades, like to 1950s.

The player development system in the minors leaves much to be desired; due largely to the rushing factor caused by continued expansion. Players with extraordinary potential have been stunted as a result of being rushed too quickly. They are not fully developed by the time they reach the majors. Prospects with exceptional ability must spend more time at Triple-A.

Minors Need More Revenue

While containing expenses, the operators of minor league baseball must constantly be thinking of generating new revenue. Sue Lazzaro, director of merchandising for the Salem Avalanche, explained "The professional game is ultimately a business and for a business to survive, costs cannot exceed generated revenue."

Strong business participation with an ample number of corporate sponsors is essential to a good season ticket base. Franchises are marketing their team as a regional attraction, and broader appeal has provided greater marketing opportunities.

Minor league clubs today are tapping all the sources of financial support they can think of. In chapter five, I have compiled lists of numerous revenue-generating ideas, successful promotions and special nights conducted by minor league clubs.

Sources of Financial Support

* Advertising sales
* Billboards, scoreboard, etc.
* Camps and clinics
* Community nights
* Concerts, musical
* Concessions (food/beverages)
* Corporate sponsorships
* Fence signs
* Mail order souvenirs
* Merchandise sales
* Parent club (salaries)
* Park reservations
* Parking fees
* Picnic area
* Program sales
* Radio-TV sales
* Restaurant/café/sports bar
* Revenue (State, local, etc.)
* Signage
* Sky boxes
* Souvenir sales
* Stadium rental
* Suites (private/luxury)
* TICKETS (day-of-game, group sales, season)

Strong Marketing the Key to Success

A strong marketing plan should have creative and imaginative concepts and techniques. Nightly promotions have contributed greatly to the high attendance figures, with major focus on family entertainment. Clubs have profited significantly from the memorabilia business, opening large souvenir shops. Merchandise sales have risen from $2.5 million to $40 million since 1991.

Good promotions can make the ball park a fun place to go and that builds family business. The most successful teams are taking an inexpensive family-oriented approach to good entertainment. "If you get tickets into the hands of kids, their parents will come," said a successful minor league president.

114

Minor league clubs learned a long time ago that they are in the entertainment business. They sell the experience of the game, not one or two star players. Fans identify with their team, not the prospects that pass through. Every game is an event – the fan's ticket to excitement. Therefore, every club's goal is to get as many people into the stadium as possible.

Successful Promotions

* Appearances by celebrities
* Autograph ball
* Backpack night
* Beer, half-price
* Breakfast clinic
* Church picnics
* Company nights
* Concerts, post-game
* Country nite
* Dollar discount
* Exhibition game (parent club)
* Fan Appreciation
* Feed the Hungry
* Fiesta Night
* Fireworks shows
* Food drive
* Fundraisers
* Give-aways (bats, balls, seat cushions, etc.)
* Hall of Fame autographs
* Kids Day/Night
* Knothole Gang Club
* Lazy Lounge chair
* Old-Timers uniforms
* Performers (clowns, etc.)
* Quarter Hot Dogs
* Scout Night
* Shopping cart race
* Team of the Night
* Theme weekends
* Turn Back the Clock
* Watermelon Olympics

Community Commitment is Vital   For small markets to survive, teams must become a focal point in their communities. A minor league team is the community's team. There has to be a strong commitment by those in the community to keep baseball alive in small towns. A greater effort must be made to keep the ownership rather than for people outside the game to buy franchises with the intent of just making big bucks.

Everyone connected to the organization, including players and managers, must be as active and visible in the local community as time permits. Players should be accessible to the fans, helping out with promotions at the park and the community. Strong community involvement must be combined with a strong business presence, with an ample number of corporate sponsors so essential to a good season ticket base. Many teams today are run like corporations, with streamlined accounting, promotions and marketing.

Creative Approach to Stadium Upgrading

The new stadium frenzy, which has rejuvenated leagues throughout the country, has caused attendance figures to soar. In doing so, minor league clubs are developing more creative solutions to paying for their ballparks. Numerous stadiums are being upgraded or new ballparks built. Some of the most attractive new features are theater-style seats, entertaining scoreboards with video screens, first-class playing fields, locker rooms and training facilities.

The multi-purpose stadium in downtown Fresno, California, is an example of creative financing. According to team president John Carbray, "The new facility will all be paid back by stadium operation." The following financing was obtained:

- Borrow $23 million in the form of privately backed bonds

- A loan of $7.5 million that was approved by the county

- $8.5 million city grant to reduce the debt from the bonds

Independent League Boom Is Over

While the independent league boom is over, teams with strong financial support and sound business practices are doing very well. But there is a significant inconsistency in the caliber of the teams, as well as how the leagues are organized. Many changes continue to occur, however, like new franchises, teams switching leagues and those who fail to make it. As in the case of National Association clubs, teams are moving to larger markets. Getting quality players continues to be a problem. Most independent teams are composed largely of undrafted collegians.

The success of independent ball grew from its old-time approach, giving teams back to cities rather than big league organizations. "Watching the evolution of independent baseball has been interesting," wrote Lingo. "At times it has been exciting, teams with new nicknames and logos in cities that had no teams in years."

116

Kevin Trainor of Baseball America believes "Independent leagues should change its emphases, from being a second-chance development league for undrafted players to a more advanced degree of baseball." But for indy teams to achieve this lofty goal, Lingo says, "they will need good owners, good markets and a good business operation. Simple, but difficult to achieve." A full alliance would be in the best interests of independent baseball. The alliance would start out with the Northeast, Northern and Frontier leagues. Once the alliance begins, other independent leagues would be welcome. "The alliance would bring uniformity," said Lingo. "It would also provide a stamp of legitimacy to good independent leagues, giving them more credibility with Organized Baseball and with governmental and business entities that the teams and leagues have to deal with."

Starting an Independent Team
Kevin Trainor, writing in Baseball America, gave the following recommendations in getting a team established:

1. Don't do all the financing yourself. Get other investors.
2. Firm up a field lease first and don't skimp on facilities.
3. Advertise and promote. Give fans a reason to show up.
4. Get an experienced minor league general manager.
5. Study the business side of minor league baseball.
6. Sign more hometown heroes, players fans identify with.
7. Establish a sufficient line of credit.
8. Avoid stadium cost overruns and political problems.
9. Don't antagonize local citizens; be positive and involved.
10. Don't schedule weekday afternoons, but weekend day games are OK.

USA Baseball/International

USA's participation on the international level has been clouded by a number of controversial issues and problems. From a competitive standpoint, the success of USA baseball teams leaves much to desired. American teams, in general, have not done well in worldwide competition, whereas the caliber of play shown by teams in a growing number of countries continues to get better.

In the Olympics and other international competitions, Cuba has had the strong advantage of a highly regimented government sponsorship that provides a highly organized development system. With no professional leagues, Cuba's best players are considered to be "amateurs". In the past, the USA National Team, with a roster of 20 and 21-year olds, have played the world's best national teams comprised of players 26-30 or older who have played together for years. America's top players are playing professionally.

Through the years, USA National teams have had difficulty competing against the powerful teams of Cuba and to a lesser degree, Japan and Korea. At the 1996 Atlanta Games, the U.S. men's team finished in fourth place by defeating Nicaragua for the bronze medal. It was the first official Olympic medal in USA baseball history. Then, during the summer of 1998, the USA team finished a distant 9th place at the World Championships in Italy. In youth baseball, going as far back as the late 1960s, Taiwanese youth, more physically advanced and better prepared, have dominated USA children in the Little League World Series, largely the result of the inequities of training and physical and emotional maturity of the American children.

The development of young baseball players in America remains the same, a non-structured system with minimal government involvement, with much of the development and training provided by the youth leagues, high schools, colleges, universities and USA Baseball, the governing body. Past failures have shown the weaknesses of America's system of player development and training.

Ever mindful that America's baseball teams have not fared well in international play, USA Baseball, with headquarters in Tucson, Arizona, appears to be on the right track with their efforts to maximize the competitive capabilities of teams on the senior and junior levels. Under the able leadership of executive director Dan O'Brien, USA Baseball's staff of coaches and administrators is striving to make

American teams more competitive and successful in a sport that continues to be upgraded world-wide. But, big league players do not belong in the Olympics, and neither should Cuba's best "amateurs" who have no professional league to play in. With many professionals representing their countries, USA Baseball now has no other choice but to use Triple-A players.

Rather than have professionals compete in the Olympics, the best players representing the top baseball countries from around the world should play in a World Cup of Baseball. A World Cup would do far more for the game than for the championship team of MLB to play a specific country in a World Series event. It would provide the clout the game of baseball needs.

Away from the ball fields, the International Olympic Committee, the organization that administers the games, has been rocked by corruption and bribery. I will discuss later how the IOC's corruption has cast shame over the Olympic movement, the need for re-organization, changes and reform in the governance structure and the restoration of Olympic ideals and values. In an editorial, the San Francisco Chronicle said, "The Olympic image, one of the most powerful in sports, has become badly tarnished. A convincing rebuilding effort, with fresh leadership, must be allowed to go forward to restore its luster."

Development System Needs Structuring

Stronger, more efficient player development programs need to be implemented by all of the youth organizations. America's system of player development, in sharp contrast to those in Cuba, Japan and Taiwan, is far less intense and regimented. School children in Cuba are introduced to baseball in the early elementary grades. Little boys in the first and second grades can be seen practicing one hour each day after school. Like American youth did a half century ago, Cuban kids play on their own, in pick-up games and at home.

To be more successful, young baseball players and teams in the future need a more structured system of development and training. They need to be given more practice time and game experience to develop a higher level of skills, instinctive nuances, and a broader knowledge of the game. A more productive and disciplined program must be developed with greater resources and commitment than ever before.

Ways USA Baseball Can Upgrade Play

- Stronger player development programs need to be implemented, a more structured and competitive system of development and training

- Attracting and developing more good athletes to baseball should be a major objective of the new organizational structure

- Baseball academies, regionally located, should be established and attended by USA's most promising 14-17 year old prospects

- A renaissance of playground baseball is urgently needed to re-introduce young children to fun-oriented pick-up games

- Coaching certification programs must be implemented by all youth leagues

- Popularizing the sport on a world-wide scale should continue to be a challenge of all baseball organizations in America

- A World Cup of Baseball will widen the sport's appeal on a global level

- A double elimination tournament of one week, similar to soccer's World Cup, should precede the MLB season and involve 4-8 teams

- There is an urgent need to reorganize the Olympic Games and to restore Olympic ideals and values

- The International Olympic Committee must reverse the decision to allow professionals to compete in the Olympic Games

- The word "amateur" should be put back into the Olympic charter and the best amateur athletes should compete in the Games

- Rather than compete in the Olympics, major league stars should play and represent their country in the World Cup

Getting young players in America playing and practicing more on their own is of the greatest importance. A renaissance of playground baseball is urgently needed to re-introduce young children to fun-oriented pick-up games their fathers and grandfathers used to play, in the backyard, a vacant lot or park-school ball field.

For these concepts to make a successful comeback, however, they will require the combined involvement and cooperation of numerous agencies and organizations in the community and on the national level, with the support of past and present major league players. The prime objective is linked to the ability to get children and teenagers to play more on their own.

Higher coaching standards, a more disciplined approach to practice and training, a greater access to instructional materials are urgently needed. A nation-wide promotional campaign should be conducted, with support from past and present big league players and the news media, to motivate children to join a "Renaissance of Baseball", a revival of pick-up games, sandlot and playground baseball, with a greater number of kids playing on their own and with their close friends and parents.

A major weakness in the player development system in America is the quality of coaching at the lower youth league levels. A large majority of those who coach at this vital stage of learning are volunteer parents who know little about coaching a team and how the game is played. Little League and other youth baseball organizations must finally take the necessary action to implement a coaching certification program, similar to the excellent model Baseball Canada has used for many years. In level one, the three components are: theory, technical and practical. On completion of all three components, coaches will receive a "passport" officially recognizing their accomplishments as a certified coach at that level. They are qualified to coach in a variety of situations.

Regional Baseball Academies

The most promising 14-17-year old prospects in the United States should attend baseball academies from 4 to 6 weeks each summer. Such an academy concept would be similar to Cuba's program, but geared to the realities of our society and culture. For years, Cuba has benefited greatly from a highly regimented government sponsorship which has produced a highly successful development system for youth as young as 9 years of age.

In Cuba, their best prospects are identified at an early age and sent to baseball schools to develop their talent. Even at the equivalent of the Little League level, coaches keep precise player records. Young children are given a rigid screening, a process which takes the more skilled to more advanced levels. At the age of 15, the most promising players are sent to a highly specialized school where they train and compete with the best in the country. Each of Cuba's 14 provinces has an academy, and the top players are placed on teams representing the various provinces. From an overall 400 ball players, about 50 are chosen to attend a training site in Havana.

In the United States, academies would be conducted regionally under the auspices of USA Baseball, with college and high school coaches serving as instructors. At each of the six regionally located academies, the top 60 young players are placed evenly on four teams. From an overall 360 players, about 60 youngsters are chosen to attend the USA Training Headquarters in Tucson.

The six regions are:

* Northeast   * Southeast   * Rocky Mountains

* Midwest   * Southwest   * Far West

USA's regional academy program should be supported financially by the various funding resources, such as Major League Baseball, corporations, commercial enterprises, service organizations, and some type of governmental assistance. Colleges, schools, park and recreation agencies would provide much needed facilities. Ideally, six colleges should be selected to host the regional academies.

Amateurs or Professionals?

As late as 1974, those competing in the Olympic Games must not be or have been a professional athlete in any sport or contracted to be so before the official closing of the Games. However, when Juan Antonio Samaranch became president of the IOC in 1979, any reference to the word "amateur" was deleted from the Olympic Charter. It was now simply "the best athletes" in each sport that competed in the Games. The true Olympic spirit was given a cruel blow by the advocates of professionalism

Still, member nations of the International Baseball Association remained opposed to the inclusion of pro's until 1996. At which time, IBA countries were forced by Samaranch to allow professionals in after intense pressure was put on the IBA. Samaranch made it clear that the future of baseball in the Games would depend on the admission of professionals in future Olympics.

The movement toward professionalism and Dream Teams has greatly disturbed many people who understand the true meaning and spirit of the Olympics. Based on polls taken in recent years, a large majority of both baseball officials and fans strongly oppose the use of pros in the Games. They believe major league stars and dream teams do not personify what the Olympics stand for. Many still have the impression that the Olympics is about amateur athletes, not a group of overpaid professional all-stars.

Contrary to popular belief, even the ancient Greek athletes were not "pure" amateurs. As David Wallechinsky wrote, "Not only were they fully supported throughout their training, but even though a winner received only an olive wreath at the Games, back home he was amply rewarded. The concept of amateurism actually developed in nineteenth century England as a means of preventing the working classes from competing against the aristocracy. The wealthy could take part in sports without worrying about having to make a living, and thus could pursue the ideal of amateurism." The qualifications for being an amateur have varied from decade to decade and from sport to sport. Following the 1988 Games, the IOC voted to declare all professionals eligible for the Olympics, subject to approval of the federations in charge of each sport.

Professional athletes must not be allowed to invade what should be the world's tribute to its finest amateur athletes. The spirit of the Olympics burned ever so brightly when the Games were the domain of amateurs who relished the sports, the competition, and the fellowship, not multi-millionaires who do it a day after day for big paychecks and product endorsements.

The Olympics should continue with amateur athletes. Those who support professionalism should conduct their own competition, but not under the cloak of the Olympiad, rather as the "Professional Games."

Reversing the Professional Movement
The true Olympic spirit was given a cruel blow by the people who advocate professionalism at the international level. When the IOC made professionals eligible for the Olympics, they committed the sports crime of the century. Having been excessively commercialized by corporate sponsors, hyped by TV, the Olympics have moved blatantly to the use of professionals.

With the word "amateurism" no longer in the Olympic Charter, the basic premise of the Olympiad has now been removed. Those oriented to professionalism should organize their own competition and allow the true Olympics spirit to return to the Olympiad as espoused by its founder, Baron de Coubertin, over a century ago.

Today's Olympic Games do not personify what the Olympiad stands for. The philosophy of professionalism, which was strong-armed by Samaranch, is wrong for the Olympics. The Olympics is no place for multi-millionaires who receive huge paychecks and endorsements. Based on its charter, philosophy and tradition, the Games are for amateurs, and amateurism should be what the Games are all about.

The IOC must reverse their decision to allow professionals to compete in the Olympics. The world "amateur" should be put back into the Olympic charter, and the best amateur athletes should compete in the Games.

How Amateurism Can Return
For the Olympics to revert back to a strict code and philosophy of amateurism would simply not be realistic. In returning the Olympics to amateurs, those who compete should be allowed to be subsidized by their countries and private corporations, receive limited benefits and be able to be employed during training.

Government and corporate subsidization, combined with a loosening of strict eligibility rules, would make it possible for the amateur athlete to regain prominence in the Games. The IOC should develop a practical and realistic code of rules, financial guidelines and limits as to how much athletes can earn. Then, with the assistance and support of each country, they must enforce the new rules and amateur code with periodic inspections by investigation teams. Countries who break the rules and do not abide by the code will be penalized, suspended, or barred from future competition.

World-wide Forum Needed   There is a long, over-due need for a world-wide forum of governmental leaders, Olympic officials and athletes, past and present, from all nations. They should convene for the purpose of airing their views and opinions, and recommending the future course of the Olympics. Today's Olympics are driven by financial considerations, rather than by sporting ones. It's about money. El Pais, Spain, in an editorial, wrote "Aside from corrupt individuals. the IOC is an anachronistic body that requires urgent reform."

Major problems and issues of the Games would be addressed, such as the movement to professionalism, its deeply negative impact on amateurism, and the true meaning and spirit of the Olympics, and the growing movement to return the Games to amateurs. The forum would cover eligibility rules, financial guidelines, limitations on subsidization, enforcement and inspection procedures. Issues on the agenda should include such problems and issues as bribery and corruption, out of control commercialism, politics involved in the Olympic Movement, and the appointment of IOC members.

Olympics Rocked by Corruption   In December, 1998, Switzerland's Marc Hodler, a longtime member of the IOC's ruling inner circle, described the systematic buying and selling of the Olympic Games. Hodler specifically cited a pattern of bribery and other ethical malpractice in the bidding and selection of at least four Olympic host cities. He also cited bribes of up to $1 million and pay-offs of up to $5 million.

"The huge windfall from television contracts and corporate sponsors spawned high stakes bidding wars among host-city candidates," wrote William Drozdiak of the Washington Post. "That fueled a combustible mix of graft and greed that exploded into the worst bribery scandal in the 105-year history of the modern Olympic Games.

Samaranch maintains he never encountered any solid proof of the improprieties, but as Drozdiak stated, "Anybody familiar with his domineering style of leadership knows it is hard to believe he was not aware of corruption in the IOC ranks." As Bob Simon reported on "60 Minutes", Samaranch's iron control over the IOC is rooted in his formative years as a fascist politician in Barcelona during the reign of Spanish dictator General Francisco Franco, when he rose to minister of sport.

Samaranch and the IOC permitted sponsorship of athletes and payment by their national federations. "Under Samaranch, the money has flowed in to the IOC and the individual federations," wrote Paul L. Montgomery in the Los Angeles Times. Corporations pay as much as $50 million each to use the five-ring Olympic logo in their ads. Now corporate executives are demanding reform or else. They have assailed the IOC's handling of the scandal. As long as Samaranch stays in office, an increasing number of sponsors will pull away. It is time for Samaranch to go.

The bribery corruption has cast a shroud of shame over the Olympics. Antonis Loudaros who carried the Olympic torch in 1996, wrote, "The scandal is leading the Olympic movement to self-destruction." In a letter to Newsweek, Anthony Melita wrote, "The image of the Olympics has been tarnished since 1928, the year the IOC elected to accept corporate sponsorship." Later, the IOC's integrity was blemished further when officials decided to allow professional athletes to participate in the Games.

Olympics Should Re-organize

Many years of greed and corruption has finally caught up with the International Olympic Committee. The authority of the IOC has eroded. "No revolution has been possible without scandal," stated Mark Hodler. "We have a great opportunity at this time. Let us make changes." But mere changes are not enough. As a headline in the Washington Post read, "To get to the bottom of the scandal, look to the top." An editorial in Christian Science Monitor stated that "The torch of idealism that has illumined the Modern Olympics for 105 years, making them worthwhile, needs re-igniting."

The International Olympic Committee is a non-governmental, nonprofit organization in the form of an association. It is financed entirely by private income, essentially from the negotiation of exclusive television rights, marketing programs, to the exclusion of any state subsidy. The general belief is that the IOC retains only 10% of these revenues, and distributes the majority to its "partners", namely federations and national committees, through the so-called Olympic Solidarity Fund and organizing committees.

"Now is the time to either scale down the Olympics or adopt the proposal by the late Greek president and prime minister Constantinos Karamanlis to create a permanent site," stated Antonis Loudaros. "Greece, where the Olympics were born in ancient and modern times, would be an ideal location. The Olympics Games belong to the young amateur athletes of the world, not to the older statesmen. Is it possible the 2004 Games in Athens, Greece, could be the beginning of the end of the modern Olympics as we know them?"

As for solutions to the IOC's corruption and bribery scandal, the following suggestions appear to be most appropriate:

- Provide complete disclosure of corruption and bribery.

- Establish strict rules and ethical guidelines; to be more open, accountable and representative.

- Agree to independent oversight.

- Be more prudent in selecting its members.

Drugs, the Greatest Threat to Sport

"The greatest threat to the image, integrity and even the continued existence of the Olympic Games and other competitions is the use of illicit performance-enhancing drugs," wrote Sharon Begley and Martha Brant in Newsweek. Many sports medical doctors, even the athletes themselves, have said that doping among world-class athletes is widespread, and the IOC and the governing bodies of individual sports "turn a blind eye". According to Dr. Charles Yesalis of Pennsylvania State University, an expert on Olympic doping, "The IOC has known about the drug epidemics in sport for the last 40 years and has covered it up."

"Better drug-detecting strategies and technologies alone won't make sport clean," said Begley and Brant. "Athletes themselves have to believe that the IOC and international sports federations will catch anyone who uses performance-enhancing drugs." But as a former American rower said, "Many Olympic records were made with the help of drugs, and people like to see records broken." The IOC doesn't want sponsors to be unhappy so they don't reveal the full extent of doping.

Salvos Exchanged over Drug Problem

At the IOC's summit on drugs in sports, Barry McCaffrey, director of the White House Drug Policy Office, attacked the IOC as too scandal-ridden to police the sports world's drug problem. He said "The IOC must institute democratic reforms and open its books to have any credibility in the fight against drugs in sports". But, the IOC shot back at American "hypocrisy" that ignores its own drug problem. Vice president Jacques Rogge, in his reference to Mark McGwire and his use of androstendione, legal in baseball but banned by the IOC, stated that, "Before lecturing people, you have to be sure your own house is in order." Rogge sneered at the American claims that androstendione is not a steroid. "Let's not be hypocritical," he said. "It's a drug that induces the formation of testosterone in the body and therefore is illegal, illicit and dangerous. Come on!"

McCaffrey told IOC leaders that the Olympic bribery scandal has damaged the IOC's credibility. He emphasized that drug-testing reform requires institutional reform. "Testing must be done by an independent agency," he said. "For complete credibility, this agency must be needed by someone other than an IOC member." McCaffrey urged the United States Olympic Committee to form a testing arrangement with the NFL, NCAA and MLB, if baseball will finally get serious about the drug problem.

World Leadership Needed in Baseball

For baseball to reach its vast potential as a truly international sport, a stronger and more assertive type of leadership is needed on all levels of play, from the governing IBA on down to the ever vital grass roots level. Popularizing the sport on a worldwide scale is a challenge that those in pro baseball shouldn't ignore. But global baseball needs leadership that will place the welfare of the game ahead of personal and commercial gain.

The needs of baseball throughout the world are many, particularly in the developing countries, which are experiencing shortages of equipment and facilities for play. There is a critical lack of qualified coaches, umpires and administrative officials to assist in the development of the game. Too much emphasis is currently placed on "elite development" such as national teams, tournaments and not enough time and resources on developing an organizational structure that will attract more young players to the sport. The International Baseball Association must continue to assist continental confederations and national associations.

Colleges and Universities

While the college game remains popular, a dilemma exists, having failed to move the season back. Northern baseball cannot compete with Southern baseball and it is not because of coaches and players. Rather, it is because of weather and existing academic calendars. Collegiate baseball has become much too offensively oriented, with powerful aluminum bats contributing to a decade of out-of-control scoring.

Still, college baseball has the potential to achieve unprecedented popularity and a higher level of play. More good programs are in existence than at any time. Tournament play has attracted record crowds. The World Series has been a big success. Coaches are the game's best teachers. Players get more instruction than ever.

Still, there are too many problems and road blocks preventing the college game from maximizing their potential. Detroit Tigers general manager Randy Smith does not believe college baseball is doing a good job of developing players. "The college game has significantly slipped in recent years," he said. "Consider the bat issue and coaches holding their jobs for one reason --- because they win. And to win, they will put their best pitcher out there as often as they possibly can, which leads to abuse."

As the 20th Century comes to a close, the college game is in a crucial period. Can collegiate baseball maximize its potential? Does it have the program resources and administrative support to do so? For the college program to be elevated to a higher level, the competitive skills of those drafted by Major League Baseball will need to be upgraded and all areas of the country share its popularity and appeal.

Will the powers to be, the university presidents, athletic directors, etc. allow college baseball to realize its full potential and attain higher standards in player development? I am inclined to believe that MLB would like the college programs to take some of the financial load off their costly farm systems. However, for this to occur, the overall structure of college baseball must be upgraded and the NCAA be more receptive to change.

Ways Colleges Can Upgrade Baseball

- Make stronger effort to maximize potential and reach higher level of play

- Become a revenue-maker and make programs self-supporting:
    - Market the game "Minor League Style"
    - Stronger and more creative efforts in raising funds
    - Build a first-class lighted ballpark
    - Move the season back to warmer weather
    - Enhance college baseball's appeal to television
    - Greater access to tournament play for all regions
    - Expand summer collegiate leagues involving non-pro play

- Closer player development ties with professional baseball, with the following objectives and needs:
    - Increase college's role in the development of pro prospects
    - Utilize the resources of a college education
    - Have MLB help subsidize wood or wood-composite bats
    - Revise the amateur draft; limit size of H.S. bonuses

- Stronger academic standards; graduation of more athletes

- Re-define what college baseball should be, what athletes should receive in education to prepare them for life

- Make College baseball a better game by correcting the following developmental deficiencies:
    - Replace aluminum bats with wood or wood-composite
    - Coaches stop calling pitches and let athletes play
    - Don't overwork pitchers; throw fewer breaking balls and work off the fastball; have pitchers pitch inside again

- Elevate the developmental ladder for college umpires

- Reinstate the program cutbacks of the early 1990s

- Control the use of performance enhancing substances and drugs

College Baseball at a Crossroad
As to the future of collegiate baseball, there is an urgent need for every program to re-define what it should be, what each academic institution wants to provide student-athletes and the underlying purposes of the program. What should athletes receive that can be both educational and prepare them for life? If collegiate baseball is to fulfill its potential and more effectively prepare students for life, the program must provide greater benefits.

In addition to providing vigorous athletic participation, physical exercise and competitive activity, the three primary missions of college baseball should be to achieve the following:

1. Stronger Academic Standards. Academics must be given greater emphasis by those involved with college sports. The strength and viability of athletic programs must be matched by strong academic standards. The goal of every student-athlete should be to obtain a quality education.

2. Greater emphasis on the development of highly skilled players. Programs should play a greater role in the development of players for professional teams. With close support from the big leagues, developmental deficiencies need to be corrected. The quality of play should be upgraded to a higher level. Having better players on the field, players and coaches with ties to the professional game, would heighten the awareness of the sport.

3. A more prominent role in preparing players for pro careers. This would involve expanded opportunities to play in college summer leagues and professional Rookie leagues and still return to play college baseball during the academic year. This option, of course, would require a new inter-pretation of an amateur athlete. The best players should be allowed to play in the summer leagues, whether they are collegiate, semi-pro, or professional. Prior to 1900, professional players were allowed to do both.

The analogy of allowing advanced players to receive professional training and experience can be compared to what students of Law and other professional fields have always done. Likewise, a college player should be allowed to hold a summer job in a professional field and be able to represent their school in baseball.

MLB Emphasis on Colleges Should Grow

Despite the current inadequacies of the collegiate system, there appears to be a growing movement by Major League Baseball to utilize colleges to a greater extent in player development. I formed this conclusion after hearing the opinions of some of the game's top leaders at Baseball America's Round Table '98, moderated by Alan Schwarz.

Most of the great players in baseball today were produced by college programs. In fact, the success rate to make the majors is nearly double for a college athlete. "College players selected in the first round have a 60 percent rate while a high school player has only 35 percent," according to player agent Scott Boras. "The difference is about academia. You learn how to learn and how to become a professional." Randy Smith said, "Intelligence is very important as to what it takes to succeed in the big leagues."

Baseball still doesn't utilize enough the resources of a college education to develop their players. They continue to sign many young prospects directly from high school. "A prime reason is that the collegiate system is not working for professional players or amateur systems", said Sandy Alderson, baseball's chief operating officer. "The colleges have too few scholarships."

But Boras asked, "Look at the premier players in the game today. Seventy-nine percent came from a college program. Of the top 20 paid pitchers, 17 are college-trained players. While it's been said the college system is not working, I'm not so sure. We would like them to use the wooden bat and have better instruction but there is something going on in the academic environment that is allowing these players to enter our profession and succeed."

In referring to how college coaches are utilizing their players and other developmental problems, Gene Orza of the players union said, "If you want someone else to help you bear your costs, you will have to help them get better." Alderson emphasized, however, "We have only attempted to place education on a higher priority. As for cost shifting, that is a whole different issue."

But Orza pressed the issue further, stating, "We must take heart of what Scott has said about some of the great players produced by college programs and see if we can change some of our hardened attitudes toward the efficacy of college baseball and divert some of our player-development costs to them."

Maximize College Baseball   Is college baseball capable of maximizing its potential and reach a higher level of play? Based on our studies, we believe it can if the NCAA would allow it to do so. For collegiate baseball to reach optimum growth, programs must have sufficient resources and administrative support. Would a higher level of play and stronger programs be in the best interests of Major League Baseball? Most definitely. Would the necessary reform and progressive changes meet the needs and satisfy the academic standards of the college presidents who rule the NCAA? I believe they would if academics and a quality education would be given greater emphasis.

Currently, top prospects drafted from college teams require from two to three years of development in the minors before reaching the majors. With stronger programs and appropriate legislation, the players couldn't be drafted until their junior year; college prospects could move quickly to the majors. More likely, they would need a season of Double-A and a short stint in Triple-A.

Could the competitive skills of collegiate players drafted by the big leagues be upgraded to a level comparable to the skills of those drafted in other sports? Possibly, but one should keep in mind that baseball is the most difficult sport to learn and become highly skilled in. Then, what would it take for college baseball to reach a higher level? Greater involvement with the pro game would be needed, with a longer regular season, more coaches with professional backgrounds, using wood-composite bats and strongly upgrading the player development aspects of college baseball.

As the majors continue to downsize their development systems, there is a strong likelihood the college game will play an even greater role in the development of prospects. If the colleges would do a better job of development, I believe the majors would pump a substantial amount of money into the college game. For college ball and MLB to have closer relations, the aluminum bat has to go. With closer ties, the majors would be more receptive to partially subsidizing wood-composite bats.

Become a Revenue-maker   For college baseball to maximize its potential, it has to become a revenue-maker. Each program and coach should analyze his or her own situation and come up with a solution to generate money for the program. If baseball can produce money, college presidents will be more apt to allow coaches and A.D.s to run the programs.

Many schools are doing just that, while others are sitting and waiting for something to happen.

Programs must be made self-supporting. More growth in revenue has to be generated. Coaches need to take the initiative to generate more revenue. They must look more to off-campus assistance. Moving the season back two or three weeks would help programs become revenue producers, but it has to be combined with an aggressive promotion and marketing campaign. Programs that are able to install lights for night games will attract even greater crowds and more revenue. Fee income for the use of the stadium, including the percentage of concessions, from a summer collegiate league and youth tournaments, can also be good sources of revenue.

Stronger fund-raising efforts should be made, like getting help from the community, business, corporations, service clubs and alumni, especially ex-players. Most definitely, college baseball needs greater support and involvement from Major League Baseball.

Build a First-Class Stadium

New stadiums are the foundations of many of the nation's foremost baseball programs. As they have done in the professional leagues, new ballparks have contributed much to raising attendance figures on college campuses. They help the whole game and interest in it. First-class stadiums have also had a major effect on recruiting. Arkansas' Baum Stadium, an $8.9 million jewel, is just one of eleven ballparks in the SEC that have been built or rebuilt since 1987. At San Diego State, Padres owner John Moores contributed $3.5 million to build the state-of-the-art Tony Gwynn Stadium. On the Fresno State campus, Bob Bennett's dream came true in 1983 when a $2 million facelift increased the capacity of Beiden Field to 4,575, including 3,575 theater-style seats.

Marketing the Minor League Style

Successful promotions, cleverly marketed, and combined with new stadiums, have contributed greatly to the success of the minor leagues. Getting people to come out to the park for the "Fun of it" has been a winning concept. Innovative marketing and promotions have made the ballpark a fun place to go. The same approach can be successfully emulated by the colleges.

Minor league clubs learned a long time ago that they are in the entertainment business. They sell the experience of the game, not a star player or two. Every game is an event – the fan's ticket to excitement. The most successful teams have taken an inexpensive family-oriented approach to good entertainment. As one club president explained, "If you get tickets into the hands of kids, their parents will come."

Strong Promotion and Fund-Raising
For collegiate baseball to become a major revenue-maker, a sound foundation of creative, exciting promotions and successful fund-raising events have to be developed. While the type of promotions held at college games have been quite diverse, those that involve corporations and commercial businesses have been some of the most successful, both in their appeal and prizes.

Promotions should appeal to students on campus, especially the fraternities and sororities. Those that appeal to families and young players are also popular. During their Youth League Day, Tallahassee kids got to mingle with their Florida State Seminole heroes on the playing field. All youth players who wore uniforms got free admission to the game.

The ability to raise money has been vital to the success of many programs. Ron Fraser, Miami's "Barnum of Baseball", believed that "It is just a question of knowing where to get the money, through the development of leads. A telephone blitz can be a good fund-raising technique. Get together former players and members of the Coach's Committee at the alumni office for a big phoning session.

Return to Wood or Wood-Composite
"The nuclear bats that helped shatter records in Omaha, the same bats that, for better or for worse, gave collegiate baseball its identity for 25 years, are giving way slowly to wood, wood-composite or 'restricted' metal bats," wrote John Manuel in Baseball America. The bat issue, which reached the boiling point after 62 home runs were hit in the 1998 CWS, had centered originally on safety and quality but now is dominated by legal liability.

Refusing to use aluminum bats, many conferences in Division III voted to use wood or wood-composite bats. Despite the new ruling by the NCAA, they wanted to use wood or wood-composite bats. The New Jersey Athletic

Conference thought the liability risk was too great using current aluminum bats. They voted to prohibit member institutions from playing against opponents who use aluminum bats for the 1999 season, including the championship.

Greater Access to Championships

For many years, college teams in northern, cold-weather regions have had a limited access to championships. In 1998, the NCAA Board of Directors approved expansion access to championships in the post-season for all divisions of play. The 64-team regional structure now has sixteen 4-team regionals, eight 2-team "Super" regionals, with eight teams qualifying for the World Series.

For bracket expansion to succeed and fiscal goals met, however, more parity is needed in the at-large selections. Regional tournaments must be placed throughout the nation geographically. Super power conferences should not have the lion's share of the field. Other deserving conferences must get an equal chance.

Among the concerns are the RPI computer ratings as one of the key tools to choose teams for the regional field. The RPI, which has been criticized as being regionally biased, measures records against Division I opponents, strength of schedule and opponents' strength of schedule.

Move the Season Back

For college baseball to become a revenue-maker, a change-of-season must be approved, and it should be more than one week. With the competitive gap between northern and southern schools growing increasingly wider, moving the season back two or three weeks will help the total national well-being of college baseball. If the college game wants to become more recognized, every region of the country should be able to compete.

The NCAA cabinet, however, voted to move up the season just one week. It amended the proposal from two weeks because of monetary concerns. This constitutes a major setback for college baseball. The one-week plan fails to address a very serious problem. In no way does it level the playing field. After years of legislative process and NCAA bureaucracy, collegiate baseball missed a golden opportunity to enhance the sport.

From a financial standpoint, moving the season back would help college baseball become a revenue-maker. Warmer weather will result in higher attendance at games, and costly spring-break trips to the South will be fewer. By moving into the summer, college baseball will discover many ways to raise money, such as collegiate leagues, youth camps and professional development curricula.

Expand Summer College Leagues

To develop their playing skills, college players need to play in the summer. Expanding the number of summer college leagues will enable a larger number of collegians to do so. An evening league at the campus stadium, combined with a youth camp and playground league in the morning, will be financially rewarding to college baseball programs, as well as providing jobs for the athletes.

This innovative program will enable student-athletes to combine summer class studies with their baseball play in the evening. Under MLB auspices, it would improve the training of the players, influencing more of them to explore a baseball career. It would also provide professional preparation and occupational education for students enrolled in the fieldwork studies in Sport Management or a related field.

Set Stronger Academic Standards

The cutbacks ordered early in the 1990s by the NCAA came as a result of breakdowns in the academic process. Some coaches and athletic directors were running out of control. Athletic graduation rates at many schools were embarrassing. The presidents took it upon themselves to assume a stronger role in their athletic programs. By imposing new rules, they tightened academic standards that athletes must attain to receive a scholarship or participate in sports. In 1995, the NCAA introduced Proposition 16, in which students need a 2.5 grade point average instead of 2.0. The higher standard sent a message to athletes that they needed to perform as students, too.

Early in 1999, a federal judge ordered the colleges to rework academic standards for athletes. The court ruled that using only test scores discriminates against blacks, whose scores are lower than those of whites. He declared the NCAA's minimal academic standards illegal. Many educators believe the judge's ruling will disrupt the high school's attempts to educate athletes. Although schools bring to the campus athletes unprepared for work, the freshman eligibility standards have helped schools press promising athletes to study.

Restore the Cutbacks

At the 1991 NCAA convention, university presidents instituted a number of damaging reforms. College baseball sustained extensive wounds, such as scholarships, coaching staffs, practice time and schedule length all were reduced. The cutbacks have given high school players more reason to choose professional baseball than they did during the 1980s. They have been harmful to the ability to prepare fundamentally sound players for higher levels of play.

Since the NCAA's "reform movement", programs have been unable to regain losses caused by cutbacks. Off-season practice and playing time has been limited. Among the many important needs it serves, the fall program allows a valuable educational process to take place, with emphasis on basic fundamental instruction.

The Majors Must Help the College Game

The time is long overdue for Major League Baseball to help the college game and amateur baseball in general. The majors would be taking a big step in solving the bat issue if it were to put its weight and money behind either wood or composite models. As David Rawnsley stated in Baseball America, "It would make those million-dollar bonus payments a whole lot less risky."

New bat standards are currently being set by the NCAA to legislate the length-to-weight ratio and the barrel size so that metal bats duplicate the performance of wood. "The door is wide open for composite bats and less powerful aluminum bats," wrote Rawnsley. "Companies such as Easton and Louisville Slugger, which profit heavily from their aluminum bat divisions, are sure to hit the drawing board hard to serve the new market. Bat manufacturers will be trying to develop a new market that could reach down into the high school, summer league and youth level. This is where MLB has to act quickly and firmly. Regardless of the quality and characteristics of composite or redesigned aluminum bats, the best alternative for professional baseball is still wood."'

If the majors truly want to rid the college game of aluminum bats, it must help colleges make the transition to either wood or composite models. How much would it cost the majors to subsidize college baseball with wood? "A figure of $3 million could start the wood bat program," said a scouting director, "plus a lesser amount annually to continue industry support." Rawnsley wrote, "That amount would work out to $100,000 a club the first year."

Closer Ties with Professional Baseball

A closer relationship would be in the best interests of both the major leagues and college baseball, as well as the game itself. The NCAA and the major leagues should work together in developing a system that encourages more top athletes to go to college. Top officials of the NCAA and college baseball should meet with Major League Baseball to discuss a closer relationship and to determine what the majors can do to enhance the status of college baseball.

Of mutual interest should be what the majors can do to enhance the popularity and appeal of college baseball, making more quality athletes available for college programs. To achieve this vital goal, the number of graduating H.S. prospects drafted by pro baseball must be reduced. A reduction would help significantly. With ever increasing signing bonuses and huge salaries, owners have considered making cutbacks in player development. By going to college, a young prospect will receive an education, and big league clubs will have the opportunity to watch him mature before determining what he's worth. It will be less of a gamble as far as signability and predicting his talent.

More Emphasis on Pro Development

College baseball should place greater emphasis on professional development like they do with other academic professions and occupational education programs, with close assistance from the majors. The benefits would be substantial. To achieve a working agreement with MLB, the colleges need to upgrade their programs, relative to developing highly skilled players. Some type of professional preparation agreement should be initiated between the colleges and the majors, which would place more emphasis on player development. For this to occur, the current developmental deficiencies of the college game must be corrected.

The most discussed concept is for the colleges to allow their players to play in professionally-supported leagues during the shortened summer season and still return to play college baseball during the academic year. For colleges to play a more prominent role in player development, a larger number of former big league players, particularly those with a collegiate background, should be employed to coach. Ex-major leaguers are some of college baseball's most successful coaches, such as Dick Siebert, Gene Baker, Jerry Kindall, and Bill Freehan. The Hall of Fame of Baseball is filled with extraordinary players who came up through the college ranks -- Lou Gehrig, George Sisler, Christy Mathewson, and more recently Tom Seaver, Reggie Jackson and Mark McGwire.

For college baseball to serve the player development needs of professional baseball, more ex-big leaguers should be coaching college teams.

Correct Developmental Deficiencies   For collegiate baseball to attain a higher level of play and to strengthen its appeal nationally, the overall resources, system of development, and the game itself, will need to be elevated to an unprecedented level. College baseball has some serious shortcomings in player development, which has the strong concern of the majors. For the colleges to maximize their potential and develop closer ties with pro ball, these deficiencies must be corrected:

1. <u>Aluminum bats are detrimental to the game.</u> From a financial standpoint, aluminum bats have been an asset to college and other amateur programs. Developmentally, though, metal bats have proven detrimental to both hitters and pitchers, as well as how the game is played. Pitchers who turn professional discover there is a big difference in the weight and density of aluminum and wood. Learning how to pitch against the aluminum bat continues to be a frustrating and developmentally damaging experience. Because pitchers are afraid to challenge hitters, they throw more breaking pitches and throw more pitches overall. Then, there is the safety problem that more powerful metal bats pose to the game.

    Colleges should go back to wood or Baum wood-composition bats. If they do, their ability to develop players for pro careers will not only be given a big boost but the familiar "crack of the bat" will return to collegiate campuses, rather than the ping sounds that turn off many people.

2. <u>Pitchers are not pitching inside.</u> Because of the aluminum bat, most college pitchers are reluctant to throw the good inside fastball. They do not want to work inside that is so effective in discouraging hitters from leaning out over the plate. As to why? Because the value of jamming hitters with inside pitches is minimized by metal bats. Inside pitches that ordinarily break wooden bats on the major league level are often driven for hard hits in collegiate baseball. Pitchers soon give up on working inside. "Pitchers must throw fastballs inside to set up other pitches," said Joe Morgan. "Instead of pitching inside, many pitchers are throwing breaking balls or changeups away."

3. <u>Pitch-calling by Coaches.</u>   Coaches who signal pitches hinder the development and potential of both the catcher and pitcher. Calling pitches from the dugout stunts the growth and maturity of pitchers who are not learning the feel of the game. Joe McIlvaine believes "The development of the pitcher's decision-making skills has been retarded at the college and scholastic levels by coaches calling pitches. A pitcher learns best from making his own decisions and mistakes. Among the shortcomings, it is very difficult for a pitcher to establish a good rhythm when he has to wait for the coach in the dugout to send the sign to the catcher. Then the catcher has to signal the sign to the pitcher on the mound. This time consuming process is another reason for longer games in college.

An academic institution should be the last place to see coaches calling the pitches, considering how detrimental it can be for the catcher. Sports therapist Alan Jaeger believes the system prevents the pitcher from reaching his full potential and may cause a deep-seated resentment by hurlers toward the coaches. A growing number of college coaches are refusing to signal pitches. They believe the game belongs to the players. As UCLA coach Gary Adams explained, "When a coach interferes with the development of a pitcher and catcher by calling pitches, he is not helping them get better."

4. <u>Over-worked Pitchers.</u> Many college pitchers are being overworked. Much too often, young, just-signed pitchers from college arrive in pro ball with tired arms, having thrown too many curves and sliders. In the 1995 regionals, for example, freshman right-hander Kyle Peterson of Stanford threw 120 pitches in a complete game victory over Arkansas, then returned with two days rest and threw 146 pitches in the Cardinals' clinching victory.

Collegiate pitchers are not only throwing a lot of pitches but even more damaging to their pitching arms and careers ahead, they are throwing an excessive number of breaking pitches. Not enough emphasis is on the fast ball, largely due to the use of aluminum bats. College pitchers are working off the breaking ball, while top big league pitchers work off the fast ball.

Reduce the Time of Games   College baseball, like the majors, must do a better job of keeping the game moving. Umpires must enforce rules designated to prevent excessive stall tactics by hitters and pitchers. Hitters need to be urged to stay in the box, or at least one foot in, and the pitcher to

deliver a pitch by 20 seconds. Hitters should not be allowed to step out following every pitch, walk several feet away, and go through their practice swing ritual again.

The practice of calling signals from the dugout can be very time consuming, contributing significantly to longer games. Too many pitching changes can slow down the time of a game, too. Coaches can save some time by indicating the relief pitcher to an umpire immediately after crossing the foul line for the second time in an inning. Umpires must enforce the strike zone as outlined in the NCAA rulebook. With the balance of the game much in favor of the offense, calling the high strike will help pitchers get ahead and it will result in fewer walks and shorter games.

Umpiring Development Needs Elevating

While the quality of college umpiring is very good, the overall ladder of development and advancement is in need of some reform. Many young promising umpires are experiencing difficulty moving up to the NCAA Division I level. Likewise, there are many highly qualified college umpires who should have more opportunities to move up to the professional ranks. "There still is not a program for young umpires to follow to break down the barriers and gain admittance to the upper echelon of college baseball," according to Jim Lane, CEO of the Mideast Collegiate Umpires Alliance.

But things are looking up. Dave Yeast, NCAA's national umpire coordinator, along with Jon Bible and other Division I umpires, have formed the Amateur Baseball Umpires Association. "The idea behind the ABUA is to bring together all the amateur umpires in America," said Lane. The ABUA will stage a minimum of three camps each year to allow umpires to gain access to the proper two and three-man mechanics employed by the NCAA. Umpires will have the opportunity to be certified by the NCAA for future competitions."

The overall ladder of development and advancement is in need of reform.

Non-Pro/Semi-Pro, Adult/Senior

The 1990s has been a decade of growth and revival for the non-pro area of baseball. Much of the growth has concentrated on leagues involving older players continuing or returning to ball diamonds. Senior leagues are more recreation-oriented, remarkable in that thousands of men are paying to play for the pure love of the game in the rapidly expanding Men's Senior Baseball League.

The semi-pro leagues, organized on a more competitive basis, are showing some signs of recovery from fiscal instability and a lack of sponsors. Known traditionally as semi-pro ball, they appear to be coming back. Yet, both managers and sponsors have expressed strong concern for their teams' financial stability. While a majority of commissioners and sponsors believe the status of non-pro ball is good, financial burdens continue to have a major impact.

The organization of more local teams and a comeback of hometown rivalries seem to have stimulated both player and fan interest. An increasing number of summer collegiate leagues are playing a major role in the revival of non-pro baseball. Significantly, the National Baseball Congress is beginning to take on a stronger and more assertive stance in its overall organization structure.

With strong support from USA Baseball, the NBC has the capability to play a greater role in the development of higher-skilled players, as well as providing competitive opportunities for young and older players alike. Should the NBC continue to assume its laid back stance of the past, the recreation-oriented programs, like MSBL and NABA, will soon dominate the non-pro level of play. While such dominance would serve the leisure needs of the nation, America's already declining and inadequate system of developing young baseball prospects would be further damaged.

Growth of men's and adult baseball leagues has been phenomenal, with players 30 and over performing in 300 cities, including such former major league players as Jerry Reuss, Jim Barr, Bob Oliver and Jose Cardenal. But the great majority are men who have never played pro ball and many have not played since high school.

Ways Non-Pro Can Upgrade Baseball

- Revive and expand non-pro teams representing towns and cities

- Re-kindle home town baseball and neighborhood rivalries

- Promote a comeback of Sunday afternoon baseball

- A broad national program by NBC to aid leagues in need

- A stronger, more viable National Baseball Congress

- NBC should take a more structured and promotion-minded stance

- Increase college involvement in hosting summer leagues

- Attract support of pro scouts by developing skilled players

- Expansion of recreation-oriented adult and senior programs

- Close cooperation between NBC non-pro and adult/senior leagues

- NBC teams should implement a creative approach to marketing

- Greater support from corporations, businesses, service clubs

- More sponsor money, corporate support, fiscal stability

- Utilize a diverse array of publicity methods to draw crowds

- Stronger support from families with post-game picnic in a park

- Get children and youth involved in various ways

- Urge park and recreation agencies nationwide to get involved

- Encourage more women to participate in organized leagues

Revival of Non-Pro Leagues

The traditional non-professional leagues of America need to be revived to provide a higher level of competitive opportunities and give player development a much needed "shot in the arm." Young players coming out of high school, particularly those with pro potential, should be given the challenge of playing against better players. Older players in the 30s and 40s, still possessing their skills and a desire for competitive action, should have the opportunity to play in semi-pro leagues.

Non-pro baseball has the potential to contribute significantly to baseball's revival. Many leagues and teams, however, are having serious fiscal problems or organization difficulties of one form or another, such as:

* Finding good sponsors
* Lack of funding
* Getting media coverage
* Poor game and practice facilities
* Declining interest by fans

Still, I believe semi-pro leagues and teams could cope and turn things around with more unified direction and assistance from national headquarters. With a rejuvenated and supportive NBC and with corporate and community backing, non-pro ball could rebound and make a strong recovery. A strong national movement, coordinated by both the NBC and USA Baseball, could strengthen the overall structure of a revitalized non-pro area of play. This would give organized baseball the balance it so vitally needs.

More and more the colleges are making available their playing fields for non-pro leagues to use. Evening leagues can be a part of the player development agreement between the colleges and professional baseball, in conjunction with Occupational Education programs at host colleges, educating student-athletes for a career occupation, both athletes and Sport Management major students. By sharing their baseball facilities with a summer semi-pro league, both the college and non-pro game will derive considerable benefits.

Re-Kindle Return of Hometown Baseball

For a major revival to occur, hometown rivalries need to make a comeback. "Years ago, thousands of small cities and communities across the country had very good hometown teams which attracted strong fan support," wrote Bill Schroeder, publisher of Lakeland Newspapers in northern Illinois. "They called them semi-pro, but essentially, it was a town playing another town."

Town pride can be the key to the growth of semi-pro ball. But, it has to be promoted by the managers and owners, business and civic leaders, and the citizens of the community. Most urgent, it must be provided with greater financial stability and resources. For hometown ball to return, teams will need more sponsorship money, corporate support, and financial stability. Colleges should be asked to host summer leagues, with support from the big leagues.

Expand Adult and Senior Baseball

The non-pro area of play has seen a sharp growth of recreation-oriented leagues and teams involving older players continuing or returning to baseball diamonds. The senior leagues, however, are more of a paying-to-play for the love of the game. During the autumn season, more than 4,000 baseball players, ages 30-70, from 44 states and some foreign countries travel to Arizona and Florida to compete in the annual Men's Senior Baseball League World Series. Competing on a national stage, their experiences, in a way, help to fulfill a lifetime dream and fantasy.

Growth of men's senior and adult baseball leagues should and must continue because they serve the needs and aspirations of an ever-increasing number of baseball enthusiasts. However, it would be in the best interests of baseball that cooperation would prevail between the NBC-administered non-pro leagues and the recreation-oriented adult and senior programs. Indeed, the program espoused by a young New Yorker, Steve Sigler, in 1986 has achieved a most remarkable success.

Upgrade Traditional Semi-Pro Leagues

Expansion and upgrading of semi-pro ball would impel Major League Baseball to place greater emphasis and priority in their scouting and player acquisition operations. Stronger non-pro leagues would serve to balance the growth of recreation-focused adult leagues. A key to the revival and expansion of the non-pro game is for the colleges and universities to host summer leagues.

For non-pro ball to achieve greater heights, the NBC must develop a stronger structure of semi-pro leagues and regional tournaments. For expansion to occur, the NBC must become more structured and promotion-minded. Even Steve Shaad, NBC's vice president, admits, "We are a loosely organized group of leagues and teams nationwide, not a strong or iron-fisted governing organization. The structure of NBC is to determine a national champion for non-pro baseball." The NBC, for many decades, has been supported mightily by dedicated, hard working commissioners. These giants of semi-pro ball have either retired or are frustrated by the lack of funding, in part the result of NBC's unwillingness to assert its presence. While this policy has been successful in the past, it will not work in the future. A more aggressive approach is needed.

Develop Higher-Skilled Players

There is an important need for non-pro leagues to play a greater role in the development of skilled baseball players in America. A larger number of well-organized and financially stabile semi-pro circuits would provide a big boost to professional baseball by developing a stronger and more in-depth farm system that will produce higher skilled prospects.

With the support of USA Baseball, the NBC has the capability to play a greater role in developing skilled players at a time when the professional leagues are in dire need of more talent. It must take a broader approach to its organizational structure than just their showcase event, the annual World Series. Instead, the NBC has to reach out and offer greater support and staff assistance to member leagues and teams nationwide.

For USA teams to be successful in worldwide competition, the development of skilled players in America has to be upgraded. Otherwise, USA teams will continue to take home bronze medals or even fail to qualify for the Olympics. With fewer minor league affiliates, an expanded number of semi-pro leagues will provide significantly more opportunities for pro prospects to develop their talent and skills. "A mutually satisfactory working relationship with Major League Baseball should be pursued," said Dick Fitzgerald who for many years has been active in adult and senior ball in the Seattle area. He says, "Extending college baseball throughout the summer months will provide a three-prong method of financing non-pro teams: majors, colleges and sponsors."

"While this method will be difficult to achieve, as a result of over-regulations, bureaucracies, etc., someday it may be the only real solution," said the veteran pitcher from Puget Sound.

Achieving Financial Stability

The future of non-pro and semi-pro leagues will be dependent on finance. Money continues to be the most serious problem, unless they are fortunate to have a large sponsorship. But team sponsors that are willing to put up $10,000 or more are difficult to find. For non-pro teams to be fiscally stabile, a strong and aggressive sales promotion and marketing campaign is needed, like the minors do so well. As Larry Davis of the NBC stated, "A team has to get people to go out and beat on doors. Everyone has to hustle."

Major keys to the financial stability of non-pro baseball are:

- An expanded NBC with a stronger organizational structure
- Significant increase in summer collegiate leagues
- Get support from corporate sponsors, large and small businesses and companies in the community
- Become a more productive farm system for big league baseball

Publicizing Semi-Pro Ball

While semi-pro baseball in the past has not had much support from the media, the problem can be attributed to a number of factors, including a lack of fan support, less interest in the competition and failure of team officials to get the word out. With the scope of sports today so diverse, members of the news media have become so spread that they don't have time to contact non-pro games and league officials, other than at tournament time or an important event or happening.

Therefore, those responsible for publicity must get the information to the news people as to how the team and players are doing. In the recreational senior leagues, not much is done to publicize and promote the games, since attendance is not a major objective. However, semi-pro ball is a much different matter. They need the spectators and sponsors to survive.

Since space in newspapers and airtime is limited, publicists must pursue other options and approaches. "Over the past 40 years, we have tried just about everything," said Merl Eberly, whose Clarinda A's have been very successful in attracting fans. "We send to all news media and our fans pocket-size schedules, flyers, signs and yearbooks. Commissioner William Stoors of the Northern Illinois Baseball League will publish a sponsor guide with ads in it. He says, "It helps raise money for the league." Larry La Mange, sports supervisor for the

Grand Rapids City Majors League in Michigan, sends news releases to the local news media. Schedules are published in papers. Game summaries are run daily, along with a story detailing the previous day's game. Standings are run daily and occasionally, the media will run stories.

Whatever the situation and the size of a city or town, the task of publicizing and promoting semi-pro teams is not an insurmountable task. There are many ways in which the team and its players can be brought to the attention of the public. Larry Davis of the NBC suggested the use of college interns in handling media relations, sending out press releases, even some promotion and sale responsibilities. "We receive many inquiries from kids graduating from college who want to come in as interns," he said. "If a team would contact us, we might be able to send someone."

More Promotions and Fund-Raising Events

Outstanding promotions have been conducted in semi-pro ball since the early days of the NBC when Hap Dumont was highly successful in drawing crowds. The NCAA's short-season Rookie leagues have done a good job putting on shows to entertain fans. Likewise, the minor leagues and to a lesser extent, the majors, stage some type of activity, a contest or give-away, nearly every game. Then, why shouldn't non-pro teams use the same methods and ideas?

With effective and creative planning, and executed with spirited enthusiasm, promotional events of various kinds can be successful in drawing crowds. To make things happen, form a team booster or a dugout club or have the wives and girlfriends organize a ladies auxiliary. Then, ask for their assistance in helping conduct the promotions and fund-raising events.

"Promotions in the Virginia Valley League are done by each of the franchises", said vice president Curtiss Dudley. "We have a lot of give-aways, celebrities and contests. A good supply of comp tickets are often available." At NBC's Midwest Regional in El Dorado, local sponsors buy out tournament nights, which allows tickets to be given away. In Jasper, Indiana, players on the Reds sell season passes. Promotions that involve corporations and commercial businesses have proven successful.

The following are just a few of the many popular promotional and fund-raising events which semi-pro teams should consider:

- Portable advertising signs on outfield fences
- Concessions and vendors
- Golf tournament (see H.S. chapter for details)
- Team yearbook; T-shirt and/or cap sales
- Alumni game, hit-a-thon, home run derby, marathon game
- Spaghetti/pizza feeds; candy, cookies, Xmas tree sales
- Bingo and various giveaways with support from businesses

Stronger Support from Families

In past decades, hometown teams have given the family a common interest and enjoyable activity during summer nights. "The pace of the game can be relaxing, social, therapeutic and rejuvenating," wrote Dudley. But, how can semi-pro and hometown baseball get more family members out to the ballpark? In building a good family atmosphere and loyal fan support, the most successful teams are those who use the Sunday game and the picnic-in-the-park. President Tom Strickland of the South Central Texas Amateur League said, "We encourage everyone in the family to attend – moms and dads, girlfriends, brother and sisters. Many of our most faithful are the grandparents." In smaller towns and cities, fan support can be very good. Fans identify with the team as representing the community. There is town pride involved, and this characteristic can be promoted by some effective creativity. "When we get kids involved to help us, we draw their relatives," wrote Marv McCown, who runs the NBC's regional tournament in Elkhart, Kansas. It really helps when you put the players in host families to live."

More Competent Umpiring Needed

Competent umpiring is as vital to the success of non-pro baseball as it is to every other level of play. The standards of umpires, the consistency of their work and their expenses are very serious concerns of those who administer the leagues. Organized baseball would best be served if more non-pro, high school and collegiate umpires, with the support of umpiring associations, would upgrade their umpiring skills, not necessarily with a professional career in mind but just to improve their skills. More information can be obtained at the web-site of the Umpire's Resource Center: http://www.umpire.org/

154

High Schools

High school baseball could well be the centerpiece in the development of highly skilled players in America. Major league scouts believe prep baseball is the key to baseball's career ladder, the most critical level of play in developing major league talent. All levels of play in baseball benefit from a strong high school program. However, baseball continues to take a back seat to football and basketball, losing athletes to sports which have higher profiles. A number of serious problems have prevented high school baseball from building much needed popularity and achieving a higher profile. To attain optimum growth, prep baseball must gain a much stronger profile, if only to be a more attractive alternative for athletes competing in football and basketball.

High school programs are not getting enough financial support to maximize their potential. The economic downturn early in the '90s had a devastating effect on prep sports in general, and baseball in particular. Budget cutbacks continue to seriously hurt high school programs. By reducing the number of games and practice time allowed, programs and the players are being impeded. Weather in northern regions has always been a major problem. The lack of adequate indoor facilities has made it difficult for the teams to prepare for the season. Poor weather often makes it necessary to delay opening the season. The high temperature for a mid-April weekend in Chicago can be as low as 40 degrees!

During the past two decades, high school ball has shown a general decline in the execution of basic skills, largely attributable to the decline of baseball at the pick-up and sandlot level. While skills have not been neglected, they aren't practiced enough. The entry level of players entering high school has declined. Young players arrive knowing very little about the basics. Furthermore, the number of quality athletes playing prep ball has diminished.

Among the positives in high school baseball, the overall quality of coaching is still very good, despite criticism that the "walk-on" coach has contributed to substandard play. The walk-on coach is a prime reason why most states now require some form of mandatory coaching certification. The ability to acquire knowledge and information necessary to teach the sport is better than ever, and a huge array of camps and clinics have contributed significantly to the improvement and development of players.

Baseball's future, in large measure, exists in our high schools. Strong prep programs are crucial to the overall development of professional ball players. They are most essential to improved Jaycee and collegiate baseball, and while they won't admit it, the youth leagues urgently need their close support. To fulfill these roles, high schools need greater financial assistance, not only from the community but also from professional baseball.

How can the high schools fulfill the promise expressed by those who have lauded its potential? What can be done to elevate the prep game to a higher pedestal, a greater profile and much needed visability? Our Plan for Baseball has recommended the following steps and provisions.

Way H.S.'s Can Fulfill Their Promise

- Establish a National High School Baseball Championship

- Expand and move the season back to warmer weather

- Become a revenue-maker by using a multi-funded approach

- Establish closer ties with professional baseball

- Upgrade playing facilities – build a pro-style ballpark

- Stress academics and good study habits to the players

- Promote entertainment and fun at high school games

- Reinstate the program cutbacks of the early 1990s

- Increase funding from community and corporate sponsors

- Develop an effective farm system by helping the youth leagues

- Strengthen the development and quality of umpiring

Organize a National Championship

To achieve a greater image and more attractive profile, the prep game should introduce a showcase event – a national high school baseball championship. Such a spectacle would provide much needed visibility and identity. The high schools of America need a national championship, similar to Japan's remarkable and highly successful event, where "the entire country is shut down."

First held in 1915, Japan's high school championship every summer is the most followed sporting event in the nation, more popular than the World Series. In his book, "You Gotta Have Wa", author Robert Whiting wrote, "For two solid weeks, the eyes and ears of virtually the entire nation are turned to aging Koshien Stadium, near Osaka, where the top schoolboy teams in the country battle for national supremacy."

More than 50,000 fans fill the stadium every day. The competition is a single-elimination tournament involving 49 teams gathered from nearly four thousand participating schools in the regional preliminaries. Every game is carried live on television and radio.

A national tournament in America, featuring the top high school baseball teams in the nation, will lift the prep game to unprecedented heights. League play would begin in mid-April and conclude late in June, with the national play-offs to follow. The single elimination tourney would involve from 32 to 48 schools competing at eight regional sites. The actual school teams will compete, not all-star teams, with eight advancing to the World Series.

While it would be most difficult to duplicate the popularity and phenomenal success of the Japanese, a national championship in the United States would provide high schools with a huge shot in the arm. There will be some time constraints. The national tournament would have to be completed sometime in July. While working out the state schedules will be complex, the event would generate considerable interest and enthusiasm at the grass root level. We have seen what a World Series event has done for other levels of baseball. Everyone, except the prep game, has a national title.

Move the Season Back

A change-of-season is needed just as much by high schools as it is for the colleges. The large majority of teams in northern and eastern regions suffer through intolerable cold weather. Games can be delayed until the middle of April, and the league season finishes as early as May 23rd.

Moving the season back to warmer weather would not only upgrade high school baseball but also it would help facilitate the staging of a national championship. A change-of-season could be a key factor in helping prep baseball become a revenue-maker. It would give teams more practice time prior to the opening game. There is an urgent need to condition and develop young arms so pitchers will not suffer career-ending injuries.

An increasing number of high schools have moved the season back. They start later and go into the summer. The state of Iowa plays almost totally in the summer. In Illinois, the State Association has increased the number of games from 20 to 35, and no more than 10 can be doubleheaders. "We're allowed 35 games in the spring and another 25 games in the summer," stated veteran coach Jim Panther of Libertyville High School in northern Illinois.

Reinstate Program Cut-Backs
In the early 1990s, high schools were squeezed drastically by the economy. The cutbacks in games and practice time were alarming and inflicted serious harm to the game. As a result of declining budgets in school districts, governing officials seriously impeded programs and player development.

"Practice time to the first game is not nearly adequate," stated Ken Schreiber, highly successful coach of LaPorte High School in Indiana. "We need to have both of these returned to the original time and number." Harvey Krupnick of Holliston High in Massachusetts, summed it up by saying, "We need better weather, a longer season, more money and better fields."

Become a Revenue-Maker
Like the colleges, prep baseball must become a revenue-maker if it is to achieve its goals and reach its potential. A growing number of schools are proving they can be self-sufficient. Otherwise, schools will continue to be underfunded, lacking resources to conduct a quality program. To become a revenue-maker, a multi-funded approach must be taken, supported by a strong marketing and promotional plan. The formation of an active booster club is most essential in gaining help and involvement from the community, including corporate support, fund-raising committees, and assistance from pro baseball.

Multi-Funded Approach to Fund-Raising
To give high school baseball much needed financial stability, the school's annual general athletic fund should be supplemented by:

1. Fund-raising committee and/or Dugout Boosters Club.

    * Spearhead numerous fund-raisers, ad signs on outfield fences, yearbooks, car washes, T-shirts, etc.

    * Golf tournaments have proven very successful with a limit of 144 golfers at $30 per person.

    * Baseball Annual. In raising over $5,000, each player sells a minimum of $130 worth of ads.

2. Corporate involvement, including the building of a scaled-down minor league (or college) model baseball stadium.

3. Assistance from Professional Baseball. In helping to subsidize high school baseball, the major leagues would contribute money to finance the conversion from metal bats to wood-composite bats. In return, school programs would purchase an agreed-upon block of tickets to major and minor league games. Players, student, family members and boosters would then buy and sell the tickets.

4. Pay-For-Play. Programs, which lack sufficient funding, have the option to utilize this concept, in which each player pays $50 up to $250, for example, to cover program expenses.

Closer Ties with Pro Baseball
A top priority of high school baseball should be the development of closer ties with professional baseball. Such a relationship would be of mutual benefit to both the majors and the schools. There is an urgent need for Major League Baseball to support high school programs financially and otherwise. Subsidization of prep baseball by professional baseball is long overdue. The majors and minors will receive in return more than they will give, in ticket sales as well as much needed good-will by the most valuable fans of all -- the baseball families of America!

Build a Scaled-down Pro Ballpark

To develop a higher profile, increase attendance, entertain fans by putting on a show, high school programs need to build a ballpark, not just an athletic field. The facility does not need to look like Lake Elsinore's state-of-the-art professional stadium, but with some creativity, hard work, and strong support from the community, a scaled-down replica of an old-time minor league or even college stadium can be built, eventually with lights!

At first thought, the idea of pursuing such a construction project has the sound of a pipe dream, but consider the fact that numerous colleges and some high schools have successfully done so, with ample volunteer labor, donated, or at cost, equipment and building materials and a lot of dedication and commitment.

DEVELOP A FIVE-YEAR MASTER PLAN:

Phase One – Build a quality enclosed playing field, complete with a backstop, tiled and sodded infield with an outfield fence, dugout, scorer's table/P.A. system, scoreboard, flag pole, restrooms, bleachers, sprinkler-drainage system, portable concession stand, ticket booth, storage building, batting cages and bullpen mounds.

Phase Two – Construction of a scaled down minor league stadium, featuring a major conversion from bleacher-seating to traditional grandstands, a permanent concessions stand with a press box above and ticket booth out in front, and two player locker rooms.

Phase Three – Install lighting equipment and poles to play night games.

Stronger Effort in Promoting Games

For prep baseball to become a revenue-maker, it has to follow the lead of the colleges in becoming involved in the promotions game. With the assistance of the drama and journalism departments and a few field trips to minor league games, I am confident that our young people today will be able to organize and conduct some very creative and exciting promotions. They only need to be asked. Then provide them with the necessary direction and resources.

A game promotion sign and billboard program can be very effective in promoting games on the high school campus. A marquee sign can be constructed with names of opponents, dates and times of home games. Billboards can be placed on outfield fences, with sponsors paying for each advertisement, like at minor league ballparks.

The time of high school games has become an increasing concern to coaches and athletic directors. Traditionally, teams start their games at 4 o'clock, not a good time since many people don't get home from work until 6 o'clock. Basketball and football play at times when there is a maximum exposure but in baseball, only Saturday doubleheaders are feasible to attract the public. If lights are available, night games once a week can be scheduled.

Better Media Coverage Needed
To promote high school baseball, better media coverage is a must. Schools should make every effort to publicize their games, to let people know about the program. Having good rapport with the news media is the key to selling and promoting a program.

Newspaper editors, writers and broadcasters need to be supplied with up-to-date information, team and individual photographs and pertinent quotes from players and coaches. Game information and results, along with records broken, should be provided. Having games broadcast over a local radio station can give a big boost to the baseball program. Those who send out reports should not underestimate the willingness of the press to support high school baseball. Major newspapers in the Chicago area, like the Tribune, provide more coverage to local and regional prep teams than they do collegiate baseball teams.

Correct Developmental Problems
Calling pitches, a practice started by collegiate coaches, has infiltrated the prep level, contributing to serious developmental problems for catchers. Professional scouts are most critical of the practice, calling it over-coaching. The large majority of coaches who responded to our survey believe both the catcher and pitcher should learn how to set up hitters.

An even greater development problem is that too many high school pitchers are being over-used. Many young prep hurlers, especially in the colder regions, are throwing too many pitches early on and come tourney time, their arms are being blown out. Coaches should be restricted from overusing their pitchers, with particular concern early in the season. A rule must be initiated where pitchers can pitch once in 72 hours, or in relief three times a week and no more than 10 innings. For schools to be more effective in player development, aluminum bats should be replaced by wood-composite bats. Pitchers need to pitch inside again. Strength-building programs should be designed for athletes to play baseball, not for football.

Convert to Wood-Composite Bats

The time has come for schools to implement strict bat performance standards and make an all-out effort to convert to wood-composite bats. Supported by a subsidization agreement with professional baseball, the long overdue conversion from metal to wood composition bats would give high school programs the impetus it needs to realize its potential. While metal bats have saved the schools money through the years, the price of aluminum bats has continued to rise in recent years. Some models cost upward of $200 to $250.

Since wood is too expensive for prep programs, a wood-composite bat is the best solution. A composite bat has the same qualities of wood without the breakability. The Baum composite bat has been used for several years by professional rookie leagues. It has a feel similar to the wooden bats, but are more resistant to breakage. The cost of these bats runs up to $75-$100 per bat, but the rewards will be worth it – the long, lost crack of the bat will return, and the ping sound will be gone forever.

More Summer Opportunities

High school players need more opportunities to play baseball during the summer. Jim Panther says, "The better players in Illinois play a lot, as many as 90 games when they combine the high school and Legion programs." In Indiana, Ken Schreiber instituted a very effective summer program made up of LaPorte players. "We have our own LaPorte summer league team, and we use this time to mold our new group of players."

Summer high school baseball leagues should be expanded. Ideally, the regular season should extend well into the summer, culminating with exciting national championship play-offs in late July. This would give prep baseball much-needed visibility and a much stronger profile. "We keep no team standings or statistics and everybody plays," said Panther. "It's an excellent way to evaluate for next year, have kids improve on individual needs.

Helping the Youth Leagues

High school coaches will benefit greatly by working closely with the youth leagues. Their help will contribute much to a higher level of play.

Whether or not they fully realize the seriousness of the problem, organized youth baseball is in dire need of assistance, and the sooner the better. The number of quality players coming out of the youth leagues is steadily declining, due largely to a lack of quality instruction and the number of practice repetitions at the lower levels.

High school coaches can be invaluable to youth baseball by:

- Conducting clinics for youth coaches before the season

- Organizing summer camps for young players at affordable fees

- Become a "hub of knowledge" for the lower levels of play

- Provide instructional materials; recommend a video library

- Invite youth coaches, even teams, to H.S. team practices

- Conduct a campaign to get kids to play more on their own

Stress Academics to Players

Coaches must stress to their players the importance of attaining good grades. Coaches should encourage their players and praise them when they do well in the classroom. Showing an interest in their players' grades can be a very important motivating factor in their striving for excellence. Student-athletes must realize they are a student first, then a baseball player.

"We are passing kids who don't deserve to be passed on," said Ken Schreiber, one of America's most successful coaches. "Therefore, this welfare child expects everything to be given to him or her. We are graduating from school kids who can't read their diploma!"

Allow Players to Play Other Sports

A growing number of coaches, particularly soccer and basketball, want their players to play all year. This is not only selfish but it is wrong and not in the best interests of young athletes. Coaches in all sports, including baseball, should not insist on year-around participation in their program. They should be flexible in allowing kids to be multi-sport athletes.

"I love my kids playing other sports," said Panther. "I don't like a coach putting restrictions on kids, or even talking in a manner where a kid should just play that particular sport. Kids today are being forced to specialize early, and they are making a big mistake." Panther likes to see 3-sport athletes. "Some of the best teams I have had at Libertyville have been youngsters that were good football and basketball players because they have taken that competitive edge and with the success they have had, have brought it into the baseball season. Athletes who have excelled at three sports have made a tremendous achievement, which is why my school gives a special award for them at our spring awards banquet."

Strengthen the Quality of Umpiring

Competent officiating is most essential to any sports contest. It is particularly important in a baseball game, where split-second calls must be made. As far back as 1956 in conjunction with my Master's degree thesis assignment at the University of Illinois, I sent a questionnaire containing 25 suggestions for "Improving High School Baseball in Two Illinois Conferences". Good officiating rated the highest of all items. Coaches today should have just as high a regard for competent umpiring.

A major effort must be made to provide the most qualified umpires possible and for those involved with the prep game to strongly support increased efforts to upgrade the competencies, training and pay of umpires. On the field, umpires should be treated with respect by coaches, players and fans.

For more information, contact the Umpire's Resource Center:

http://www.umpire.org/

Youth Baseball

Youth baseball leagues in America continue to provide competitive opportunities to millions of children, with strong involvement by their parents. When administered effectively and excesses controlled, organized youth league competition can provide beneficial athletic and emotional experiences. From a perspective of Little League's enrollment numbers, its broad international scope and pro-type uniforms and facilities, perhaps the program should be celebrated, not indicted. In its 1998 report, the Sporting Goods Manufacturers Association said, "The combined enrollment of youth and children 18 years or younger in amateur leagues grew from 1.8 million players in 1985 to 4.6 million in 1996, an impressive 156% growth over 12 years. " But how can there be celebration when so many serious problems and needs exist?

The most serious problems and weaknesses in America's player development system are in youth baseball. The excesses and abuses of Little League continue to hinder the growth and development of young baseball players. Even more significantly, society and our culture today have had a profound influence on play at the youth levels. While there are more organized leagues than ever, children are not playing enough on their own. In greater numbers, kids are quitting organized baseball far too early.

Organized league play in Little League is too short, due to heavy emphasis on all-star teams and play-off tournaments. Summer ball opportunities have declined. For most kids, the baseball season is over in June and the great majority are not playing during the summer and not improving their skills. For the top players, being an all-star is an exciting experience, but for equally deserving players who are left off the team, it is a shattering experience for them and their parents.

Little League is much too organized, competitive, and structured for most young children. Adults have completely taken charge of what was once the play of children. The basic framework of the organization is actually a junior replica, a model of big league baseball. Contrary to what the founders of Little League had in mind, children have a basic right to play as a child and not as an adult.

Since Little League began, emphasis has always been on making the program bigger and bigger. The only variables have been size and numbers. Very seldom have administrators referred to the quality of play, skill development, standards of coaching and having fun. Instead, we only hear of enrollment figures and making something bigger, like doubling the number of teams in the World Series.

The pressure-packed and highly competitive atmosphere of Little League can be a nightmare for many young children. Older athletes may be able to handle the emotional stress but most children cannot. Too often, there is a sense of failure, anxiety and pain, sleepless nights, and bad dreams. Lewis Yablonsky and Jonathan Brower wrote that "In a sense, Little League is a game of errors, and the manner in which children's errors are handled can prove to be a positive or negative experience for their fragile egos." The pressure of the Little League World Series is so intense that one has to wonder, "Why should a program be geared from start to finish to play in Williamsport when the problems it produces are so detrimental to young children? Participation, player development and fun should be what Little League is all about.

There is a disturbing absence of fundamental instruction at the younger age levels. Coaches lack coaching skills and knowledge of the game. The large majority are untrained and non-certified, mostly volunteer parents. Too much emphasis is placed on winning. As a result, the basic skills are not being practiced as much as they have in the past. Fewer fundamentally sound players are coming through the youth leagues. An even greater concern, too many young players are giving up baseball as early as 13 or 14 years of age. They have been burned out and too often abused.

Young children are starting organized competition at earlier and earlier ages. Programs are now taking 4 and 5 year olds. According to many child development authorities, rigorous competition so early in life has diminished markedly a child's enthusiasm for sports. Highly structured leagues run by hypertensive adults and urged on by over-enthusiastic parents have turned off many kids.

Ways to Upgrade Youth Baseball

- Conduct national campaign to urge Little League and other programs to make constructive, meaningful changes

- Organize task force committee to study need for reform in youth baseball

- Cut down on excesses and abuses which undermine the emotional and physical well-being of young children

- Reduce competitive and emotional pressure on children, over-demanding coaches and excessive parental scrutiny

- Replace or modify the professional model of youth league organization with a child-centered model

- Scale down the massive post-season tournament schedule, particularly for children 12 and under

- Provide safer playing conditions by implementing bat and ball restrictions and ban curveballs for kids 12 and under

- Upgrade quality of coaching; train and certify the coaches

- Get kids to play more on their own, to go out and have fun

- Give children a choice, an alternative to Little League, such as Playground Baseball of America

- Promote a revival of pick-up games, playing catch and the fundamental approach of baseball play

- Urge cities and towns to organize playground baseball programs

- Establish American System of Player Development by building and operating regional baseball academies

The need for a renaissance or reform in youth baseball is greater today than ever. A revival of the game would involve not only the youth leagues but would re-open parks and playgrounds to baseball. A nationwide reform would be highlighted by the return of sandlot baseball and a revival of pick-up games. Little League and other programs do not need to be abolished but their excesses must be curtailed. A plan of reform is urgently needed.

Reform in Youth Baseball

Little League Baseball and other youth league programs are in need of restructuring, to reduce the competitive pressure on children, and allow young children to play the game without over-demanding coaches and excessive interference by parents. A strong attempt must be made to urge youth leagues to initiate meaningful changes. The main focus and objectives of organized youth leagues should be directed to the children. This can be achieved by de-emphasizing winning, learning fundamental skills and giving them a positive experience, a fun time, without undue pressure from coaches and parents.

Little League Baseball must take a hard look at their excessive approach to play-offs, all-star teams and national travel. Youth baseball continues to be driven toward national championships. There is too much pressure to win. The many excesses have had a damaging and often unhealthy repercussions on American children. Youth leagues must become more interested in skill development than getting to the World Series. For many years, medical and child development experts have strongly criticized the excessive pressure and emotional stress which young children are subjected to in World Series competition. Now, Little League has doubled the number of teams and their stay at Williamsport.

Reform is needed to address the problems of coaching, the lack of quality leadership, excessive emphasis on fathers and mothers and their lack of baseball knowledge and coaching skills. Meaningful and constructive changes must be made. Society's emphasis on organized play must be supplemented by more unstructured play and sandlot programs which emphasize fun and skill development. Young children need to have alternative opportunities in the summertime and after school play in safe, supervised areas.

Will Little League reform and make needed changes? Not likely considering the fact that the organization is dead set in its ways. But, either Little League must reorganize and reform, or cities and communities across the nation will take the initiative and make program changes themselves.

Organize Special Task Force   A special task force committee should be organized to study the need for reform in youth baseball, addressing the following:

- The overall impact of Little League's short season, long play-off schedule and heavy emphasis on all-star teams

- Determine how programs can provide more skill development, participation, and fun, rather than get to the World Series

- Recommend meaningful, constructive philosophical and program changes and reform to eliminate excesses and abuses

- Urge programs to place greater emphasis on player development, training and the certification of coaches

- Recommend less emphasis on winning and strive to remove the pressurized atmosphere which prevails in Little League today

- Hold national forum on youth baseball for the purpose of airing viewpoints relative to the status of organized leagues

- Form a select planning committee to implement recommendations of the forum and a Plan of Action

Philosophical Changes Needed   Little League has always been overly ambitious with an overpowering desire for world-wide expansion. Making the professional model increasingly identical to Major League Baseball has been a long-time goal, while making the program bigger and bigger.

A basic change in philosophy by Little League is long overdue. It is time for youth league programs to give the games back to the kids. Let young children go out and just have fun. Youth baseball must finally recognize the need and responsibility to serve two different interests: organized leagues and un-structured play. The professional model has to be modified. This type of organized structure doesn't serve the best interests of young children. Highly pressurized competition is not emotionally and psychologically sound. Young kids need to see baseball as a fun activity, not something they must do because of peer or parental pressure.

The goals of Little League should be designed to meet the basic needs of children. In survey after survey, children in the elementary grades have ranked "having fun" as the No. 1 reason for being involved. Winning, the most pursued goal in sports, has always been a relatively poor motivator for kids.

Replace or Modify Professional Model

The professional model which has prevailed in Little League Baseball since its inception has to be replaced or significantly modified. A child-centered model is more appropriate and would be far more beneficial. This model focuses on the intrinsic needs of children to participate and have fun, rather than a professional focus on achievement and success – winning!

Philosophical changes need to be made from a professional characterization to a child-centered program. The youngest age levels of Little League, 12 and under, are in need of change and restructuring that would reduce the competitive pressure on children, and allow children to play the game without over-demanding coaches and excessive parental scrutiny. The needs of youth are to participate in sports and to have fun.

Alternative Programs Are the Key

A revival or renaissance of youth baseball is not to replace Little League and other programs, only to give young kids alternative opportunities in a game more to their liking. An alternative program is just what the name implies – to give young children a choice, an opportunity to play baseball without the highly competitive pressure and atmosphere which prevails in Little League today. Kids play in the mornings without parents present.

An alternative program is designed to provide the sandlot type of atmosphere that many of us experienced. "The key is to get children to see baseball as a fun activity," stated Bill Erickson of Beverly Hills High School, "not because they have to or something they will embarrass themselves." Two examples of summer playground programs are the Wildcat Baseball League and Playground Baseball of America, the one I would like to propose.

Return of Playground Baseball   Back in the 1950s and 1960s, neighborhood kids across the nation could be seen gathering every morning at the local playground for pick-up baseball. Every park had a leader or supervisor. Today, however, children seldom play by themselves. The game of baseball has become so highly organized at an early age that many kids do not know how to play pick-up games on their own, and they are not playing on their own.

What can be done to get the kids back to playground and sandlot baseball? The key to the return of sandlot ball are the thousands of public park and recreation agencies nationwide. A major effort should be made to have local recreation agencies spearhead a multiple-sponsorship of Playground Baseball of America, a non-profit organization in coordination with the National Recreation and Park Association and state affiliates. Such a national movement would require the joint cooperation and support of local and regional recreation agencies, ably supported by national service organizations, school districts, professional baseball, law enforcement agencies, the news media, and funded by corporate sponsors.

Similar to the highly successful Wildcat Baseball League in Fort Wayne, Indiana, Playground Baseball will re-open playfields and parks to sandlot baseball, a mixture of informal, casual types of play activities, pick-up games and leagues, combined with instruction. The program will feature a revival of old-time games like Scrub, Work-up and Catch-A-Fly-You're-Up, which will be described in chapter 10. League play will be organized by the local park and recreation department, with emphasis on drop-in participation.

A summer playground type of program would begin in mid or late June and run for 4 to 6 weeks. It would operate on a half-day schedule, such as 9 a.m. to 12 noon. Supervision would be provided to lay out the bases, hand out equipment, and on occasion, settle the more serious disputes and lend first-aid assistance whenever necessary. Perhaps a coach could come by once a week to offer instruction and evaluation, watch some games and make suggestions. No set schedule would be followed. Instead, games would be played at the youngsters' interest in pick-up fashion, altering the rules when there are not enough players.

For a playground baseball program to be successful nationwide, however, it must have the support and sponsorship of recreation and park agencies, schools, and parent-teacher organizations. "This is exactly the way this great game has evolved into the national pastime," wrote Bob Merritt, baseball coach at Crestwood High in Ohio. "American youths are secretly crying out for a more skill-based, fun-resulting recreational program, as opposed to high-pressurized, result-oriented little leagues."

The key to the program's success will be funding, to handle equipment expenses, with bases and catcher's paraphernalia loaned from the recreation agency. For Playground Baseball to succeed as a national movement, it will be most urgent to obtain sponsorship and funding.

As for prospective sponsors, I polled numerous high school coaches as to the most appropriate. They ranked sponsors in the following order:

1. Major League Baseball
2. City park/recreation agency
3. Corporation/commercial
4. National service club
5. Youth leagues (providing parallel leagues)

Revival of Pick-up Games

The best way to get children to play more baseball on their own is to promote a return of pick-up games. These are the simple, low-organized games we grew up with as kids, without close adult supervision. Most children today, even their parents, have not even heard of the various games children used to play. Therefore, the youngsters of America and their parents need to be taught how to organize pick-up games on their own.

Young children today should be encouraged to play pick-up games at home, at a neighborhood park or school playground. They need to play more catch. It is what defense is all about. Play catch every day and make it a habit.

The large majority of young kids today do not play pick-up games, nor do they and their parents know how. Therefore, in chapter 10, I have selected and explained in detail ten Favorite Pick-up Games, which hopefully will return to park and school playgrounds and around the homes of American children and youth across the country.

Favorite Pick-up Games

- **Work Up**
- **Scrub**
- **Wall Ball**
- **Army Ball**
- **Catch-A-Fly and You're Up**
- **Stickball**
- **Play Catch**
- **Pepper**
- **Wiffleball**
- **Over the Line**

Playground Baseball of America

Playground Baseball of America is a national organization established to provide and promote summer sandlot baseball opportunities for youth between the ages of 7 and 14. The program has been designed for those who prefer FUN and PARTICIPATION. The primary objective of Playground Baseball is to offer children a much-needed and overdue alternative program, in contrast to over-structured youth leagues. With supervisory support from a local recreation agency, young children organize themselves in a playground, sandlot atmosphere, with no league champions, no all-star teams and national titles.

As a subsidiary of Baseball Play America, PBA has been formed to coordinate and assist individuals, groups and public agencies who want to join the movement and organize a Playground Baseball program. A major effort will be made to have recreation and park agencies nationwide spearhead a multi-sponsorship of Playground Baseball of America. Rather than serve as a youth league, PBA is a playground program which hopefully will be jointly administered by local recreation agencies, the national Recreation and Park Association, and a national service organization.

A national organizational structure is now being developed, with the goal of locating programs in cities and towns throughout the country. A national board of directors will be selected, followed by the assignment of regional directors. Current plans are to hold a Playground Baseball Conference during the annual Congress of Parks and Recreation convention in the fall.

Baseball Play America, the national base for Playground Baseball, will provide organizational materials to those who wish to become a member. Membership will include the following benefits:

- Program organization booklet (sample schedules, how-to-play instruction, checklists, favorite pick-up games, funding, etc.)

- Quarterly newsletter and membership card

- Web site access to information, materials, progress reports, instruction, downloading sequence photographs on basic skills, etc.

- Free membership in Baseball Play America

- Official report of the Plan for Baseball

Annual dues of $36.00 will provide membership in both Playground Baseball and BPA. This can be paid by check or charged to your credit card.

To receive membership information and how to organize a Playground Baseball program in your city or area, write: Playground Baseball of America, P.O. Box 4182, El Dorado Hills, CA 95762-0014. Telephone: (916) 933-7459 Fax No. (916) 933-7447.

The E-mail address is: plaground@worldnet.att.net. Or visit our web site at: www.baseballplayamerica.com.

Wildcat Baseball League (Ft. Wayne, IN)

The Wildcat Baseball League was organized by Dale W. McMillen, Sr., founder of Central Soya Company, whose personal motto – "This Day I will Beat My Own Record" – is a worthy challenge for Fort Wayne's "Wildcatters"! McMillen believed in community service, and he practiced it. Mr. Mac also believed in youth, and in adequate recreational opportunities for their development as good citizens. As he put it, "If the Wildcat Baseball League can save just one boy who may have turned out wrong, then it's worth all the time, effort and money that has been put into it.""

It was decided that the League's three main purposes would be:

1. To provide guidance, counseling and leadership for the players
2. To give the proper instructions on how to play baseball
3. To give all youth between the ages of 7 and 15, regardless of race, creed, or family background, a chance to play baseball. The Wildcat motto became, "Everybody Makes The Team."

Wildcatters are scheduled at least three times per week, one practice session and two games. Through this program the Wildcat League seeks to create a wholesome atmosphere in which youth can learn correct attitudes, habits, language usage and sportsmanship, as well as kindness, tolerance and wholesome competition. To accomplish these aims, it is necessary to hire personnel of high moral character with experience in working with youth. For each of its sites, the league selects a director, and assistant director (a college student), and two junior assistants (high school students).

The uniqueness of the Wildcat Baseball League can be found in its philosophy, which is unchanged since it began. The program provides an opportunity for the youth of Fort Wayne, ages 7-15 ½, to develop socially, physically, and spiritually underqualified, salaried staff members. The League is divided into four divisions, by ages: Kitten (7 and 8), Kitty (9 and 10), Kat (11 and 12), and Tiger (ages 13 to 15 1/2).

Athletic ability is not the primary emphasis. Nurturing the self-image of each child and developing good, solid citizens is the most important part of the Wildcat philosophy. John S. Grantham, president of the League since 1965, says, "We create a situation where kids can be successful. The only cost is for T-shirts and caps ($7), and if a kid can't afford that, he will work for it, helping the coach chalk and groom the diamond before games."

Staff members are salaried, not volunteers. Games and practice sessions, unlike those for Little League and other groups, are in the daytime. The governing body is the Wildcat Recreation Association. The McMillen Foundation pays for insurance and other costs, while the board of directors approves the overall policies and the budget.

The coaches are called site directors. All site directors are teachers and coaches from local public and parochial schools. Average participation during the league's existence has been more than 4,000 youth during the summer. The eight-week instructional baseball program interfaces with the Parks and Recreation Department and school systems for facilities, giving the league access to 40 baseball diamonds.

Wildcat teams get together at least three times a week for one practice session and two games. The baseball teams have been coed since 1971. Wildcat Baseball differs from Little League in another way: parents are not encouraged to attend games. They can attend if they wish, but any parent who becomes unruly or puts down his or her child for making a mistake is asked to leave.

"Wildcat games and practice sessions involve the children in a positive educational experience," wrote Barbara Sieminski in Business People. "If a player makes a mistake, he or she isn't yelled at. Instead, something wonderful happens. Enter: "The Teachable Moment." For example, if a player fumbles a grounder, the coach may stop the game and briefly, without anger, explain the correct way to do it."

New Development System Needed   America's system of player development has failed at the youth levels of play, largely the result of organizational and leadership weaknesses and the various social and cultural forces in society. A new and more efficient system is needed, coordinated by a national director for player development, in conjunction with USA Baseball and Major League Baseball. Major focus would be on the grass roots of baseball, from little league on up through high school and college.

A more structured and productive system of development and training is urgently needed. Players on all levels, beginning with those in the Little League Division, would receive more training and instruction to develop a higher level of skills and a broader knowledge of the game. Higher coaching standards, a more disciplined approach to training and practice, and greater access to how-to instructional materials are primary goals of the system.

A nation-wide promotion campaign would be conducted with the able assistance of past and present major league players and the news media to motivate kids to join a renaissance of baseball, a revival of pick-up games and playground baseball, with a greater number of children playing on their own, with friends and family.

An American System of Play

Baseball in America needs a strong, more efficient development system with all youth baseball programs involved. In contrast to the growing number of nations who have developed systems for training baseball players, there has never been a structured system of player development in the United States.

While the USA does not need Cuba's highly regimented program, a more systematic approach to development would be beneficial, not only for our most promising 14-17 year old prospects but every level of play. Our best players in the 14-17 year age bracket should have an opportunity to attend a baseball academy. These academies would be conducted regionally under the auspices of USA Baseball, with top college and high school coaches instructing.

While a definitive national style of play does not appear to be practical, national coordinators are needed to promote and teach players and coaches on all levels how to execute baseball skills the fundamental way. The director or coordinator would be responsible for the overall growth, development and well-being of young baseball players in the United States.

Baseball Academies in the USA

Major League Baseball has spent millions of dollars building and maintaining academies and training facilities in other countries. But there are no academies within the United States, either subsidized or sponsored by big league baseball. Other than USA Baseball's training headquarters in Tucson, only a few privately owned centers for young amateurs exist.

There is an urgent need for player development academies to be built in this country, created primarily for American athletes. For decades, Cuba has been very successful in developing highly skilled players, and a big part of their success can be attributed to training academies at each of their 14 provinces. As many as 400 players participate on 14 teams and play a 92-game season. Cuba's top players are then chosen to train near Havana.

Challenges for Little League

While the basic philosophy and program framework of Little League Baseball has drawn strong criticism, the organization itself has achieved remarkable success, expanding to phenomenal proportions. Unfortunately, the success and quality of Little League and other youth leagues have been marred by their excesses and abuses, particularly in the younger age divisions.

For Little League and other programs to be more responsible and more effectively serve the best interests of young ball players, we challenge you to respond to the following recommendations:

Limit Post-Season Play
Emphasis on post-season tournaments and all-star teams is excessive and should be reduced. Tournament play for Little League begins early in July, which means the baseball season for most children is over in June. Only the very few players who make the all-star teams are playing baseball during the summer.

From a positive view, tournament play that is limited to local, state and even regional competition provides young people with new experiences of travel and association. But for the 11 and 12-year old children who play at Williamsport, the pressure, nervous anxiety and emotional stress is much too excessive. In 1999, the problem was magnified when Little League officials decided to double the number of teams in the international championships.

Should the Little League Division World Series be abolished? In his August, 1995 article for Baseball America, Casey Telertiller wrote, "Little League is a program with many benefits, but there is no need to place 12-year-olds on an international platter to spin for the rest of their lives. The time has come to view the Little League World Series as a misplaced anachronism of a confused generation. Children are far too precious to mess up their lives with artificial goals and unrealistic glory."

"We are slowly becoming aware of what should have been obvious many decades ago: children never should be exposed to the pressure of high-level competition under national and international spotlights," said Telertiller. "Little League should be a time to learn the pleasures of baseball, not the pressure."

Ban Curve Balls for Kids 12 and Under

Young pitchers are still throwing excessive numbers of breaking ball pitches. In a typical Little League game, half the pitches thrown are curve balls. In doing so, pitchers are doing serious harm to their throwing arm. Still, Little League officials who have the responsibility for the health and safety of the players have largely ignored the curve ball problem. As a result, a great many pitching prospects through the years have ruined their arms and had their baseball careers sharply curtailed.

The "Little League elbow" is the nemesis of kid curve-ballers. As early as 1968, Dr. Joel Adams studied the elbows of 80 Little League pitchers in San Bernardino, California. His study found that X-rays of 39 of them showed damage to the medial epicondyle, compared with only six of 47 little leaguers who played in the other positions. This small bone in the elbow is wrenched loose.

Increasing numbers of local Little League presidents are expressing opposition to curve balls for children 12 and under. Bob Taillefer shared with me some of his frustrations by saying, "Little League should just say, 'No curve balls for the 9-through-12 year olds' because they will do serious harm to the boy. Time after time, I see a young pitcher throw an excessive number of curves and when they come up to the Senior Division, they pitch one year and are gone, because their arm is damaged."

Growing numbers of youth leagues, like Middleboro and Springfield in Massachusetts, are protecting their young pitchers from injuries by banning the curve ball: No curve balls for pitchers 9 through 12 years of age. The rule was drafted after a 10-year-old broke his wrist throwing a curve. In our survey of

1,000 veteran college and high school coaches, we asked them, "Should the curve ball be banned from the Little League Division competition?" 64.9% answered "Yes". Many coaches, in explaining their views, cited the stress on a developing arm and improper throwing mechanics.

De-emphasize All-Star Teams

For many years, all-star teams and play-off tournaments have been a major part of the Little League program. But, a growing number of administrators, coaches, and parents are saying there is too much emphasis on all-star teams and tournament play.

"All-star teams create many problems," says John Grantham, president of the Wildcat Baseball League. "The many who are rejected, the method of choosing all-stars, and the time and effort spent for a small percent of the total participants are reasons not to have all-star teams." In expressing his opposition to all-star teams, Hall of Fame manager Walter Alston pointed out, "Too often the right boys are not selected. Consequently, the children who are not chosen have the feeling they are inferior. At age twelve, no child should be made to feel inferior."

In sharp contrast to Little League and other youth leagues, the American Legion program is based on the team concept and does not involve all-star teams. Al Anicich, retired commissioner of District 6, Sacramento, explained, "One of the biggest advantages of Legion Baseball is that if you play in the league and win, your team and not an all-star selection, will go up to the next level. The process continues on up, district and regionals, state and nationals. In doing so, players develop a team identification."

Get More Qualified Coaches

Better trained coaches are urgently needed in Little League and other youth baseball programs. The level of coaching skills at the lower levels is a very serious problem in player development. Most youth leagues have been recruiting fathers and mothers to coach, regardless of their knowledge of baseball. While their intentions are good, a large majority of them have little knowledge of the basic fundamentals. As a result, children who need instruction on the basic skills are not being taught correctly.

Youth leagues are having difficulty recruiting qualified and experienced coaches. Bob Taillefer, former president of the Citrus Heights Little League in suburban Sacramento, admitted, "It is a source of headache trying to get qualified coaches and managers. It is a very hard problem that we have to deal with every year. This is why 80 percent of the coaches are parents of players."

Many years ago, Dr. Arthur A. Esslinger, one of America's foremost educators, wrote "If Little League is to become qualitative, then we must do something positive about improving the quality of leadership in its day to day operation. The quality of leadership represents our biggest problem, and until we solve it, we never will realize the full potential we have."

Based on extensive studies the past five years, Little League has failed to achieve the goal and aspirations so eloquently expressed by Esslinger. What is most frustrating to educators like the author, Little League officials, through the many years, have not placed a high enough priority on the quality of coaching in their leagues, nor have they made it mandatory for their coaches to be certified, and their efforts to train and instruct inexperienced parents have been minimal at best.

In selecting people to coach, Little League has a responsibility to recruit more qualified coaches and provide the current volunteers with better training. College students who are pursuing careers in teaching and coaching who possess baseball knowledge, should be strongly considered. Since the current policy of Little League emphasizes the use of parents as coaches, pairing them with young college and high school students would be an ideal solution to the coaching problem.

Certify Youth League Coaches
The qualifications and training of youth coaches must be strengthened. For this to be achieved, Little League must certify its coaches. A much greater commitment has to be made to upgrade the quality of its coaching. There has to be some type of standards for youth coaches in America. To coach in the youth leagues, an individual must go through a certification program instructed by an experienced high school or college coach.

As to how youth leagues can implement a certification process, a very practical way is for the local community college to offer a class in Youth Baseball Coaching. Students who successfully complete the class will receive a certificate to coach, including an emblematic patch to wear. Training methods should be "hands-on", skill-oriented, where they learn the basic fundamentals, how to organize and conduct a practice session.

Youth coaches should be required to attend clinics and training sessions. Give them a manual containing instructional materials on the basic fundamental skills. In addition, coaches should receive suggested practice organization plans, lists of drills, their explanations, check lists on basic skills and techniques.

Another certification approach, particularly if the league itself provides the training, coaches would be required to attend a set number of hours of instruction. Similar to the class conducted by the college, participants would be required to take a written and practical exam. Give them an incentive to become certified with a patch on their shirt or jacket.

A number of youth leagues have obtained the assistance of NYSCA and ACEP, two national organizations, which provide youth coaches with training and certification services. Founded by Fred Engh, the National Youth Sports Association has provided thousands of coaches with training, supervision and instructional materials. The addresses of NYSCA and ACEP are given in chapter 10.

Control Parental Pressure   Parental pressure and interference is a very serious problem of Little League. In too many instances, parents can not separate themselves from their children's successes and failures. They expect too much too soon. Many parents will yell, scream and humiliate their children in front of peers and friends. Perhaps the most damaging type of interference are parents and coaches out of control, unable to restrain their desires and frustrations.

Parental pressure is one of the reasons why fewer quality players are coming to high school programs. "By the time the boys reach us, most of them have turned to other interests," explained George McKinnon, baseball coach at Cleveland Heights High School. "Their parents made baseball so frustrating they turned to something in which there was less parental pressure."

Children's sports should be about participation, sportsmanship, character and the development of playing skills. Those who jeer and bully players and coaches provide a distraction and an atmosphere youth sports does not need.

Still, parents can be a very positive force and strong influence in their children's baseball participation, the development of skills and practice habits. Here are some effective suggestions for parents who want to help their children succeed in baseball:

- Urge children to play baseball more

- Take time to practice with your child

- Encourage them to play pick-up games

- Read how they are played and teach them to your kids

- Build some practice facilities around the home, such as a wall to throw at, batting tee or machine, pitcher's mound

- Limit the time your kids can watch TV and video games

- Don't make a child live your dreams. Let him follow his own heart

- The best thing to spend on children is time

The YMCA's of the USA are to be commended for helping parents and their children learn about sports and sportsmanship. Everyone involved in youth sports would do well to heed the following YMCA Spectator's Code:

1. Remember that children play organized sports for their own fun

2. Don't use profane language, harass players, coaches, officials

3. Applaud good plays by your own team and the visiting team

4. Show respect for your teams' opponents

5. Never ridicule or scold a child for making a mistake

6. Condemn the use of violence

7. Respect the officials' decisions

8. Encourage players to always play according to the rules

Uphold Respect and Integrity of Umpires

Disrespect toward umpires seems to be increasing, especially in amateur baseball. More umpires are being taunted or even threatened with physical abuse. Such actions on the part of those at the ballpark – coaches, players, parents, and fans, should not be tolerated. Considering that those who umpire in the younger youth leagues are volunteers trying their best makes such actions even more intolerable.

Umpires are hired or recruited to be arbiters of the game to oversee the contest and make appropriate rulings, and they must be allowed to carry out their responsibilities. Respect for officials must be maintained and they deserve the support of officials. However, those who administer organized youth leagues have a responsibility to provide as high a level of competency and skills as possible. To achieve this goal, umpires, including those who volunteer, must be qualified and trained and participate regularly in rules meetings with other association umpires. The need for certifying umpires is just as essential as for those who coach.

Keep Kids from Quitting
Approximately 25 million young people between the ages of 6 and 15 participate in organized sports outside of school. However, by the time they are 13, about 75% of youth league players drop out of baseball. A dramatic drop-out rate occurs after age 12. As the game gets more difficult, many youth league players start dropping out.

As to why so many young players are quitting, many of them have literally been "burned out", as a result of too much pressure, publicity, and recognition. Burn-out is often caused by too much participation, success, and pressure at too early an age. Or, it was due to the lack of playing time, not enough improvement and success, or "I didn't have fun." Young children prefer fun over achievement. The coach was a poor teacher. There was too much pressure to excel. Or, the coach played favorites. In many cases, the demand has been too great, from the manager, parents and fans. Quite often, they receive too much criticism from their coaches who overemphasize winning even to the point of abusing players. Or, their parents were overzealous and expected too much.

Then how can organized youth baseball keep kids from quitting and help them enjoy playing the game?

- Keep the game FUN. What young kids want out of sports is fun

- Let the kids play and teach them the game

- Try to eliminate or curtail the fear of failure

- Build the child's self-esteem and confidence

- Set realistic performance goals; emphasize skill development

- Put the fun back into the basic fundamental skills

- Develop a better winning and losing perspective

- Find a way for every kid to play; otherwise, add more teams

Reduce Competitive Stress
Little League continues to be strongly criticized for its emphasis on winning and being overly competitive. Much of the criticism is the result of the nervous anxiety and emotional pressure experienced by young children at highly intense tournaments. When faced with defeat in do-or-die games, children are crying, unable to control their emotions.

For years, medical doctors and child psychology authorities have stated strongly that such competition isn't in the best interests of young children. Highly competitive games ultimately harm the self-esteem of certain children. They believe excessive emphasis on post-season play-offs and all-star teams should be reduced.

Yet, children need play and competition in order to develop. As the renowned author, James Michener, wrote in his fine book, Sport in America, "Competition is essential to the full maturity of the individual. Children should have the widest possible experiences of play, but heavily organized competition with end-of-the-season championships should not be initiated before age twelve, if then.

Competition should not be to such a degree that continued failure and losses leaves children devastated and emotionally upset. Quite often, it depends on the child and specific situations. Therefore, coaches are often the crucial element as to whether children's sports are helpful or harmful to the players. Of course, failure is a part of the game as it is in life. It requires mental toughness. To play baseball, young athletes must deal with failure. It is not easy. In hitting, a .300 hitter is successful three out of ten times at bat. The best baseball teams lose 60 games a year.

Is competition healthy or normal in Little League Baseball? From an overall perspective, it is not, particularly when teams move into post-season tournament play, when a World Series berth is at stake. For those who move on to Williamsport, the intense competitive atmosphere of the championship game, televised around the world, has proven to be both exhilarating and traumatic for the 11-12 year-old children who experience the joy of winning or the devastation of losing.

Get Kids to Play on Their Own

A major challenge of those in youth baseball and everyone else in the game is to get kids to play more on their own. Children today are not playing enough on their own to develop a high level of skills. The few swings, throws and catches that kids normally take at a little league practice or game is not enough. Twenty minutes of practice and undivided attention in the backyard can give a young player far more swings and throws than an hour-and-a-half on a little league field with 15 other children.

Young children and their parents need to know how to play pick-up games, what they need and where they can play. For children just learning the game, practice at home, a nearby park or school playground promotes not only skill but also safety. A baseball field is not necessary to develop playing skills. Young children can use their yard or driveway as a diamond. Using a rubber ball or tennis ball, they can throw against a hard wood or concrete wall or the garage door.

At an early age, kids need to be taught how to play catch and why it is so important. Every child has a friend that he can call and play catch and throw with. Or a father can say, "Son, let's play catch!" Coaches must demand that players play catch correctly and often. Try to make it challenging, competitive, like throwing for a target, the chest area or glove. Start close, then move back.

Provide Safe Play Areas

Children have a basic right to participate in safe and healthy environments, such as parks and playgrounds. The premise that "Kids can no longer go to a park, playground, or schoolyard to play" must be eliminated in our society. Young children need to feel safe to go to a playground and play ball. Cities and towns should provide children with safe play areas where they can go without fear and play among themselves.

More supervised programs of play are needed. While park agencies cannot afford to assign leaders at all facilities, as many parks as possible should have someone in charge, supervising and monitoring the areas. Public play areas must be made safe enough for parents to allow their children to play there. Law enforcement agencies working closely with public and private institutions must make a greater effort to provide safer and more secure play areas for children, as well as young and old people alike.

In a brilliant portrayal of a city mayor in the movie City Hall, actor Al Pacino spoke eloquently to grieving relatives of a young child, "Until we can stroll along the streets, congregate at a park without fear, families mingling and children laughing, we have no city. Our task must and should be making them safe and livable. Is this too much to ask?"

Children today need to be able to play in their neighborhoods, like kids used to do. For this to occur, however, families must get together to take charge of their neighborhood as opposed to just hiding indoors. This type of cohesion and cooperation can do much to reduce crime, resulting in more community policing, tougher penalties and greater juvenile crime prevention.

**Players, represented
by the Players Union**

**Ownership, administered
by the Commissioner**

Baseball's Equation

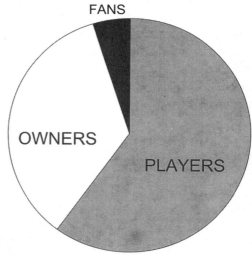

FANS

OWNERS

PLAYERS

Baseball Fans

**When will the
fans truly
become part of
baseball's equation?**

4 Major Leagues

As baseball approaches the 21st century, Major League Baseball is showing some signs of recovery. Sparked by exciting home run races in two consecutive seasons, the overall popularity of the game is on the rise again. Overall attendance climbed from 63.1 million in 1997 to 70.3 million in 1998. The 1998 season was a year of individual achievements and one remarkable team achievement by the New York Yankees.

The drama of the home run battle between Mark McGwire and Sammy Sosa made even casual fans pay attention. Michael Knisley of The Sporting News wrote, "Perhaps one of the reasons baseball seems to have come to life during the advance on the home run record is the case with which fans connect to the game's history at moments such as these."

Baseball is back, but as Pete Schmuck wrote, "What does the sport do for an encore? When the luster begins to fade, the industry will be faced with some of the same old problems that were so happily obscured in 1998." While the home run race was said to have "saved" baseball, why did the 1998 World Series between the Yankees and Padres produce the lowest television ratings for any World Series ever? Increasing competition for an audience, cable, the Internet, and a Series that wasn't competitive.

There are still many dark clouds hanging over the game. Competitive balance has been severely damaged. Two-thirds of baseball's 30 clubs cannot compete. The economic stability of Major League Baseball has been shaken. Over half of the clubs reported substantial budget deficits, forcing them to boost ticket prices even higher. Only teams with large payrolls can win a pennant anymore. Only large revenue clubs can sign the best players. Operating costs and ticket prices have soared. Some teams are charging as much as $50 a game, while World Series prices have doubled to $150. They're even thinking of putting advertisements on uniforms!

The already sky-high player salaries continue to rise. The average major league salary is $1.72 million, while the total team payroll for the 30 teams is a staggering $1.5 billion! Who is paying the price of higher and higher salaries? The fans. Ticket prices are being raised to maintain high payrolls.

As for the pennant races, they have become almost non-existent, attributed largely to the wild-card system, competitive imbalance and unequal payrolls. The wild-card format continues to prevent what used to be some dramatic races. The season is too long, and it doesn't mean as much anymore. In 1996, the Padres and the Dodgers had clinched post-season berths, and neither cared much whether it won the division or instead took the wild-card.

The people who are running baseball are showing little respect for the game's traditions and continuity. And they continue to push for radical realignment, which will make more than 100 years of history obsolete. It appears that Commissioner Bud Selig has not given up, despite the fact that an overwhelming number of fans and the game's foremost authorities are vehemently opposed to excessive realignment.

The most talked-about problems of the 1997 World Series were poor TV ratings, the unbearable cold-weather of late October, too long a season, the lengthy three-tier season, and long, slow-paced games. For many years, baseball has been too preoccupied with ratings, which prompted Jayson Stark to write: "The more this sport lets its ratings fixation drive the train, the less popular it seems to get." While good ratings provide clubs with substantial TV money, Stark said, "No amount of TV money is enough, given this sport's insane salary spiral."

While Commissioner Selig tries to downplay the low ratings, he needs to understand more fully the reasons for their decline, which I will cover later in the chapter when I address the following issues and areas of concern:

- The league season is too long
- The big increase in postseason games
- Games start too late and last too long
- Overemphasis on night games
- The World Series weather problem

The gorgeous New York autumn is crying out for day games!
- Bruce Jenkins

The home run races of 1998 and 1999 have thrilled many fans and created renewed interest in baseball, but like many other big league hitters, McGwire and Sosa have resorted to performance-enhancing substances. Androstendione, steroids, and other chemicals would be illegal if baseball did what other pro sports organizations have done. Instead, Major League Baseball has been derelict in their responsibilities, not only as to the health and future lives of its players but to thousands of young athletes who are resorting to the same practices as their heroes. Baseball must ban andro, require mandatory drug testing, and implement a responsible drug policy. In putting baseball's plight in proper perspective, John Feinstein wrote that, "Fans look at the game's flaws - - the tiny strike zone, the games that won't end, the ludicrously late starting times of the World Series, the lack of a financial playing field - - and wonder, "Why doesn't someone fix these things?"

Baseball, of course, will survive as it always does because as Tony LaRussa once said, "The game is better than all of us." However, for the game to be restored to its past luster and grandeur, the fans, who have been taken for granted and left out of baseball's decision-making will have to become a bigger part of the equation. With the establishment of the Baseball Fans Association of America, U.S. Sports Fans, and the looming presence of Ralph Nader, and other fan activist organizations, they could in the future make a stunning impact on the game.

Ever Changing Home Run Records

"Baseball's home run records have no longevity these days," wrote Daniel P. Finney in USA TODAY. In 1998, a season-record 5,064 were hit, and this mark is already in jeopardy. In mid-August, 1999, home runs were 11.1% ahead of the pace, one that would produce 5,593. "The way players are bashing balls, almost every day is home run record day," said Finney. On Friday, August 13, 55 were hit, the most on one day. The following day, the Colorado Rockies and Montreal Expos hit a combined 10 homers. With September approaching McGwire aand Sosa were locked in a home run race that was nearly a rerun of 1998.

The phenomenal hitting records that hitters are compiling today are inflated primarily because the ball was juiced up in 1993 to increase offense in the game. Other conditions in modern baseball, of course, have contributed significantly to increased offense. The new and smaller ballparks are home run havens. Much more emphasis is on muscle development among ballplayers, and two expansions in the '90s have added 40 pitchers to the majors. From 1961 to the 1990s, nobody hit more than 52 homers. Now 50-plus seasons are commonplace, highlighted in 1998 by McGwire's incredible 70, followed closely by Sosa's 66 round-trippers.

Must Baseball Live On Home Runs Alone?

The "Great Home Run Race" in 1998 was not only good for the game but America, too. As Jay Feldman wrote in SN&R, the home run duel "put us in touch with America, reminding us of the central place that baseball occupies in our national mythology. It also gave us two desperately needed heroes." Tim Keown stated that "People paid attention to the game, and baseball needs to build on that." But baseball cannot and should not live by home runs alone. As Keown said so eloquently, "Now the task is to emphasize the aspects of the game that don't include slow trots around the bases. The home run, now that it has done its main job, needs to take a well-deserved rest. Give us subtlety, a double in the right-field corner scoring a slow runner from first, just barely, to win a crucial September game between teams locked in a pennant race. We don't need another 70-homer season."

Despite the Years of the Slugger, some outstanding seasons by pitchers, and those in the field and on the basepaths have been overshadowed. The home run has almost totally dominated other aspects of the game, phases of the game baseball badly needs. But Keown says, "This is probably a traditionalist's folly. The increasing number of bandbox ballparks, bad pitchers and pharmaceutically inflated forearms make homerun hysteria an accepted, desired part of the landscape."

Baseball should reflect on what else beside the home run mania would be good for America. If those in baseball would look at the game from a broader perspective, they will see that there is so much more going on than to obsess on whether McGwire or Sosa will eventually hit 80 home runs. Off the field, it needs to consider the widening fiscal disparities between large and small-market franchises which has created a very serious competitive imbalance in baseball.

Baseball has a moral responsibility to protect the overall health and best interests of the youth of this country, which it has failed to do. Considering their negative response to McGwire's use of androstendione, major league officials have shown a glaring lack of concern for fair play and the health of children and teenagers who idolize the many big leaguers taking performance-enhancing substances and steroids.

The home run races in 1998 and 199 were very exciting and enhanced the popularity of the game, but as Keown wrote, "Enough is enough. Another year of it and we'll be lobotomized. If it continues along its current pace, the spectacle of McGwire and Sosa will become less important and less impressive."

How Can Pitching Rebound?   In response to the many complaints about the lack of quality of pitching in the majors, Deon Snyder in USA TODAY Baseball Weekly offered 10 suggestions on how to improve the serious plight of baseball's often shell-shocked moundsmen. In his featured article, "Pitcher protection program", Snyder bluntly stated that, "With apologies to Pedro Martinez, Randy Johnson and a short list of others, pitching stinks." My overall assessment on the state of pitching, however, is less severe because baseball has done everything it can for the hitter while doing nothing for the pitcher. Yet, baseball does not appear to be concerned at all.

Here are Snyder's top 10 ways to improve pitching:

1.   CALL STRIKES   Nothing would have a more dramatic effect on the game than calling a strike a strike. <u>Enforce the strike zone!</u>

2.   CHECK THE BALL   "If baseball wanted an immediate effect," said Yankees' pitching coach Mel Stottlemyre, "they can take the rabbit out of the ball."

3.   IGNORE THE READINGS   "Velocity seems to be the thing that gets everyone's attention," said pitching coach Dave Duncan. "The ability to control the ball can be as effective as power pitching."

4.   LOSE THE ALUMINUM   By the time most pitchers reach the minors, their psyches have been battered by aluminum bats. The complaint that "nobody pitches inside" can be traced to the aluminum bat.

5.   LOOK IN THE FIELD   Because of the DH rules, many players chose other positions because they liked to hit and be in the lineup.

Raise the Pitcher's Mound

The higher 15" mound of the 1960s (Don Drysdale)

The current 10" mound since it was lowered after the 1968 season.

Remove the "rabbit" from the ball and stop tampering with it.

Move fences back and make batters hit genuine home runs.

6.   TINKER WITH THE PARK   Move the fences back and raise the mound. Raise the walls and increase the foul territory.

7.   START 'EM EARLY   "People are looking for shortcuts to gain arm strength", said Cubs general manager Ed Lynch. "The basis of a good arm is throwing. Weights help only marginally."

8.   PLAY GOOD GLOVES "Improved fielding is the No. 1 way to improve pitching," said manager Larry Dierker of the Houston Astros.

9.   BE RADICAL Since good pitchers are hard to find, coming up with four could be easier than with five.

10.   SHRINK IT "Contraction is the simplest way to overcome the effects of expansion," wrote Snyder. "Instead of having 30 teams, requiring 360 pitchers, you'd need only 336 pitchers."

"Unless baseball starts incorporating some of the above, or other ideas, don't count on those scores, hits, runs, homers – or ERAs – coming down anytime soon," concluded Snyder.

New Stadium Controversy

In baseball today, a new stadium has become as essential as the market size of the franchise. With their luxury suites, club-level seats, and "sweetheart" leases, new facilities can double stadium income and increase significantly the value of a franchise. New ballparks provide the extra revenue that gives the ownership a chance to be competitive. When going to a ball game today, fans expect more than a team to watch. They expect intimate settings, elaborate sound systems, brewpubs, or other amenities. Designs include children's play areas, putting greens, shopping malls, and picnic grounds.

On the downside, the stadiums being planned today offer much less seating than in past eras, Jacobs Field in Cleveland, as well as ballparks in Denver and Phoenix, have been sold out almost every game since the parks opened up. All of these stadiums have been limited to 40,000 seats, with major emphasis on season tickets, corporate-oriented luxury boxes, etc. In too many instances, low-income families, and others, have few opportunities, if any, to see a major league game, particularly with tickets steadily rising. These small ballparks typify the current thinking "fewer seats make a park more fan-friendly". As Tom Tingle of HOK Sport, the nation's leading designer of new sports facilities, says, "People want to be in a park that is full of people."

But what has made new stadiums so controversial is the issue of who should pay for them. Team owners and stadium enthusiasts maintain that public support is justified because teams generate business and job growth. However, a new study by University of Maryland economists Dennis Coates and Brad Humphreys argues that sports teams and stadiums actually reduce per capita income in their hometown.

The 1990s have been a decade when taxpayers have paid millions of dollars to help finance ballparks and keep teams from leaving. Unfortunately for sports franchises, stadiums are getting tough to build with public money because rising player salaries offend taxpayers. Fans are saying it doesn't make sense for team owners to pay huge salaries while asking for help to build stadiums. I can understand the viewpoints of both sides, but it seems to me that the demands of major league clubs would be more favorably received if owners would use greater restraint in giving ridiculously excessive salaries to the players. In 1997, 61% of the $2.05 billion industry revenue was spent on player salaries. Surely, baseball and the taxpayers would best be served if a reasonable amount of this would be used for privately financed ballparks.

Radical Realignment in 2001?

Evidently, Commissioner Selig still does not get the message from the fans. In his USA TODAY column, Hal Bodley wrote, "Expect realignment to be radical in 2001. When it does, Major League Baseball will have another new set of standings. Look for radical unbalanced schedules, the possibility of four, four-team divisions in the National League and at least two teams changing leagues." The most-discussed major changes move Tampa Bay to the National League, Arizona to the American League and Texas from the AL West to the AL Central.

"Selig apparently has scrapped his end-of-the-world travesty where countless teams would switch leagues," said Bruce Jenkins. "The new strategy would divide the 16-team National League into four divisions, conveniently eliminating the need for a wild-card playoff entry."

Need For Economic Stability

No problem is more crucial to the state of the game than baseball's economic problem. As far back as 1985, Peter Ueberroth, then commissioner of baseball, stated that, "Financial decay is prevalent among many of the teams in the major leagues." Salaries, averaging an alarming $1.7 million per player, have forced ticket prices and overall costs to soar. Teams not prepared to have a $50 million payroll have no chance to compete.

When will this fiscal insanity end? Will owners finally realize that they do have the power to control their costs, to reverse the increases in player salaries and show some profits. Someday, owners will say "No", and the madness will be over.

Competitive Balance Hurt By Disparities There
is a huge divide between large and small-market teams that threatens competitive balance, the game's lifeblood. Small-market franchises simply cannot compete, and they continue to unload their high-priced talent. Clubs with the most revenue and new stadiums are winning consistently.

The most serious problem with small-market teams trying to compete with large-market clubs is in the local television contracts. A team like the Yankees receives $50 million just from television, far larger than the entire operating budget of most teams. Since TV is baseball's prime source of revenue and many teams are owned by organizations with major television interests, the game continues to serve TV's best interests.

In baseball, there is no cap and only partial revenue sharing. Jim Van Vliet wrote, "Baseball split up the revenue from national TV and radio contracts but are allowed to keep all monies from local broadcast rights. That's where the disparity begins. Teams like the Yankees can meet their payroll just by using their radio-TV money." The current TV and radio deals in the New York Yankees market are worth $55 million a year, about ten times more than some teams. Local broadcast rights for the Giants, for example, are about $10 million a year.

And what have baseball's powers done about the problem? Very little, considering the magnitude of competitive imbalance. The other major pro sports in America have devised a means to prevent free-spending, big-market teams from dominating and cash-strapped, little-market franchises but baseball hasn't been able to do so. "The NBA, NFL and NHL have all implemented salary caps and revenue sharing," wrote Van Vliet. "All radio and TV money goes into a league fund and given out in equal proportions. As a result, a team like the Green Bay Packers, playing in the smallest market in the country, can win Super Bowl championships."

The Watered Down Luxury Tax
The luxury tax was designed to prevent high-revenue teams from even higher payroll escalation. Over half the teams have payrolls above $50 million. While the luxury tax originally was to be levied on 35 percent of the amount of payrolls above $51 million, the union insisted on a clause, limiting it to only the teams with the five highest payrolls. Because of that, the threshold will be a minimum of $59.9 million rather than $55 million, and the 1999 threshold was at least $64.2 million instead of $58.9 million. Another failure to control rising salaries!

Salary Arbitration is Very Costly
What the owners have found to be most difficult to control is salary arbitration, more costly than free agency. Arbitration has proven the player's strongest vehicle, with mediocre players making far more than they would without the process. Average salary for the 80 players who filed for arbitration in 1997 increased 152.8%, a jump that more than doubled 1996's increase of 73.1%.

The approach many clubs are currently taking is to avoid arbitration by signing players to long-term contracts, giving them security but taking a big risk. However, once young players enjoy success and reach arbitration after three years in the majors, small market teams can no longer afford them.

Increased Revenue-Sharing Needed
For baseball to prosper in the future, small-market teams need more help. More competitive balance is needed. Big city teams maintain a huge financial advantage over small-city teams. Baseball needs a more effective form of revenue-sharing that will keep small-market teams from dealing away their best players. An

increasing number of teams are finding they cannot keep up with the high salaries.

An equitable system of revenue-sharing must be realized, one that would contribute to fiscal viability and competitive balance. However, baseball's new agreement between the owners and players still favors the rich. Low-end clubs are only being paid $3 to $4 million per season. Even with its tax on excessive payrolls, it has not slowed down the free spenders.

For revenue-sharing to really work, the share of total revenues among clubs must increase significantly. This goal can be realized by sharing more revenue from television and licensing. Disparity has grown as a result of local media contracts becoming relatively more important. Profitable teams must share a larger portion of their income with the struggling teams.

Revenue-sharing would provide a restraint on salaries, in that the most profitable teams would have less money to spend on salaries. It could make teams less willing to pay for free agents, thus reducing salaries.

**Baseball should follow the NFL's example
of splitting revenue more evenly.**

Correcting Baseball's Fiscal Imbalance

If baseball's salary structure and revenue distribution system made sense, its revenue and fan base would be quite sufficient for the game to prosper. But, until they do, any quick infusion of funds won't matter. As Bob Costas pointed out in his excellent essay in The Sporting News, "The amount of money each individual team makes from these "quick fixes" is less than the amount each routinely wastes on one or two mediocre players. These maneuvers don't get near the heart of the problem."

As for what can be done to correct baseball's perplexing fiscal imbalance, the clubs, of course, should have done things differently in 1993 with a work stoppage on the horizon. In what should be the "Golden Rule of Baseball", Costas said, "It makes no difference how much money is taken in if an insane system guarantees more than that will go out. The owners should have presented their plan for realignment, expansion, and interleague play, selling it as vision for baseball in the 21st Century." Baseball can still reshape the game in a positive way, but it must be done in the spirit of cooperation, doing what is in the best interests of the game.

Salary Cap System Needed

Some type of a cap has to be put on baseball that owners have to abide by. Salaries have sky-rocketed overwhelmingly out of control. A soft-salary cap system similar to the NBA would be fairer and more rational than baseball's free labor market constrained by an insignificant luxury tax. Jerry Colangelo, owner of both the expansion Arizona Diamond-backs and the Suns' NBA franchise, explained that "The NBA system lessens payroll disparity between large-market and small-market clubs, encourages personnel stability, and rewards intelligence over wealth. Baseball's system does the opposite."

The luxury tax contained in the 1996 settlement was implemented to penalize free-spending teams, but it is not stiff enough to act as a deterrent. But, revenue-sharing is a halfway measure, because it allows clubs to dig into their pockets and deficit spend, as Florida owner Wayne Huizenga did in the winter of 1997.

The solution is a system of near-equal payrolls and development budgets. In 1994, the owners tried to implement such a system, a move that would have set up baseball in fine style for the 21st Century, but the players union struck over the issue. The players union opposes near equal payrolls "on the basis that salaries are suppressed if clubs are prevented from spending as much as they possible can." Can you believe this? As difficult as it is to believe this statement, the union's opposition to near equal payrolls is about as selfish and greedy as anyone can get, certainly a flagrant disregard for the game's economic health. In arguing its position, the union insisted that competitive balance is not disrupted by allowing some clubs to outspend others by multiples of two and three. Nonsense! Competitive balance is disrupted.

The players union is against near equal payrolls

"The players union thinks a system of near-equal payrolls would penalize its members," wrote Steve Marantz of The Sporting News. "But what happens when more teams decide to survive with payrolls under $20 million rather than fail, inevitably, at $30 million or $50 million? A progressive system would preclude this, forcing some clubs to spend more than they might otherwise. Eventually the union must recognize its members are served by payroll equality, and not by the existing bell-curve model with built-in failures."

As baseball moves into a new century, major league owners appear to be more determined to change the game's financial state of affairs. Despite the lucrative free agent signings late in 1998, more teams are demonstrating greater control of salaries, especially if they downsize. Rather than go into debt, many are placing greater emphasis on developing their own players. Peter Gammons wrote in Baseball America that, "It is quite clear there isn't enough money in baseball for everyone to make $6 to $10 million." He believes, "A massive correction is finally taking place."

Better Control of TV
Television money has been the owners' lifeblood, the great equalizer in the baseball economy. However, the contrasting local TV contracts continue to be a most serious problem, with small-market teams trying to compete with large-market clubs. A team like the Yankees receives $50 million just from TV, far larger than the entire operating budget of most teams.

To reduce the payroll disparity between large and small-market teams, baseball must increase revenue sharing. A new system should be implemented whereby clubs will split not only the revenue from national TV and radio contracts, but monies from local broadcasts rights as well. Major League Baseball has to follow the lead of the NFL, NBA and NHL by placing ALL radio and TV money into a league fund and given out in equal proportions.

Super-stations have saturated the market place, widening the disparity even further. They need to be curbed. They have contributed significantly to a fiscal imbalance. While providing more exposure to the game, they have overloaded TV with baseball, undercutting the value of everybody else's TV right. In cities with weak teams, a hot super station club can overshadow the hometown team.

Baseball must regain control of the game from TV interests who call the tune, such as scheduling all night games for the World Series and virtually no free nationally televised games on weekdays during the regular season. Post-season games have become just another prime-time TV show. Games often run past midnight in many areas. As a result, a large number of children do not have an opportunity to see the World Series and post-season games. Much too often, it is a case of "Whatever television wants will happen," and not always in the best interest of the game.

More Responsible Ownership is Needed

Despite all their wealth, earned largely with the corporations they represent, owners have not been good baseball businessmen. What business would pay its employers more than it can afford? The owners talk of salary cap and budget-cutting, yet they continue to sign players at unbelievable salaries.

Owners have it in their power to take control of their costs. With some self-control and holding back their spending, they could reverse the increases in player salaries and organization losses. More teams would find themselves in the profit column, and from the fans standpoint, clubs would be able to reduce costs at the ballpark, such as ticket prices, concession costs, and parking.

Corporate owners are revolutionizing the economics of professional sports, although they are not new to baseball. Sports franchises are quickly becoming the core asset in the sports communications business, and as Roy S. Johnson wrote in Fortune, "The long-ball hitters are getting into the game. What attracts these companies is a powerful mix of potential strategic alliances."

Still, Peter Ueberroth believes, "Corporations will tend to be more responsible. Operating records will be more public and thus available to communities and fans. Ultimately, they are more responsible to shareholders than to fans, which should bring some reasonableness to the cost of salaries." But Johnson added, "It's a nice thought, but probably not a very realistic one."

Baseball Urgently Needs Leadership
Baseball needs a strong and independent commissioner, one who will have the power to serve the overall best interests of the game. He must be committed to the fans and to the future of baseball. I firmly believe many of the problems and wrongs of the 1990s could have been prevented, or at the very least alleviated, had there been someone truly governing the game – a strong commissioner with authority.

Ruling by consensus is not the way to operate a professional baseball league. During much of the 1997 season, for example, Bud Selig was constantly on the phone, sending faxes, trying to convince fellow owners that moving to the other league would benefit them. He was always trying to change someone's mind or influence the thinking of another owner. Shouldn't owners think for themselves, without constant badgering? As the spokesperson for ownership, his conduct was clearly biased, personally motivated, and relentless, like his attempts at radical realignment.

The commissioner's office today, however, has been strengthened by the presence of two outstanding baseball administrators, Paul Beeston and Sandy Alderson. I have noticed a significant change following the arrival of both men. Sandy would make an excellent commissioner. He has the leadership skills the game needs at this time, what with many difficult and vital issues ahead.

What the Commissioner Should Be
The commissioner should be a "solid baseball man", with a good feel for the game and its traditions. He should have the vision, passion and foresight to help bring the game into the 21st century. More than ever, baseball needs someone with strong leadership, a neutral voice, speaking for the best interests of all of baseball. It is essential for the commissioner to stay in touch and serve the interests and concerns of all levels of play.

To be truly effective, the commissioner has to be able to gain the trust of both sides. He should have the ability to get along with people, an understanding of what is important for the clubs, players, fans, and yes, the umpires. A major factor why the NFL is considered the model for professional sports leagues is because past and present commissioners urged owners to "look beyond their own narrow interests and try to do what is best for the league as a whole. Baseball needs that kind of approach, too.

Developing Better Relationships

For baseball to prosper at the big league level, more positive relationships must be established, not only between players and owners but with umpires, fans, and the news media.

Players and Owners

Greater harmony is needed between players and owners. Although player-owner friction is almost as old as the game itself, the continued conflicts, confrontations, and an unwillingness to compromise has alienated and turned off a large number of fans. Rather, it should be owners and players working together in the best interests of the game and the business of baseball. The players and owners need each other. What is needed is a change of attitude from animosity to alliance, both earning each other's trust.

The Players' Association has become the most powerful collective bargaining union in sports. Every important idea or change proposed in baseball has to be run through the union, and as a result, the players continue to thrive under the new labor agreement. The players continue to oppose a salary cap because it limits the amount of money the clubs can spend on salaries.

Players and Fans

Following two decades of turbulent labor strikes, there is an urgent need for all players to contribute more to the game than their highly skilled efforts on the field. For baseball to prosper for everyone involved, the players must realize that they do have a P.R. responsibility to those who pay their salaries, the fans, and it has to be genuine, not superficial. Unfortunately, fans today have a low degree of tolerance for millionaire players who complain that they should be bigger millionaires.

Players, however, can counter these feelings by making a stronger effort to communicate and show a greater concern for the fans, young and old alike, and their best interests. They need to try to be thought of a real people, friendly, with a sense of humor. Many fans get turned off by athletes who are arrogant and insensitive and refuse to sign autographs. Not all big league players are like Cal Ripken, Jr. or Tony Gwynn who demonstrate this responsibility day-in and day-out. Still, I believe there is less misconduct by big league baseball players than athletes in other sports. The large majority of major league players play hard, and they play to win. Fans relate to and appreciate this type of work ethic.

Players and Umpires
Baseball should take action to relieve tensions between players and umpires. Strained relations and the constant friction both on and off the field are not in the best interests of the game. While tensions have existed for many years, their negative relationships have not only diminished the quality of play but has made the game less appealing to the fans who have to put up with it.

Through the years, umpires, in general, have used their authority to deal appropriately with players and managers who abuse them, with profane language and, occasionally, some physical contact, and umpires were given strong support from league officials. However, during the past couple of decades, relations between umpires, players and managers have deteriorated, the result of any number of reasons, like millionaire players, ever conscious of their stats, not giving umpires their due respect.

Umpires, however, need to come down from their high haunches. More than ever, they are inclined to have short tempers and are more thin-skinned. Some seem to be too willing to toss players from a game. Umpires should allow a little showmanship and crowd-pleasing antics of manager, but there is, of course, a limit to some of their shenanigans. Even National League President Leonard Coleman agrees disputing an umpire's call is a part of the game. But when Atlanta Braves manager Bobby Cox jawed with umpire Ed Montague, kicked dirt, sprayed chewing tobacco and stepped on his feet, Coleman fined him $1,500.

Baseball must back up the umpires, while being fair to players and managers, too. Players are less tolerant today than those a few decades ago. Perhaps players and managers have gone too far too long. How much are umpires supposed to take from them? What the Umpires Association is seeking are swifter and more severe penalties that are in line with the million-dollar salaries of suspended players. A code of conduct is needed to get tough on both players and managers who abuse umpires, provided umpires show a greater willingness to work within the organizational structure of Major League Baseball, which in recent years, they have failed to do at times.

Players and the News Media   Players should be more accessible to the media, to be in front of their lockers after every game, instead of hiding in the trainer's room.   Much too often, the news media find the atmosphere in the clubhouse uncomfortable. Players should realize it is in their best interests, as well as the team and baseball, to cooperate and respond positively to requests from the writers.   Writer Bus Saidt's credo when approaching a player, and he acts as if he is being bothered is to just say "Thank you" and walk away to find somebody else.

Developing positive relations with the news media is very important. "You have to learn to help the writers do their job but keep your sense of privacy," said the Orioles' Jeffrey Hammonds. "This fosters a more constructive attitude among players and the media, fewer negative incidents, and a better image of baseball as a whole for the fans."

Profile of a Player Agent   Scott Boras has become the most powerful agent in baseball today. Boras has been labeled by many as the most-disliked man in the game, not only by owners but by fans disgruntled with soaring player salaries. "To the players he represents, he is unquestionably the product of a Virgin birth," wrote Jim Van Vliet of the Sacramento Bee. "To baseball's general manager, Boras is the Grinch who threatens to steal baseball."

For over a decade, Boras has not only lined the pockets of dozens of players, but he's changed the way baseball does business. He's found loopholes to get players into more lucrative situations. In the amateur draft, Boras got a $1.3 million contract for Texas schoolboy Todd Van Poppel in 1990. He squeezed $7 million out of the St. Louis Cardinals for J.D. Drew in 1998.

Boras now operates a stable of about 50 major leaguers and 40 or so coveted minor leaguers. He has a staff of two dozen employees, including labor lawyers, economists, a psychologist and a "NASA whiz" running his million dollar computer system. He takes an entourage of a dozen lawyers, stat analysts and staff members to arbitration hearings.

Don Wollett, one of Boras' professors at McGeorge Law School in Sacramento, says that "Baseball salaries are outrageous, but it takes two to tango, and Scott's just doing his job. That's the free-market system."

Stronger Marketing Needed

Baseball has done the poorest job of marketing itself and its players than any other major pro sport. It is essential that baseball launch a dynamic but practical marketing campaign. It should hire a national spokesman whose role is selling the game and lobbying for baseball's best interests, with a master plan coordinated by MLB and the Players Association.

Baseball's best-kept secret is that the game is still great, but for it to try to be like the NBA and NFL would hurt the game badly. The appeal of baseball is something different. Its appeal is timeliness and continuity. There are those who believe baseball should speed up the game and make it more exciting. But Lee Garfinkel, creative chief of ad agency Low & Partners/SMS in New York, said, "You can't make baseball seem like a super-fast game with action that never stops."

Those in baseball must do a better job of capitalizing on the uniqueness of the game. The beauty, charm and essence need to be exploited more fully. The game unfolds at a leisurely, pastoral pace under blue skies and bright sunshine. Baseball has more humor than any other sports. While watching a baseball game, spectators have time for other pleasures as well, such as food, drink, and conversations. They enjoy conversing at a baseball game, in a way they cannot during the continuous, never-ending pace of other team sports. Above all, those in baseball must remind people how much fun it is to watch and share a baseball game, with the family, a friend or loved one. It must get out the word that the game is by far the least expensive of the four major sports.

Sell and Market Players
Major League Baseball should do a better job of selling and marketing its best players. They can do so by the following ways:

- Get players before the public eye, such United Way campaign.
- A series of public service messages should show players as regular human beings and members of the community.
- A stronger effort should be made to make players household names.
- Players should spend more time talking to fans, signing autographs, etc.

Selling The Game To Kids

To spark a true revival of the game, there is an urgent need to market the game again to children. This is the key to baseball regaining its stature as America's No. 1 Pastime. They are the season ticket-holders of tomorrow.

Baseball must get a better hold, a feel, on the imagination of young people. Kids need to be convinced that baseball is contemporary, in addition to having great tradition and heritage. Make the game more relevant to youth. Nostalgia won't work because the younger generation can't relate to nostalgia. Still, young people should be made aware of it. But more important, baseball should enlighten young fans as to what the game is, help them develop a greater understanding of the game, the subtleties and unique qualities.

Educate the kids on the great traditions and heritage of baseball but point out that the game is also contemporary and hip. Get them to appreciate the nuances of the game. So much of the enjoyment in baseball is the tactical strategy, tension, and drama, and our youth like these aspects.

Additional ways to sell the game to kids:

- Get youngsters into the ballparks, like baseball marketed the game in 1969. Make available free tickets and reduced rates.

- Bring back the Knot Hole Gang Club; MLB has already begun its Kids Club, a national promotion that will help children attend games, learn more about baseball, compete in skill/trivia games.

- Do some other innovative things to make the game more appealing to younger people; the time length of games needs to be shortened, considering our culture's ever decreasing attention span.

- Encourage more of the youth to get into the game; to really appreciate baseball, one has to play the game.

- Baseball should expand its RBI program to more inner cities.

How TV Can turn Kids On To Baseball
Television can play a vital role in nurturing baseball's appeal among the younger generation. Young people today must develop a greater interest and fascination for the game if they are to be drawn to the ballparks and develop the desire to play the game.

Strategy should be emphasized more by baseball announcers. While baseball lacks football's power and the sheer speed of basketball, it makes up in the tense strategic interplay between pitcher and batter, defense and baserunners. If announcers would emphasize this aspect of the game more often, the younger generation would be more inclined to tune in.

Baseball should televise more day games, particularly during the postseason playoffs when kids can view them. Since the prime time ratings of the World Series have hit all-time lows in the 1990s, why not move a couple of games to daytime hours? Young fan-oriented TV shows prior to game will further attract more kids to baseball, including personal interviews with the players on how they first started out playing baseball. More Saturday afternoon games and doubleheaders should be scheduled, with a larger number of post-season games earlier in the day.

Dealing with Competition Issues

The essence of baseball is the competition of play, and this is where the focus of the game should be, rather than on economics. From the early years to the present, the primary goal of any baseball league has been to offer a meaningful game between well-matched opponents.

Four competition issues appear to be foremost in baseball now: realignment, interleague play, wild-card system, and the designated hitter, with slow games, the length of the season, and the division series close behind. "Realignment and interleague play are tricky, but should not be insoluble," said Bob Costas. "The game's real issues, salary structure, revenue-sharing, and marketing are the most problematic." Then, there is the matter of the sharp increase in the number of offensive records which have been attributed to a number of reasons, such as a livelier ball, hitter-friendly ballparks, performance-enhancing drugs, substances, etc.

In baseball today, having the right idea about issues is not enough. Those in charge still must deal with the owners and the Players Association. For example, baseball had proposed what appeared to be an excellent solution to the designated hitter dilemma, but as Costas explained: "It faced a Players Association, which, as always, finds no merit in any idea that doesn't enrich its membership."

The League Season Is Too Long   By lengthening the post-season three weeks into late October, baseball has created a serious problem it can no longer ignore. The World Series, of course, has always meant baseball with a chill in the air. However, in 1997 at Cleveland's Jacobs Field, the Indians and Florida Marlins played in the snow with temperatures in the 30's because Major League Baseball had added an extra layer of playoffs without any compensation in the schedule. The bitter cold wind was so severe pitchers had great difficulty gripping the ball.

A logical solution, other than eliminating one of the playoff series, is for baseball to return to a 154-game schedule. The current schedule of 162 games, with few days off, followed by a grueling three-tier post-season, is simply too much. Certainly, snow makes for a good case for a shorter season. The earliest start of any season in history, March 31, 1996, was a disaster.

Following the 1997 Series in which severe cold weather hindered play in Cleveland, Commissioner Selig indicated he would propose such a schedule for the 1999 season, but the owners refused to go along. Consequently, the 1999 World Series could conclude on the last day of October, and players and fans will likely be freezing in such northern cities as Cleveland or New York.

A reduced season would be a good move for the game. It would mean the season would start a week later to avoid the early postponements because of weather and to accommodate the extra playoff games. The regular season would end the last Sunday in September, and the World Series would begin no later than the second week of October. Reducing the league season would accommodate expanding the divisional playoffs from best-of-five to best-of-seven. The return to 154 (or 156) games would provide a boost to the quality of play. The game would benefit if players had more days off. Teams would have much needed rest, and an occasional doubleheader would prove a big hit with fans.

The Big Slow-Down

Games are running longer than ever. Younger fans, with their dwindling attention spans, have become increasingly turned off by long, slow-paced games. Today's average nine-inning game lasts well over three hours. Florida's 14-11 victory in the 1997 World Series lasted 4 hours and 12 minutes – two minutes short of the Series record for a nine-inning game. But the pace of the games is a greater problem than the length. "Baseball is a game that has a pace to it," explained Joe Morgan. "I think we have gotten out of the pace and rhythm during the past decade." Former great hitter Frank Robinson, who was given responsibility by baseball to help speed up ball games, agreed by saying, "We're not trying to fool with the pace of the game itself, but if we can cut 10 to 15 minutes off, it will make a big difference."

The game has to become more "TV friendly", and that means speeding up the tempo. Rules were put into place to address the problem, the time between innings and pitches, batters stepping in and out of the box, but umpires have been slow to enforce them.

Long games can be attributed to various causes, but the most often time lapses can be attributed to the shrunken strike zone and a frustrated pitcher. Umpires are not calling the higher strike, so there are longer counts, and too many walks. Calling the high strike will do much to make games move faster. Many pitchers become upset in that their pitches are in the official strike zone, but umpires will not call the high strike nor the inside corner. As a result, many counts are going 2 and 2, 3 and 2. Hitters are taking their sweet time at the plate, stepping out too often.

Another major cause of lengthy games is that baseball is in the era of set-up men, situation pitchers, and closers. Adding to the problem is that many pitching changes are made by managers who must always play the percentages (right against left, etc.). Managers have become over-dependent on bullpen specialists. They are too quick in relieving starters, with the exception of Larry Dierker. A very annoying aspect of the modern game is the employment of the "one-out specialist", the reliever who comes in for one batter and one batter only. This one-out beast slows up the game! St. Louis manager Tony LaRussa is most responsible. In 1996, he used a one-batter-only pitcher 47 times!

Baseball must take steps to speed things up, without disrupting the natural rhythm of the game. If games were not so long, I believe TV viewership would improve. A major problem is that baseball does not effectively enforce stall tactics between pitcher and batter, other than an occasional urging from the umpire to "get going". Umpires must continue to urge the batter to stay in the box, or at least one foot in, and the pitcher to deliver a pitch to the hitter by 20 seconds.

Excessively long television commercials have contributed to longer games, particularly in post-season play. The players are ready to go, but the umpires must hold up play. Between inning commercials are running far beyond the 2:25 allotted time. Commercials should be limited to 2:05-2:25 minutes, with some short messages worked in between plays.

While many people favor speeding up the game, there are those who are not concerned with the length. George Will wrote that baseball contests do seem to drag "until you understand the game and then you wonder how they pack so much action into such a short time." Jerry Hoover, a fan from Asheboro, North Carolina, wrote: "The possibility that a game could go on for infinity is one part of the game I love. In a world where time constraints are always prevalent, baseball gives us a wonderful escape."

Among the new rules to speed up games:

- Require pitchers to throw the ball within 12 second of getting it from the catcher when nobody is on base. Failure to do so means an automatic ball.

- Hitters will not be allowed to step out of the box with nobody on base.

- For managers and coaches to move more quickly when visiting the mound and making pitching changes.

- Umpires to start innings on time after mandated breaks for commercials.

Moderate Approach to Realignment

As early as January 1997, interim commissioner Bud Selig had begun pushing for radical geographic realignment, in which fifteen teams would have switched leagues. When that plan failed to gain support, he proposed a seven-team switch that was squashed by the Giants and the players union. Finally, despite Selig's never-ending phone calls and fax memos to owners, including reported special deals and favors, baseball's owners on October 15 voted to approve a modest realignment plan that sent one team, Selig's Milwaukee Brewers, from the American League to the National League in 1998.

For awhile, it appeared that the owners were in favor of extensive realignment in which numerous teams would switch leagues. The belief was that the proposal would foster regional rivalries and stimulate interest. The owners could see financial benefits from less travel and playing most of their games within the same time zone, thus providing television with higher ratings. But, support gradually eroded from those owners who evidently started to listen to their fans.

Despite strong opposition to radical realignment, Selig appears to be still determined to reach his personal goal. Undaunted, he will likely keep trying despite the overwhelming results of USA TODAY's poll, in which 82% believe "Let Baseball Alone", while only 18% want to see the league changed. Baseball America polled its readers, known for being knowledgeable and objective, and also found them overwhelmingly against realignment.

Proponents say realignment is a matter of distance, in that teams travel as many as 50,000 miles per season, and realigning is a way to curb costs. The fact is, however, that teams spend an average of just $700,000 to $1 million on annual travel, the salary of a mediocre utility infielder. Even Selig concedes, travel costs is a very secondary factor.

Then, what is the prime reason owners are pushing for increased realignment? The team's local television ratings, along with the profit motive! And what are the consequences? Radical realignment would destroy 121 years of baseball history and tradition. David Kindred of The Sporting News explained: "It would abolish the National League and the American League. The names would continue to be used, but with 15 teams moving from their traditional positions, the names would become meaningless. In their places would be eight divisions (four each) based on geography, not custom or habit."

"These owners are threatening to rip the fabric of this most traditional sport by a stunning miscalculation," wrote George Will. "They believe this year's novelty of interleague play boosted attendance because of regional rivalries."

Does baseball really need realignment? Mike Lopresti answered this question by saying: "Never mind that only four years ago, in 1993, baseball set records and made millions. Then, came the lunacy of the strike. The fan desertion that followed had nothing to do with alignment. It is the wrong medicine for the symptoms."

When Major League Baseball is ready to expand to 32 teams, four eight-team divisions will provide an ideal setup. Each league will send its two champions into post-season play. By ridding itself of the wild-card system, exciting pennant races will again return. Each division will be reminiscent of the classic leagues and pennant races of the past.

But, Major League Baseball would be making a major mistake if it arranged the 32 teams in eight four-team divisions, resulting in an absurd eight "pennant races".

The independence of the two leagues must be retained.

Division Series Format is Unjust

The present division series has created serious problems for baseball, another big mistake by the governing owners. "The owners were so preoccupied with realignment, they ignored how unjust the division series format is," said Bob Costas. According to the original agreement, it was decided that teams with the best records should have an advantage in the short series. So somebody decided the home-field advantage would be the last three games. "In a best-of-five, the first game is the most important, followed by the second," wrote Hal Bodley in USA TODAY. "Lose the first two, and teams with 'home-field advantage' might be out after one game at home".

The division series had a new look in 1998, but kept its best-of-five format. Baseball has made a wise decision in discarding the ridiculous 2-3 plan. By using the seeding concept, the 2-2-1 plan will give the higher percentage teams games 1, 2, and 5. While the general managers want the series increased to best-of-seven, the council decided there should be further study relative to the season schedule.

Interleague Play Should Be Limited

From a positive standpoint, interleague play, at least in its first two seasons, boosted interest and attendance by creating new rivalries. It created a new level of excitement with teams coming into other ballparks that people have never seen. However, from a negative viewpoint, interleague delivered a blow to the century-long tradition and uniqueness of baseball. One of the major reasons baseball is different from the other sports is because the two leagues don't play each other. As a result, interleague play has diluted the importance of the World Series and the All-Star Game.

Mel Antonen of USA TODAY wrote that, "Interleague play will diminish the popularity of the World Series, cheapen a century of statistics, and cause baseball to lose credibility." Costas, the most ardent spokesperson for the preservationists, said, "Under the right circumstances, a small amount of interleague play could be a good idea, but just as was the case with realigning and the expanded playoffs, this plan reflects the quick-fix mentality that rules baseball."

To accommodate interleague play and three division alignments, Major League Baseball felt it had to adopt so-called balanced schedules, where teams played many more games outside their division. But, in doing so, it necessitated a glut of two-game series, and divisional teams had few games with each other down the stretch. With an unbalanced schedule, more games will be played between teams in the same region, thus creating better rivalries. The quality of play will be improved, too, with less travel and the elimination of two-game series.

Handled properly, a limited number of interleague games could work well for baseball. Natural rivalries are very attractive to the fans. However, the identity of the two leagues are very important to baseball, and Major League Baseball should be most hesitant to remove or diminish this mystique, as well as the respective identities of the two leagues.

Delay Expansion

With the number of major league teams now at 30 teams, expansion should be delayed until baseball's diluted talent product has recovered. While 32 teams will provide baseball with an ideal organizational structure, the game isn't ready now to take on two more teams without significant dilution of the player pool or appreciable fall-off in the quality of play. On the plus side, expansion has resulted in more jobs and a greater demand for big league players. It has also created new, innovative ballparks. There are many baseball observers, however, who believe expansion has been a mistake. Rushing of prospects is the direct result of continual expansion. "Relocation and stabilization was the answer," said Yankees owner George Steinbrenner.

Continual expansion over the past two decades has done much to thin out batting orders and weaken pitching staffs. There are fewer quality fourth and fifth starters, as well as dependable left-handers. The huge demand for pitchers has driven up their salaries greatly. There are simply not enough big league caliber players to fill the current number of team rosters. Prospects are spending fewer years in the minors, and the development of pitchers has had to be speeded up. Too often, young pitchers are not ready for the majors.

The next round of expansion could be a decade away, according to John Harrington, chairman of MLB's schedule-format committee. If so, it would be a wise decision, what with teams floundering financially, combined with a shallow talent pool. The priority of baseball should now be focused on dealing with franchises that are struggling in low-revenue markets.

Wild-Card System Mars Pennant Races

Baseball fans are unanimous in stating that nothing beats a great pennant race, but the wild-card prevents that from happening. It rewards mediocrity, holding the possibility of teams having an incentive to lose games on purpose, like the Dodgers and Padres fiasco in 1996. The wild-card extends the postseason, unworthy teams meet in the World Series, and division titles mean nothing.

The wild-card system has diminished the game. It was supposed to heighten interest in playoff races, but instead, the 162-game regular season has been stripped of much of its meaning. It was one of the worst mistakes baseball ever made, a gimmick, a hoax to get fans into the park.

In his superb article in The Sporting News, Bob Costas wrote: "The wild-card was created at the expense of everything that was legitimate about baseball's regular season and authentic pennant races. The ebb and flow of a true pennant race or division title was one of the unique pleasures of baseball. A pennant race has specific competitive and dramatic characteristics. Virtually all of these characteristics are destroyed by the wild-card system."

Baseball's three-division, wild-card format is a loser. As Tim Keown wrote, "With the extra round of playoffs, the cynical fan is more likely to reserve his emotions until the team makes the playoffs. With three tiers to the postseason structure, a team that makes the first round is just beginning."

The World Series Weather Problem

ABC's Nightline asked one stern question during the 1997 Fall Classic, "Whatever happened to the World Series?" While this question drew a number of responses, I tend to agree with the one Tim Keown wrote in his San Francisco Chronicle column, "Nothing happened to the World Series, at least nothing that couldn't be cured by a little warm weather, a healthy dose of desperation and Game 7." The unbearable cold weather brought the play down several levels. Games played near or after midnight in late October in Cleveland are going to be altered by the weather, but baseball does not want to admit it.

Baseball urgently needs to consider the realities of playing late October baseball. Since the game is largely controlled by television, Major League Baseball has chosen to go exclusively with night games, like the 8:22 p.m. EDT first pitch. Consequently, in numerous World Series, severe cold weather has marred the play of the players and provided discomfort for the fans. Games have ended after midnight with kids going to school the next day.

In 1976, the first all-night World Series was played through frigid temperatures in Cincinnati and New York. Commissioner Bowie Kuhn, so sensitive to complaints about playing games in the cold, defiantly watched the games without a topcoat. It was 43 degrees at the start of Game 2 and kept getting colder. Poor Bowie almost came down with pneumonia. Two decades later in Game 3 of the 1997 Series in Cleveland, another commissioner, Bud Selig, sat in icy cold conditions, with the wind blowing off of Lake Erie, but he was wearing a top coat. The 1999 W.S. could finish the day before the first of November!

Whatever happened to the World Series? Among the many reasons given by Steve Marantz in The Sporting News:

- The big increase in postseason games has definitely hurt the appeal of the World Series.
- Games started too late and lasted too long, precluding children from the audience.
- The best teams were not participating.
- Too many pitchers lacked good control and command in the cold.
- Baseball is not meant to be played in light snow with a wind chill of 15 degrees.

Still, Commissioner Selig said, "Baseball won't move the World Series back to the daytime." Selig added that, "We put quite a few day games on during the playoffs and the ratings were terrible." His reaction, of course, goes to show how baseball and the TV networks are influenced and controlled so heavily by the ratings.

The time has come, however, for baseball to start demonstrating a greater concern for the game's future -- the children of America. An all-day schedule is highly unlikely, simply because the networks would demand a big reduction in rights fees to make up for the loss in advertising revenues. Larry Baer, the Giants' chief operating officer, believes "A simpler solution is to play a couple of afternoon games while starting night games no later than 7 p.m. in the East, even if it means everybody, players included, settles for less money."

Baseball's Umpiring Controversy

The on-going feud between Major League Baseball officials and the Umpires Association has gone far too long, and it does not serve the best interests of the game. Umpires have been upset that certain players and managers seem to complain constantly with exemption from punishment. They are unhappy that controversies are replayed constantly on television.

In recent years, however, the umpires have come under increased criticism by fans, players, and team management, not only for their inconsistent interpretation of the strike zone but their overall arrogant and belligerent attitude with players and managers. There are many who believe the umpires aptitude is less a problem than their attitude. As one National League pitcher said, "You don't say anything because you can't take the chance of getting run." In fact, the umpires' intolerant stance has instilled some fear on the field, removing some gamemanship. For a player or manager to argue a call, even if it ends up nose-to-nose, is a team's only means of holding an umpire accountable.

Until recently, baseball has failed to address the problems between players and umpires, but as I discussed earlier, the situation has now changed greatly. As the Sacramento Bee News Service reported, "Fearful baseball would lock them out after their labor contract expires December 31, umpires announced in July that they would quit en masse to try to force an early start to negotiations. But the strategy backfired when their union split and 27 of the 68 umpires either refused to resign or withdrew their resignations. Baseball then hired 25 new umpires from the minors."

Dating back more than a century, umpires had always been under league control, but the commissioner's office has indicated their intentions to handle this responsibility, with one set of standards, and one way of teaching umpires in the minors, and one pool of umpires. This will mean no more separate styles for each league. The best officials will work the most important games. A merit system will be used to determine which ones qualify for the post-season.

Baseball should institute a process that increases accountability of the umpires, and it must provide consequences for those unable to meet the standards. The very best umpires should survive, just like the players. When the skills of players aren't high enough, they are gone. The same should apply to the umpires.

Baseball's Antitrust Exemption

Baseball's antitrust exemption stands alone among professional sports. In 1922, the Supreme Court declared that baseball was not a business, nor involved in interstate commerce, and was not subject to the country's antitrust laws. The high court reaffirmed this decision in 1953 and again in 1972 relative to the Curt Flood case. On both occasions, the Court stated that if baseball's exemption is to be lifted, it should be done by Congress. That exemption deprived players of some of the protections enjoyed by other professional athletes and has been blamed for baseball's many work stoppages, including the disastrous strike in 1994-95.

Yet, no bill to lift the exemption has ever made it out of committee in either the House or Senate. Through the years, baseball's legal monopoly has been able to withstand a number of challenges contending that baseball was abusing its privileges. In 1998, the U.S. Congress, followed by President William Clinton's signature, voted to overthrow part of a 76-year-old Supreme Court ruling that exempted baseball from antitrust laws on the grounds it is a game and not a business.

Amateur Draft   Implemented in 1965 to save teams money and distribute talent evenly, the draft process accomplished those objectives quite well in its early years. But recent drafts have literally shaken the system from its foundation, as a result of huge bonus payments to high draft picks and international free agents. Record-shattering $10 million bonuses were paid in 1996 to Matt White and Travis Lee.

"An amateur draft is absolutely essential to the future of the game," said Sandy Alderson, Executive Vice President for MLB. "But the amount White signed for is one-half of a team's entire payroll. If these lavish bonuses should continue, neither the player development or free agent routes will be available to many teams. I seriously have to question paying those kind of dollars for players who haven't proved anything on the big league level."

Changes to the draft process must be made and it appears likely Major League Baseball will alter the process, probably in the form of a cap on Player-Development cost, including signing bonuses. A cap on Player-Development costs, which would increase each year by a prescribed amount, would leave teams more willing to draft players based on ability than signability.

There is increasing pressure from the Commissioner's office to implement a worldwide draft. "The theory is that small-market-teams need the worldwide draft to compete in the foreign market," wrote David Rawnsley in Baseball America.

Baseball's Drug Policy Needs Overhaul

While there are many who believe baseball does not have a drug policy, Major League Baseball does have one, but it is greatly out-of-date and in need of a major overhaul. C.W. Nevius wrote in the San Francisco Chronicle, "Until now, baseball's muscle-building drug policy was simple: Don't ask, don't tell!"

Baseball's tolerance for andro has hurt anti-doping programs in other sports. What baseball does not want to admit, though, is that McGwire's performance was enhanced by substances and drugs. What will Major League Baseball do if the study conducted by two Harvard physicians determines that a slugger taking andro has a competitive advantage? "Both management and labor will attempt to shoot down the study," wrote Rick Reilly in Sports Illustrated. "Or they will bite the bullet on the McGwire legacy and ban andro, hoping the public thinks the issue has disappeared. It won't have. Until baseball decides to test for drugs, the ban isn't worth the paper the news release is printed on."

McGwire states emphatically that, "Weight training and nutrition transformed everything." But there are many prominent medical and health authorities who strongly question McGwire's regimen, like Dr. Charles Yesalis, a Penn State professor of health and human development and author of the book, The Steroid Game. "Androstendione is a steroid, and honest-to-goodness drug," said Yesalis who has watched the growth of muscles in baseball with suspicion.

Yesalis says the talk about supplements is a smoke screen, that 25-30 percent of major league ballplayers are using anabolic steroids. "Over the last decade, I've seen lean-mass increases in players that I frankly cannot attribute to changes in strength training alone. Forget about Creatine. To me, it's very obvious that anabolic steroids have taken a major foothold in baseball."

For baseball to control the use of steroids, drugs and performance-enhancing substances, it must set a policy and then enforce it. According to Dr. Gary Wadler of Cornell University who co-wrote the book Drug and the Athlete, says, "The only way to catch offenders is to conduct random testing, including the off-season.

The time has come to have meaningful, reliable drug testing. I like to believe the large majority of players would like to see a return to the level playing field of the pre-steroid era. The best hope for this to happen lies with the athletes themselves, but their union has opposed random drug testing, contending it is an infringement of an individual's rights. Why should the union oppose random testing? The reasons are not hard to figure out.

Ban Andro and Require Drug Testing

Baseball must follow the lead of the NFL, NCAA, IOC, and other organizations in banning androstendione. The Association of Professional Team Physicians, comprised of doctors from all the major sports, have recommended that andro be taken off the consumer market and classified as a controlled substance available only by prescription, legitimate medical uses, not for athletes.

If baseball fails to ban androstendione and continues to refuse to make drug testing mandatory, the future of players and their families will be in jeopardy. Baseball, of course, doesn't want to take any action that would diminish McGwire's record-breaking 70 home runs. But it would be wrong and highly irresponsible for Major League Baseball not to take action because of a desire not to tarnish the record.

The most effective way to avoid the steroids controversy is to require mandatory drug testing. Players union chief Donald Fehr doesn't believe there is a steroid problem. Therefore, the union prohibits random testing for any non-drug offender. Obviously, Fehr refuses to recognize that there is much more to baseball's problem, one far more serious than the use of andro and Creatine. Players are using andro and other supplements to mask strength gains from actual anabolic steroids. Players are not bulking up with steroids during the actual season. Rather, it is happening during their workouts over the winter.

The Downside of Steroids

Anabolic steroids, the blight of modern sports, have a very unhealthy downside. Certainly, the tragic early-age deaths of numerous athletes as a result of steroid drugs should deliver a powerful object lesson to every athlete looking for an artificial edge. Steroids increase significantly the risk of kidney and prostate cancer, heart and liver disease, the shrinkage of testicles, raise blood pressure and enlarge the heart. Steroids, particularly testosterone, have a powerful effect on the central nervous system. Many unexplained fatal heart attacks have been linked to concealed steroid use.

"There is no doubt that a wide variety of drugs improve sports performance," stated Dr. Michael Colgan who directs the Colgan Institute of Nutritional Science in San Diego. "But they also pose serious dangers for both physical and mental health. When athletes take steroids, they do so at the risk of physiological and sexual alterations, which cannot be reversed. That's too high a price."

On the playing field, steroids are a major cause of the excessive number of suspicious injuries. "Injured tendons are one of the most frequent problems we see with steroids," said Dr. Colgan, author of Optimum Sports Nutrition. "In addition to the injury itself, they immediately ruin your training. As tendons get sore, first it's knee and wrist wraps. Then, it's big doses of anti-inflammatories, elbow and ankle wraps, elephant size wraps up the thighs, and good-bye Charlie."

"If that's not enough, steroids can cause rapid hair loss in some individuals," says Dr. Colgan. "Of course, all the young athletes we see shaving their heads is probably just high fashion and nothing to do with concealing sudden baldness. Sure! And impotence? Many young men today are spending big bucks on hormone treatment trying to get back their manhood."

"But an even worse consequence of drug use," said Colgan, "It's that it destroys your pride, integrity, and your concept of self. Drugs inhibit the pursuit of excellence, because you never know whether you could have done it without them. You do not have to use drugs to achieve your potential. Do you want to give powder the credit for the good work you do in the weight room and on the field?

Chicago Cubs first baseman Mark Grace does it the old-fashioned way, working out four to five hours a day, five days a week, with a personal trainer. Mark adamantly refuses to use Creatine, andro, steroids, or any other muscle-enhancer. "I'm scared of that stuff. The short-term gains are positive, but the long-term effects are scary."

Sooner or later, the rest of the story will be written. Surely, the long range health and longevity of McGwire and other athletes who have used extensively drugs and growth hormone substances will be under close scrutiny in the years to come.

Is Androstendione Dangerous?
Many team physicians in the big leagues consider androstendione dangerous and have advocated a policy in which it be taken off the shelves in the United States. "Despite how the manufacturers of androstendione try to position it as a natural substance, it is still an anabolic steroid," stated the Association of Professional Sports Physicians. "Simply put, its effects are anabolic, i.e. muscle building. As with any steroid,

there is a wide range of potential side effects, from minor ones, to much more serious ones, such as personality disorders, liver abnormalities, elevated cholesterol or even heart attacks."

Androstendione is a synthetically produced form of a substance naturally produced by the body in the adrenal glands and gonads. However, the pills and capsules deliver it in concentrated form. As a precursor to the human hormone testosterone, andro is transformed by an enzyme into testosterone, which then promotes muscle growth by helping stockpile nitrogen, a key component of muscle fiber. Therefore, androstendione is an anabolic (muscle-building) steroid hormone.

Player Development

A strong player development program can help offset competitive imbalance caused by the various economic disparities. More and more, teams are developing their own players. Teams are giving their farm directors more responsibilities and authority, like overseeing international scouting. Every team has become more involved in the worldwide market, but why not the proven athletic prowess of African-Americans here in America?

A strong farm system is most essential. It is the best guarantee for a competitive team year-in and year-out, and it's cheaper. Major League teams each spend from $6 to $7 million annually on their farm systems. This amount includes scouting expenses, signing bonuses, spring training costs, medical expenses, player and staff salaries and meal money.

Start At Home!   In delivering a strong message to big league scouts, Don Newcombe, former outstanding pitcher for the Dodgers, said, "Baseball should start at home, but the color barrier still receives little action." In voicing his strong concern, Newcombe, a close friend of the late Jackie Robinson, believes there actually is a smaller percentage of African-Americans in MLB today than when baseball became fully integrated in 1959. In 1959, 17.25% of the big league players were African-Americans. Today, 14.1% of the Opening Day rosters had African-American players. Even more alarming, 47.9% of the African-American players in the big leagues today are 30 years or older.

"Something is terribly wrong," wrote Bob Nightengale in Baseball Weekly. "Remarkably, today, there were nearly as many players from the tiny islands of the Dominican Republic and Puerto Rico (96) as African-Americans (119) on the opening day roster."

"You see these teams with all of these beautiful academies in the Dominican trying to get these kids," Newcombe says. "You don't see them getting kids out of Watts, Compton or the inner cities. We're reverting right back to where we were 50 years ago. If the baseball industry really wanted to make a full-fledged commitment," said Newcombe, "teams would start building baseball academies in their own cities. It's time we develop ballplayers in the United States instead of some other country. Let's give a chance to our kids in the inner cities."

Building A Good Farm System

The roots of the modern farm system began with Branch Rickey in the 1920s, when he began buying minor league teams at various levels to develop players. In 1962, following an almost devastating decline, the relationship between the majors and minors was formalized in the Player Development Plan. The standard number of teams in a farm system is six: Triple-A, Double-A, High Class A, Low Class-A, Short-season, and Rookie-level affiliates. The best systems have more than six, while the worst have fewer and force players to skip a step in their development.

Why don't more teams buy their own affiliates? As usual, money is the answer. Franchises are expensive to buy these days, and they still don't produce revenue on a daily basis. Owning affiliates is a practice that few teams engage in anymore.

Scouting

Scouts are still the foundation of a big league baseball organization. Scouting and player development are the heart and soul of the game. Instead of shrinking, a distinct possibility early in the 1990s, scouting departments are expanding. Clubs today have a separation of powers in the scouting department between professional and amateur coverage.

Scouting has now become a science, consisting of readouts and graphs. It is far more than just pointing a radar gun at the player. As Peter Pascarelli wrote in The Sporting News, "While physical skills can be assessed relatively easily, what makes a player succeed or fail goes beyond how he throws the ball or swings the bat. The personality makeup of young players is just as important, and it is the most difficult aspect of scouting." In assessing a player's makeup, scouts are using psychological tests and evaluations. Still, physical ability is what will get a prospect to the big leagues.

Greater Focus on Global Competition
The time has come for professional baseball to be marketed on an international scope to showcase the "best sport in the world." The fan base for baseball is huge and fanatical in Japan, Korea, and many Latin American countries. U.S. baseball gets higher TV ratings than the NBA in Japan. According to officials of Major League Baseball International, baseball on a worldwide basis is a sleeping giant, ready to explode relative to competitive play, spectator entertainment, and televised coverage.

WORLD CUP OF BASEBALL Major League Baseball should take the lead in proposing a World Cup style tournament. The time has come to consider an alternative to the Olympics. A true World Cup of Baseball every 2 or 4 years would do more for the game than having professionals compete in the Olympics or staging a World Series event with a country like Japan. A format similar to soccer's World Cup would provide the clout and exposure baseball needs on a worldwide scope. The event could precede the MLB season, like March 24-April 1, or in early November, with games played in warm-weather areas.

While the idea of a World Cup involving major league players sounds very attractive, it presents two major obstacles and problems. First, the current major league season is long and demanding. Second, the World Cup type of competition in soccer and ice hockey could not be duplicated in baseball.

The most practical approach would be to stage the Cup every two or four years and limit competition to eight countries and no more than 7 to 10 days. A double elimination tournament would be similar to the international format the Little League World Series features each year. Or, the competition could be set up similar to Latin American baseball's Caribbean Series, where the champions of four leagues compete. The latter part of March would appear to be easier for major league players to work in than immediately following their grueling season. And, too, a World Cup wouldn't interfere with Latin American leagues.

TURFACE Sports Field Maintenance

Proper field maintenance is vital to the quality of play and safety of the players. There is no substitute for conditioning fields to maximize performance and safety. For over 30 years, TURFACE has set the standard for sports field maintenance. It has been selected by 3 out of 4 major league groundskeepers. "Compaction, bad ball hops and rainouts are significantly reduced," said Mark Razum, head groundskeeper of the Colorado Rockies. Floyd D. Perry, 1997 Sportsturf Magazine Man of the Year, said, "TURFACE Pro LeagueTM has allowed groundskeepers the ability to create the finest fielding and sliding surface a player could wish to play on."

SOIL SELECTION Razum prefers a 65% clay, 10% silt, and 25% sand mixture which passes through a 1/8" screen. He then conditions the soil by incorporating TURFACE Pro LeagueTM at about a 20% blend, 4" deep to absorb excess water and keep the clay from becoming too hard (See cover picture of the Coors Field infield).

TURFACE TOP 10 TIPS FOR FIELD MAINTENANCE

1.	Know your field	6.	Use proper dragging techniques
2.	Create safe, high performance infields	7.	Build safe, durable mounds and batter's boxes
3.	New construction (Build it right the first time)	8.	Water is your most important maintenance tool
4.	Make puddles a thing of the past	9.	Use the right equipment
5.	Maintain the perfect base path	10.	TURFACE for outstanding turf

For more information about the TURFACE PRO LEAGUE-TM, call 1-800-207-6457, or visit them at **www.profileproducts.com**. Their mailing address is: PROFILE Products, 750 Lake Cook Road, Suite 440, Buffalo Grove, IL 60089.

Administration of Major League Baseball

OFFICE OF THE COMMISSIONER

Mailing Address:
    245 Park Avenue, New York, NY 10167
    Telephone: (212) 931-7800
    Web Site: **www.majorleaguebaseball.com**

Commissioner: Allan H. "Bud" Selig
President, Chief Operating Officer: Paul Beeston
Executive Vice President, Baseball Operations: Sandy Alderson
Executive Director, Public Relations: Richard Levin
    Public Relations:
    Telephone: (212) 931-7878   Fax: (212) 949-5654

AMERICAN LEAGUE

Mailing Address:
    245 Park Avenue, 28th Floor
    New York, NY 10167
    Telephone: (212) 931-7600

President: Gene Budig
Senior Vice President: Phyllis Merhige

NATIONAL LEAGUE

Mailing Address:
    245 Park Avenue
    New York, NY 10167
    Telephone: (212) 339-7700

President: Leonard Coleman
Senior Vice President, Secretary: Katy Feeney

The '90s, the best era in minor league history.

Despite boom in attendance, profit margins remain thin.

Entertaining fans is a major priority for the minors.

Players take time to talk to fans and sign autographs.

The minors are the training ground for the majors.

5 Minor Leagues

The decade of the 90's could be the best era in minor league history. Attendance is at its greatest level since the late 1940s, sparked by new ballparks and affordable family entertainment. Franchises have become one of the best investments in the country. Overall attendance, from class AAA to rookie leagues, climbed 4.3% to just under 35 million, the highest season total since 1949. Annual gross revenues over the past five years have doubled to nearly $300 million.

Most minor league teams are privately owned and subsidized by the major league club with which they are affiliated. The National Agreement between Major League Baseball and the National Association continues to be a stabilizing force in professional baseball. Despite all their cut-back talk, the major leagues seem to be convinced that their arrangement with the minors is good for them. As Will Lingo wrote in Baseball America, "It develops players, of course, but it also develops baseball fans."

In contrast to the lack of strong leadership on the major league level, the minors have had the benefit of a dynamic and visionary president, Michael Moore, who has always emphasized togetherness and the best interests of the minor league system. The minors, unlike the majors, have not forgotten the fans. They continue to administer the policy of "The Fan as No. 1". The large majority of teams have been successful in providing quality entertainment in a clean wholesome environment. Fans can still get a good seat for $4 and parking is free.

Despite the boom in attendance and franchise value in the last decade, the profit margins remain thin. The disparity between large and small markets is even wider than in the majors. Like the majors, an increasing gap is developing between the haves and the have-nots. Teams in the same league can have total operating budgets from $400,000 to $4 million. While the big markets are generating millions of dollars of revenue, teams in small cities are being left behind. About 10 percent of the clubs account for 60 to 70 percent of the operating profit.

The cost of doing business in the minors continues to increase. Many teams are moving into new stadiums and new cities to keep the money flowing. Cities and towns across America are spending millions on beautiful, but expensive, stadiums. While upgraded parks have boosted the game's popularity, facility requirements and standards of the Professional Baseball Agreement have been a financial burden for many of the clubs. Some clubs are in heavy debt due to acquisition costs. Still, the stadium boom is expected to continue.

Even the big market teams are having problems, such as more overhead, more employees, and more operating costs. Despite feelings that minor league franchises have become "cash cows", Lacy Lusk of Baseball America pointed out that "Those who made fortunes in minor league baseball did it by buying franchises when they were relatively cheap and then selling them for millions. The operating margins have always been pretty thin, and they have become even more so with the ever-increasing cost of baseball." Minor league presidents have had difficulty finding owners who are capable of operating Double-A and Triple-A expansion franchises.

While television has boosted overall interest in the game, the proliferation of major league games on cable television does not serve the best interests of the minors. Big league games continue to flood the market. Playoff attendance is a serious problem since fans care little about the postseason. When September comes around, the excitement and interest of fans has dwindled.

Many major league teams are not happy with their farm systems as they exist now. The efficiency of the player development system in the minors leaves much to be desired, due largely to the rushing factor caused by continued expansion. Today, there are about 6,000 players in the minor leagues competing for one of 700 roster spots in the majors. Only 7-8% of the players in the minors will play even one day in the majors. About 10 out of 11 players will fail to make the big leagues. Furthermore, there has been a general decline in play at the minor league level. Players are not as fundamentally sound as those of a decade or two ago. Many clubs are moving players too quickly through their farm systems. Prospects are not spending enough time in the minors.

The development of minor league umpires also appears to be a major problem. In addition to being grossly underpaid, they are not receiving adequate supervision and guidance. According to Jim Honochick, "The umpiring situation in the minor leagues is terrible." He believes that, "Each minor league should have a supervisor to observe and assist the young umpires, someone knowledgeable in umpiring, perhaps a retired major league umpire."

Despite the boom, the minors are making plans for slower times ahead. National Association president Mike Moore wants clubs to be prepared when the explosive growth finally slows down. Moore said, "Despite the current robust economy of the minors, the one thing that may be missing is vision, a sense of where the minors should go and why."

Controlling expenses should be one of the minor leagues' biggest concerns. Both Moore and vice president Pat O'Conner have been pleading for years for minor league leaders to address the growing gap between the big-money and small-money franchises.

The widening gap between large and small-money franchises must be addressed.

What the Minors Are All About
The tradition, atmosphere, and charm that used to characterize baseball are still alive in minor league baseball. Seeing future major league players develop almost matches the thrill of seeing them in The Show a couple years later. The minors offer affordable family entertainment and a fun place to go, in a casual, relaxed, and festive atmosphere. The minors sell an experience, not just a game. For many fans, being at a minor league game is more fun than going to a big league game.

Minor league ballparks have always had an intimate personality, local cuisine, and inventive promotions. Life in the stands is a great part of the minors. Small parks, in particular, lend an air of intimacy to the game and a proximity to the field. It is easy to get a seat close to the field at a minor league park. Players are far more accessible than big league stars with their large-sized egos. They take time to talk to the fans.

Many of the new stadiums are designed to look like the old ones. In many ways, the minors are moving back in time closer to the minors of old, like the Durham Bulls moved into in 1994. Parks are being renovated in old style, with grandstand roofs held up with pillars and flags flying from the tops.

**Development of future
Major League Stars**

The Diamond Is A
True Gem!

**Lake Elsinore Storm Professional
Baseball Club
(California League – Class A)**

Small Town,
Big Crowds
Packing The Stands For a Night of Fun

**"Hamlet" the
Sea Serpent**

Indeed, the minor leagues offer an appealing alternative to the major leagues where one has to spend well over $100 to take a family to a game. There are no incentive bonuses and agents, sky boxes, and price gauging card and collectible shows. People tend to believe it was the majors that made the national pastime, but those who have studied the history of professional baseball maintain it was in the minor leagues that baseball truly became the national pastime. To be sure, the great stars of the majors attract the headlines and the TV spotlight, but the tales of the 125 years of minor league baseball are just as fascinating. The lifeblood of baseball flows from the thousands of small towns which have supported minor league play. It has been the minors which have brought professional baseball to the grass roots of America's population.

How The Minors Are Classified
The minor leagues are classified by the caliber of play and size of the home city. The minors consist of fifteen leagues in North America and 150 teams. Four thousand players are employed, fulltime professionals, whose contracts are mostly owned by a major league club. The standard number of teams in a farm system now is six: Triple-A, Double A, high Class-A, low Class-A, short-season and Rookie-level affiliates.

Many people don't understand what all the different classifications mean, especially at the lower levels. Will Lingo believes they should be made easier to understand. He recommends that "After Triple-A, Double-A, and Class A, the minors should restore the old classification of Class B and Class C and do away with all the short-season and Rookie-level nonsense."

Realignment of Triple-A
The top level of the minor leagues has undergone a major realignment. Triple-A teams have realigned from three leagues into two. With the merging of the Pacific Coast League and American Association, the two remaining leagues, International and the Pacific Coast, will consist of 14 and 16 teams.

Why did Triple-A realign to just two leagues? After all, the three-league arrangement had worked very well for so long, but as Lingo explained, "It seems that owners wanted a bigger variety of opponents and a resumption of a Triple-A postseason series." The return of a junior World Series was one of the driving forces for those who supported new alignment. While the new alignment will provide Triple-A with a much-needed jolt of energy, Lingo thinks, "It will be sad to lose one, or possibly two leagues with nearly 100 years of history."

Triple-A World Series Has Potential The new Triple-A World Series has the makings of a world-class event. However, it remains to be seen whether Las Vegas is the right place to have the event. The Nevada show-biz and gambling city will attract casual fans because it is a true tourist destination, but as Lingo wrote, "With so much going on, the Series can get lost in the shuffle." There is also the gambling presence and atmosphere that baseball is so very concerned about.

In the inaugural game, the crowd was fewer than 3,000 people in a ballpark that seats nearly 10,000. The national TV audience was on ESPN2, watching a game that ended after 3 AM Eastern. Many of those who attended the inaugural event came away with a positive feeling about the first Triple-A World Series. "Given time, it could become minor league baseball's big event," said Lingo.

"Major league officials say they care about the Triple-A Series, but they don't care that much," wrote Lacy Lusk. "As one might expect, the big league teams' considerations still take priority over a minor league event. "Prior to their championship series against Pacific Coast League champion New Orleans, the Buffalo Bisons were hit hard by major league call-ups. Then lefthander Eddie Priest was promoted the day the Triple-A Series started, and Jason Jacome, the team's best pitcher, was off the roster by the time the team traveled to Las Vegas.

Farm director Tim Purpura, in trying to defend the Jacome promotion, said, "If that's the best arm you have in your system, you should call him up. The goal is to win in the big leagues. What's best for the organization is to have success at the major league level." Tim, isn't winning important at the minor league level, too?

Relations With The Majors The minors' relations with Major League Baseball are as good as they have ever been. "The major leagues have accepted the success of the minors," said Lingo, "and the minor leagues have accepted that their success means they'll have to pay more of the expenses of putting on minor league baseball." Jimmie Lee Solomon, MLB's executive director for minor league operations, says, "It's hard to point to real problematic stuff."

The Winter Meetings returned to their former glory in December, 1998, making the big leagues a formal part of the meetings again. "It was great to have the major leagues back," said Lingo. "It added to every aspect of the meetings, bringing more media interest, and more major league executives."

The All-Star Futures Game proved a big success at Fenway Park in July. It showcased the best prospects in the game, a somewhat different approach from that of the minor league all-star games, which reward minor leaguers having good seasons.

PROFESSIONAL BASEBALL AGREEMENT The Agreement is the document that binds the major leagues and the minors. It is the governing lifeline between the two levels of play. Unity is vital to the future of the game. A closer, more amicable relationship appears to have emerged between the majors and minors, a tribute to their negotiators. The two sides had known little about how the other operated until the last few years. NA officials and owners learned a lot about MLB's economic troubles, forced on them by their salary structure, and the majors learned that the minor leagues do a very good job of operating their business and are more aware that the minors are not getting rich.

Under the terms of the past two PBA's, the minor leagues have had to bear a greater percentage of the day-to-day costs of running a club. The minors now assume the expenses of umpire development, which cost the majors $5 million in 1996. They also pay a greater share of equipment and uniform costs, saving the majors about $500,000 a year. In exchange, the minors now are part of the lucrative licensing program of the major leagues, which now earns over $60 million a year. While the minors gained operating revenue, they lost a lot of control. The majors now have a much greater say in minor league affairs.

Minor's Historical Background

The minor leagues have been in operation since 1877, when the first organized professional minor league was founded by James A. Williams of Columbus, Ohio. On February 20, seven clubs "banded" into the International Association. During 1877, thirteen professional teams in the Midwest formed the League Alliance. The continuous playing history of minor league baseball began in 1883 when the Northwestern League and Interstate Association were established, and by 1884, as many as eight minor leagues were in business.

The early minor leagues experienced a most turbulent history. Without the financial stability of big league teams, leagues and teams would come and go. The majors were snatching their stars in midseason and lower clubs could lose an entire roster at the end of each season. In 1882, a basic reform was instituted, permitting minor league clubs to reserve up to 14 players per club. The player-purchase system had arrived.

By the end of the century, twenty-one official minor leagues were operating with more than 150 teams, in addition to over twenty semi-professional leagues. As Bruce Chadwick wrote in his excellent book, Baseball's Hometown Teams, "With minor-league and semi-pro teams playing games several days a week and doubleheaders on weekends, the ballpark had become an entertainment mecca, providing inexpensive entertainment for millions of Americans from coast to coast. Tickets at most ballparks cost just a quarter, and trolley rides to and from the stadium a nickel."

INVASION BY THE MAJORS   At the turn of the century, however, the minors were being raided more than ever by the majors, greatly angering those in towns and small cities for stealing their best players. According to Chadwick, "It reached a crescendo in 1901 when Ban Johnson's brand-new American League opened play, and launched a full-scale invasion of the minors, signing more than 150 players from across the country."

Despite a National Agreement, the minors had become orphaned by the stormy war between the major leagues. Finally, when the Agreement was scrapped in 1901, the minor leagues decided on the Ben Franklin credo, "We must all hang together or assuredly we shall hang separately." According to Hy Turkin and S.C. Thompson in the Official Encyclopedia of Baseball, "The minors' own "Fourth of July" came on September 5, 1901, when representatives of seven leagues gathered in Chicago and proclaimed their Declaration of Independence." As Chadwick wrote, "The leaders formed the National Association to represent themselves. They also organized themselves into leagues on different levels of talent to prevent some of the runaway games that bored fans. Teams would now play in four classifications: A, B, C, and D."

Big league clubs were bluntly told by the minor leagues that "We will no longer release any of our players without compensation, and that any efforts to take even one more player would result in costly lawsuits. It was war!" By 1903, the majors, realizing they needed the minors as a talent pool, came to an agreement with the minors. A payment of up to $7,500 would be made to the minor league club for any player signed to a big league contract. The agreement provided the minors with a new source of revenue and much needed stability.

With 19 leagues, the National Association was able to operate without a crisis until World War I when only one league, the International, was able to survive 1918. Then, when the troubled minors demanded an end to player options and draft by the majors, the majors terminated their mutual agreement. However, at the end of 1920, the appointment of Judge Keneshaw Mountain Landis as commissioner of baseball led to a new minor agreement. The 1921 agreement effectively exempted five of the strongest minors from the major league draft. Under the new agreement, an owner in the five-draft-exempt leagues was free to ask whatever he wanted for his stars.

THE NEGRO LEAGUES were flourishing in the 1920s, with the many outstanding black players playing on all-black teams. The black minors provided sports entertainment for the black community and gave talented young people the opportunity to be ball players. "But in the highly segregated society of America in the 1920s," said Chadwick, "they had an additional function, shared with black churches, schools, night clubs, and theaters: they built the foundation for a separate black culture that fostered heritage, pride, and opportunity."

How good was the level of baseball played in the black minors? "Very competitive," said Ernie Banks, who played with the Amarillo (Texas) Colts in the late 1940s, followed by the Kansas City Monarchs before moving directly to the Chicago Cubs. "The players I faced were just as good as the players in the white minors."

During the Depression, promotions started to appear. Ladies' Days were marketed heavily, with fans receiving dishes at the ballpark like they could at the movie theatres. The popular Knothole Gang promotion provided kids with free season tickets. By the mid-1930s, many teams were using lights for night baseball, and attendance soared.

GOLDEN ERA, THEN SHARP DECLINE World War II caused a shut-down of much of the minor league operation as it did during World War I, but in the postwar years, the minors picked up just where they left off. In 1949, there were a record fifty-nine leagues, 464 teams, and ten thousand players in minor leagues in the United States. It was the golden era for the minors. The 1950's, however, brought minor league baseball close to the brink of destruction. Television, the exploding popularity of organized youth baseball, increased travel, the arts, etc. almost devastated them, reducing the minors to fifteen leagues in 1963. As Chadwick explained, "Minor league owners assumed television, which started broadcasting baseball in the late 1940s, would help them even more." By the middle of the 1950s, Americans were watching three or four hours of television a day. With all kinds of free entertainment, who needed to pay the price of admission to a minor league park?"

By 1956, minor league attendance had plunged to just seventeen million. Thirty-one leagues and some 240 teams had gone out of business since 1949. The minors were in serious trouble. Fully aware that the loss of the minors would destroy them, the owners created a $500,000 stabilization fund to save the minors. In 1959, hundreds of thousands of additional dollars were given to the minors in a player development fund. In subsidizing the minors, the majors assumed most of the minors' operating costs.

As Chadwick explained, "The parent club would now pay players' salaries and most of their expenses, but did not have to pay a fee when it brought a player up to the majors. Owners of the minor league team, freed from the responsibility of bearing so much of the costs of their players, would in turn work harder to promote and run the club, and would profit from sales of tickets, souvenirs, food and beverages. The majors could keep their farm systems and development programs."

A new Class A, combining classes C and D, was created, in addition to rookie leagues for raw recruits. In addition, the new agreements included a structured draft system in which the big league club drafted each player, signed him to a major league contract, and assigned him to one of their minor league teams. As Chadwick emphasized, "The minor league teams no longer "owned" any players."

After bottoming out in 1963, attendance climbed the following year, reaching 9.9 million. While attendance continued to rise slowly, it only reached twelve million by the mid-1970s, less than a third of what it was in the late 1940s. By the early 1980s, however, the minors were booming once again, with forty new ballparks, and a dozen more were refurbished. Franchises were popping up throughout the country. Today, there are more than 150 cities and towns with minor league teams.

Resurgence of Interest

Minor league baseball is drawing big crowds again. The strong resurgence began sweeping across the country in the mid-1980s. Class A franchises, in particular, have sprung up everywhere. For the fourth year in a row, attendance exceeded 33 million fans, the highest totals in 50 years for leagues that comprise the National Association of Professional Baseball Leagues. The National Association and Major League Baseball Properties extended their licensing agreement through 2001. Under the partnership, retail sales of licensed minor league merchandise have grown from $2.5 million to an average of more then $38 million.

In giving several reasons for the renewed interest, Chadwick believes, "Televised games, which once kept fans from baseball parks, are now boosting attendance, the success of major league baseball on TV has whetted the appetite of fans for baseball. People are growing tired of life in the fast lane. The small-town atmosphere many people seem to want is to be found not in the huge, multi-million-dollar, cookie-cutter sports complexes of the majors, but in the tiny old bandbox stadiums of the minors."

Fans have become more interested in the development of future stars. They are aspiring a return to baseball's simple roots emulated at minor league parks. Interest in the minors received a boost from such Hollywood films as The Natural, Bull Durham, and Field of Dreams, glorifying the simplicity and the spirit of the game itself.

Traditionally, there has been a tendency for sports fans not to take the minors too seriously, that the game is more of a sideshow. To enhance their appeal and popularity, the minor leagues have organized all-star games of their own. "The Double-A and Triple-A classifications have been successful in making the all-star game viable," said Lingo, "an event that cities and teams want to have. They have added television and are getting their top prospects into all-star games."

Saving Baseball in Small Towns

I have always thought that bringing baseball to small towns that would not have baseball otherwise was what the minor leagues are all about. But in checking the Baseball America Directory, it is quite apparent that minor league baseball is leaving small-town America. The short-season New York-Penn League, for example, moved its Watertown, N.Y. franchise (population 28,700) to Staton Island, and Pittsfield, Mass. (46,315) may soon move to Brooklyn.

George Spelius, president of the Midwest League, believes "In the long run, it is going to be a hardship for small markets to compete. They are disappearing." Spelius said that of his three small-market teams, two were close to breaking even in 1998, and the other was going to lose money. "The only thing that keeps them hanging on," says Lingo, "is the guaranteed player-development contracts that the PBA brings."

Teams keep leaving traditional markets, however. "The Kinston Indians of the Carolina League, supported by a population of only 25,072, is making a go of it," said Lingo, "but may be the last hope for small-town baseball in the affiliated minor leagues."

The National Association appears to be taking an individual approach to the problem, which Lingo believes will not provide a solution. "With every club looking at its problem individually, the trend will not change. Operating a club will get more and more expensive, and smaller towns will slowly but surely disappear from the National Association."

"As more people outside the game buy franchises looking to make bigger dollars, small towns are going to lose out," said Johnson. "That's sad to me. That's supposed to be what minor league baseball is all about."

Striving for a Balanced Franchise   For over a half-century, the primary goal of the minor leagues has been to develop players and prepare them as prospects for the majors. They do it because major league teams spend a considerable amount of money on player development.   Player development is the lifeblood of any organization. Therefore, it is essential that the development system be supported so as not to eliminate the minor leagues.

Traditionally, a successful minor league franchise has meant the development of players for the parent club, fielding a competitive team, providing fans with fun and entertainment, and, hopefully, showing a profit at the end of the year. Much too often, however, there is a missing ingredient. During the stretch drive and the play-offs, many teams lack sufficient talent in their quest for the league championship. Most of their best players, particularly pitchers, have been called up, without replacements.

While the minors must continue to maintain a major commitment to player development, overemphasis on development has and will continue to turn off an even larger number of fans. Since their team rosters are predominately owned by the majors, players are subject to quick call-ups, with little return. As one general manager said, "We believe in the player development concept, but there seems to be a fine line when moving players up and down continuously." As a result, minor league fans share little identity with players who are shuffled back and forth on a farm director's whim. Championships are virtually meaningless with the roster instability. Fans find it hard to understand why their team is penalized when there is a call-up and no one to replace.

If the minors are to serve the game' best interests and those of the fans, clubs on all levels should be given the opportunity to strive for a "balanced franchise". Too much major league control can be detrimental to the minors, because tight controls can diminish initiative. Overemphasis on development has turned off many local fans who would like to see more emphasis on winning. On too many occasions, managers make decisions to develop players, not to win in all situations.

Is Player Development Working?   The minor leagues are the training ground for the major leagues. They exist today for the primary purpose of developing talent for the majors.   Big league clubs spend a

considerable amount of money on player development. Quite understandably, they want to make sure it is being spent efficiently.

But is the cost of player development too much? Major league owners claim that with average expenditures of $5.5 million per team on their farm and scouting systems, with a typical promotion rate of three minor leaguers per year to the active 25-man roster, the cost of developing an average player in the minor league system was $1.83 million.

Expansion has resulted in a dilution of talent, and as a result, players are moving too fast through the farm system. They are advancing without perfecting or improving their skills. Time and seasoning restraints does not permit skills to be taught and practiced as in the past. Application of the basic skills continues to decline, as has the knowledge and appreciation of the game. Fielding fundamentals have given way to offensive output. Team play and winning are stressed to a much lesser extent.

Most major league teams support six or seven minor league teams and promote players up through the ranks. Some minor leaguers move up through three levels of play in three years. Others do it in a single summer! Big league players who have had successful careers believe being held back in the minors actually helped them. Wade Boggs, for example, spent six years in the minors before getting the call. "When I went into pro ball at age seventeen, I was immature. I needed to learn the game, read pitchers, to hit to different fields. When I did move up to the majors, I was ready."

WHY SO FEW SUPER STARS? The major leagues today are not allowing the minors enough time to fully develop prospects. As a result of baseball's player development timetable, major league prospects are not maximizing their potential. In sharp contrast to the number of Super Stars in earlier decades, players with extraordinary potential are being stunted as a result of being rushed to the majors.

Potentially talented hitters, in particular, are receiving minimum minor league experience by their rapid promotion to the majors. Promising young hitters with natural talent are overmatched and hurt by being brought to the majors too early. Likewise, young pitchers are not getting enough time in the minors to perfect their craft. Prospects today are not getting enough seasoning and professional game experiences to develop their skills, instincts, and knowledge of the game.

The large majority of rookies are not fully prepared when they play their first game.

MORE TIME AT TRIPLE-A   An ever increasing number of prospects are skipping the Class AAA level entirely or just making a brief stop before being rushed to the majors. Consequently, these players have to learn and develop at the big league level. The scouts I have talked to strongly believe this has hurt the development of many players.

"There is no question even the exceptional players will be better off when they get to the majors if they have spent time at Triple-A," said Pirates general manager Cam Bonifay. "I only wish our club had the time and caliber of roster that would allow us the luxury of having our young players spend more time at Triple-A." At the AAA level, young players learn that if they make a mistake or two, it can change the overall outcome of the game, like missing a sign or the cut-off man with a throw.

Status of Play in Minors   Although fundamentals are being stressed in the minors, players are advancing without perfecting or improving their skills. Major league expansion has resulted in a dilution of talent. The lack of time and seasoning does not permit skills to be taught and practiced as in the past. Players are not as well-rounded in all phases of the game. The application of basic skills continues to decline, and this has caused a general decline in play at the minor league level. A large majority of minor league managers we surveyed, 73.8%, believe there has been a decline.

Players are not as fundamentally sound as those of a decade or two ago, when young players would learn to do things the Dodger way, the Yankee or Cardinal way. They would learn the same system in the lowest level all the way up to the majors, and the fact that players were in the minors for 4 or 5 years, they learned the basic fundamentals very well.

Players today are blessed with a combination of greater speed and strength. "Often a 6'4" player has not only power but also speed," said Bob Romero, general manager of the Yakima Bears. "However, the knowledge of the game and appreciation for it have decreased. While athleticism is on the rise, execution of the basic fundamentals has declined." Players are not always focused and do not work hard enough on the basics.

With the majors placing more emphasis on offensive production, fielding fundamentals have given way to offensive output, largely the long ball. Players are not as well-rounded in all phases. Team play and winning are stressed to a much lesser extent. Few players like to bunt. Bunting, baserunning skills and hitting behind the runner seem to be "lost arts". Young players get to AA who cannot execute a sacrifice bunt. They do not know how to run the bases. Players are lacking in defensive skills. Rundown plays are botched, and cut-off men are missed. Many young pitchers coming up today have not learned how to pitch, largely because they haven't had enough time in the minors to learn their craft.

Entertaining the Fans

Entertaining fans continues to be a major priority for minor league clubs. As the competition for the entertainment dollar grows, the minors have done an excellent job of providing high quality entertainment in a clean, wholesome environment. Their commitment to maintain affordable entertainment is unique and highly commendable in professional sports today.

Many teams emphasize an intimate family atmosphere, making the games a fun place to go to. "Every night should be FUN," North Johnson said, "It might be their first ball game together so it will have an everlasting impact." A competent, entertaining public address announcer can keep their attention with the promotions. Strong emphasis has been given to encouraging more young players to come to the ballpark and help them develop an appreciation and understanding of the game. They are the future for baseball.

From an entertainment standpoint, those who have to view such an ugly spectacle, brawls are not needed, and the minors have wisely come down hard on brawlers. Tough rules have proven a good deterrent to on-field fights. A player deemed by the league president to be an instigator or a primary combatant will receive an automatic fine and a minimum three-game suspension.

Fielding a Competitive Team

Although the minors have a major commitment to player development, every club has a responsibility to its fans to field a competitive team that plays hard and goes all out to win. A strong desire to win makes a big impression on fans. The most successful franchises are those who can field a continuity of strong teams, year after year. While many minor league people believe winning doesn't matter, I think it should. Despite the contention of many that winning plays a small part in attracting a good minor league crowd, major league farm directors should have more concern and help affiliates become more competitive.

A team's overall popularity and crowd appeal has to be enhanced if they can win. It has been said many times that "Winning is contagious", and the sooner prospects develop the winning spirit and attitude, the better off they and their organization will be. Winning is especially important at AAA because the right tone or frame of attitude has to be set for players to succeed at the big league level.

Dick Balderson, scouting director of the Chicago Cubs, said, "I don't know if seeing them win or lose is that important. It is "What are they giving away tonight?" But shouldn't more emphasis be given to team success and players accomplishments? Certainly, they would add even more to the popularity of minor league ball. If there were restrictions on the number of player moves a major league club could make each season, fans could better identify with players and more meaningful rosters would be established for championship competition.

Community Involvement By stressing their role as members
of the community, teams have found it easier to work out promotional deals with local businesses and to get help from local government. Indeed, a minor league team is the community's team.

Everyone connected to a minor league organization should strive to be as active and visible in the local community as time permits. Involvement in the community not only by the front office but the manager and players can go a long way in developing strong relations with local citizens, business people and governmental officials. Players should be accessible to the fans, helping out with promotions at the park and the community. Kids respond positively to autographs, handshakes, and conversations with their favorites. This is why the public relations and sales marketing staff work so hard at keeping the team visible in the community. Strong ties with the press can generate a positive following by the news media.

Economic Problems Grow   While the overall financial status of the minors is good, some clubs are still in debt due to acquisition costs, rising operational costs, and adhering to stiffer standards of stadiums. As a result of the current agreement, the majors have made it harder for the minors to operate financially.

An ever-increasing problem of the minors is to keep the small-market teams alive, as the big-market teams grow even bigger. "The yearly attendance disparity among Class-A teams in the same league often is tenfold," wrote Paul White in Baseball America. "By comparison, the best-drawing team in the majors does not attract even four times as many fans as the worst." Teams in the same league can have total operating budgets from $400,000 to $4 million. In the Midwest League, the operating budget of the Lansing Lugnuts is about 10 times that of the Clinton Lumber Kings. The differences are less dramatic at the higher levels.

Increased costs are a significant factor in the growing subdivision. As a result of the last two agreements, more financial burden has been placed on minor league teams. Prior to the attendance boom of the late 1980s, much of the operating costs were subsidized by the majors. Now the minors are sharing more of the costs. Umpire development costs more than $4 million a year, and the ticket-tax increase requires teams to pay a percentage of their gate receipts to Major League Baseball.

The minor league post-season continues to be a disappointment. The fans and the excitement usually are missing. For the most part, fans care little about the post-season, and as a result, it is difficult to sell play-off tickets with season-ticket packages. Texas League president Tom Kayser believes "It gets down to people not promoting post-season games as well as they do the regular season. In promoting the playoffs, teams should work as hard and operate in the same manner as they do during the regular season."

The Stadium Boom   Minor league cities are spending millions of dollars on beautiful new stadiums with no signs of stopping. The new stadium frenzy is re-shaping leagues throughout the country, causing attendance figures to soar. More minor league clubs are developing creative solutions to pay for their ballparks.

The big increase in new stadiums has been driven by demands from big league owners that their affiliates improve their facilities. The stadium building provisions of the 1990 PBA was unprecedented in minor league history. It contributed significantly to the decision of well over 60 franchises to construct new ballparks since 1987. To meet the new standards, numerous other stadiums were upgraded over the last few years.

Sec Taylor Stadium, home of the Iowa Cubs, was one of the first of the new wave of minor league parks. "In Des Moines, you can look across the river and see the gold dome of the capitol," said Branch Rickey, president of the Pacific Coast League. "It's as enjoyable a place to watch a baseball game as I've ever seen."

The seating capacity of the large majority of parks vary from 5,000 on up to 10, even 15,000 seats. The cost of construction also has a wide range, from several million dollars to the $22 million, 7,500- seat ballpark of the Lake Elsinore Storm of the California League.

NEW STADIUMS HAVE LOCAL INVOLVEMENT The new ballparks have all required some type of taxpayer assistance. In Oklahoma City, Southwestern Bell Park is perhaps the premier facility in all of minor league baseball. The $32 million stadium is part of a $350 million redevelopment project. Bob Burns wrote in the Sacramento Bee, "The redevelopment plan, which includes a new library, performing arts center and sports arena, is financed through a one-cent sales tax approved by Oklahoma City voters in 1993." In New Orleans, Zephyr Field, which cost $26 million, was financed by Louisiana's hotel and motel tax.

"I'm a real believer that cities or states should get involved," said former Oklahoma City mayor Ron Novick. "The ballpark has been a real focal point for entertainment and social activity." Although it was a tough sell at the time, the 13,066-seat stadium is already paying itself off. The Oklahoma Redhawks averaged more than 7,100 fans in 1998 at their new park which features 26 luxury boxes and 652 club seats.

Arthur Johnson, author of "Minor League Baseball and Local Economic Development", differs slightly with Novick's assessment. "No community's going to get back dollar for dollar what they invest in a team," he said. "But the investment can still be worth it if they develop new stadiums as part of a larger comprehensive community development plan."

After a 20-year absence, the PCL returned to California in 1998. The Fresno Grizzlies are playing at Pete Beiden Field on the Fresno State campus until a proposed downtown stadium opens in 2000. The Diamond Group, which owns the Grizzlies, has invested $20 million in the 12,500-seat stadium and will receive an additional $8.5 million grant from the city and county after the park is built.

Still, not everyone is anxious to spend money to build a new minor league park. Lingo wrote, "Many cities and counties have not chosen to spend public money to renovate old ballparks or build new ones. But the reality is that in today's minor league marketplace it probably means that city will lose its franchise."

Anti-Trust Threat Has Eased

In 1998, the Congress, followed by President Clinton's signature, voted to overturn part of the Supreme Court's ruling in 1922 that exempted baseball from anti-trust laws. The partial repeal applies only to the terms of employment between major league players and clubs, not to the minor leagues. The minors' concern about the exemption is with player movement, specifically the draft and the reserve clause.

If the exemption was repealed, the reserve clause and the amateur draft could be struck down. "If those things happen," said Stan Brand, NA vice president, "big league teams would have little incentive to spend millions on a player development system because they could not control players long enough to make development worthwhile."

Without that financial support, many minor league markets would not have professional baseball. The larger cities would likely survive but the franchises of small towns could be devastated. This is why the minor leagues will continue to help Major League Baseball defend the exemption.

Changes in Amateur Draft Expected

Baseball's amateur draft could soon undergo far-reaching changes. Major league officials are now studying all aspects of the very controversial draft and will likely make changes that will have a strong impact on Organized Baseball.

Players enter professional baseball through the annual June draft when they are selected by a single club that has the exclusive right to sign them. The player has the right not to sign, but if he exercises that right he then has to stay out of baseball until the next June, at which time another club may draft the exclusive rights to bargain with him.

Once signed, the player is bonded to the team for at least three and a half years. Beyond that, the major league club can keep the player in the minors and control him for another three years by placing him on the forty-man major league roster and optioning him to a minor league affiliate. A maximum of fifteen such optioned players is allowed per team. After the initial three and a half years, any player not put on the forty-man roster can be drafted by another big league team at the Rule-5 Draft held yearly at the Winter Meetings. A drafted amateur faces the prospect of six and a half years in the minors without the right to offer his services to another team or to accept competitive bids from other teams.

Exploitation of Minor Leaguers? Major League Baseball has often been accused for exploiting the conditions of minor league players. It is quite apparent that the salaries, benefits, and living conditions of minor leaguers are excessively poor compared to those of big leaguers. In 1950, the average salary in the majors was only 3.37 times the average salary in the highest classification minors. But in 1990, the average salary at the major league level had become 24.5 times the average Triple-A salary!

What caused the contrasting salaries to widen so greatly? The explosion of major league salaries can be attributed to such forces as free agency, arbitration and the inability of owners to control their spending. As to why the minors' salary scale failed to rise, those in baseball have always maintained that the minor leagues involves an extensive farm system for Major League Baseball, that the teams are all affiliates of the majors. Serving in a player development system, the large majority of players are essentially apprentices preparing for professional careers in the majors. Most of them are young, without families. Only a small percentage of them actually make it to the big leagues.

Just how low are the salaries of minor league players? Salaries begin at $850-$1000 per month (paid over two and one-half months) for first-year players and range up to an average of $6,000 per month for Triple-A players. The median Triple-A salary, however, is approximately $2,000 per month. The average is skewed upward by top draft picks and former big leaguers who sign minor league contracts.

While the employment conditions of minor league players need to be upgraded, there are obvious questions to be asked and consequences considered. What would happen to minor leaguers if they were not reserved by one club? How much greater remuneration should they receive? Who would get what? And, could the majors and the minors afford to pay more? Already, baseball's player development system is very expensive, approximately $1.83 million for an average player. The minor leagues would surely have to bear the brunt of the higher costs, and the current affordability of the minors would no longer be possible.

Minor league players have no union to fight their battles or file grievances on their behalf. Why doesn't the MLB Players Union include the minors? According to an official with the MLBPA, the logistics of having several thousand minor leaguers under the MLBPA umbrella would be overwhelming, because farm clubs exist on major league subsidies. During his tenure as the first executive director of the players union, Marvin Miller told minor league players if they couldn't organize, no one could do it for them. He explained that "Most organizing is done by employees with some help from the outside. In other words, the spark and initiative have to come from the inside."

Dick Balderson, vice president of Player Personnel for the Colorado Rockies, doesn't look for any attempt on the part of minor leaguers to organize. He told Jerry Crasnick of Baseball America, "There's no money to be made by representing minor leaguers." Balderson pointed out that the Rockies have a 401(k) retirement plan for their minor leaguers and pay 100 percent of the health insurance premiums. He added that "Minor leaguers with salary grievances have the right to appeal to the president of the NA.

Should playing baseball in the minor leagues continue to be regarded as an apprenticeship? The fact that no one, even Congress, has challenged the contrasting salaries of the two levels makes one believe that the system is working and is in the best interests of the game. As for being apprentices, perhaps Andrew Zimbalist said it best, in comparing minor league players with their counterparts in the performing arts and other professions. Zimbalist wrote, "It is not clear that minor leaguers have it so bad."

Building a Successful Franchise   The success of most minor league teams has been built on making games a fun and family-oriented event. Teams have become heavily involved with the community. "Community

is literally our middle name," said general manager Dan Mason of the Rochester Red Wings. An even more important factor in their success is because they have become businesses. Strong business participation with an ample number of corporate sponsors is essential to a good season ticket base. Of course, a positive working relationship with the major league affiliate, with good local support and cooperation from governmental agencies can provide much needed stability.

As Al Mangum, general manager of the Durham Bulls, told Bruce Chadwick, "Teams now run like corporations, with streamlined accounting, promotions and marketing. In the Sixties, teams were run by one or two guys who opened the ballpark and hoped somebody would show up."

Franchises are marketing their team as a regional attraction, even those on the lower levels. "A broader appeal gives the franchise more marketing opportunities," said North Johnson, "allowing the team to target different groups and a healthy supply of promotions." To achieve this goal, a strong marketing plan has to have creative and imaginative concepts and techniques.

Still, the key to boosting attendance is a new ballpark. The Charleston Riverdogs more than doubled their attendance by building a beautiful new ballpark on the river and getting the promotional genius of president Mike Veeck.

OWNERSHIP In earlier eras of minor league baseball, many clubs were owned by local civic leaders who had very little interest in the profit-and-loss statement. In the late 1970s and 1980s, however, a resurgence of interest in minor league baseball began sweeping the country. As Chadwick stated, "A new breed of minor league owner has replaced the old guard, introducing new, streamlined marketing and promotional campaigns, and convincing cities that it is in their economic interest to help keep teams and refurbish ballparks."

Today, as minor league franchise values soar, local ownership increasingly are selling out to wealthy businessmen from distant cities who have no stake in the community. While they lack the close ties their predecessors had with the community, many of the out-of-town owners have given the game the same no-nonsense business approach they used to make millions with their banking, law firms, and real estate companies.

In examining minor league teams as investments, Bloomberg Personal magazine wrote: "Minor league baseball today is best left to those with plenty of money and business savvy." It noted that the days are gone for deals like that of college professor Jerome Mileur, who bought the Harrisburg Senators (Eastern) for $85,000 in 1982 and sold them after the '94 season for $4 million.

FRONT OFFICE STAFF   The front office of minor league clubs today are run like corporations, with advanced accounting systems, creative promotions and imaginative marketing, combined with plenty of hoopla and give-aways.

Having a dedicated, hard-working front office is most essential for success, with creative, quality employees with energy, who are visible in the community, and spearheaded by a strong sales staff. Selling season tickets is still No. 1.

A good example is the San Bernardino Spirit franchise in which eight full-time people work in the front office:

- ✓ General Manager
- ✓ Assistant General Manager
- ✓ Director of Business Operations
- ✓ Director of Stadium Operations
- ✓ Director of Media/Public Relations
- ✓ Director of Sales/Marketing
- ✓ Director of Merchandising
- ✓ Director of Ticket Sales

FIELD MANAGER   For his team to succeed, the manager must have control in the clubhouse and the respect of his players. He can achieve both of these goals with good communication and showing a genuine interest in his players. Rather than be a tough, overdemanding disciplinarian, the manager has to enforce discipline and team rules.

Along with his duties on the playing field, a minor league manager should understand the business side of baseball, the marketing philosophy, that promotions are part of the game. He will please both the owner and the front office staff by sharing in the efforts to get people to the park.

ROLE OF MANAGER AND COACHES

- Be a teacher and don't assume players know the fundamentals
- Place greater emphasis on fundamentals in daily workouts
- Devote more time on the basics in spring training
- Follow-up with regular refresher practices during season
- Greater repetition of basic skills. Repeat, repeat, etc.
- Better evaluation of performance during games and practice
- Have more individual instruction, by conducting workouts with only 2 or 3 players participating
- Place emphasis on winning, not individual stats

FUNDAMENTAL APPROACH TO DEVELOPMENT   To achieve a more fundamental approach to player development, a good farm system should adhere to the following:

- Give prospects more seasoning and development
- Slow down the "Rushing Factor"
- Be better prepared during spring training
- Place more emphasis on instructional leagues
- Provide an environment in which young players can receive daily coaching and refinement of their skills
- Have fewer games to allow more time to practice and rest

Innovative Marketing/Promotions   Successful promotions, cleverly marketed, have helped the minors a great deal – getting people to come out to the park for the FUN of it. "Promotions make the ballpark a fun place to go and that builds family business," said Larry Schmittou, who has owned several minor league teams. Multimedia packaging has worked very well for Lou Schwechheimer of the Pawtucket Red Sox. One company can purchase television, radio, billboards, yearbook ad, etc. in a "packaged price".

Every minor league game is an event -- the fan's ticket to excitement. Therefore, every club's goal is to get as many people into the stadium as possible. "An empty seat never bought a hot dog," said one veteran owner.

Every season should be preceded by a strong and intense sales campaign. Norfolk general manager Dave Rosenfield said it best, "Success is built on something very simple: SELLING TICKETS. We have very reasonable pricing, so it's something people can afford." Among the multitude of giveaways are caps, tee-shirts, baseball card sets, and seat cushions. Some of the favorite events are home-run derbies, fire works displays, softball games, and concerts. Team mascots are always popular, like the Durham Bull, Carolina Chicken, and Tony the Tiger.

Team names, logos and nicknames that have appeal and are catchy sell more merchandise. Nicknames are starting to make a comeback, thanks to Motorboat Jones, Bubba Smith, Skeeter Barnes, and others. Giving a guy a nickname is a sure way to add more appeal and popularity. New teams are taking the names of now defunct teams that once played in the same towns, such as the Wilmington Blue Rocks and Scranton-Wilkes Barre Red Barons.

Mike Veeck, son of baseball's legendary promotional wizard, the late Bill Veeck, has provided his own type of promotional flair and crowd appeal. His successes with the St. Paul Saints and elsewhere have featured many creative and crazy ideas. Prior to the game, Mike spends about 45 minutes at the turnstiles, taking tickets and sharing laughter with the fans. Veeck learned from his father that "If you promote it, they will come."

Independent Leagues Seek Stability
Following their explosive growth in the mid-1990s, independent leagues are still flourishing, despite a high failure rate. Many changes continue to occur, like new franchises, teams switching leagues and those who fail to make it. Teams are moving to larger markets. With many leagues downsizing, league presidents are constantly looking for better markets in their quest for stability.

In 1997, indy leagues drew more than 30 million fans. The Winnipeg Goldeyes drew 22,081 fans to one game. There were eight independent leagues with 58 teams. With box seats to a big league game selling for $25 and more, independent teams are charging $4 to $6. Team names range from the Ohio Valley Redcoats to the Adirondack Lumberjacks to the Moose Jaw Diamond Dogs.

Without big league affiliations, many clubs are having difficulty getting quality players. Most independent teams are composed largely of undrafted college players. Teams that survive are those who have sufficient cash flow to get their operations rolling. Those who don't are either underfunded or too ambitious. Most of the failed teams were owned and operated by the league presidents. When attendance falls short, the cash flow is not available.

The man who led the independent renaissance is Miles Wolff, the Northern League commissioner and publisher of Baseball America. In 1994, Wolff revived the Northern as an independent league with no major league subsidization. As Bruce Chadwick wrote, "Owners were confident that a well-organized league, with salary caps to keep down costs, would permit local teams to make money, play good baseball, and provide a competitive game. League officials promoted the league heavily, worked with local merchants on advertising and ticket campaigns, and invited major league scouts to check out the players. All of the opening day games sold out."

The Northern League continues to be the elite organization in independent baseball, attracting more than a million fans in a season. The St. Paul Saints, Northern's flagship team, have played to near capacity since they opened, outdrawing the Minnesota Twins on at least one occasion. The Saints are unique due to their metropolitan location and having benefitted by the promotional wizardry of former co-owner and president, Mike Veeck. The Northern League has a salary cap of $78,000, covering the entire team for the season. Jim Caple wrote in Athlon Sports Baseball 1998, "The cap provides a level playing field throughout the league and makes the players more appealing. Fans can relate to the independent players who squeeze by on as little as $600 a month to keep their baseball dreams alive."

Good markets are still in short supply. While the financial stability of independent leagues will be an on-going problem, their long term success will be determined largely by how many viable markets they are able to move into. The Texas-Louisiana League has reestablished itself as a topflight league, after struggling to recover from the woes of a couple of bad franchises and an expansion plan that was too ambitious.

Despite the explosion of independent minor leagues, there is still a significant inconsistency in the caliber of the teams, as well as how the leagues are organized. Since a major concern is the quality of players, many teams have taken steps to upgrade the playing talent and to recruit some hometown heroes, players that fans can identify with. Additional concerns are: where to find ballparks, how much to pay players, and how to win fans.

If and when the minors downsize, and it appears they will eventually, many look for independent leagues to take up the slack. Because of their market size, some good, well-supported minor league teams will lose their teams. The economics of operating those teams will become so great that baseball will outprice itself to operate in those communities. At which time, independent teams will take over. If the amateur draft was held later on in the summer, players could use indy leagues as a place to enhance their draft status.

More than ever, there is a market for independent baseball in America. While attendance has improved, the question remains as to how many fans will support indy leagues in the future. Kevin Trainor, correspondent for Baseball America, believes a change in emphasis should be made "from being a second-chance development league for undrafted players to providing a more advanced degree of baseball." Meantime, the leagues are striving to gear themselves for long-term survival.

Women in Professional Baseball
After an absence of over 50 years, a growing number of women's baseball leagues are being organized or in the planning stages. The concept of a women's professional league has been attempted several times but without much success. In 1943, the Chicago Cubs owner Philip K. Wrigley came up with the idea of women playing pro baseball when he created the All-American Girls Professional Baseball League.

During baseball's 1993 winter meetings, the formation of an all-woman baseball team, the Colorado Silver Bullets, was announced by Bob Hope. The creation of the Silver Bullets ended baseball's ban on women, established in 1931 when Commissioner Keneshaw Mountain Landis deemed the game "too strenuous for women." Hope, the Silver Bullets' owner and president, and manager Phil Niekro, assembled the highest quality of women baseball players available in the country.

Sponsored by Adolph Coors Brewery, the Silver Bullets lost 21 of their first 22 games. The losses continued even though the team lowered the quality of competition from professional teams to local men's semi-pro and all-star squads. The Bullets finished 6-38 in their maiden season, followed by an 11-33 mark in 1995. After switching from wood to aluminum bats in 1996, they were 14-16 with metal but only 4-17 with wood. In 1997, the Bullets finished above .500 for the first time in the team's history, with a 23-22 record. However, the following season after losing their sponsor, the team folded and were unable to find another.

Pamela Davis, a 21-year-old right-hander with the Silver Bullets, was the first woman to play for a major league farm club under the current structure of the minor leagues. On June 4, 1996, Davis pitched a scoreless fifth inning and got the victory in the Jacksonville Suns' 7-2 exhibition victory against the Australian Olympic team.

WOMEN'S PRO LEAGUES ORGANIZE   The Ladies Professional Baseball League opened its second season in 1998, bolstered by nine former members of the Colorado Silver Bullets. Founded by President Mike Ribant, the six-team league is comprised of the Arizona Peppers, Long Beach Aces, San Jose Spitfires, Buffalo Nighthawks, Florida Legends, and the New Jersey Diamonds.

A 56-game schedule culminate with a best-of-five World Series. Each team has 18 players, making from $850 to $1,500 a month, about the same for a Class A men's player. Ribant has a three-year plan that calls for securing corporate sponsorships. Otherwise, the league could be in trouble. "The Silver Bullets folded because they lost their sponsors," Ribant said. "Not many can operate without one."

Peter Kirk and his Maryland Baseball Limited Partnership appears to have discovered the right formula. Kirk's group, which owns the Bowie Bay Sox (Eastern), Frederick Keys (Carolina), and Delmarva Shorebirds (So. Atlantic) started a four-team women's league in 1998, using its three ballparks and another in the area. Kirk believes this league could avoid similar problems because they control three ballparks and have good relationships with other minor league teams in the area. Schedules are coordinated so that their games are played when minor league teams are on the road.

Serving as chairman/CEO for the Bowie Baysox, Kirk can be contacted at the following address:

Bowie Baysox, P.O. Box 1661, Bowie, MD 20717
Telephone: (301) 805-6000   Fax: (301) 805-6008

FIRST WOMAN TO START PRO GAME Ila Borders, a 23-year old left-hander with the Duluth Superior Dukes, continues to blaze a trail for women in baseball. On July 9, 1998, she became the first woman to start a professional game when she pitched five innings in the independent Northern League. At one point in the season, Borders ran off 12 straight shutout innings. Mark Derewicz wrote, "She spots her pitches well, changes speeds and throws her curve ball so that it falls just out of the strike zone." Ila says she wants to get better and isn't fixated on being one of the few women to ever play professional baseball.

"She's a true role model for young, aspiring female athletes who want to play baseball," said Derewicz of Baseball America. According to Kostya Kennedy, "Ila isn't big league bound but she's holding her own among the boys." On CBS's "60 Minutes" show, Borders was asked by Mike Wallace, "Do you feel like a pioneer?" She replied, "No. To me, I'm playing the game because I love it. I'm really in a dream, playing professional baseball. Everything that has happened to me is what I have wanted since I was 10 years old."

CAN WOMEN MAKE IT IN PRO BALL? In her article, "Playing hardball" in The Sporting News, Susan Fornoff thinks, "The physicality of women could very well enable them to reach unprecedented heights." She explained that "Women's natural inferiority in upper-body strength generally limits her ability to hit the ball hard or far, but her lower-body strength and agility may allow her to pitch adequately and field well."

"Baseball, more than any other team sport, forgives the physically flawed and embraces the short player, the skinny player, the fat player, even the player born without a hand (such as the remarkable accomplishments of southpaw Jim Abbott). Someday, baseball will open its arms to a woman."

"But that can't happen," said Fornoff, "until the woman player's training and preparation equals that of the men, particularly during her teen years. The mentality that softball is for women and baseball is for men has steered young girls away from their first love, baseball, to the game they think they should play."

Baseball and softball are very different sports. Hitting is where women playing baseball have had to make the most adjustments. They are swinging heavier bats now and the swing is completely different. Aluminum bats used in softball, for example, are at least 5 ounces lighter than the wood models a baseball player must swing quickly enough to make contact with a smaller ball traveling at a higher speed. Since their average weight is about 145 pounds, not many women are able to hit home runs. They need to concentrate on hitting the ball hard. Women on the Bullets were used to swinging 25-26-ounce aluminum bats. Then they had to swing 30 to 32-ounce bats and they just were not conditioned physically.

Indeed, Ila Borders does not throw like a girl. In fact, the phrase "You throw like a girl" is just a myth," according to Erika Salemme of Inside Sports. "The wrong foot forward, the elbow bent at a ridiculous angle, the entire motion looking like some sort of spastic fit."

"With the same training, women can throw just as hard as their male counterparts," stated the Penn State Sports Medicine Newsletter. "Recognizing obvious anatomical differences between men and women, no scientific data indicates that those differences prevent either gender from correctly throwing a baseball. The differences that do matter are in muscle development, proper training, and experience."

"Women traditionally don't receive as much early sports instruction as men do," said Salemme. "In many cases, by the time a girl becomes involved in sports that involve throwing a ball, her motions already are off and she has lost flexibility in her shoulder – two important elements in correcting bad form. With the correct training, muscle development, flexibility, and most importantly, practice – women are just as able to throw like major leaguers as men are," said Salemme.

NATIONAL ASSOCIATION

National Association of Professional Baseball Leagues
Office Address: 201 Bayshore Dr. SE, St. Petersburg, FL 33701
Mailing Address: P.O. Box A, St. Petersburg, FL 33731
Telephone: (727) 822-6937   Fax: (727) 821-5819

President/Chief Executive Officer: Mike Moore
Assistant to President: Carolyn Ashe
Vice President: Stan Brand (Washington, DC)
Treasurer/Chief Operating Officer
   and V.P. Administration: Pat O'Conner

Baseball Around The World

Baseball on a global scale is a sleeping giant ready to explode.

The Olympic Games used to be the exclusive preserve of amateur athletes.

A World Cup of Baseball will widen the sport's appeal on the international level.

Now the Pro's have taken over in the Games.

Major League Baseball is becoming more involved internationally.

Should professional athletes compete in the Olympics?

The future of big leaguers in global competition should be in a World Cup.

Strong opposition to the dilution of Olympic spirit by the invasion of pro athletes.

6 USA Baseball/ International

As baseball continues to grow throughout the world, teams representing the USA are becoming more involved in international competition. For many decades, the majors and minors have had a strong international flavor, but competitive opportunities for American teams against other nations have been limited primarily to the Little League World Series, occasional competitions for teenagers, collegians, and the Olympic Games.

The spread of baseball worldwide has grown rapidly since the IOC made baseball an official sport, starting with the 1992 Barcelona Games. At the 1996 Olympics in Atlanta, baseball ranked No. 3 among all the sports in attendance. The number of baseball playing nations has increased from 60 to over 100 since the IOC's 1986 decree. In many parts of the world, baseball has become the sport of the future.

USA Baseball, as a result of an Act of Congress in 1978, became the National Governing Body (NGB) for the sport representing all of amateur baseball in America, the U.S. Olympic Committee and the International Baseball Association. USA Baseball is responsible for putting together the teams that represent the country at junior and senior level international tournaments, including the Olympic Games. With 16 national and 57 regional member organizations, USA Baseball governs over 20 million amateur athletes in this nation. In essence, USA's primary mission is to provide leadership for growth and development both nationally and internationally for baseball.

Major League Baseball is becoming more involved internationally. As Will Lingo stated in Baseball America, "International baseball is gaining unprecedented momentum and MLB appears ready to capitalize on it." However, the future of major leaguers in international competition will be in a World Cup tournament, not the Olympics. A World Cup will do far more for the game than for the championship team of Major League Baseball to play a specific country in a World Series event.

Challenges Faced by USA Teams

A number of problems and controversial issues have clouded the picture relative to USA's participation on the international level. While Major League Baseball has most of the greatest players in the game, United States teams on other levels have not done well over the years in worldwide competition. There is a serious need for everyone connected with USA Baseball to address the shortcomings of America's system of player development and, in particular, place greater emphasis on the development and training of players at the youth league level.

The success of USA Little League teams, dating as far back as the 1960s, leaves much to be desired. Taiwanese youth, far more physically advanced and better prepared, have dominated American children in the L.L. World Series, largely the result of the inequities of training and physical and emotional maturity.

In the Olympics and other international competitions, Cuba has had the strong advantage of a highly regimented government sponsorship that provides a development system for youth as young as 9 years of age. Players are developed with extraordinary training discipline and practice commitment. The USA Olympic team, in sharp contrast, has consisted mostly of young college players put together in June following the College World Series. With a 20-man roster of 20 and 21-year olds, Team USA has competed against the world's national teams comprised of players 26-30 or older who have played together for years. With no professional leagues, Cuba's best players are considered "amateurs".

After considerable review, however, including lengthy discussions with Major League Baseball, the decision was made by USA Baseball to use professional players. The team, which represented the USA at the 1999 Pan Am Games in Winnipeg, was comprised of veterans and top prospects in the minor leagues. As to who will play on USA's team in the Sydney Olympics is still in question. MLB has stated that players on 40-man rosters would be allowed to play.

Should professional athletes compete in the Olympics? A growing number of fans detest the dilution of Olympic spirit by the invasion of pro athletes. There

USA teams have not done well in global play

Making USA teams more competitive

Systematic approach to player development is needed

Stronger youth development programs coordinated by USA Baseball

Higher level of coaching at the Youth levels

Nation-wide, regionally located academies and training centers are most essential to developing a systematic approach to player development

are also those who like to believe the barriers between amateurism and professionals are crumbling. But are they and should they be? While top minor leaguers were used in the Pan American Games, a large majority of those who responded to our national survey believe the pro's have no place in the Olympics. The Olympics should be for amateurs, they said, with the pro's competing in a World Cup. Later, I will compare the two philosophies, formulate conclusions, and make recommendations.

Systematic Approach To Development

Through the years, the development of young baseball players in America has remained the same, a non-structured system with minimal government involvement, with much of the development and training provided by the youth league organizations, high schools, colleges, and USA Baseball, the governing body. America's system of development has been highly successful in producing the best players in the world, the major leaguers, but where the system is failing is at the youth league levels, a result of modern society, combined with the shortcomings of organization and leadership.

In sharp contrast to our system, Cuba has developed a sophisticated training system that identifies potential stars as early as 9. By the time they are teenagers, many are in specialized baseball schools, playing the year around. No, America does not need Cuba's regimented system. The present system developed by USA Baseball, for the most part, appears to be working, but a more systematic approach to development is needed throughout the youth league levels, from Little League on up. The current system lacks sufficient cohesion and coordination.

Making USA Teams More Competitive

To be more successful, USA teams in the future need a more structured and productive system of development and training, implemented by all youth baseball organizations in the country. It is most essential that players be given more time and experience to develop a higher level of skills and a broader knowledge of the game. A more efficient and disciplined program must be developed with greater resources and commitment than ever before.

A more systematic approach to development would be particularly beneficial to our most promising 14-17 year old prospects, by having them attend baseball academies from 4 to 6 weeks. Such an academy concept would be similar to the Cuban program, but geared to the realities of our society and culture. The academies would be conducted regionally under the auspices of USA Baseball, with top college and high school coaches serving as instructors. The program would conclude with an Academy National Championship, with the regional winners competing for the title. While USA's headquarters are now centralized in Tucson, there is still a need for regionally located academies.

Getting the kids of America playing and practicing more on their own is of the greatest importance, a renaissance of playground baseball, re-introducing young children to fun-oriented pick-up games, in the backyard, a vacant lot, or on park-school diamonds. For these concepts to make a successful comeback, however, will not come easy, but grassroots programs and activities are most essential to their growth and development. Young children need to play more on their own, in parks, schools or around the home.

Stronger Youth Development Needed
The systems of training and developing young baseball players in such countries as Cuba, Taiwan and Japan are superior to the American system. The advantages are numerous, largely the result of greater involvement and assistance from their governments, school systems, specialized training, and physical and emotional maturation at earlier ages. For many decades, young American children have had to compete against these inequities of development.

Little League and other youth baseball programs in the U.S., with the help of recreation and park agencies, schools, service clubs, and corporate America, should develop a more efficient and productive system of development and training for our children. The system that has been used the past four decades is not working. To compete favorably with teams from Latin America and the Far East, a better program should be developed, with greater resources and commitment than ever before.

Higher coaching standards, a more disciplined approach to practice and training and greater access to how-to instructional materials are much needed. In addition, a nationwide promotional campaign should be conducted, with the support of past and present major league players, with support from the news media, to motivate children to join a "renaissance of baseball", a revival of pick-up games, sandlot and playground baseball, with a greater number of kids playing on their own and with their buddies.

Hit, Run And Throw   The most successful and innovative program to develop baseball skills is Honda's Hit, Run and Throw contest which is offered to schools, parks and after-school programs in a growing number of countries. It has created great awareness of baseball in schools by offering quality lesson plans, free equipment for physical education classes and recreation programs.

Canada's program began in 1995 at over 200 local sites throughout the country, with the winners advancing to about 50 regional sites, followed by 10 provincial finals. The program consists of five age divisions: boys 12-13, girls 12-13, and mixes 10-11, 8-9 and 7 and under. The champions from each of the provinces are flown to Toronto's Skydome to compete for the Canadian championship prior to a Toronto Blue Jays' game in September.

Higher Coaching Standards Urgently Needed

A major weakness in the player development system in America is the quality of coaching at the lower youth league levels. The large majority of those who coach at this crucial level are parents who know very little about coaching a team and how the game is played. Still, Little League and other youth baseball programs in the U.S. refuse to take the necessary steps to train and certify their coaches.

Many years ago, countries like Canada and Australia developed model certification programs for their coaches, a major factor in the rapid development of young players. As a result of the National Coaching Certification Program (NCCP), baseball in Canada has more than 60,000 certified coaches. The fact that the certification of coaches in the U.S. is not a high priority is a major weakness in America's player development system.

Comparing Development Systems

For years, baseball teams representing the United States have had difficulty competing against teams from Cuba, Taiwan, Japan and Latin America. Surely, the success of the Cubans, Taiwanese and Japanese can be attributed to the unique advantages of their development systems. The following shows how contrasting their systems are compared to how young players are developed in the United States.

United States

America's system of player development, in sharp contrast to those in Cuba, Taiwan, and Japan, is far less intense and regimented. Most children in the United States start playing baseball at an early age, usually with local youth programs such as Little League. Volunteer parents serve as coaches, helping organize the leagues, draft the players, manage the teams, umpire the games, maintain the fields, and operate the concession stands. Boys and girls from age five to six are taught the basic techniques of the game by volunteer coaches, many of them inexperienced and uncertified, using various methods and levels of instruction.

When players reach high school age, they try out for the school team, and the best players earn the right to represent their schools. After graduating from high school, many players enroll at a college or university to continue their education, and the most talented players try out for the college team. The best players receive scholarships. The most skilled high school players choose to sign professional contracts instead of going to college, and begin their pro careers in Rookie Leagues. Each year, USA Baseball invites the top prospects who reach 18 and 19 and the most talented college players to try out at the National Training Center in Tucson, Arizona.

Cuba

School children in Cuba are introduced to baseball in the early elementary grades. Little boys in the first and second grades can be seen practicing one hour each day after school. Cubans, of course, have the distinct advantage of the Caribbean climate which allows them to play baseball the year around.

The sheer pleasure of playing baseball, a strong passion and love for the game, and the drama of competition they exude is quite evident among Cuban children and adults. Like American youngsters did a half century ago, Cuban kids play often on their own, in pick-up games on vacant lots, even on dusty streets. It is common for both boys and men to play the game during their free time. Despite a limited amount of equipment, Cubans have an intense loyalty and devotion for baseball, combined with an undeniable amount of discipline and commitment.

The top prospects are identified at an early age and funneled into baseball schools to develop the talent. Young children are given a rigid screening, a process which takes the more skilled players to more advanced levels. Coaches' manuals set year-by-year standards for young players. Even at the equivalent of the Little League level, coaches keep precise player records. At the age of 15, the most promising players are sent to a highly specialized school where they train and compete with the best of the country. From an overall 400 players, an estimated 50 young baseball players attend the elite academy in Havana. Each of Cuba's 14 provinces has a baseball academy, and the best players are placed on teams representing the various provinces.

Like a major league club, Cuba's national squad has its own farm system, run by the government, recruiting players as young as 10 years old. Technically, the Cuban players are not paid as baseball players. Rather, they perform for the Cuban national as amateurs. While they have jobs and receive certain advantages, players receive only about $20 a month.

Japan

The Japanese baseball player begins playing at a very young age, partly because of the Japanese cultural need for group activity. Parents want their children to learn spirit and discipline. "In Japan, even from the elementary school level, you join one team, or one club, and you are a member for life," wrote Larry Fuhrmann. "If a kid in elementary school chooses to play baseball, he will not likely play any other sport."

Unlike American baseball, the heritage of the game in Japan is rooted in amateurism. College baseball rivalries are the oldest in the nation. The nation's single biggest sporting event is the National High School Baseball Summer Championship tournament, an event that rivals the Olympics in its pageantry and appeal to the Japanese people.

"Once they arrive in professional leagues, Japanese players are expected to take on the role of sameness, fully integrating themselves into the group," said Fuhrmann. "Individualism is frowned upon and this sameness has its root in the Bushido code of the samurai. Although ideas are changing, this unofficial code of honor still remains strong. For instance, a player is expected to follow the manager's orders without question, no matter how difficult, harsh, or unusual they seem."

Because of all their training, the Japanese are some of the most superbly conditioned and disciplined athletes in the world. They are also well schooled in the fundamentals. The Japanese place great emphasis on long and hard practices. Training camp is intense and exhausting. There are endless hours of conditioning, batting, fielding and pitching, with numerous drills on the basic fundamentals. Managers still hold rigorous 3 or 4 hour workouts before a game.

Players on Japanese Olympic teams are regarded as amateur players who come from the nation's industrial leagues. Typically, older and more experienced internationally, they receive most attractive salaries for playing baseball all year for a corporation to promote their products.

Taiwan   The overpowering domination of American teams by Taiwan in the Little League World Series is largely the result of two highly contrasting programs of development and training. Youth teams from Taiwan have benefited greatly by strong governmental promotion and sponsorship through the school system. For example, the Ministry of Education in Taiwan identifies about 150 target schools with the potential to develop championship teams. The government will then provide living expenses for 50 coaches at these schools. In addition, the government provides baseball equipment to all needy schools.

While most American elementary schools have fewer than 1,000 students, some schools in Taiwan have more than six times that. But the number of students in a team's area is not the major reason for Taiwan's domination of American Little Leaguers. Rather, the one-sided competition is because of many other factors, such as significant differences in training, instruction, practice time, discipline and commitment, governmental sponsorship and payment of coaches, all of which have given Taiwanese players huge advantages over USA children.

Taiwanese teams and their coaches have had an intense, all-out approach to winning, with strong emphasis on sound fundamentals. Their players are superbly trained. Since volunteerism is not a well ingrained concept and volunteer coaches are difficult to find, Taiwanese coaches are paid, usually teachers at schools. Baseball is offered in all the schools, from elementary schools through junior high and high school. Players at target schools will practice 90 minutes before school and 90 minutes after school. Teams work out an average of three hours per day during summer and winter vacations. The weather permits year-round play.

USA Baseball

USA Baseball is responsible for promoting and developing the game of baseball on the grassroots level, both nationally and internationally. It is a resource center for its various membership groups, fans, and players. Nearly every major national amateur baseball organization in America has been united as a national member of USA Baseball. As a governing organization, USA Baseball strives to coordinate, not duplicate, individual member organizations, programs and projects, so as to provide services unique and essential to amateur baseball.

Ever mindful that America's baseball teams have not fared well in international play, USA Baseball appears to be on the right track in maximizing the competitive capabilities of teams on the senior and junior levels. Under the leadership of executive director Dan O'Brien, USA Baseball's staff of administrators and coaches is striving to utilize all available resources in an effort to put stronger squads on the playing field.

All three of America's national baseball teams train in Tucson, Arizona, with centralized planning and quality personnel and facilities. Each autumn and winter, USA Baseball conducts its National Trials at Hi Corbett Field to evaluate players for consideration for the following summer's National Team.

USA Baseball has an annual budget from $3 to $5 million. In addition, the U.S. Olympic Committee allocates $10,000 per athlete per year to affiliated programs which finish with a gold, silver, or bronze medal. Since the U.S. has 20 players on the Olympic squad, USA Baseball will receive $800,000 for the next four years.

Mailing address for USA Baseball's Corporate Headquarters is:
Hi Corbett Field, 3400 E. Camino Campestre, Tucson, AZ 85716.
Telephone: (520) 327-9700. FAX: (520) 327-9221. E-mail address, usabasebal@aol.com. Web Site: www.usabaseball.com.

Chairman: Cliff Lothery   President: Neil Lantz

Executive Vice President: Tom Hicks
Executive Director/CEO: Dan O'Brien Sr.

International Baseball Association   In 1975 at a

meeting in Mexico City, amateur baseball agreed to form the International Association of Amateur Baseball, later becoming the International Baseball Association. The IBA is the governing body for world baseball, responsible for conducting world championships and invitational tournaments at different age levels. It assists the IOC in organizing competition in the Olympic games. The IBA now has 108 national federations, more than double the 1993 number. Of the 14 current members of IBA's executive board, five are from Europe, three from the Americas, and Asia, Africa, and Oceania each have two representatives.

The IBA is responsible for developing baseball world-wide by providing coaching, instructional materials, equipment, as well as technical and financial assistance to its membership. "The IBA gives money to the continents for development," said Aldo Notari, president of the IBA, as well as the European Baseball Confederation. "Every continent decides what is the best system on their continent." As the IBA strives to develop baseball in the world, the quest for progress continues to be stymied by poverty. Despite strong development in many parts of the world, poverty remains a major problem elsewhere.

When one considers the remarkable growth and development of the IBA, Dr. Robert E. Smith, who served as president for well over a decade, deserves a great amount of praise and gratitude, which is why he was honored by more than 15 foreign governments and organizations for exemplary services. Smith played a major role in convincing the IOC to approve baseball as an official sport. As president, he made a major impact on the game worldwide.

IBA headquarters is located in Lausanne, Switzerland, close to the IOC and other international sports governing bodies. Mailing address of the IBA is: Avenue de Mon-Repos 24, Case Postale 131, 1000 Lausanne 5, Switzerland.

Telephone: (41-21) 3188240.   Fax: (41-21) 3188241
E-mail address: iba@baseball.ch.   Website: www.baseball.ch.

Major League Baseball International

Established in 1989, Major League Baseball International (MLBI) has done much to globalize baseball in the fields of marketing, broadcasting, licensing, sponsorship and development of the game. During the 1990s, this enterprise has contributed much in expanding the understanding and appreciation of baseball world-wide. It has introduced the game in a growing number of nations.

Major League Baseball International has sent numerous American college coaches and organized baseball instruction to countries throughout the world as part of its envoy coaching program. During the summer of 1996, for example, thirty-one coaches traveled to 23 countries for two months of teaching and training in each nation. In schools and during clinics, they taught the fundamentals of the game to the local teams. Most deserving of recognition for their strong contributions to MLBI are such dedicated people as Bill Artz, David Osinski, and Tim Brosnan.

"The Envoy Program is an integral part of our top-down and bottom-up strategy to develop the game," explained Brosnan, chief operating officer of the MLBI. "World-wide television exposure, coupled with grassroots development, will ensure baseball's long-term growth internationally."

MLBI's game development strategy includes tours, clinics, instructional videos, exhibition games, team exchanges and equipment donations and Fan Fests. The highly successful Pitch, Hit, and Run program has been expanded to Germany, Great Britain, Japan, Korea, and Taiwan. In its first year in Germany, the program was adopted in almost 200 schools, including 20,000 students aged 12 to 14.

Mailing address of MLBI: 245 Park Avenue, 30th Floor, New York, NY 10167. Telephone: (212) 931-7500. Fax: (212) 949-5795.

Senior Vice President, Licensing: Tim Brosnan

The Olympic Games

The Olympic Games used to be the exclusive preserve of amateur athletics. For three-quarters of a century, the Olympic Games provided amateur athletics with competitive opportunities in sports. Traditionally, the purpose of the Olympics was "to conduct a world-wide sports festival, a universal celebration of sport and sportsmanship. The Olympic spirit burned ever so brightly when the Games were the domain of amateurs who relished the sport, the competition, and the fellowship.

Baron Pierre de Coubertin was a strong advocate of "sport for sport's sake." For 31 years, de Coubertin worked actively as president of the International Olympic Committee. Even in 1894, he warned against what later became known as "commercialization" of sport. To the end, de Coubertin fought to keep athletics on a lofty plane. "What greater motivation is there for young athletes than to participate in the Olympic Games, to strive for an Olympic championship medal, and the opportunity to represent their country? The Olympics should truly be a world-wide sports festival traditionally conceived."

The eloquent words of de Coubertin still appear on electronic scoreboards at opening ceremonies of the Games: "The most important thing in the Olympic Games is not to win but to take part, just as the most important thing in life is not the triumph but the struggle. The essential thing is not to have conquered but to have fought well."

In 1930 at an Olympic Congress in Berlin, a new definition of amateurism was adopted: "To be eligible for participation in the Olympic Games, a competitor must not have received any financial rewards or material benefit in connection with his or her sports participation, except as permitted in the bye laws to this rule." Later, in 1967, the Congress ruled that "Individuals subsidized by governments, educational institutions or business concerns because of their athletic ability are not amateurs." In 1974, a new draft rule stated that, "A competitor must not be or have been a professional athlete in any sport or contracted to be so before the official closing of the Games."

Avery Brundage gained worldwide fame as president of the International Olympic Committee from 1952 to 1972, the first American to hold the highest office in the world of amateur sport. An ardent advocate of amateur athletics, Brundage faced an array of troubling issues during his presidency, including commercialism, nationalism, politics, gigantism, doping, etc. In the early 1960s, however, a number of sports federations were expressing their dissatisfaction with some of the IOC's actions and decisions. They felt they should have a more significant voice, and many formed the General Assembly of International Federations.

When Juan Antonio Samaranch became president of the IOC, any reference to the world "Amateur" was deleted from the Olympic charter. It was now simply "The best athletes" in each sport that competed in the Games. The true Olympic spirit was given a cruel blow by the advocates of professionalism. To support this revolutionary change, Samaranch, himself, selected those who would agree with his philosophy, those who represented corporate and commercial interests.

While professional athletes in other sports have been allowed to compete in the last few Olympiads, member countries of the International Baseball Association remained opposed to the inclusion of pro's until 1996. At which time, IBA nations were forced to allow professionals in after intense pressure was put on the IBA by the IOC. Samaranch had made it clear that the future of baseball in the Games would depend on the admission of professionals in future Olympics. A negative vote for pro's would almost have sealed baseball's death as a future Olympic sport.

The growing movement toward professionalism and Dream Teams is disturbing to those who understand the true meaning and spirit of the Olympic Games. The true Olympics is about amateur athletes, not a group of overpaid professional all-stars. Peter Ueberroth, president of the 1984 Los Angeles Olympic Organizing Committee, had the right idea when he said, "Our goal is to make the Olympics a sporting event again, to put on a Games that goes back to the early principles of the Olympics, to celebrate sport."

Baseball in the Olympics

Olympic baseball, as a demonstration sport, goes back as far as the early 20th century when a game was played at the 1912 Olympics in Sweden. The game was held July 15 at the Ostermalm Athletic Ground (without a pitching mound!), with the final score 13-3 in favor of the United States.

276

At the 1936 Games in Berlin, a capacity crowd of 125,000, one of the largest crowds ever to watch a baseball game, watched two American teams play a "not too lighted" night contest. The game was highlighted by Leslie McNeece's dramatic home run for the winning "World's Champions" team over the U.S. Olympics team. Baseball was given its chance on the Olympic program and came through magnificently. It appeared that baseball was headed for world-wide play. Nearly three decades later, following one-game exhibitions at the 1952 and 1956 Olympics, a team from the United States in the 1964 Olympics in Tokyo, Japan, defeated the Japanese, 6-2, in a single game, although the Americans played several games against Far East All-Star teams.

An attempt was made to get baseball included as an official Olympic sport as early as the 1968 Olympics in Mexico. However, in 1972, the IOC voted to eliminate all demonstration sports. Even though the IOC had voted to eliminate demonstration sports, many people in amateur baseball refused to take no for an answer. During the 1970s, Carlos Garcia of Nicaragua and former president of the IBA, traveled constantly to lobby IOC members. In 1978, after lobbying president Samaranch, Peter Ueberroth announced that baseball would make its seventh start in the 1984 Olympics as a demonstration sport. Peter O'Malley, owner of the Los Angeles Dodgers, pledged the assistance of his organization, and Bowie Kuhn, commissioner of Major League Baseball, reaffirmed pro baseball's support.

An eight-team tournament was held at Dodger Stadium at the 1984 Games. Before more than 385,000 fans, it set the stage for baseball's eventual inclusion as an official sport. Japan defeated the USA team, 6-3, to capture the gold medal before 35,290 fans. At the 1988 Games, the last Olympics with demonstration status, the United States met Japan again in the final and won the world title, 5-3. Baseball finally made its debut as an official Olympic sport in the 1992 Barcelona Summer Games. On July 26, more than 80 years of hard work by amateur baseball leaders worldwide was rewarded when the game made its debut as an official Olympic sport. Cuba downed a surprising Chinese Taipei team for the Gold Medal, while Japan defeated the USA to capture the Bronze.

The 1996 Atlanta Games may have had the "official" distinction of being the last Olympics tournament in which only amateurs competed. Atlanta-Fulton County Stadium, known as "The Launching Pad", lived up to its name. The eight teams combined for 110 homers in the 28 games, for a .325 batting average. Following their 11-2 upset victory over the USA, Japan was defeated by a powerful Cuban team in the Gold Medal game. A record 1,134,203 tickets were sold for the baseball competition in Atlanta, while 8.6 million were sold to all other sports. Baseball ranked No. 3 in attendance among the 32 different Olympic sports, certainly an exceptional achievement.

Amateurs or Professionals?
Who should represent the USA in the Olympic Games? IOC officials want major leaguers to play in the 2000 Sydney Games. Based on our polls, however, a large majority of both baseball officials and fans strongly oppose the use of pro's in the Olympics. They believe big league stars and dream teams do not personify what the Olympiad stands for. The impression that many people have about the Olympics is about amateur athletes, not a group of overpaid professional all-stars. Those who oppose professionals in the Olympics say that their use would give stronger baseball countries an unfair advantage. They maintain that the Dream Team concept is getting to be a bore in basketball and would be the same in baseball.

There are many who believe that if the pro's take control of baseball, it will destroy the framework of competition at the other levels. If major leaguers pass up Intercontinental Cups and world championships, which they will likely do, will college players be satisfied with "the crumbs"? The use of professional baseball stars means that amateur players will not have a chance to compete in the Olympics. The use of professionals will result in an even wider disparity in the competitiveness of nations. Some countries will field very strong teams, while the great majority will simply not be able to compete. Those who support the use of pro's in the Olympics maintain that times have changed, and the IOC should go after more money and television exposure. They point out that the Games will gain greater visibility and sponsorship opportunities if top professional baseball players are competing.

Certainly, the professional will provide a more highly skilled product and a more competitive athlete on the field. No one will dispute this, but winning is not what the Olympics is all about. For top collegiate athletes to have the opportunity to train, practice and play games over a two-year period, touring American cities, will do far more for baseball than having big leaguers show up a few days before the Olympics begin. A Dream Team of top stars from Major League Baseball is not likely, since their owners will not allow their best players to be taken away during the season. Dream teams provide their sport with a higher profile and TV ratings, but they are unfair to the amateurs they compete against. It prevents qualified amateurs from the college ranks from competing for a possible medal.

Another viewpoint considers the fact that USA national teams in the Olympics and international competition have not fared well against teams from Cuba and Japan. For several decades, American teams have not won consistently. Proponents of professionalism believe the USA cannot compete against the Cubans with a college all-star team. It must seek talent from AAA professional clubs to enable our country to be competitive. The team should be a mix of top collegians and pro players who shuttled between Class AAA and the Majors that season.

Who Should Compete?

Professional athletes must not be allowed to invade what should be "the world's tribute to its finest amateur athletes." The Olympic spirit burned ever so brightly when the Games were the domain of amateurs who relished the sport, the competition and the fellowship, not multi-millionaires who do it day after day for big paychecks and product endorsements. The Olympics should and must continue with amateur athletes. Those who support professionalism should conduct their own competition, but not under the cloak of the Olympiad, rather as the "Professional Games", or better yet, a World Cup of Baseball. If the IOC continues to push the professional movement, it will be time to consider an alternative to the Olympics.

World Cup Of Baseball

Rather than have professionals compete in the Olympics, a true World Series would be a far more meaningful and appropriate form of competition for them than the Olympic Games. The best players representing the top baseball countries from around the world would meet in a format similar to soccer's World Cup, which matches national all-star teams. As to who should administer the World Cup, perhaps a newly formed committee of Professional Baseball Leagues should have jurisdiction over the event. Major League Baseball should take the initiative in proposing a World Cup-style tournament to be held in early November, or late March, every four years. Since the World Cup of Hockey precedes the National Hockey League season, baseball's World Cup should precede the MLB season, like March 24-April 2. A double elimination tournament could involve from 4 to 8 teams.

While there are some serious concerns, the potential of such an event is so strong that Major League Baseball should make it happen. The long 162-game schedule, with nearly a month of post-season play, has to be considered. Certainly, a reduction in the season by 6 to 8 games would benefit both the major's game and the proposal for a World Cup. In addition, baseball's event has to be limited to 8 countries and no more than 10 days. The double elimination schedule, ideally, should be limited to one week.

Reversing Professional Movement
The true Olympic spirit was given a cruel blow by the people who advocate professionalism at the international level. With the word "amateurism" no longer included in the Olympic Charter, the basic premise of the Olympiad has now been removed. Those oriented to professionalism should organize their own competition and allow the true spirit to return to the Olympiad as espoused by its founder, Baron de Coubertin, over a century ago. Samaranch and his committee of selected appointees have tarnished enough the sacred name of the Olympics.

Today's Olympic Games do not personify what the Olympiad stands for. The philosophy of professionalism which was strong-armed by Samaranch is wrong for the Olympics. The Olympics is no place for multi-millionaires. Skip Bertman who coached Team USA in the 1996 Atlanta Games, said, "The Games are not about taking guys from pro ball and getting together for two weeks and having them lopsidedly beat the opposition."

The future of the Olympic Games must not be decided by Samaranch and those whose interests lie in commercialized professionalism. The philosophies of amateurism and professionalism are so contrasting and divergent that the future of the Olympic Games is in jeopardy. Based on its charter, philosophy, and traditions, the Olympics are for amateurs, and amateurism should be what the Games are all about. The IOC must reverse their decision to allow professionals to compete in the Olympics.

The world "amateur" should be put back into the Olympic Charter, and the best amateur athletes should compete in the Games.

The IOC - - - Who Are The Members?

Juan Antonio Samaranch, president of the International Olympic Committee, handpicks the 118 members, whose term is for life. In taking the oath of allegiance, they pledge loyalty to the movement, whose meetings and books are closed.

Who are the members of this incomparable, select committee, accountable to absolutely no one but themselves? As Bob Simon revealed on CBS's 60 Minutes early in 1998, the IOC is comprised of "A smattering of royals and nobles, sporting czars, Olympians, businessmen, such as the directors of Coca Cola and Visas, those who happen to be sponsors of the Games. The IOC is not quite as aristocratic as it used to be, but some of Samaranch's appointees have seemed highly curious, like Uganda's defense minister under Idi Amin; a former member of the KCIA, Korea's notorious intelligence service; Erich Honecker, the man who built the Berlin Wall; and Nicolae Ceausescu, often referrred to as the "Butcher of Bucharest". In 1985, Samaranch gave both Honecker and Ceausescu the IOC's highest honor, the Gold Olympic Order. The IOC's response in 1998 was "no regrets". Samaranch, himself, for three decades, was a loyal follower of Spain's Fascist leader, Francisco Franco, holding a high office in his regime.

Until recently, criticism of the IOC has tended to remain in the shadow, but as Simon reported, "Four years ago, one athlete did speak out, Vegard Ulvang of Norway, who won three gold medals and a silver at Lillehammer in 1992. Ulvang said, "Samaranch's past is nothing to be proud of, and I think the IOC should be organized in a much more democratic way." And how did the IOC react? It threatened to disqualify Ulvang from participating in the Games.

On numerous occasions, the IOC has succumbed to bribery and an excessive showering of gifts. To win Nagano's bid to host the 1998 Winter Olympics, for example, Japanese industrialists donated millions of dollars to the Olympic museum, in addition to taking IOC members on various shopping trips. However, every city bidding to become an Olympic city, including Salt Lake City and Atlanta, have been doing the same thing for many years.

PRESERVE THE IDEALISM
OF THE OLYMPIC MOVEMENT

Pierre de Coubertin founded the modern Olympics in 1896 to promote fairness, understanding, peace and goodwill. These values set the Olympics apart from professional sports leagues.

The spirit of the Olympics burned ever so brightly when the Games were the domain of amateurs who relished the sports, the competition, and the fellowship, not multi-millionaires who do it day after day for big paychecks and product endorsements.

"The IOC must preserve the idealism of the Olympic Movement. Otherwise, its worst nightmare – the loss of Coubertin's vision and the eroding of public confidence and corporate sponsorship – will lead to its downfall.
-- *Sharon Raboin* USA TODAY

OLYMPIC IDEALS AND VALUES
MUST BE RESTORED

Restore Olympic Ideals and Values

The IOC bribery scandal and corruption has so tarnished the Games that many believe it threatens to undermine the very foundations of the Olympic Movement. The Olympic value lies in its ideals, goals that are highly desirable and worthy of emulation. "From the very beginning, the Olympics have been about a moral high ground, "said USA TODAY's Sharon Raboin. "Pierre de Coubertin founded the modern Olympics in 1896 with the romantic notion of promoting fairness, understanding, peace and goodwill. This unique set of values is what sets the Olympics apart from professional sports leagues."

The IOC today exists in a material and idealistic world. During the last three Olympiads, the increased participation of professional athletes has devalued the meaning athletes expect from the Olympic Movement. As two-time Olympian Betsy Mitchell said, "There is a fundamental difference between professional and amateur. In the most naïve sense, the professional is motivated primarily by money, the amateur by love. Or so I thought."

In the 1980s, the Olympic Movement was scarred by widespread findings of medal-winning athletes testing positive for performance enhancing substances. The '80s also saw a big increase in "Money for medals" programs created by the IOC and national governing bodies. More recently, Olympic leaders and members of the IOC who should be standard bearers have let all Olympians down. "The competitive creed and value of sportsmanship that I hold so dear was replaced by the nationalistic need for political domination," said Mitchell in USA TODAY. "We must not let go of the thought that ideals, values and standards mean something and that we need them to endure. Looking into the next century, I wouldn't mind a clean Olympic slate: one where love of the sport (not the reward) and a balanced perspective could right the wrongs of the recent Olympic history."

Admittedly, those lofty ideals were not enough to sustain the Olympics financially. In 1976, the city of Montreal nearly went bankrupt after putting on the Summer Games. Still, the IOC must preserve the idealism of the Olympic Movement. Otherwise, as Raboin stated, "Its worst nightmare -- the loss of Coubertin's vision and the eroding of public confidence and corporate sponsorship -- will lead to its downfall."

The success rate to make the majors is
nearly double for a college athlete.

College baseball has had to endure a decade of
out-of-control scoring, produced by power-laden bats.

College coaches are the game's best teachers.
Players get more instruction than ever.

Collegiate baseball is attracting record
crowds to post-season tournaments.

Great disparity exists between programs in warmer
climates and those in cold weather areas. Snow in
April has covered this baseball field in Massachusetts.

Despite the imbalance of the game, many
college teams are fundamentally sound.

7 Colleges/Universities

Collegiate baseball, it has been said, is at an all-time high, capitalizing on the success story of the College World Series and record crowds at post season tournaments. The success rate for a college athlete to make the majors is nearly double that of a high school player. Increasingly, college baseball appeals to fans of all ages, from all walks of life. In describing his experiences at Stanford's "Sunken Diamond", Doug Albert wrote, "Beautiful scene, with only trees beyond the outfield, small bleachers and sloping grass beyond the diamond, good competitive baseball and the players all hustle and show a lot of spirit."

However, a problem that has been smoldering for many years among northern teams could soon shake the stability of college baseball and bring about dramatic change. Great disparity exists between baseball programs in warmer climates and those in cold weather areas. There is not a level playing field, and cold-weather teams need a major change. Minnesota baseball coach John Anderson stated that "There's clearly only one choice – we need to create an alternative -- probably a dramatic alternative." As to what action could be taken, Anderson said, "Perhaps making a move to create a different league, an NIT kind of post-season championship."

For collegiate baseball to maximize it's potential, much needs to be done. There are a number of problems which must be solved and for needs to be realized. The collegiate game, like the pro leagues, has become much too offensively oriented. The imbalance of the game and various developmental deficiencies need to be corrected. Baseballs flew off aluminum bats at a record pace in 1998, creating serious safety dangers. Despite the NCAA's attempts in 1999 to reduce the bat speed, the bats performed much the same way they did in previous years. The safety factor and exit velocity have not been addressed.

Programs are not making revenue and have some serious development shortcomings. To be a revenue sport, college baseball will have to look off campus. The season has to be moved back so that all programs, northern and southern, can benefit by warmer weather. Schools need to know how to deal more effectively with gender equity. There is an urgent need for the development and training of athletes to be upgraded to a higher level. To achieve this goal, college baseball has to place greater emphasis on professional development like they do with other academic professions and occupational programs.

Based on our studies, collegiate baseball is capable of maximizing its potential and reaching a higher level of play, providing the NCAA would allow programs to do so. I firmly believe a closer relationship between Major League Baseball and the colleges would be in the best interests of both levels of play. From my talks with big league scouts, I have the feeling that if the colleges would do a better job of development and closer working relations could be developed, the majors would look for ways to support college programs financially.

The most skilled college players would be allowed to be contracted to play in shortened professional summer seasons and still return to play college ball. This would, of course, require a new conception of the amateur athlete, but the current distinction between pro and amateur athletes is already open to various interpretations.

For these goals to gain the support of college presidents and be successful, campus administrators will want to see a much higher number of graduates, with a larger number of student-athletes seeking vocational career goals. Stronger academic standards must be the goal of every institution, and everyone involved has to promote more effectively the need for a college education.

College baseball has the potential to achieve unprecedented heights and popularity. However, the NCAA's current legislative process and bureaucratic chain of committees, cabinets and boards make it very difficult to make progressive changes and improvements. A prime example is the failed change-of-season proposal, which could have given college baseball a big boost in nationwide stature and popularity. Not only did the Management Council oppose the three-week change, it rejected moving the season back one week! However, Dave Keilitz, ABCA's executive director, has not given up. He plans to take the proposal back to the Committee for reconsideration and another try. He said, "It took us nine years of hard work and many tries to get the bracket expansion."

Showcase of College Baseball   The Division I College World Series is a sporting spectacle that has become one of the most popular events in all of sports. Some 279 teams begin practicing in the fall and only 8 of them manage to get to Omaha. As Tim Brando of CBS so eloquently said, "What other championship event would you have 20,000 people watching youngsters for the most part, they know very little about, just enjoying the pure aspects of the game of baseball. That's what makes this so special."

The 50th anniversary was celebrated in 1996, with 46 years in Omaha.   Nebraska, America's heart-land, has been host to many of college baseball's greatest moments. In Omaha, there is a community pride in staging the College World Series, and it is every player's dream to perform at Rosenblatt Stadium. For many, it is the thrill of a lifetime, since many will not go on to play pro ball. "The College World Series is their bowl game," said Brando. "This is their time to really get attention and show people what they can do. It is an event filled with emotions, mistakes coming from some of those emotions, yet outstanding individual play. Games can be very unpredictable. You never know what to expect."

For the large majority of Division I schools, however, there is the other side of the coin. Teams that play in the Omaha tournament are, with few exceptions, from the warmer-weather southern states or the West coast. The term World Series is a misnomer, as it is on the other levels of play. The term National Series is not even applicable, considering the overwhelming domination of the game by warm-weather teams. It has become a "Southern Championship" and northern schools do not have a chance. The problem has existed ever since the post-season tournament began, and teams from the north have begrudgingly accepted the inequities of the competition. Unless they are corrected, however, I look for many of the northern schools to form their own leagues and schedule their own seasons during the warmer months.

Collegians Have Greatest Potential   Studies reveal that college-trained players have far greater potential for professional stardom than those who enter pro ball following graduation from high school. College coaches produced 200 percent more major league players for extended careers in the mid-80s than high school coaches.

College coaches are baseball's best teachers

Sunny skies and warm spring weather in California. How about college games in the northern regions?

Powerful aluminum bats have distorted the delicate balance between offense and pitching

Juco Flavor. Jaycee transfers have made a major impact on 4-year college programs

Colleges are the major source of supply for major league players. A study conducted by Scott Goldby, recruiting coordinator at Arizona State University, stated that an analysis of major league rosters in 1994 showed that 661 major leaguers had signed out of college, while only 290 big leaguers signed out of high school.

Goldby's study reaffirms the need for high school seniors to understand the importance of a college education. He stated that "Players experiencing college baseball are stronger, more mature, in many cases better coached than some players in the minors.

Less than 5% of those drafted, and less than one percent of high school players actually make it to the major leagues.

Strong Juco Flavor   Junior college transfers have made a major impact on colleges and universities across the country. They are a growing trend, one that has made a mark in Division I programs. With NCAA scholarship limitations reduced from 13 to 11.7, and pro teams making a greater effort to sign high school draft picks, college teams have had to rely more heavily on juco transfers. Louisiana State, college baseball's team of the 1990s, won its fourth national championship with four juco transfers in the Tigers' lineup. In the '99 CWS, righthander Mike Neu of Miami, a jaycee transfer from Sacramento City College, saved the title game against Florida State by fanning Kevin Cash.

Indeed, junior college programs serve as a farm system for four-year schools and professional baseball. Jack Carey wrote in USA TODAY, "In an era when the NCAA has toughened admission standards for freshmen, junior college transfers, although they usually stay only two years at Division I schools, can have an effect that's immediate and immense."

Origin and Background

When Oliver Wendell Holmes, the noted author, confided to a Boston reporter that baseball was one of his favorite sports in college (Harvard, class of 1829), he undoubtedly meant some version of New England town ball, forerunner of our modern game. The first intercollegiate baseball game was played on July 1, 1859, between Amherst and Williams College at Pittsfield, Massachusetts. Cappy Gagnon wrote that "Amherst won by a 73-32 score, on a playing field unrecognizable today. The pitcher was 35 feet from the batter, with the teams using 13 players on each side."

Early college baseball thus preceded the National League by seventeen years. Intercollegiate championship baseball history began with three great universities, Yale, Harvard, and Princeton with the first title going to Harvard in 1868. "By the time the pro's formed their first league in 1871," said Gagnon, "college teams were good enough to be scheduled for numerous exhibition games. The practice continued for many decades. Collegians occasionally managed to beat the pro's, too."

Baseball became the most popular sport on college campuses in the 1880s and 1890s. Gagnon wrote, "Spectators saw highly skilled players at college games, all the more so because some schools permitted minor leaguers to play on their teams. Hundreds of minor league players earned college degrees while playing seasons for different universities."

From the founding of the National Association in 1871 to the present, there has been a collegiate influence on the national pastime. Big leaguers came from virtually every college, including smaller and lesser known schools, such as Christy Mathewson of Bucknell, Jack Coombs of Colby, and Eddie Plank of Gettysburg. The USC Trojans, Texas Longhorns, and Arizona State Sun Devils are the three top schools in producing major leaguers.

When USC's Rod Dedeaux returned to his alma mater as coach, he increased the Trojans' big league output dramatically while winning ten collegiate championships from 1958-1978. The Michigan Wolverines are the only school to have produced a major leaguer in every decade since the founding of the National Association in 1871. In 1921, Lou Gehrig, later to become baseball's "Iron Man" as a result of his consecutive game streak, enrolled at Columbia. Ray

Colleges have produced many of Baseball's greatest players

Christy Mathewson
Bucknell

Lou Gehrig
Columbia

Tom Seaver
Southern California

Jimmy Key
Clemson

Robinson wrote in his fine text that "Gehrig used to hit tremendous fly balls off the steps of Low Library and off the walls of the Journalism building -- some traveling 500 feet from home plate."

College athletes were not always warmly received into the major leagues. Gagnon acknowledged that "The crude, often ill-educated pros were more than a little resentful of the more cultured and better educated collegians. Because of the harsh conditions they faced, many star baseballers took their schooling seriously and skipped the majors. Another factor is that player salaries were often not attractive enough to persuade a bright college man to give up a career in a profession."

Early in the century, college baseball was barely subsidized. Only a few colleges gave the game an adequate place in their athletic programs, because of the emphasis placed on football and basketball. As Robinson said, "Few college teams played extended schedules and the major leagues depended on a network of high and low minor leagues to train talent." Soon after World War II, however, a foundation was being laid for a truce between pro baseball and the colleges. Branch Rickey stated, "I will continue to scout and sign collegians because I feel that some college teams have relationships with major league teams that are akin to their being farm clubs."

With minor league teams increasingly unable to sign and develop their own players, fully dependent upon "Working agreements" with big league teams, long-term player development became a function of college baseball programs. College facilities and coaching were at least as good as the low minors. Players were signed to scholarships and nurtured by the colleges. Major league scouts could watch their playing and learn something about their competitive abilities, injury history, and maturity. After two or three years, the best players would be drafted and sent to Rookie Ball or higher. From the 1950s on, the major leagues changed their relationship with the minors dramatically, thereby thrusting the college game into an even more prominent role. Baseball Commissioner Bowie Kuhn estimated in 1978 that more than two-thirds of major leaguers were college men.

Indeed, there have been many significant events in the long and successful history of collegiate baseball, but two of them surely must be regarded as the most meaningful in its development. In 1945, collegiate coaches organized the American Association of College Baseball Coaches. Two years later, the College

World Series was introduced, affirming baseball's recovery, and the game has grown steadily on collegiate campuses.

The year 1995 could have been the game's most distinguished. The American Baseball Coaches Association celebrated its 50th anniversary convention and clinic in Chicago, with a record number of coaches attending. Then later in the year, with enlarged facilities, a record crowd of 22,027 witnessed the CWS Championship finals between Cal State-Fullerton and Southern California.

The College Game—Status Report

College baseball has changed greatly from what it was like two or three decades ago. The game used to be based primarily on pitching and defense. Today, the bunting game, hit and run and base stealing is rarely seen. There are not many teams playing Small Ball anymore. Aggressive base running is missing. Teams are not running. They are swinging from their heels. Teams are playing for the home run and the big inning.

"Bulked-up players swinging feather-light aluminum bats have produced gaudy offensive numbers," wrote Mike Dodd in USA TODAY. High-tech alloys have made metal bats lethal weapons, raising strong concerns for safety, even the integrity of the game. In addition to the health and well-being of the pitcher and infielders, coaches and officials are very concerned about the many 20 plus games that run longer than four hours.

Many college teams are fundamentally sound, particularly those who perform in the World Series. However, more players entering college are lacking not only in good skill techniques but a well-rounded knowledge of the game. Seventy percent of the college coaches we polled believe there has been a general decline in the execution of the basic skills. The reduction in practice hours by the NCAA has also been a factor. Fielding, bunting and sliding skills are not up to par. Good baseball instincts are lacking with many players. Throwing skills have definitely deteriorated, particularly basic arm speed. Although players are in good overall physical condition, the heavy emphasis on weight lifting has contributed to tighter throwing arms with less velocity on their throws.

Imbalance of the Game

The College game is out of balance, the ball is flying, scoring records shattered, and those who make the rules and keep score are scratching their heads. The game has evolved into a procession of home run trots and 4-hour scoring sprees. College baseball has gone to a 10-9 game, and more. As a result of the scoring explosion, many of the finer points of the game have been lost. Players are not developing skills for the short game. Few teams are playing for one run early in the game, to bunt a runner over, because one run will not stand up. They are looking for the home run.

More home runs are being hit and they are traveling farther and deeper than ever before. The major reasons are:

- Greatly superior alloys are being used by bat manufacturers
- Lighter and unbreakable aluminum bats have great reflex, a trampoline effect that springs the ball farther and faster
- A more tightly wound, harder baseball
- Bigger and stronger athletes
- Outfield fences have been moved in
- Fewer quality pitchers, with many H.S. pitchers going pro

Super bats have created an imbalance favoring batters and are responsible for many of the game's problems. They have contributed significantly to numerous developmental weaknesses in college baseball. Each year, a technologically more advanced bat enters the market. Caps should have been put on bat technology long ago. Both the bat and the ball have been juiced up.

Impact of the Aluminum Bat

Powerful bats have distorted the delicate balance between offense and pitching in the college game. Sean McDonough of CBS Sports explained, "Teams are able to score runs in bunches. You don't see college teams bunting, hitting behind the runner and playing hit and run. Why give up an out when just about anybody can hit the ball out of the park."

Then there is the strong concern of Major League Baseball about the difficult transition of the aluminum bat to wood. "There is a huge adjustment," said former big league slugger Joe Carter. "In the majors, there is a sweet spot of maybe 2 to 3 inches, but the aluminum bat has a sweet spot of 7 to 8 inches."

Along with safety concerns, that's what college coaches are concerned about most. As for the players, many come into professional ball unprepared. They would prefer that the wooden bat be used.

There are, however, college coaches like Mike Martin of Florida State who believe the bat is overrated, that people like to see offense. Carter, who starred as a collegian at Wichita State, said, "Look at the '98 major league season, what McGwire and Sosa did. People want to see offense. They don't want to go to a game and see a one to nothing game."

Games Too Long and Slow-Paced Many of the college games today are taking from 3 to 4 hours to play. In 1997, UCLA and Miami played the second longest game in CWS history, 4 hours and 42 minutes. With each pitch, the irritation factor in the stands goes higher. Not only are college games running longer than the pro's, but the pace is an even greater problem. In addition to score-fests and home run mania, the long games can be attributed to the delaying tactics by hitters and pitchers, the time-consuming process of signal-calling from the dugout and many pitching changes. The long pitching counts and base-on-balls are the result of pitchers' frustration with metal bats and the reduced strike-zone. In the 1997 CWS, UCLA pitchers issued 21 walks in two games.

Batters are stepping out on pitchers, and pitchers will step off the mound when hitters take too long. The intent of most hitters is just to disrupt the timing of the pitchers. Some hitters use the first 15-seconds to get into their pre-pitch ritual. As Lou Pavlovich, Jr. wrote, "They will routinely receive signals from a coach, take a dry swing, and then get into the visual system to execute hitting properly." Excessive pitching changes, referred as "Pitching by Committee", is another reason for marathon games.

Competitive Disparities Because of the warmer weather, southern and Far West schools are not only dominating play in the NCAA Division I but host nearly all the regional tournaments. Of the eight-team CWS in 1997, the Southeastern Conference claimed one-half. Southerners, of course, are dancing in the streets, but those in the northern regions of the nation, including the news media, are turned off. As a result, the Southeast, Southwest, and Far West have come to dominate the game, in large part because those are the warm weather areas of the country where players can play the year around.

Developmental Deficiencies

Despite its success in producing numerous players for the major leagues, collegiate baseball has a number of shortcomings in player development. Most definitely they have the strong concern of Major League Baseball. For college baseball to develop a closer relationship with the professional game, they will have to be corrected. The most harmful can be attributed to the use of aluminum bats which have created many problems.

Hitters have a difficult transition when moving from metal bats to wood. Generally, it takes a hitter from two to three years to adjust. MLB has urged the NCAA to return to wooden bats but have not responded to the suggestion the majors subsidize the conversion. Likewise, pitchers develop bad habits pitching to hitters with aluminum bats, having to throw too many breaking pitches, not throwing off the fastball, failure to pitch inside, etc. Many prospects have to be taught to pitch all over again.

Many college pitchers are being overworked and are given insufficient rest between starts. Too often, just signed pitchers from college arrive in pro ball with tired arms and bad habits. As a rule, college pitchers throw an excessive number of breaking ball pitches. While top big league pitchers work off the fast ball, college pitchers are working off the breaking ball. There have been many instances of coaches running up excessive pitch counts, bringing back starters in relief a day or two after a complete game, and other serious abuses. Most recently, righthander Matt McClendon of Florida threw 183 pitches in a complete game.

Pitch-calling by college coaches continues to be a serious developmental problem for both catchers and pitchers. It is apparent that coaches are more concerned with winning than the development of players. Surely they have to realize it develops a deficiency. Perhaps they should get an earful from professional coaches who have the difficult task of helping players make the transition.

Access to Championships Still Lacking

For many years, college teams in northern, cold-weather regions have had limited access to championships. In 1999, the number of Division I regional sites was expanded from eight to sixteen locations. While the new 64-team structure attracted overflow crowds, 14 sites were warmer climate locations, eleven in the South and Southwest. "It's abundantly clear that a great disparity exists," wrote

Dr. John Winkin, columnist of Collegiate Baseball. "There is not a level playing field for northern programs competing with warmer area institutions."

"The reality of Division I college baseball is that we play a different game than warm climate teams," explained Geoff Zahn, University of Michigan coach. Among the comparisons cited by Zahn, northern teams like Michigan must compact a 56-game schedule in 13 weeks, whereas southern teams spread their games over an 18-week schedule. Essentially, the RPI System of rating teams is not valid in determining teams for the NCAA regionals. Zahn has proposed the idea of regionalizing the system so that the top teams play each other in their own regions. In addition to selecting the best teams from each region, the season would be moved back three weeks.

ABCA's Dave Keilitz pointed out that "As long as the philosophy of the NCAA Executive Committee is to get the best teams to the finals in sports, it will be difficult to regionalize the RPI approach currently used." In all fairness to all regions, however, there is a long overdue need for regionals to be scheduled throughout the country, instead of centered in a few areas. Southern schools should not continue to dominate college baseball, like the large market teams do in Major League Baseball.

Even though northern schools have accepted this unfair weather disparity far too long, the NCAA should not underestimate the strong resolve and determination of programs in the colder climates of the Midwest and northeast.

There is not a level playing field for northern programs competing with warmer area institutions.
- Dr. John Winkin

Maximizing College Baseball

Although collegiate baseball is more popular than ever, it has yet to reach its potential. There are numerous reasons why the game has been unable to do so. Earlier in the chapter, I wrote that major problems are holding back the growth of the game on college campuses. Is college baseball capable of maximizing its potential and reach a higher level of play? Based on our studies, we believe it can if the NCAA would allow it to do so.

What would it take for college baseball to reach a higher level? Greater involvement with the professional game! As the majors continue to downsize their player development systems, there is a strong likelihood the college game will play an even greater role in the development of big league prospects. Unquestionably, player development would be much more productive with the support of professional baseball. If college programs would do a better job of development, I believe big league teams would pump more money into the college game. For college baseball and MLB to have closer relations, the aluminum bat has to go, and with closer ties, the majors could be receptive to partially subsidizing wood and wood-composite bats.

Now we need to address the problems that are preventing college baseball from reaching its potential, with recommended solutions, which will help programs achieve this much sought after goal.

Become a Revenue-maker
Perhaps the biggest downside in college baseball is that very few programs are producing revenue. Colleges today have too little money for all the non-revenue sports, like baseball. As Danny Hall said, "Until we can generate money, we're going to be part of the problem for our AD's and presidents, of having too little money for all the "non-revenue sports".

As gender equity continues to swallow up entire programs, the prosperity of college baseball, the survival of programs, will be dependent on becoming financially solvent. It does not appear programs will get much support from their own campuses. They are going to have to be on their own. Therefore, they will need to look more to off-campus assistance, with the realization they will have to fight for their survival. Developing a closer relationship with Major

League Baseball could be the key for college baseball to solve their financial woes.

Still, those involved in college baseball must work harder at getting more assistance from the community, such as corporations, service clubs, and alumni, particularly former players. In all fairness, the community and Corporate America will be assisting the women as well, but the "proof of the pudding" will be who wants to work the hardest. College programs must do a better job of marketing and promotions, enticing fans into the ballpark, getting behind their team's fund-raising efforts. There are many ways to raise money. Collegiate Baseball's program, tied in with Wilson Sporting Goods, honors the best promotions of the year, providing an insight into some of the best methods which teams and coaches use to raise funds.

Stronger Promotion and Fund-raising   To become

a major revenue-maker, college baseball must develop strong programs in promotion and fund-raising. Ron Fraser, a great promoter during his highly successful coaching career at Miami, emphasized, "You never know about a promotion until you try. Sometimes these promotions do not work, but if it does work, you can raise a lot of money and publicity, which can turn around your program. " Judging from the impressive array of promotion projects and events entered in Wilson's Best Promotion Award each year, it appears that a large number of college baseball programs are getting on the promotion bandwagon.

Promotions that involve corporations and commercial businesses have been some of the most successful. Prime examples were the "Ole Miss Home Run-Free Motorola Cellular Phone" promotion, and Wichita State's "Pack Your Bags Night", in cooperation with a Las Vegas hotel. At "Businessman's Night", the person who donates a hundred dollars gets to throw out the opening ball that night. Nightly events and contests can be very effective getting fans in the stands. A team yearbook can be very effective for recruiting and as a showcase for the baseball program. A telephone blitz is another good fund-raising technique. Get together former players and members of the coach's Committee at the alumni office for a mass phoning session.

Wilson Sporting Goods company, in conjunction with Collegiate Baseball, annually selects the best promotion of the year in an effort to spotlight the nation's most attractive programs and to help college baseball offer more excitement, fun, and appeal for fans. "Since the award was established, many more programs have stressed promotions," said Lou Pavlovich, publisher of Collegiate Baseball. "It has produced a dynamic domino effect to our game."

"Fund-raising is the salvation to having a first-class program," said Fraser. More and more, raising money is being done by the coaches, but it is so vital to the financial stability of the programs. Ron's advice to coaches: "First, sell yourself, then the program, and get publicity to let people know about the program." As one veteran college coach said, "To keep our program among the top 20 every year, we must fund-raise $25,000. That' a lot of money and takes a lot of time."

FRESNO STATE'S BULLDOG FOUNDATION The Bulldog Foundation of Fresno State has been highly successful in raising funds and promoting sports. The Foundation has a $6 million budget through ticket sales and donations to help augment the athletic department's budget. The Foundation has over 5,000 members, with 350 fund-drive workers. Many of the members represent a large segment of the business community.

Community support has been the key to Fresno State's success. The 1,000-member Dugout Club is the largest in the nation. The group helped with the fund-raising for various renovations, and helps organize the Pepsi-Johnny Quick Classic, one of collegiate baseball's best tournaments. Prior to the Sunday home games, the Club stages a brunch for players, parents, coaches and boosters.

Build a First-Class Stadium
New ballparks have contributed significantly in attracting larger crowds to college baseball games. They contribute to the entire game. First-class stadiums have also had a major effect on recruiting. As Auburn coach Hal Baird said, "There was no question that to compete, we had to upgrade. We had little more than a high school operation before, and it really hurt in recruiting. There definitely is a direct correlation between the stadium and recruiting."

An informal poll by Baseball America concluded that Arkansas' Baum Stadium at George Cole Field, an $8.9 million jewel that opened in 1996, is the nation's top college baseball complex. Yet, it is just one of eleven ballparks in the SEC that have been built or rebuilt since 1987. In his article, "Building Blocks", John Manuel stated that "The trend began when Mississippi State's Dudy Noble Field, a 2,200-seat bleacher and covered grandstand structure, was dismantled. In its

First-Class Stadiums have a major effect on spectators, recruiting, and becoming a revenue-maker (Central Michigan University)

Indoor facilities are invaluable to programs in northern, cold-weather areas (University of Maine at Orono)

place rose a 6,700-seat facility with 3,700 chairback seats, as well as the Left Field Lounge, where rabid Bulldog fans pull their vehicles up to the stadium and tailgate before, during and after games. A total of 18 skyboxes have been constructed."

Rice will replace its baseball stadium, Cameron Field, with a $6.4 million facility for the 2000 season. The facility, to be funded by private donations, will have a capacity of 5,667, including 3,427 permanent seats and 2,240 temporary seats. The stadium, with its bigger capacity, will make the Owls eligible to host an NCAA regional.

In addition to theater-style seats, Fresno State's Beiden Field features a state-of-the-art press box, a shower/locker room, new restrooms and concession stands, offices for the baseball coaching staff, four batting cages, and six mounds in two bullpens. The facility includes a $140,000 electronic scoreboard, featuring a complete score by innings, game totals and message center. The field lighting includes 98 fixtures on eight towers generating 100-foot candles of light in the infield and 80 average foot candles in the outfield.

Give Athletes an Education

A college education is in the best interests of all athletes who aspire to play professional sports. Even top high school draft picks should attend college before playing pro baseball. Unless they are paid a lot of money, prep stars should go to college. While bonuses of $200,000 and up might seem difficult for prep standouts to ignore, in all likelihood, they will receive a much larger bonus after a few years of college baseball.

A very small percent of those who enter professional baseball actually make it to the big leagues. As for the great majority who fail, without a college education, they will almost certainly get involved in low wages or minimum wage positions. Many major league players who jumped right out of high school into pro ball, without the benefit of a higher education, have learned to regret this decision. When their playing careers are over, they find themselves without marketable skills.

Education for life ahead is far more important than signing a pro contract. Joe DiMaggio, widely known as the Yankee Clipper when he starred for the Yankees in the late 1930s and 40s, deeply regrets skipping college. "If I could relive one day in my life," he told Art Cohn of the San Francisco Examiner, "it would be the day I quit Galileo High School at the end of my third year, to go into professional baseball. It was a big mistake. I should have stayed in school, graduated and then gone through college. From a money standpoint, it might not have been wise, but you don't play baseball all your life. I believe education is the most important thing in life."

Emphasize Professional Development

Scouts and farm directors have expressed the view that professional baseball will be relying more and more on the development of college baseball to produce more and better players for them. For professional development to be truly successful, the colleges and Major League Baseball should implement "Apprentice Baseball" through a professional preparation program. The task of getting the NCAA to adhere to change might appear to be an unlikely proposition but nonetheless, the Commissioner's office and the NCAA should renew negotiations begun in Fay Vincent's regime to allow the best college players to play in pro leagues during the summer.

By playing in professional leagues, players would gain the advantage of playing in a pro environment with wood bats, and would be that much better prepared when the time came for them to pursue baseball as a job. Scouts could better determine a prospect's worth, making bonus money well spent.

Professional Baseball Preparation

Progressive changes are needed in college baseball, such as the implementation of a professional development agreement between colleges and Major League Baseball. Through the Occupational Education Program (OEP) on each campus, student-athletes would be educated for a career occupation --- professional baseball, similar to the long standing programs in other fields. While professional baseball is a game, it is also regarded as a business and a part of the entertainment world. Baseball is also an occupation, and a highly attractive one at that.

What makes professional baseball such an attractive occupation?

- Average salary in Major League Baseball is over $1,500,000
- Major League Baseball has 30 teams, with two more planned
- Over 100 countries are playing the game, with an increasing number organizing professional leagues

Already players who play in the various NCAA-sanctioned summer leagues are being compensated financially. By playing in professional leagues, they would have the same advantage of playing in a pro environment as Law and Medical student, entertainers, corporate and business interns, etc. The curricula would be professionally oriented, classes such as business math, economics, etc.

The Professional Baseball Preparation program would have three primary goals: (1) player development; (2) sport management; (3) baseball administration, leadership training, and methods of coaching. The most skilled college players would be allowed to contract to play professional ball during a shortened summer season and still return to play college baseball during the academic year. Modest compensation would be given to both the college players and the Sport Management field students responsible for running the front office and conducting the youth programs.

During the summer, the PBP program will sponsor non-pro play in the evening, both twilight and night action, combined with youth baseball camps, clinics, and playground leagues in the morning. Conducting these programs will be the players and those students enrolled in the college workstudy program. If successfully implemented, this program could provide a dramatic impact on the development of young players in the United States, from the colleges on down to the youth leagues.

To implement such an innovative and progressive program, college coaches, athletic directors, and faculty advisors must sell the campus administration and academia on a closer relationship with professional baseball. Allowing college players to play in a short summer season and still return to play college ball will require a new conception of the amateur athlete.

Move the Season Back
College baseball's potential to become a major sport would be significantly enhanced by a change of season. It would contribute much to the stability and popularity of the game. According to Dave Keilitz, "The change of season plan will take college baseball to a much higher level nationally. Without it, college baseball will only exist competitively in the South, Southwest, and Far West. For many years, 80 percent of Division I programs have had minimal opportunity of ever being rated in the top 30 teams, of ever being selected as an at-large team to a regional, or ever getting to Omaha. It is impossible for a player in a northern state to approach his full-skill potential because of the conditions he must practice and play in."

Warm-weather teams enjoy nearly ideal playing conditions, while 80 percent of the baseball schools suffer through frigid weather well into April. In all fairness, all teams should begin their seasons when the weather is more attractive. Many years ago when an April 1 starting date was first proposed, Bobby Randall, Iowa State coach, asked his players, "What do you think?" They replied, "That sounds great not to have to wear long johns for our first 20 games."

Because of inclement weather, most northern teams can't begin their seasons or even practice outdoors until March at the earliest. As a result, they must play early-season games on the road, usually expensive trips to the southern states, and cram several games into a shorter time period. Warm-weather schools can play many more home games and spread their schedules out, which exacts less of a toll on their pitching staffs. From a recruiting standpoint, it is very difficult when cold-weather schools go head-to-head against warm-weather schools for a top player.

The idea to play college baseball later into the summer has lingered for over two decades. In 1996, the Big Ten Conference sponsored Proposal 129. The measure created an NCAA Ad Hoc Committee to study the possibility of redefining the seasons for baseball and softball by moving those sports national championship tournaments. Minnesota baseball coach John Anderson, chairman of the Big Ten Baseball Coaches Committee, said, "The unlevel playing field is the reason the Big Ten sponsored the proposal."

While the change-of-season would have pushed the CWS back two or three weeks, Anderson said, "Schools may want to push it back even further for all schools to develop their teams outdoors before the season. If we don't move the season, I think you'll see the Big Ten and other people break away and form our own season. We don't have a chance to go to Omaha in the current system."

The NCAA Division I Baseball Committee, strongly supported by a large majority of college coaches, had recommended a change-of-season plan. However, the Management Council rejected a "one-week" change by a vote of 15-18-1. Many coaches thought the vote was "unbelievable", in that even council members representing northern and eastern conferences opposed the change. The plan would have pushed the season back two weeks by moving the start of the CSW to the fourth Friday after Memorial Day. The problem with selling the plan to college presidents and athletic directors is cost. In many cases, teams would have to remain on campus after classes have ended, meaning added expenses for the school.

Open Up Tournaments Geographically
There is a long, overdue need for the regionals to be scheduled throughout the country, rather than being concentrated in southern and warmer-weather areas. The new regional structure has sixteen 4-team regionals, eight 2-team "Super" regionals, with eight teams qualifying for the CWS. But, only a few northern schools received invitations and only two, Ohio State and Notre Dame, hosted regional tournaments.

A major criticism over the years is that NCAA's Baseball Committee "goes south with everything", which is still the case. The Sun Belt again dominated the regional sites, with four in Texas, two in Alabama and two in Florida. Asked why the NCAA chose four Texas hosts, Committee chair Dick Rockwell replied, "Texas is a big state." I agree, Dick, but the USA is a big country too!

For Division I's expanded tournament concept to be fair to all schools, more parity is needed, particularly in the at-large selections. More teams in the east and north should have a better opportunity to receive a bid. The need to spread selections around is more important now than ever.

FORMATION OF A SUPER DIVISION?   Should the NCAA fail to sufficiently open up regional tournaments geographically, I look for a large number of Division I colleges to either create a different league, or as Anderson said, create an NIT kind of post-season championship. A new "Super" division of college sports has been proposed, an organization that would not be under the NCAA's scope of operation. Over 100 college baseball programs across the country are suppressed by the current structure and have considered forming their own division.

Should 100 or more baseball programs decide to break off into their own association, the college season would begin on April 1 and continue well into the summer, with a 64-team championship in early August. Teams would play over 100 games. Requirements for membership would be rigid, like a commitment to self-sufficiency, a minor league-caliber stadium, strong marketing and promotion, allotting the full number of scholarships per team, and subsidizing wood and wood-composition bats.

By installing lights for night games, college baseball could attract record-breaking crowds. Indeed, night ball will give the college game the type of impetus the majors received back in the 1940s. Surely, the Super conference will appeal to television, and college baseball's longtime goal of their own "Game of the Week" will finally become a reality.

Correcting Developmental Deficiencies

For college baseball to be more effective in player development, aluminum bats should be replaced by wooden or wood-composition bats. Pitchers need to pitch inside again. Coaches should let their catchers call the signals and not overwork pitchers, and players must have more practice time to develop. Strength-building programs should be designed for athletes to play baseball, not for football.

There is no doubt the aluminum bat has been detrimental to scouts evaluating talent. It is very difficult to predict how a player will hit after he switches to wood. Metal bats give hitters a false sense of security. Aluminum bats penalize pitchers who throw inside and who have good fastballs. "Because the aluminum bat doesn't break, the hitter who gets jammed frequently collects a base hit," wrote David Rawnsley in Baseball America. "The professional hitter has a broken bat, hands that sting until the next inning and a pop-up to shortstop in the scorebook."

In the field, infielders are often "eaten up" on the hop, the strong overspin on the ball. Rather than coming forward, being aggressive, and getting the good hop, infielders get caught in between, often times back pedaling. As a result, many middle infielders position themselves at the edge of the grass and are not in position to make the all-important double play.

"Fundamentally, baseball needs a complete return to wood in all leagues," wrote Phil Garner, former Milwaukee manager. He believes a college hitter's chances for the majors are much better with wooden bats. Cost-wise, Garner realizes the financial hardships that all-wood bats would mean at the lower levels.

Stronger Bat Controls Are Needed

Based on the overall scoring and home run totals during the 1999 college season and tournament play, many coaches believe aluminum bats are still too lively and dangerous. There are still too much scoring and home runs. In an initial attempt by the NCAA to reduce the bat speed of aluminum and increase safety, two changes were made in 1999:

1. Reduce diameter of bat one-eighth of an inch to cut down the sweet spot.

2. To reduce bat speed, the weight of a bat must be within 3 ounces of its length in inches.

Despite the new bat standards, however, the record high batting averages and runs per game were down only slightly during the 1999 season, from .306 and 7.1 in 1998 to .301 and 7.0. In the CWS, reductions were modest. In fact, players at Omaha were unanimous in saying they didn't notice any difference in the way the ball came off the bat.

NCAA officials are now calling for more bat changes. A newly formed Baseball Research Panel has recommended that college aluminum bats perform like the wooden bats used in the majors. "In terms of both risk and integrity, the panel concluded that wood should be the standard," said chairman Milton Gordon, president, Cal State-Fullerton.

Then, what is the solution? While much of the talk at the CWS focused on bat performance standards and control measures which aluminum bats should comply with, Sean McDonough of CBS Sports asked, "Why not just go to wooden bats? I have heard people say aluminum bats have been "cost- saving" over the years for the colleges, but now high-tech bats have become very expensive. When you do the math and figure out the financial aspects, the cost factor between aluminum and wood has become very close."

Return to Wood or Wood-Composite

College baseball should follow the lead of the New Jersey and Wisconsin conferences and return to wood or wood-composite bats. As the NCAA attempts to find a bat that behaves more like wood, simulated wood appears to be the solution, to bring the feel of wood bats back to college baseball. Wooden bats provide the stroke of tradition in baseball, the sweet swack of ash on cowhide that has echoed from Mudville to Cape Cod through the years.

As a cost-saving alternative in the minors, the wood-composite bat has been a remarkable success. The bat developed by Steve Baum is the first non-wood bat to win over the traditionalists in professional baseball. This bat is being used by all of the teams in pro baseball, in Rookie leagues and A-ball, and all of the summer leagues sanctioned by the NCAA. A shell of white ash wrapped around a core of foam plastic, it preserves the genuine crack-of-bat meeting ball. But it almost never breaks. It sound like wood, and reacts with the same dynamics as wood. The cost is $95 to $115 per bat and will last longer than the thinner-walled aluminum, which cost up to $300.

George Brett, one of the greatest hitters in baseball history, has gone to bat for wood. Brett, with 3,154 major league hits, and brothers Ken, Bobby and John, have formed Tri Diamond Sports in Spokane, Washington. Co-owner Joe Sample and his partners had developed the bats with researchers at Washington State University. The bat is said to be 20% stronger than wooden models used in the majors. Their process electronically scans each piece of ash for imperfections that cause a bat to break. Three strips of northern white ash are glued together, shaped into bats, and laminated for extra strength. For more information, call the Brett Bros. Bat Company (509) 891-6435. Their web site is: http://www.brettbros.com or http://www.tridiamondsports.com

Expand Summer College Leagues

To develop their playing skills, college baseball players must play in the summer. By expanding the number of summer leagues will enable more college players to do so. The number of summer college leagues are growing rapidly, many of them certified by the NCAA. The leagues play with wooden or wood composite bats, instead of aluminum used during the college season. The Gems of the Central Illinois Collegiate Summer League are averaging more than 3,400 fans, including a season-high 6,137. "The biggest thing about the Gems is that we're family-oriented," said general manager Jeff Jansen. "As long as the young kids continue to enjoy the atmosphere and the prices are affordable, I don't see it stopping."

Cape Cod, the Model Summer League

For over a century, the Cape Cod League in Massachusetts has been the most prestigious summer college baseball league in America. Since switching from semi-pro to a collegiate league in 1963, the league has attracted numerous scouts and professional prospects. David Grunebaum of USA TODAY, wrote, "Sitting on beach chairs and bleachers, fans at McKeon Field can smell the fresh cut grass and hear the cracks of wooden bats launching baseballs into Hyannis' cool, salt air. It has been that way at the Cape Cod Baseball League for well over 100 seasons."

"Early in the 70s when colleges began using aluminum, I didn't think that was baseball," said Fred Ebbett, former commissioner of the Cape League. "The scouts were always complaining that they could not evaluate the hitters accurately when they were using aluminum." With a $10,000 grant from Major League Baseball, the league bought wooden bats and began to attract professional prospects all over the country. As many as 4,000 spectators watch the game at the ten seaport towns that make up the Cape Cod League. Admission is free.

"The atmosphere promotes a strong link between ball players and fans," wrote Dana Heiss. "Munching on pop corn, they discuss players, games, and strategy. Generally, players stay with host families (at a cost of $40-50 a week), who provide housing, food and often a friendship that lasts well beyond the summer."

The majors provide the 12-team league with close to $100,000 to cover bats, balls, umpires, and scorers. For this amount, it has been a highly productive "minor-league" system. Cape Cod was the first to switch to wood in 1985, a move that contributed to their reputation as the top summer league. Players know that scouts find it easier to evaluate players with wood bats instead of with aluminum.

Umpiring Development in Reform   While the overall quality of college umpiring is very good, development and advancement has been a major concern. Many young promising umpires have had difficulty moving up to the upper echelon of college and professional ranks. However, conditions are improving, a result of the organizational talents of Dave Yeast, NCAA's national umpire coordinator. Yeast, along with Jon Bible and other Division I umpires, have formed the Amateur Baseball Umpires Association.

The primary mission of the ABUA is to bring together all the amateur umpires in America. According to Jim Lane, CEO of the Mideast Collegiate Umpires Alliance, the ABUA will stage a minimum of three camps each year to allow umpires to gain access to the proper two and three-man mechanics employed by the NCAA. Umpires will have the opportunity to be certified for future competitions.

As a service of the ABUA, the Umpires Resource Center is now on the Internet, providing a wealth of information for active and aspiring umpires, including the policies, procedures and guidelines of the NCAA's Baseball Umpire Program. "One of our program's goals is to communicate with as many college baseball umpires as possible," said Yeast. This web page is an excellent database, with information about the Amateur Umpire Association, Major League Baseball and NCAA umpires. In addition, it offers articles about umpires from recent publications, along with information about clinics, equipment, etc.

For more information, contact Dave Yeast, NCAA National Umpire Co-ordinator, 572 Oak Valley Dr., Froupenac, MO 63131. Telephone: (314) 821-5164, FAX: (314) 821-5165. Web site: http://www.umpire.org.

Major Problems and Issues

In addition to those that deal with developmental deficiencies, collegiate baseball has many problems and issues that relate to the program as a whole. I am referring to gender equity, lack of scholarships, amateur draft woes, declining academic values, rigid money-work rules, sportsmanship and ethics, steroid abuse, etc.

Gender Equity

Title IX, known as Gender Equity, continues to be a stumbling block in college baseball's efforts to upgrade their programs. Title IX is the civil rights law that prohibits colleges getting federal money to practice sex discrimination, especially on the athletic fields.

The Proportionality rule in Title IX has seriously damaged men's sports, including baseball. The current trend is to continue to slash rosters of men's baseball teams and other sports. Hopefully it will not jeopardize efforts to become more closely involved with professional baseball. With gender equity constantly looming over the program, college baseball really needs the close support of Major League Baseball.

College administrators are trying to find a solution so men's sports are not further eliminated, rosters cut even more, and program budgets drastically slashed. The University of New Hampshire no longer has any men's spring sports, despite an emergency eight-week period in which a monumental $520,000 was raised. Yet the school went ahead and eliminated baseball, along with men's golf and lacrosse.

The problem of gender equity will continue to worsen until both sides, administrators, AD's and coaches of both men and women teams, work together to generate sufficient funding that will enable both sides to prosper. By all means, women should have athletic opportunities but not at the expense of the long established men's programs. As a result of the current cost-cutting atmosphere of college athletics, many universities are finding it easier to reduce men's programs than to increase women's. College presidents and athletic directors should focus on areas other than sports programs to make budget cuts.

Programs threatened by Title IX must not be eliminated. I have read of numerous instances where the strong efforts of students, alumni and community have kept college baseball programs afloat. Cal State-Northridge approved a $586,000 loan to keep baseball and three other programs going. Central Washington University students voted in favor of a $35-a-quarter fee increase that prevented elimination of baseball, wrestling, and cross-country. It was projected to raise about $700,000 annually. Temple's Board of Trustees voted baseball back. Skip Wilson, the Owls' head coach, credited his players and their parents for a lot of politicking, successfully getting through to the student body, which played a major role. But, many other programs have not been so fortunate.

Baseball's Lack of Scholarships
More than ever, college baseball programs need a larger number of scholarships, particularly with MLB throwing huge bonuses at promising high school graduates. Despite producing the second most dollars in the NCAA championships, baseball is the most underfunded sport in college athletics. Programs have the fewest scholarships and coaches per student-athlete. Most players are on partial scholarships that can be withdrawn on a year-to-year basis in the case of poor performance or injury. Full-ride scholarships are very scarce. The gross inequity of Title IX is that baseball may have 11.7 scholarships split up among 40 players, while women's softball has 16 full-ride scholarships and only 17 athletes.

"Relief does not appear to be on the horizon," wrote John Manuel in Baseball America, "certainly not under Title IX which mandates equal athletic opportunities be provided for men and women in college athletics."

College baseball programs must find a way to get more scholarship money for their athletes. With limited scholarships, college baseball coaches must be as creative as possible. As an example, getting football players who are on scholarship to play baseball can ease somewhat the scholarship problem.

How can collegiate baseball get more scholarship money?

- Corporations, businesses, and service clubs active in the campus communities.
- Former players now in the big leagues who may feel they want to give something back to the program that prepared them.
- Major League Baseball should consider providing funding through the NCAA for scholarships.

Money/Work Rules Too Rigid
Until just recently, the NCAA had barred athletes from working for extra money. But in 1998, the governing body of intercollegiate athletics finally approved their right-to-work measure and relaxed restrictions on athletes' employment. Approval was given by the NCAA to allow student-athletes on full scholarships to hold part-time

jobs. The revision ended the NCAA's longtime ban on employment for full-scholarship athletes during the school year.

Division I athletes who have been enrolled for one-year will now be able to earn up to $2,000 annually. They can work while their sport is in season, and the jobs can be arranged by the athletic department or boosters. There is the concern that the decision will ignite a wave of cheating. However, Bridget Niland, head of NCAA's Student-Athlete Advisory Committee, does not think it will be abused. "The only way it will be abused if coaches and athletic directors find a way to abuse it."

Still, the NCAA continues to adhere too rigidly to amateurism. While the U.S. Olympic Committee has abandoned all pretense of amateurism, the NCAA prohibits its student-athletes from making money at their sports. To keep their sports stars in college, the NCAA should pursue various ways of easing their financial difficulties, while at the same time assist other hard-working, needy student-athletes. Financial restrictions on college athletes should be relaxed, and new ways should be found to allow college athletes to receive money and more financial aid. ACC commissioner Gene Corrigan believes the association should re-examine the possibility of some kind of cash stipend for athletes in lieu of the jobs allowance. But who pays for this stipend? Certainly, the NCAA does not want to reopen the door to boosters paying athletes for "no-show" jobs.

More Minority Athletes Needed

College baseball finds itself today with very few black and other minority players, and their athletic prowess and competitive skills are being missed. "Young black kids are not playing baseball like they used to," wrote John Manuel. "They are programmed into other sports, particularly basketball and football."

According to coaches at black colleges, two facts explain the lack of African American baseball players: (1) Fewer black youngsters play and stay with baseball; and (2) Money for youth and college programs is often scarce.

"Young black athletes see that much greater money is spent in basketball and football," explained Manuel. "In comparison to those sports, very little money is spent on baseball at the high school and college levels. The only black schools that give 11.7 scholarships are Southern, Florida A & M, and Bethune-Cookman. "We have a larger mission, said Southern coach Roger Cador. "Our selling point to recruits is that we have an 80 percent graduation rate, and our young people are doing so well in society. We give kids the opportunity to play and get an education."

Amateur Draft Woes

Baseball's amateur draft continues to give problems to college baseball. Those drafted have no deadline to sign their contracts. Many of the athletes do not officially sign their contract until July or August, which leaves the college coach in a predicament. One program lost $720,000 worthy of drafted players over a two-year period.

Despite pleas from college coaches, professional baseball still refuses to have a signing deadline of mid-July so programs can at least get a replacement for a player who decides to sign. An earlier signing date deadline would appear to be in the best interests of everyone. However, the majors say they need more time to evaluate players after they are drafted. Another serious concern of college coaches is that more of their players are being drafted early, following their first or second year in school. Because of the lucrative bonuses being offered, top draftees are either signed right out of high school or after a year or so in college.

For colleges to be given a greater role in player development, the drafting of college players should be delayed until they have completed their senior year. By waiting, big league clubs, like the NBA and NFL, could more effectively evaluate players to insure a more predictable performance once they become professional players. Too much money is currently being spent on player development in an industry where the development of players is very uncertain.

Acts of Violence by Athletes

An increasing number of young athletes are committing acts of violence. "Coaches can become a big factor in helping eradicate the threat that is so prevalent in our country," wrote Elmer Kosub, retired coach at St. Mary's of Texas. "Every coach likes to see players who are aggressive but be aware of the ones who are violent, who express sudden bursts of anger and uncontrollable emotions."

In Collegiate Baseball, Kosub gave the following suggestions for coaches in handling problems associated with violence problems:

- Set policies concerning violent behavior

- Formulate a plan to deal with on-field acts of violence

- Attend clinics, seminars, lectures, and meetings

- Make your policy of handling abnormal behavior known to parents and report any abnormal behavior to them

- Consult with local mental health agencies and visit with local police officers to obtain information

- Be a good example to your players concerning your conduct, behavior and language

- Teach respect and demand it from players, umpires, parents and fans

Lapses in Sportsmanship, Ethics

Sportsmanship and ethics in sports continues to take a back seat to money --- how to make it and distribute it. Of all the pressing issues facing college sports, none are more critical than sportsmanship and ethics. Russ Gough of The Sporting News wrote, "Every time sportsmanship-ethics are about to get their rightful place in the spotlight, they get side-tracked in favor of the most dominant topic in college sports: MONEY." At the 1996 NCAA Convention in Dallas, despite the fact that the convention's official theme was "Integrity: Sportsmanship and Ethical Conduct in Intercollegiate Athletics," the real name of the game, said Gough, was " how to make, control, and divvy up the almighty dollar."

What should be the objectives of participation in sports?

- Promote the physical, mental, moral, social, and emotional well-being of the individual players
- Play for the joy of playing and the success of the team
- Exemplify good sportsmanship and ethical conduct
- Not to quit, cheat, bet, grandstand or abuse the body
- Playing the game fairly. Playing hard to the end
- Uphold the best values of the game

- Contribute to a meaningful educational experience
- Show cordial courtesy to visiting teams and officials
- Respect the integrity and judgment of sports officials
- Understand and accept the rules of the game
- Encourage leadership, initiative, and good judgment
- Always remember that an athletic contest is only a game
- Coaches can and should control the behavior of their athletes
- Perhaps the number of victories is least important

Supplements Imperil Eligibility

"Nutritional supplements could be a ticking bomb," said an editorial in Collegiate Baseball. Gary Green, NCAA Committee member on Competitive Safeguards and Medical Aspects of Sports, wrote, "We know from surveys that at least 20 to 30 percent of NCAA student-athletes are taking supplements, and the actual numbers are probably much higher. A significant number of athletes already have been suspended for one year for taking supplements that violate the NCAA drug-testing policy.

While Mark McGwire was allowed to take androstendione in his pursuit of the all-time home run record, NCAA athletes may not use that supplement or a number of others. "Mark McGwire makes the cover of Sports Illustrated for taking androstendione," said Green, "but an NCAA athlete receives a one-year suspension."

Why does the NCAA ban drugs such as androstendione, DHEA and 19-Norandrostendione when they are allowed by other sports organizations such as Major League Baseball? "All of those drugs are precursors of anabolic steroids," said Green, "which means if you take enough of them, they are converted to anabolic steroids. The NCAA strongly believes that anabolic steroids offer an unfair advantage and are unhealthy. Taken in high enough quantities, androstendione will cause the same health problems as anabolic steroids."

In his message to all young athletes, Green told them, "If you test positive, it is not your friends or the guy at the nutrition store who will be serving the suspension, it will be you! So, you better know the NCAA rules."

More Research Studies Needed

There is a strong need for college professors and post-graduate students to engage in more research studies, particularly the type of experimental laboratory work done on the Master's and Doctoral levels. Most definitely, the research efforts of our colleges and universities have made many important contributions to the game, but much more needs to be done. There are many problems and issues, which need laboratory analyses and evaluative study, such as the controversies over bat and ball standards, value and effectiveness of training aids, etc. From what we have learned, many coaches either do not have the time or are not sufficiently interested in doing experimental and other forms of research. If this is the case, they should request assistance from professors who serve as advisors of graduate students in the areas of sports, kinesiology, physiology of exercise, etc. and recommend meaningful subject areas.

The current chairman of the research committee for the American Baseball Coaches Association is: Jerry Haugen, St. John's University, Box 7277, Collegeville, MN 56321-7277. Telephone: (320) 363-2756; FAX: (320) 363-3130.

Maintenance Scholarships and Award

TURFACE Sports Field Products and the American Baseball Coaches Association have teamed together to offer baseball coaches two opportunities to earn free grounds maintenance supplies for their fields.

1. ABCA/TURFACE Pro League Maintenance Scholarships are awarded to coaches in need of upgrading their field to a safe, playable level. The winning field receives 3 tons of TURFACE MVP for their field, in addition to $250/year for two years to be spent on maintenance equipment.

2. ABCA/TURFACE Pro League Maintenance Awards are awarded to coaches who have outstanding maintenance programs in both infield and turf care. Winners receive 1 ton of TURFACE MVP and $400 for maintenance equipment and a plaque recognizing their excellence in maintenance.

For more information, write: PROFILE Products, 750 Lake Cook Road, Suite 440, Buffalo Grove, IL 60089, Attn: TURFACE/ABCA Award Scholarship. Entries must be submitted by November 1. For complete details and a set of rules, call: 800-207-6457, or visit their Web site: www.profileproducts.com.

Winning Coaches

Over the years, collegiate baseball has had many outstanding coaches who knew how to win and did. To win, their teams have had to play good fundamental baseball. While space does not permit me to acknowledge all of them, I would like to discuss briefly the basic style and approaches of three contrasting philosophies of coaching:

- Skip Bertman (Louisiana State), whose teams play LONG BALL
- Augie Garrido (Texas), the guru of the SHORT GAME
- Pete Beiden (Fresno State), legendary former coach, a master teacher

Skip Bertman (Louisiana State)

After experiencing failure at College World Series, Coach Bertman changed his philosophy. Rather than recruit players who could run and play defense, he decided he better score more runs and play long ball. His teams now "live and die" with the home run. The results have been extraordinary, winning four national championships – 1991, 1993, 1996 and 1997.

When Bertman became head coach of Louisiana State, he realized that the only way to win a national championship was with offense because no team can have enough pitching depth to dominate opponents throughout the postseason. Bertman's success can be attributed to his long ball approach to the game and having several big thumpers. Part of his system is motivation, inspiration to reach goals beyond their expectations and developing team camaraderie.

Bertman is relentless, tireless, and goal-oriented. He demands excellence from his players. He works on things that other teams don't, such as pickoff moves and bunt defense. Skip teaches a "pitch-by-pitch mentality", a total concentration of the game. Bertman spends much time on motivation and team orientation. Before every game, he gathers his players in front of a TV and pops in a tape from among the 60 or so from his private collection. In using visualization, he asks players to spend time picturing themselves starring in their own baseball movie as the hero who makes the big play or hits the game-winning home run.

Augie Garrido (Texas)

During his long and highly successful career at Cal State at Fullerton, Illinois and now at Texas, coach Garrido has been known as the guru of the short game. Numerous coaches have attempted to copy his high pressure offensive style which includes bunting, push bunts, drag bunts, and stealing bases.

His teams have never been power laden ball clubs. He loves to manufacture runs. His teams scratch for runs. They are very aggressive on the basepaths. Augie likes to have his baserunners make a false break to the next base and try to get some movement on the defensive infield and help his hitters find a hole. They try and get breaks, figuring out ways to just come up with a run.

A great innovator, Augie loves to teach the game. His teams do a lot of bunting. It is not unusual to watch Garrido-coached ball teams lay the bunt down in any situations, regardless of the hitter, his average, or the situation. When playing a team coached by Garrido, expect the unexpected.

Garrido teams are adept at scoring a run without a hit. How do they do it? Tim Brando of ESPN explained: "Steve Nedeau, lefthand hitter for Cal State-Fullerton, is up there. What does he do? He coaxes a walk, so there is a start. A typical one. Runner moving on the bunt. The only play is to first base. Now, you have a man in scoring position. Then, the wild pitch. Getting to the top of your order, and Mickey Lopez. Not trying to pull the ball, he does a nice job of hitting the other way. Cal State comes up with a sacrifice fly. They get a run without a hit."

The ball clubs of Garrido have always been known for their "Run and gun" style of offense, which has produced well over 1,000 wins for Garrido during his distinguished career. "We try to score first in every ball game we play," he said. "It takes pressure off your defense and pitcher, and the opposition then has more pressure on their pitcher and players."

Pete Beiden (Fresno State)

Pete Beiden, the man for whom Beiden field is named, coached at Fresno State University from 1948 through 1969. He and Bob Bennett, who played for Pete, are largely responsible for developing the Bulldog baseball program into a national power.

"Coach Beiden is a true pioneer of baseball coaching fundamentals," wrote Bennett. "His interest in teaching the basic skills was unparalleled. He was a disciple of Branch Rickey, and like Mr. Rickey was ahead of his time. He really, truly outcoached a lot of people. Our program at Fresno State is based on the teaching of fundamentals, and that's what Pete started a long time ago and something I've continued," said Bennett. "I often marveled at the way he taught. When he talked, people listened."

Perhaps the greatest single thing in Beiden's legacy is that he dispensed with each of his baseball lessons the simple fundamentals of the game. As Bennett explained, "Coach Beiden felt that the most important things to teach were the simple fundamentals. Whatever the skills, the basic fundamentals improve the level of play. Fundamentals are the roots. Improvement, adjustment and correction find a genesis in the fundamentals. Later the teaching of these fundamentals was passed on to the players, and those players now make up large numbers of coaches in the Fresno area and elsewhere from Little League all the way to the majors.

Wayne Hironaka, a southpaw pitcher of Beiden, explained how the Beiden approach to the game has remained strong in the Fresno area. "Many players, who played for Pete, stayed in the area to coach high school, Legion and other amateur teams. As a result, his coaching philosophy and teaching methods were carried on down to the lower levels and were brought up through the system. High school coaches would send their kids to a Pete Beiden graduate, who then sent them on the Coach Bennett, another Beiden graduate. Coach Beiden taught the Baseball Theory class at Fresno State, as well as helping prepare countless numbers of Physical Education Majors and players who went on to coach. So, there was a strong continuity of fundamentals taught."

Legacy of Pete Beiden. Beiden coached at Fresno State
University from 1948 through 1969. His coaching philosophy
And teaching methods have carried on through the years.
Beiden Field, below, was named after the "Master Teacher."

Administration of College Baseball

NCAA   At its first special convention in August 1993, the National Collegiate Athletic Association voted to establish national championship competition in each of three divisions for its active membership. The three divisions were designated Divisions I, II, and III. A discussion group initially, the NCAA undertook one of its most vital functions shortly after World War II, when the membership voted itself legislative and executive powers.

In 1996, however, the governing procedure of the NCAA and its schools changed. Following major restructuring, a different format was enacted as to how legislation is passed. The change allows a framework where chief executive officers at each school serve as the primary decision-makers. Dave Keilitz explained that "Instead of having an NCAA convention where proposals are voted on by the entire group (A.D.'s, faculty reps, presidents, etc.), there are no more votes in front of this total group. It is now broken down into cabinets, committees, etc."

The 44-member Presidents Commission has been replaced by a 16-member executive committee made up of university presidents, 12 of whom will come from Division I. The governing bodies of each division now have unprecedented independence to set policies and rules, and the regulations of a division. The change-of-season   plan,   for   example,   was   brought   before   the Championships/Competition Cabinet, comprised of faculty reps, conference commissioners, athletic directors, etc. The next step for the proposal was the Management council, made up of 24 persons. If endorsed by this body, the next hurdle was the Board of Directors made up of 14 people.

The mailing address of the NCAA is:
        6201 College Blvd., Overland Park, KS 66211
        Telephone: (913) 339-1906   FAX: (913) 339-0043
        President: Cedric Dempsey   Championships: Dennis Pope

NAIA   The National Association of Intercollegiate Athletics is a completely autonomous association, currently administrating programs in nearly 400 fully-accredited four-year colleges and universities. Established in 1940, the NAIA is organized into nine geographic regions spread across the 50 states. Among a large number of major league players developed in the NAIA are two current big league managers, Mike Hargrove from Northwestern Oklahoma and Sam Riggleman from Frostburg State. Recently, Steve Baker, a former major league pitcher, became the new chief executive officer for the NAIA.

A great strength of NAIA baseball is its geographic 8-regional format for getting to the national championship. Other strengths include a 65-game schedule, 24-week practice schedule, tryouts, recruits can be contacted anytime, and no time limits for practices for each week, which has to make NCAA coaches very envious.

The mailing address for the NAIA is:
> 6120 South Yale Avenue, Suite 1450, Tulsa, OK 74136
> Telephone: (918) 494-8828   FAX: (918) 494-8841

NJCAA   In 1937, 13 junior colleges met in Fresno, California to organize an association that would promote and supervise a national program of junior college sports. In 1949, the National Junior College Athletic Association was expanded to 16 regions and by 1983 was re-organized into the present region structure of 24. Baseball entered the national spotlight in '58 when the NJCAA Invitational Tournament was held in Miami, Oklahoma. The NJCAA membership includes 530 junior colleges and sponsors 28 national championships in 15 men's sports.

For over 30 years, junior college baseball recognized only one division. In the 1990s, however, the NJCAA administration and its Baseball Coaches Association took a look at the equality of the "playing field" and agreed it was not level for all competing colleges. Their solution was to form divisions (I, II, and III) with restrictions on granting financial support depending on the level of participation. To date, the divisional play system has been very positive and has had a strong impact on junior college baseball.

The school's geographic proximity plays an important part in the NJCAA's divisional system. According to Marty Dittmer, former secretary-treasurer, "It has helped to equalize the weather and climate instability which many feel is a tremendous disadvantage, particularly for the northern schools."

The mailing address for the NJCAA is:

> P.O. Box 7305, Colorado Springs, CO 80933
> Telephone: (719) 590-9788   FAX: (719) 590-7324
> Executive Director: George Killian

CCLC   The Community College League of California supervises the administration of the intercollegiate athletic programs of the 107 community colleges. One hundred colleges offer programs for both men and women in 13 sports. California community colleges stage their own state championships while the NJCAA stages its own. The two have not been involved in any type of championship since the mid-1950s. The CCLC has proposed having its state champion play the NJCAA winner, but NJCAA officials rejected the proposal. This impasse is unfortunate, the fact that junior colleges in California do not have membership in the NJCAA. Such a reality would be in the best interests of both organizations. A true national championship in jaycee baseball will only occur when the California champion competes in the NJCAA tournament.

Looking at juco programs academically and developmentally, jaycee athletes are playing too much. Players in California and Florida, in particular, are playing the year around. The season runs from January to May, followed by summer college leagues, and semi-pro ball; then, the fall program, involving games on the weekend from early October into December. It is rather apparent that many student-athletes do not have enough time to study and prepare for careers, which for most of them may not be baseball.

Mailing address for the CCLC is:

> 2017 O Street, Sacramento, CA 95814
> Telephone: (916) 444-1600   FAX: (916) 444-2616
> Commissioner of Athletics: Joanne Fortunato

American Baseball Coaches Association

American Baseball Coaches Association Since its beginning in 1945 when a group of collegiate coaches gathered in Chicago, the ABCA has enjoyed remarkable growth and stature. Through the years, the ABCA has developed into what is commonly called "the world's finest, largest baseball convention and clinic". The prime objective of the ABCA is still to promote baseball and share coaching knowledge with other members.

Record numbers of coaches attend ABCA's convention each year, highlighted by the popular clinic sessions. With the use of a big screen, "walking mike's", and video tapes, instruction is at its finest. Each year, college baseball's most distinguished coaches are inducted into the Coaches Hall of Fame.

The strong growth of the ABCA in recent years can be attributed in large part to the administrative efficiency of Dave Keilitz and his hard working staff. In 1994, Keilitz succeeded the retiring Dick Bergquist as the ABCA's fourth executive director and has done an outstanding job. The association has become a lobbying group to help out in issues that are so critical at each level. According to Carroll Land, chairman of the board, "We have spent big dollars and much energy to lobby effectively in the legislative processes for amateur baseball."

The ABCA is a nonprofit tax-exempt organization located at:
    108 South University Avenue, Suite 3, Mt. Pleasant, MI 48858
    Telephone: (517) 775-3300; FAX: (517) 775-3600
    Web site: http://www.abca.org   E-mail: abca@abca.org

    Executive Director: Dave Keilitz
    Assistant to the Executive Director: Betty Rulong
    Administrative Assistant: Nick Williams

The annual National Baseball Congress in Wichita, Kansas continues to be the major showcase of semi-pro baseball.

EL DORADO OILERS
VS.
STEARMAN AIRCRAFT
OF WICHITA

OTHER FEATURES:
Band Concert

Starting 7:15

Battery For First Pitch
J. C. Truman and
Frank L. Seymour

Plenty of Entertainment

Children Under 12 Years of
Age Admitted Free!

ADMISSION—30c

El Dorado Times (Kansas), Thursday, May 23, 1940

The non-pro area of play has had a sharp growth of leagues and teams involving older players.

James Donaldson Park

For baseball to remain America's sport, the revival of hometown rivalries is crucial.

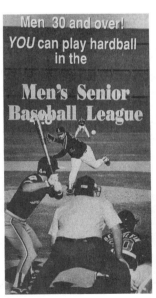

Men 30 and over!
YOU can play hardball in the

Men's Senior Baseball League

In 1986, Steve Sigler started Men's Senior Baseball on Long Island. The program has been a huge success.

Summer collegiate leagues like Cape Cod are playing a major role in the revival of semi-pro baseball.

8 Non-Pro/Semi-Pro/ Adult

There was a time when nearly every city and town throughout the country fielded semi-pro teams that were the pride of their communities. They used to be the big draw. "On game day, watching the local ball club was the social activity, the only game in town," wrote David Jackson in the Evansville, Indiana Press. "Go to church, hustle out to the park, spread out the blanket, and razz the right fielder."

Indeed, semi-pro baseball was one of the most popular pastimes for local fans, but times have changed in recent years. Attendance at semi-pro games has declined over the years. Many of the small town teams fare quite well at the gate, but teams from the bigger cities have experienced a lack of fan support. Spectators are mostly family members, parents, girl friends, and house parents of the players involved, along with some senior citizens and a few professional scouts.

The non-pro area of play has enjoyed a strong growth of leagues involving older ball players continuing or returning to ball diamonds. Senior leagues locally are more of a recreational format, in that players actually pay to play. Age brackets and drafts keep teams competitive. Thousands of men are paying to play for the pure love of the game in the rapidly expanding Men's Senior Baseball League. The league's growth has been phenomenal, with players 30 and older, more than 27,000 of them in 300 cities, including former major league players. It's a whole new generation of players. The Senior's World Series has been a big hit, drawing 4,000 players ages 30-70, from 44 states. They have the opportunity to compete for a national championship!

Semi-professional leagues, on the other hand, are organized on a more competitive basis, like the professional game. In the Seattle area's Pacific International League and many areas of the country, semi-pro, rather than non-pro, is a far more descriptive term relative to the makeup and philosophy of the teams. Having no age limits, the ability to produce is the foremost criteria. Some teams consist only of college players, while many clubs have former professionals and college graduates. "Semi-pro baseball is a player's game," wrote Steve Reich, commissioner of the Central Florida Baseball League. "They play for themselves, with the hope of moving up in the game, holding on if they are ex-pros, and for the 'pure fun of it,' if they have no further aspirations."

Although the objectives of non-pro baseball vary, the purpose of many leagues is to allow as many players as possible to continue the sport that they love. Young college players play to work on their game, improve their skills, keep in shape, and attract the attention of pro scouts. Older, more experienced players are playing for the pure love of the game and the opportunity to participate in post-season tournaments. Talented players out of high school have opportunities to be seen by pro scouts or earn a college scholarship by drawing interest in various summer leagues.

Ideally, semi-pro leagues and even the senior programs should provide fans with a highly competitive brand of baseball, wholesome family atmosphere, and plenty of entertainment. Many teams and leagues on the non-pro level, however, have yet to capitalize on the entertainment and crowd-pleasing methods used so successfully by professional baseball.

Semi-pro baseball appears to be coming back. There is increasing interest in local baseball, where more players are rediscovering the thrill of playing America's game for fun, enjoyment and self-satisfaction. For baseball to remain America's sport, the revival of hometown rivalries is most crucial. For "Sunday Afternoon Baseball" to make a comeback, however, there has to be far more involvement and interest of the family and community, with players getting involved in the community, greater emphasis on social and family aspects -- and, a town playing another town!

Non-pro baseball has the potential to contribute as much to the game's renaissance as any other level of play. The National Baseball Congress, with the support of USA Baseball, has the capability to play a greater role in the development of higher-skilled players, at a time when the professional leagues are in dire need of more talent. Rather than place too much emphasis on the World Series, the NBC, taking a broader approach to non-pro ball, needs to reach out and offer greater support to its member leagues and teams. Failure to do so, more semi-pro teams will fall by the wayside and players, young and old, will have to settle for recreational baseball only.

Stronger Presence by NBC Needed

The highly competitive National Baseball Congress, highlighted by the excitement and drama of the World Series, continues to be the major showcase of non-pro baseball. However, with the steady growth of recreation-oriented adult leagues across the country, the NBC needs to step up and develop a program that can provide a balance with National Adult and Senior programs.

For the NBC to expand and be more competitive with the growth of recreational adult and senior leagues, it has to take on a stronger presence in non-pro baseball. The organization has to reach out and spread its wings, rather than remain roosted in Wichita. To do so, it has to become more structured and promotion-minded. The NBC's overall organizational structure nationwide has to be more responsive to local and regional needs and concerns.

Semi-pro baseball has to upgrade its player development capability and quality of play so as to attract the interest and support of professional baseball. The NBC and semi-pro leagues nationwide must play a stronger role in the development of skilled players in America. Otherwise, USA teams will continue to be dominated in worldwide competition, and the number of foreign players on major league teams, now 30%, will become even greater, much to the disappointment of our American players.

For many decades, the NBC has been supported mightily by the many dedicated, hard-working commissioners of the past. One by one, however, these giants of semi-pro ball are either retiring gracefully or frustrated by the lack of funding, too often the result of an organization not willing to assert its presence, like young Steve Sigler is doing with MSBL and NABA. Even Larry Davis, the NBC's long-time commissioner and tournament director, admits that his organization has traditionally taken "a more laid back" approach. While this policy has proven successful in the past, it will not work in the future. A more aggressive approach is needed.

In his strong and emotional challenge to the National Baseball Congress, Mickey Deutschman, the veteran manager, sponsor, and guiding spirit of the San Diego Stars, stated that, "The NBC must step up and develop a program to compete with the MSBL and NABA, or else we're going to lose semi or non-pro ball and have to settle for recreation baseball only."

Among the most serious problems and concerns that the NBC should address:

- Finding good sponsors
- Lack of operating funds
- Competition from many other leagues
- Lack of good facilities
- Getting media coverage
- Shortages of good talent to be competitive
- Lack of fan interest
- Availability of responsible managers
- Difficulty in conducting a profitable tournament
- Inconsistency in the umpiring

Cooperation is needed, however, between the NBC-administered non-pro leagues and the growing number of recreational programs. The two areas of organized baseball must help each other because there is a need for both, the highly competitive NBC leagues and teams from the recreational leagues. In the Seattle area, the two programs understand their differences. As the president of Pacific International League, Steve Konek, pointed out, "We help each other and cooperate for mutual success, even to the extent of recommending players. Both need to be a plus, rather than a minus, an adversary, not a competitor."

College Hosted Non-Pro Leagues   Perhaps the key to the revival of semi-pro and hometown baseball is the steady increase in the number of summer collegiate leagues across the country. They could be the catalyst to a stronger, more stable NBC and the revival of semi-pro baseball. The NBC must develop a closer association with colleges and universities. Traditionally, college players have provided a large source of talent in NBC's program and this must continue. However, team rosters should also include as many local athletes with whom the fans can identify and be familiar with. In doing so, the popularity of semi-pro baseball would increase significantly. A growing number of college players desire to play summer baseball, to develop their playing skills, and they need to play a more competitive brand of baseball.

Semi-pro ball would receive a big boost if a sufficient number of colleges and universities would host summer non-pro leagues, utilizing the Professional Preparation Agreement plan I described in chapter 7. By making available their facilities for semi-pro oriented summer collegiate leagues, every level of play would benefit. By bringing semi-pro ball back into prominence, the player development needs of the major leagues would be served. Stronger non-pro leagues will contribute to the farm systems of the majors, similar to the independent leagues. Both college players and students would be involved in both the morning youth baseball program and the evening semi-pro league.

Student-athletes of the colleges would receive valuable playing experiences, as well as receiving leadership and coaching training at the morning youth camp and playground league. The morning and evening programs would also serve the needs of youth baseball such as the player development and training of youth coaches. The league in the evening would be part of the agreement between the colleges and pro baseball, in conjunction with Occupational Education programs at host colleges, educating both student-athletes and Sport Management majors for a career occupation.

Hometown Rivalries Should Return

For the game to remain the nation's pastime, fan interest can best be revived by the organization of more local teams and hometown rivalries. Years ago, numerous small cities and communities had very good town teams, which attracted strong fan support. They used to call them semi-pro, but essentially, it was a town playing another town. Of course, the task of reviving town teams today will be far more difficult because of the many options available to people, such as television, many other sports, outdoor recreation, and travel. In past decades, there was a greater tendency for people to stay home.

"The revival of the home town concept is baseball's only chance to re-establish itself for what the game really is," wrote Bill Schroeder, publisher of Lakeland Newspapers in northern Illinois. "Years ago, every town worth its salt fielded a team in the days before television hype and national media fawning on today's plastic heroes. The hometown diamond Warriors were the pride of grassroots America. Big leaguers were mystical characters in far off cities. Our heroes were home grown."

Club baseball would help fulfill the need for teams and people in towns and small cities to identify with, to give children and young players the opportunity to look up to, idolize, and strive to emulate their hometown heroes. "I knew them all by name," said Schroeder. "A 10-year old kid in those days revered guys who were good at baseball."

Baseball became the nation's pastime not because of the major leagues but because of the hometown heroes. "If the game is to remain the national pastime," said Schroeder, "fan interest must best be revived in the local teams. Their game hasn't changed - - twi-light and Sunday contests, merchant names on the uniforms, passing-the-hat admission prices and a pretty good brand of baseball. Semi-pro!"

The hometown concept is still alive, but it has to be cultivated, nurtured and re-kindled. Unquestionably, bringing it back will not be easy because of the many more options available to people today. In older days, baseball was the only professional sport of any stature in America. People weren't mobile like they are today. The job of building up the support of loyal fans is not going to be easy, but it represents a worthwhile challenge and a most necessary need for the movement to be a success.

"This revival must start with dedicated individuals in the small towns and communities," wrote Willis Steenhuis, commissioner for the State of Mississippi for the National Baseball Congress. They must strive for better team organization, and in some way, create more revenue for their teams.

Strong efforts should begin soon, with the assistance of Major League Baseball and USA Baseball, to spark a revival of hometown baseball and expand the number of teams representing communities and towns. The nation-wide movement would be spearheaded by a more aggressive and community-minded National Baseball Congress.

The NBC must take the initiative in organizing and promoting an upgraded program that will be more structured and geared to local and regional needs and concerns, as it is to its very successful national tournament. It has to be promoted by the managers and owners, business and civic leaders, and the citizens of the community. Most urgently, it must be provided with greater financial stability.

Remarkable Growth in Adult Play

The non-pro area of play has had a sharp growth of leagues and teams involving older players continuing or returning to baseball diamonds. Among the thousands of players are many former major league players, including Jim Barr, Bob Oliver, Jerry Reuss, and Jose Cardenal. In addition, there is a "feeder" circuit of over 14,000 players between the ages of 18 and 29. But the great majority are men (and a few women) who never played pro baseball, and in many cases, have not played since high school.

More than 4,000 baseball players ages 30-70 from 44 states and a growing number of foreign countries travel to Arizona and Florida to compete in the annual Men's Senior Baseball League World Series. Taking a week's vacation during the autumn season, they buy 30-70 from 44 states and a growing number of foreign countries travel to Arizona and Florida to compete in the annual Men's Senior Baseball League World Series. They buy plane tickets, check into hotels, rent cars, and spend a week playing at sites used by major league clubs for spring training.

A young New Yorker, Steve Sigler, thought middle-aged men should have another mid-life option. In March of 1986, he placed a two-sentence item in a Long Island newspaper, seeking players over thirty who wanted to play "hardball" again and play it with men their own age. Sigler wondered, "Am I the only one who feels this way?" But over sixty men responded, and Steve started a league with four teams. He started Men's Senior Baseball on Long Island with a few local teams. Today, the program stretches across the country and abroad. Sigler also administers the MABL (18-plus).

In Los Angeles, 28 teams compete in the "Thirty-Plus League" from March to September. All are members of the nationally, non-profit MSBL. The teams are from Los Angeles and Orange counties and are divided into three divisions: American, National, and minor league Jet-Hawk Stadium in Palmdale, with teams entering from all over the world.

"No, it is not a 'fantasy league', but the real package," wrote John Herbold in Collegiate Baseball, "with games every Sunday, uniformed (names on the back), two paid umpires and strictly regulated. No players are allowed who played professionally in the last three years. Any pitcher who hits three batters in a game is ejected." In this league, the players also pay to play, about $2,900 a team

334

and $250-375 a player. The quality of umpiring and playing fields are generally better in the MSBL, but more expensive than the NABL. World Series rings go to the players who win the Senior Men's tournament.

"It makes us feel young again," said Ken Cronan, manager of the Indians. "Sure, it's Field of Dreams stuff, and yes, we're Weekend Warriors letting off the steam of a long week at work. But all of us look forward from Sunday to Sunday to smack the ball around a little bit, and tell your wife and kids that Daddy can still 'go deep'!" Herbold wrote, "The players take the game seriously. And the talk is 'ball talk', like 'Around the horn, baby!" (throwing the ball around the infield), and occasionally, you'll hear "Ham 'n eggs' for a double play."

Of the several father/son combinations in the MSBL, perhaps the most unusual is sixty-six-year-old Jerry Thornton, a former outfielder for the University of Washington, and three of his five sons. In the Seattle area, the Red Sox of the Puget Sound League include Thornton in center field; Jeff (39), catching; J.B. (36), at second; and Jon (33), at shortstop. The grandfather of ten, Thornton said, "They can outrun me, but they can't outhit me."

Crowds at MSBL games consist largely of members of the family and friends. "It's old-time Sunday afternoon town ball, with different towns playing against each other in a festive atmosphere," said Sigler. "No games are played on Easter, Mother's Day, Memorial Day, or the Fourth of July. That's so the players can spend the entire day with their families."

In addition to the MSBL and MABL, the National Adult Baseball Association (18-65) is administered in Denver, Colorado by Brad Coldiron, president. Roy Hobbs Baseball (open, 30 and over, 40 and over, 48 and over) is based in Akron, Ohio, with Tom and Ellen Giffen directing operations. Information on these and other adult and senior leagues is given at the end of this chapter.

The Thirty-Plus League is not a fantasy league, but the real package.
- John Herbold

Father and Sons Play Together. Sixty-six years old Jerry Thornton, former outfielder for the University of Washington, and three of his five sons are members of the Red Sox of the Puget Sound League in the Seattle area

Baseball as it was meant to be played

Photographs by Douglas Merriam

The biggest and most competitive of old-time baseball programs is at the Old Bethpage Village Restoration in Old Bethpage, Long Island, New York

Baseball, As It Was Meant To Be Played

"To most people, the idea of playing baseball without a glove probably sounds like canoeing without a paddle," wrote Doug Stewart in the October, 1998 issue of Smithsonian magazine. However, at the Old Bethpage Village Restoration in Old Bethpage, New York, "It's the only sporting way to play."

Vintage baseball is booming around the United States. At least 70 programs are fielding teams that play by rules of past eras, which range from 1845 to 1924. The biggest and most competitive is the Old Time Base Ball Program at Old Bethpage. The program involves 130 players, all volunteers, on ten teams in two leagues, over a 60-game season. Stewart, a pitcher known as "the Scrivener", said "Our baseball contest is played by 1866 rules, with bare hands and a single, hard, hand-sewn ball."

"Ours is the only program with full-blown leagues," says Ken Balcom, the museum village's assistant site director. Old-time baseball games have been played at Old Bethpage since 1980 as one of the village's living-history demonstrations, like quilt making and blacksmithing. Stewart said, "The program got a boost in 1994 when hundreds of baseball-hungry Long Islanders, disgusted that the major leagues' millionaires were out on strike, converged on Old Bethpage to watch or to play an older, purer game."

The program involves 130 players, all volunteers, on ten teams in two leagues, over a 60-game season. The 1866 league, with underhand pitching, is open to anyone with basic ability. Its 1887 counterpart is a faster, more hard-nosed game with overhand pitching and fixed rosters. Participants in both include a handful of women (dressed like the men) and range in age from 17 to 67. As it did a century ago, the baseball season climaxes in October at Old Bethpage's revived Long Island Fair. Amid band concerts and cornhusking bouts, the play-off games take place during the first two weekends, followed by the league championships.

"The ballpark at Old Bethpage," said Stewart, "is nostalgic incarnate: a grass field, a wooden backstop, a vine-covered split-rail fence at the edge of the outfield, a red barn and gambrel-roofed house of 1840 vintage just beyond. Spectators begin gathering on rough wooden benches in the shade of an oak grove."

"This is baseball in its purest form," said Dan "The man" Moskowitz, 48, a bald, goateed pitcher of the Glen Head Zig Zags. "It's a window back into our youth, but also into America's past. It's a real counterpoint to the commercialism of modern day baseball, where the focus is on marketing and skybox seats." The teams' names, like their uniforms and many of the players' nicknames, are copied from their 19th-century predecessors. Moskowitz himself dug up 1880s game accounts of the Zig Zags in the local newspaper archives.

At Old Bethpage, Al "Old Dutch" Dieckmann, 54, the Hicksville Ozones' captain, is the acknowledged sage of bygone baseball trivia. A resident of Baldwin, New York and a SABR member, Dieckman and the other vintage ballists comb old game accounts for clues about how the game was actually played. Stewart wrote, "One morning, Dieckmann arrived at game time wearing a minister's long black frock coat, black flat-brimmed hat, black vest and gold pocket watch, looking like an undertaker in an old cowboy movie. He saw the getup in a Currier and Ives print of an old-time baseball umpire and borrowed all the garb from the museum's costume room."

Old-time baseball programs are popping up everywhere. Clubs in Pennsylvania, Connecticut, Florida, and Rhode Island have recently fielded teams. Colorado already has 6, and Ohio 13, including four women's teams and the pioneering Ohio Village Muffins, founded in 1981 by the Ohio Historical Society. "None of these play in leagues," said Stewart. "For the most part, they play exhibition games, often at 19th-century restoration villages." Most programs play by 1860 rules. Since the old rulebooks were fairly sketchy, today's vintage clubs are still refining their games.

Background of Semi-Pro Baseball

Non-pro baseball, better known as semi-pro ball, has existed in various forms since the 1900's. Originally organized around town and factory teams, the local and regional rivalries provided both a social and entertainment function for the fan. A crazy mix of minor league and town ball, semi-professional ball became wildly popular after the turn of the century. Although the players were amateurs, teams often passed the hat so the players could go home with a few dollars for their efforts. A local town would support a team of its own, paying the players a seasonal salary or a fee of $5 to $20 per game.

Semi-pro games were big events, especially in rural areas where two-hour-long picnics often preceded the game, usually a Sunday doubleheader and often a band concert followed. Semi-pro games in Cincinnati were so successful they had to rent the Reds ball park to accommodate their crowds, while Cleveland alone had as many as twelve semi-pro leagues in 1907. On the Fourth of July in 1913, there were four semi-pro doubleheaders going on at the same time in Lima, Ohio, all preceded by picnics. Most major cities had their own semi-pro city leagues in addition to major league franchises. Teams thrived because they offered good baseball and gave local fans an opportunity to see up-and-coming stars and future major leaguers. The city leagues would consistently draw as many as 8,000 fans a game.

Just how good were some of these teams? Some of them were just good former high school stars, but some were very good. In 1901, the Memphis team of the semi-pro Southern Association beat three major league teams in exhibitions, but was defeated by a semi-pro team from tiny (Population 750) Friars Point, Mississippi. In a much-hyped challenge, New York's Bush Wicks defeated the Brooklyn Dodgers 2-1 in 1916.

Beginning around 1905 and continuing through the 1940s, semi-pro teams made a practice of hiring big league players to join their team in a single game. Walter Johnson often pitched on his days off for semi-pro teams that would meet his price of $500 a game. Babe Ruth was a frequent semi-pro "ringer", playing for anyone for $500 to $700 a game. Lou Gehrig played regularly for a semi-pro team in Morristown, New Jersey. Two fans reportedly measured off one of his long home runs at 400 feet! The star pitcher of the Negro Leagues, Satchel Paige, earned so much money pitching for different semi-pro teams that he bought his own plane to fly from town to town.

John McGraw got his start playing semi-pro ball for $5 a game. Casey Stengel played on a barnstorming semi-pro team for a dollar a day, and Christy Mathewson, later a great star for the New York Giants, earned $25 a day in a semi-pro league. A young Dwight D. Eisenhower played semi-pro ball under an assumed name in 1910.

Most of the thousands of semi-pro teams across the United States and Canada, however, were made up of young men who just wanted to play baseball. For them twenty or thirty dollars was more than enough because they were confident their experiences in semi-pro ball would be a stepping stone to the minor leagues and then, the majors. They hoped that major league scouts were in the stands watching them.

By 1915, there were more than a thousand semi-pro teams, which culminated in the establishment of the National Baseball Federation and a national championship. Indicative of the strong popularity of semi-pro ball, a championship game attracted a crowd of 100,000 fans to Brookside, a natural grass-bowl stadium in Cleveland. Teams were receiving both trophies and money. In the mid-1930s, the various national championships were awarding $5,000 in prize money, giving each player as much as $300, a big sum at the heights of the Depression. More and more good prep and college players were joining semi-pro teams, driven by the desire to earn extra money playing ball in an era where an average weekly salary for blue-collar workers was just $75 a week.

The driving force of semi-pro baseball's modern boom was Raymond "Hap" Dumont, former newspaperman and sporting goods dealer in Wichita, Kansas. He inaugurated a statewide tournament in 1931. Within four years, it blossomed into a series involving hundreds of clubs, drawing 50,000 fans and paying $5,000 in prize money. By 1935, Dumont's brainschild was ready to go national, staging a national tournament, an invitational event. It was such a huge success that the following year, he organized the National Semi-pro Baseball Congress.

Dumont was most unique, a man who loved the game and saw a need to fill a gap between high school and the pro's. He had a vision and worked hard to make it a reality. Hap had the foresight to lure Satchel Paige to come down from Bismarck to pitch. Paige won four games at the national tournament, including the title game. His 60 strikeouts is still an NBC record.

On July 3, 1971, as he was preparing for the Kansas tournament, Dumont was to have a meeting with chief umpire, Jerry Gilas. When Gilas arrived in the early afternoon, he found Hap face down on the floor, dead at 66, a victim of a heart attack. "Hap received a stirring tribute from a dear friend, Bob Gadberry," Bob Broeg wrote in his book, "Baseball's Barnum". Following Dumont's death, Davis got several people together and purchased the estate. With the organization and people skills of Davis, NBC's tournament continued to operate quite successfully, although the organization itself went through a heavy turnover in ownership, including businessman Dee Hubbard, a team sponsor who made a strong effort to keep the NBC in Wichita.

Bob Rich, Jr., owner of the Buffalo Bisons and a highly successful businessman, responded to the appeal of Joe Ryan, another friend of Dumont, by purchasing the National Baseball Congress. He also purchased Wichita's American Association farm club and moved it to Buffalo. Then he challenged Wichita to upgrade Lawrence-Dumont Stadium so that he would add a Wichita Double-A team, the Wranglers, to his baseball holdings.

Under Rich's ownership, the National Baseball Congress entered a new era in Wichita. With four staff members having a combined 68 years of experience in promoting and operating sports, Rich had put the NBC on solid footing, ably administered by an experienced staff. Wife, Melinda, in charge of the Entertainment Division of the Rich Products, has provided creative support for Steve Shaad, Larry Davis, Di Overaker, and Mike Yearty. In praising the Rich family ownership, Davis said, "The Rich Corporation is not here to make money. If we make money, they turn it right back in the program. They love sports and take a very serious interest in whatever endeavor they might undertake."

NBC's World Series

Every August since 1935, the top non-pro baseball clubs in the world have battled to decide the national championship in the National Baseball Congress World Series. Eight regional tournaments are held throughout the country, with the champions of each qualifying for the NBC classic in Wichita, Kansas. Non-pro teams can qualify for a berth either as a winner of a sanctioned NBC state or regional tournament. In addition, the top four finishers in the previous year's tournament receive an automatic berth.

"The niche that the National Baseball Congress fills is that it bridges the gap between scholastic and professional baseball," said Steve Shaad, vice president of NBC and the Wichita Wranglers of the Class-AA Texas League. "As a result, we are a fairly loosely organized group of leagues and teams nationwide. The NBC is not a strong or iron-fisted governing organization. The structure of NBC is to determine a national champion for non-professional baseball. Beyond that, we do not burn the teams in the leagues with a very complex structure."

The National Baseball Congress is less structured and much more geared toward grassroots baseball than professional baseball is. As Shaad explained, "We may have a team in Alaska with a $200,000 budget, and they may meet a team in the NBC finals from Carney or Beatrice, Nebraska, that operates on a shoe-string budget from $5 to $10,000 for the whole year. So it becomes a real challenge to market and organize."

The NBC is sensitive to the expenses of traveling to the tournament. More teams are trying to win the national championship on as few dollars as possible. "They don't have millionaire owners," said Shaad, "nor big businesses backing them. Sometimes, there is an individual manager who is paying for all the expenses out of his own pocket, so we try to accommodate these teams and not have them sit for 2 or 3 days in between games."

"Scheduling is one of the big problems," said Davis, "bringing in teams from long distances. It is almost an impossibility to bracket. We just pair them round by round, to defer the teams expenses. Some teams in a round might play three games by the time another team comes into play their first game."

Prize money continues to rise at the national tournament. "From $32,000, we are up to $50,000 and we intend to keep on raising it if the tournament continues to be successful," said Shaad.

NBC's Home Run Craze
In the 1990s, major league hitters have been blasting home runs like never before, but the ball has been flying out of Lawrence-Dumont Stadium for decades. To what can all the home runs be attributed to? JUICED BALLS!! "Fans like to see high-scoring games," said Davis, tournament director since the 1960s. "They just like to see the ball go out of the park."

As to the NBC's use of rabbit balls, Davis explained that "We like to please the fans." Back in the 1970s, he ordered a special baseball from the now defunct DeBeer Sporting Goods Company. The ball was named "Jet" for one special reason: It flew like one, thanks to a solid rubber core and tightly wound, stitched seams. "I'd start off those tournaments with a dead ball to try and keep from having too many one-sided games," Davis said. "Then I would bring the jet in, and we'd go from maybe one home run a game to three or four." Well, at least the NBC people are honest enough to admit the use of juiced balls.

Hall of Famer Satchel Paige led Bismarck, North Dakota, to the first national title in 1935.

NBC National Commissioner Larry Davis presents 1978 title trophy to Boulder, Colorado, Collegians Bauldie Moschetti

Bob and Mindy Rich, owners of the National Baseball Congress, get a skybox view of Lawrence-Dumont Stadium

NBC founder Raymond "Hap" Dumont with an umpire and player

Hap Dumont, with Harry Walker, demonstrates one of his innovations, the 20-90 Second Timer

Whitey Herzog is congratulated by his Springfield, Mo, teammates during the 1954 national Tournament

Through the years, the national tournament has been one home run barrage after another. The Midlothian (Illinois) Mid-Sox set a record when they hit 28 home runs during the 1990 World Series. Two years later, Midlothian put on another smashing power display in winning its first national title. The Mid-Sox hit 27 round-trippers, including seven in the championship game.

Baseball Around the Clock

This very innovative event was first staged by Hap Dumont, but was put on the shelf. Then in 1990, the NBC started the event again when officials learned that Wichita State's field was being renovated and would not be available. They had to get in as many games as possible, so they offered fans the following deal: Pay one admission to Friday's session, starting at 4:30 p.m. and stay for 17 games in 56 hours. Those who check in for all 17 games would receive prizes.

Keeping fans in the stadium "Round the Clock" is a marketing challenge. "We felt we could draw a crowd just about any time of the day," explained Shaad. "By developing it into a kind of promotion, we put together a contest. We encouraged fans to stay for the whole weekend and allow them to camp out in the stadium and give them prizes if they stayed for all the games. With fans coming in from other states for the weekend, it has become a "badge of pride" that they survived 'Baseball Around the Clock' at the NBC World Series."

More popular than ever, half the tournament field, 34 teams, play a total of 17 games in a span of 56 hours. A record 502 fans registered for the marathon contest in 1993, and 272 fans actually stayed throughout the grueling weekend schedule. Those hardy fans won sleeping bags from the Coleman Company along with T-shirts that stated, "I survived Baseball 'Round the Clock!"

How do the players react to playing at 3 o'clock in the morning? Is there the feeling, "What am I doing here?" Shaad said, "Many of them are college players, and they are up and ready to go at 1 a.m. We get more complaints from the people who have to start that first game in the morning at 8 a.m. than the ones who play at night, because when night comes, players are ready to go and the juices are flowing. There's always a big crowd at 1 a.m."

Baseball's Barnum – Hap Dumont

Raymond H. "Hap" Dumont founded the National Baseball Congress in 1931. He soon became overwhelmed by the possibilities of amateur and semi-pro tournaments. Since he felt the first national tournament had to offer something extraordinary, Hap convinced legendary pitcher Satchel Paige and his Bismarck, North Dakota team to play in the tournament. He offered the club a $1,000 appearance fee, but he admitted later that he didn't even have $1,000 at the time. "I was just hoping we'd draw it at the tournament," Dumont explained. Paige, one of the greatest pitchers of all time in the Negro League, led Bismarck to the first national crown, striking out 60 batters in the tourney, including 16 in one game, a record that still stands. Dumont believed that the appearance of Paige was the key to the great success the tourney has enjoyed since.

Hap continually demonstrated his abilities as a promoter. He was a master at scheduling tournament games. He first introduced a timer to speed up play, an automatic plate duster, and a microphone that emerged from the ground near home plate. He designed red, white and blue bases. He had an orange ball 20 years before Charles O. Finley, who took credit for it. Hap even placed microphones on umpires one year so the crowds could hear the rhubarbs. But the language got a little foul for that and was discarded.

Buoyed by overflowing 9,000 crowds, Dumont quickly became baseball's "Barnum". "Good or bad, the gimmicks fostered interest in the tournament," wrote Broeg. "Hap was very media conscious and had very good rapport with the media and baseball people." Dumont worked seven days a week the year around, said Davis, who joined the NBC as a part-time ticket seller in 1950. "Hap expected a lot out of the people who worked for him because he gave so much himself."

"Hap devoted considerable time and attention to scheduling, a masterful orchestration by which the NBC flourished over the years," wrote Broeg. "Many a manager has grinned or groaned over it, but Dumont's ignoring conventional tournament seeding was integral to his success." Davis said, "Hap ignored brackets. He wanted to pit the teams adjudged weak against the strong so that the tournament cream, the box office attractions, would rise to the top. The challenge was to build up so that two strong teams would not face each other until the finals. If both teams were unbeaten, then you would get not only an exciting climax but also a possible extra game in a double elimination tournament."

"Dumont was truly dedicated to the National Baseball Congress," said Broeg. "What Hap did for aspiring semi-pro baseball players, many of them destined for stardom in the big leagues, will never again be matched by anyone. The National Baseball Congress is an enduring legacy to his memory."

Manager For the Ages

In 1931, George Long, a warehouse laborer in Muscatine, a small town in Iowa, founded a semi-pro baseball team and became its manager. After the team he was on folded, he got enough money to form his own. As of 1998, the 92-year old Long, born in 1906, was still Muscatine's manager, having compiled an impressive 1222-613 record. In the July 1, 1996 issue of "Sports Illustrated, Jack McCallum and Kostya Kennedy wrote in the "Scorecard" that "The Muscatine Red Sox are still going strong today, playing in Iowa's seven-team Blackhawk Valley League and aiming for a 68th winning season.

Remarkably, Long continues to manage from the third base coach's box. "Just having him shouting encouragement is an inspiration," says Muscatine coach John Robinson. "George has an unbelievable devotion to baseball. You can just feel how much he loves the game. Opposing players come over to shake his hand." For over 30 years, Long played in addition to managing. In the late '30s, Babe Ruth, barnstorming around the country, played with the Red Sox, and as Long recalled, "He hit two out for me."

Clarinda, Iowa, A Baseball Capital

When Clarinda won NBC's national tournament in 1981, it brought back memories. Not since the unheralded Drain, Oregon Black Sox won the crown in 1958 had such a Cinderella Story come true at the Wichita World Series. The A's scored in the last of the 11th to beat heavily favored Liberal, 8-7.

"We've had amateur baseball in Clarinda since 1954," said Merl Eberly, who managed the A's from 1961 to 1997, "but we didn't get the NBC concept going until the early 1970's." C.E. Nichols, a local optometrist, headed a committee to ensure the future of the game in Clarinda. The committee budget $8,000, established an eight-man board of directors, asked Eberly to manage the team and made the decision to recruit top college players.

Over 150 young players have used Clarinda's strong work ethic to hone their skills into professional baseball contracts. Among the many standouts who used Clarinda as a springboard to the majors include Ozzie Smith, Von Hayes, Bud Black, and Chuck Knoblauch. "The Clarinda A's is a monument to Merl Eberly and his family," wrote Bill Clark, "and to a commitment to baseball by the city's leaders and its citizens, who show a fierce love and loyalty to the game and their community."

Clarinda, located in southeast Iowa "Where the work ethic still works", is in operation only because the townspeople want a ball club. The A's now have a 22-member board that works year around, a very active boosters group and strong ladies auxiliary. For many years, the team operated on a shoestring budget. "We had to battle to raise $25,000 a year," said Eberly. Today, however, the annual budget is reported to be in excess of $40,000 a year. The larger budget supports the upkeep of a 1,000-seat stadium, additions such as new lights, a new scoreboard and concession stand. Clarinda draws a couple hundred fans to their games, however on "Baseball Day", they attract as many as 2,000 spectators. The A's playing field is truly a "Field of Dreams", with a corn field behind the right field fence. The annual banquet, which draws overflow crowds to the high school gym, is a major source of income.

In 1976, the A's auxiliary was formed to help organize a house parent program. "Since them, more than 100 Clarinda families have opened their homes to the Boys of Summer, treating them as their own," wrote Bill Clark. "Players from 45 U.S. states and growing number of countries have enjoyed their Iowa summers with the families of Clarinda. Over two dozen have married Clarinda girls, and more than 30 ex-players are residents of Clarinda today. Wife Pat became the A's heart and soul, a summertime mother for hundreds of young players", wrote Clark. "There was a time when the Eberly family housed as many as seven players in their basement. Besides looking after her children, Pat had to raise funds, answer letters, handle the telephone work and be in charge of concessions at the park."

After 37 years as field manager, Eberly, following the 1997 season, turned the job over to a longtime A's player, Noel "Bo" Bogdanski. However, he continues to serve as the general manager and fund-raiser, and Pat and the girls are back in the concession stand. And as Clark wrote, "Clarinda will welcome back baseball in 1998 just about corn-planting time."

100th Anniversary of Jasper Reds

100th Anniversary of Jasper Reds   Since 1893, there has been a semi-professional baseball team in Jasper, Indiana, the oldest continuing non-pro organization in the United States. Originally known as the Jasper Acmes, the team had reorganized and began playing all their games against teams from other towns. When the Reds celebrated their 100th Anniversary in 1993, Hak Haskins of The Herald, wrote, "With such strong tradition, the team has never let the community forget they were still around."

The Reds, like many other hometown teams in America, represent not only the spirit and tradition of the city but semi-pro baseball as well. The team symbolizes what the town and people are all about. Players keep coming back, season after season, to keep alive the tradition and play the game they love. During the past century, the city of Jasper has produced many outstanding players for the pro ranks, most recently the talented Scott Rolen, third baseman of the Philadelphia Phillies.

Organized baseball started in Jasper in 1868, soon after the end of the Civil War. Throughout the 1870s and '80s, teams flourished in Jasper," wrote Tom Alles in one of his 10 articles celebrating Jasper's anniversary. "The Golden Years in Jasper could have been the late '30s and early '40s when talent was more bountiful than broken bats." In 1940, the three Pfeffer brothers, Urban, 'Riff', and Roman, had much to do with Jasper's success. During World War II, major league pitcher Van Lingle Mungo, who was stationed at Fort Knox, Kentucky, pitched two games for the Reds.

In the late 40s and into the 50s, semi-pro ball was at its peak in southwestern Indiana. At one point, there were 10 teams in Dubois County alone. Crowds of more than 1,000 spectators were common. However, in the early 1960s, interest in the Reds began to diminish. Semi-pro baseball's popularity decreased in proportion to a growing number of other options one-time Jasper fans were being given. David Jackson wrote in the Evansville Press, "Going out to the park with kids on a mid-July southern Indiana day just doesn't hold the same allure when there's a doubleheader on the tube and a couple of frosty tasties in the fridge."

In April of 1974, the Reds were on the verge of folding. The future of the Reds was in serious jeopardy. The crowds were getting smaller and no one was actually interested in managing or handling the business affairs of the team.

for the
Love
of the
Game

In Jasper, semi-pro baseball survives

WEEKEND WARRIORS
Jasper fields semipro squad because players 'love game'

In 1974 when the Reds were about to fold, Bob Alles took over as manager. He is still at the helm.

History of Jasper Reds goes back 100 years ago to Acmes

Jasper Reds - 1906

The Herald
Dubois County, Indiana

They had no money, no manager and only a few returning players. Jerry Birge, sports editor of the Herald, wrote an article appealing for a "Committee to Save the Reds." That's when Bob Alles, a 19-year-old University of Evansville sophomore, entered the picture. A former player for the Reds, Alles agreed to take on the mission of saving a team in which his father and three brothers had played for and his father-in-law had managed.

For the next twenty years, Alles managed the Reds team to an impressive 353-191 record, highlighted by the team's best season ever, a 29-10 mark, the year Jasper celebrated its 100th anniversary. Players wore patches that proclaimed the extraordinary achievement. This banner season for the Reds was capped with an unprecedented trip to the NBC World Series. Playing in Wichita on artificial turf and with crowds of 2,000 a game was a story book finish to Jasper's century-long anniversary.

Following the 1993 season, however, Alles decided to relinquish his managerial duties, but not for long. Still handling the Reds' business affairs, Alles, a popular high school teacher, returned as field manager in 1996, at age 43, and now has collected over 400 victories in 24 years, everyone for his beloved Jasper Reds.

In contrast to many less fortunate semi-pro teams, money has not been an overly difficult task for the Reds. With the exception of a few lean years, area businesses have donated enough to cover most expenses. Team finances were given a major boost following the 1981 season when wealthy Jasper businessman, Alvin C. Ruxer, an avid fan of the Reds who once pitched for the team, set up two $10,000 trust funds for the team. The interest from certificates of deposit has helped significantly to defray season costs, such as new baseballs, umpire fees, etc. Several years ago, Jasper's Recreation Field was renamed in memory of the late Ruxer.

To meet their budget needs, however, Alles and his players must each year solicit funds to keep intact a tradition that without strong support of Jasper citizens and businesses would have faded away like so many teams. And nobody seems to want to see the team die. The team does it by selling season passes, raffle tickets and a few donations here and there. As semi-pro clubs have done for so many years, the names of merchants in this German-flavored town have bought uniforms emblazoned with names – "KREMPP LUMBER", "STERNBERG FURNITURE/TV", etc. Kimball International, for over 20 straight years, has bought the team's insurance.

The Reds still have to depend on their gate receipts to help carry the load. Unfortunately, it does not bring in a large amount of income, but helps pay for equipment, long distance phone calls and the cost of umpires. "During the 50s and 60s, crowds as large as a thousand fans were at the game," said Alles, "because there wasn't anything else to do. Now, many more big league games are being televised, softball has grown in popularity, and many other recreational sports occupy the time of people."

"But we don't get discouraged because we love to play," said the hefty, sunny-faced manager of the Reds. "As long as you have that feeling, it doesn't matter if there are five or 5,000 people in the stands. That's what has made hometown baseball. There must always be a local semi-pro team, not just for the fans but for the young men who want to play baseball."

Revitalizing Semi-Pro Ball

The traditional semi-professional leagues of America need to be revitalized, not only to give more young and old adults increased and more competitive opportunities to perform but to give player development in the United States a much needed shot in the arm. There is an urgent need for a reverse in the number of semi-pro teams experiencing financial and other organizational difficulties. With the strong support of a rejuvenated NBC, non-pro baseball can rebound and make a dynamic recovery. Such a development would give organized baseball in the United States the balance it so vitally needs.

Unquestionably, the NBC has the capability, with strong support from USA Baseball, to play a much greater role in providing competitive opportunities for young players and the older veterans. It needs to take the initiative in promoting more hometown and regional rivalries and helping local leagues obtain more funding. The hometown concept is still alive, but it has to be re-kindled, nurtured and cultivated, and most importantly, provided with greater financial stability.

An increasing number of summer collegiate leagues are also playing a major role in the revival of semi-pro baseball. The historic Cape Cod League in Massachusetts, for example, has given many collegians the opportunity to play baseball, using wood bats instead of aluminum. College coaches love the summer leagues because they give athletes a place to play. Cape Cod is one of ten summer leagues officially sanctioned by the NCAA and supported by Major League Baseball. Area fans, big league scouts and vacationers flock to scenic baseball diamonds across the Cape to see the same 10-team alignment as in past years.

The keys to the revival of non-pro/semi-pro baseball are:

- The NBC must develop a stronger structure of leagues and tournaments, which will attract the support of pro baseball.

- Encourage more adult men and women to participate in organized league competition.

- Re-kindle and promote the "Hometown" concept; the return of town rivalries, with teams representing towns and cities.

- Increase involvement of colleges in hosting summer non-pro leagues on campuses across the country.

- Seek stronger interest and active involvement by the family and community.

- Use the Sunday game as a social affair, with a post-game picnic in the park.

- Encourage more women to participate in organized league competition.

- Seek support from corporate sponsorships, large and medium-sized companies, as well as organizations in the community.

- Get park and recreation agencies nation-wide to get involved.

Need for Financial Stability

The future of semi-pro teams and leagues, to a large degree, will be dependent on finance. Financial burdens, combined with a lack of sponsors, have proven devastating, such as the cost of playing fields, equipment needs, insurance, travel, etc. Money continues to be a major problem for many teams, unless they are fortunate to have a large sponsorship. NBC teams do not play in front of big crowds in their local area, which means that operating revenue must come from other financial sources, such as advertising, season tickets, and increased admissions at the gate. But team sponsors who are willing to put up $10,000, a very conservative budget, are difficult to find. Sponsors are being hit from so many different areas.

William Storrs, a frustrated general manager in Downers Grove, Illinois, voiced an emotional concern. "After 18 years, my team, the Crestwood Panthers, is close to the end, mainly because of the money needed to operate. Our budget is between $14-18,000 a year, of which I have to raise. It is beginning to be an impossible task. Major League Baseball should help with some money, not large amounts, just enough to help teams along."

While it appears to be too huge a task, for non-pro teams and leagues to be financially stabile, a strong and aggressive sales promotion and marketing campaign is needed, like the minors do so well. As Larry Davis said, "A team has to put together a solid marketing program, getting people to go out and beating on doors. Everyone connected to the team must get out and hustle. However, in many cases, the general managers don't have time for it. Too often, the manager is also the business manager."

"The number one key is having a business or general manager who understands the business side of sports," said Steve Shaad. "It takes someone who can devote the time and energy to operating it. Teams who run into financial problems are generally operated by someone who has a sincere love of baseball, but has neither the time nor the business experience."

Corporate America, the large and small businesses and companies of cities and towns, could well be one of the three keys to the resurgence and fiscal stability of non-pro baseball. Secondly, semi-pro baseball should become a more efficient farm system for Major League Baseball. This can be achieved with the assistance of the majors and an expanded National Baseball Congress, involving a significant increase in summer collegiate leagues. Thirdly, the success of such an expansion would receive a big boost if both two-year and four-year colleges would host summer leagues.

Promotions and Fund-raising

Outstanding promotions have been conducted in semi-pro baseball since the early days of the National Baseball Congress when Hap Dumont was so highly successful in drawing crowds. Recently, the various franchises in NCAA-sanctioned short-season rookie leagues have done a good job of putting on a show to entertain the fans. On the professional level, the minor leagues and to a lesser extent, the majors, stage some type of activity, a contest or give-a-way, nearly every game. But why shouldn't all semi-pro clubs consider using some of the same methods and ideas? With effective planning, some creativity and executed with spirited enthusiasm, they can be successful. To make things happen, form a team boosters or dugout club, or have the wives and girlfriends organize a ladies auxiliary.

"Promotions in the Virginia Valley League are done by each franchise," said Curtiss Dudley, vice president for public relations. "We have a lot of give-aways, celebrities, and contests. "A good supply of comp tickets are often available." At the NBC's Midwest Regional in El Dorado, Kansas, local sponsors buy out tournament nights, which allows tickets to be given away. In Indiana, players on the Jasper Reds sell season passes. Promotions that involve corporations and commercial businesses have proven very successful, such as cellular phone promotion and Businessman's Night.

Fund-raising is another area of team management, which not enough non-pro teams make a strong enough effort. The problem of many teams is not because they didn't try. They probably used tried and proven methods but their application was not organized and presented effectively, and more than likely, the business or even field manager tried to do it all by himself, instead of having others involved.

Adult, hometown teams deserve just as much support from the community as all the other levels of play. They represent a town or city, and the community pride, spirit and loyalty that is gained is ample justification for business, service organizations and citizens to support such a cause. And be prepared to compete with fund-raisers from other organizations and sports. At certain times of the year, there will be a beehive of activity but never forget that competition is what made America great.

Publicizing Semi-pro Ball   While semi-pro baseball in the past has not had strong support from the media, the problem can be attributed to a number of factors, including a lack of fan support, less interest in the competition, and the failure of team officials to get the word out. With the scope of sports today so diverse, members of the news media have become so spread that in general, they don't have time to contact semi-pro teams and leagues, other than at tournament time or an important event of happening.

Since semi-pro ball usually has the last priority, especially in the larger markets, those responsible for publicizing teams must get the information to the news people as to how the team and the players are doing. But, much too often, no one connected to a team has the time, nor do they see the need to publicize and promote, or quite likely are not really sure how to go about it. In the recreation-oriented senior leagues, not much is done to publicize and promote the games, since attendance is not an objective. Players pay to play, thus providing the necessary revenue for the team to operate. However, semi-pro ball is a much different matter. They need spectators and sponsors to survive.

Steve Konek, Sr., president of the Pacific International League in the Seattle area, emphasized that "Any success we have enjoyed can be attributed to a determined dedication on the part of many individuals, such as our board of directors and advisory board." Recognizing that obtaining media support can be difficult, Mickey Deutschman of the San Diego Stars, "tries every way possible", including posters, newspapers, and radio, but "mostly through baseball participants, area scouts and coaches."

Whatever the situation and the size of a city or town, the task of publicizing and promoting semi-pro teams is not an insurmountable task. There are numerous ways in which the team and its players can be brought to the attention of the public. As Eberly wrote, "persistence can pay off." It need not be confined to game schedules and box scores in newspapers. There are many ways to communicate information and promote the team. Publicity can be done through a network of media contacts, a statistical office and hot line. The media depends on such information and most writers and editors will appreciate the consistency.

Larry Davis of the NBC suggested the use of college interns by teams in handling media relations, sending out press releases, even some sales responsibilities.

"We get as many as 100 inquiries from kids graduating from college that want to be interns. If a team would contact us, we may be able to send someone."

While TV's coverage of semi-pro baseball has been minimal, the NBC is hopeful that more games in the World Series will be televised, thereby exposing non-pro ball to more people. ESPN has done some of the finals that were picked up by various regions.

Stronger Support From Families

In past decades, hometown teams have given the family a common interest and enjoyable activity during summer nights. "The pace of a baseball game can be relaxing, social, therapeutic and rejuvenating," said Curtiss Dudley. But, how can semi-pro teams and hometown baseball get more family members out to the park? How can the games appeal more to families? "In building a good family atmosphere and a loyal fan support, our most successful teams are those which use the Sunday game as a social affair, the post-game meal, and the picnic-in-the park," said Tom Strickland, president of the South Central Texas Amateur League. "We encourage everyone in the family to attend -- moms and dads, girl friends, brothers and sisters. Many of our most faithful are the grandparents."

In smaller towns and cities, fan support can be very good. Fans identify with the team as representing the community. There is town pride involved and this characteristic can be promoted by some effective creativity. "When we get kids involved to help us, we draw their relatives," said Marv McCown, who runs the regional tournament in Elkhart, Kansas. "We draw a large number of senior spectators." Elkhart, a small town in western Kansas, draws 400-500 people a night. How do they do it? McCown explained, "First, there is not a whole lot else to do in Elkhart, but it really helps when you put our players in host families to live. They become acquainted with the local people. Naturally, many family members will be out there watching the kid who is living with them play."

More Competent Umpiring Needed

Competent umpiring is as vital to the success of non-pro baseball as it is to every other level of play. The standards of umpires, the consistency of their work, and their expenses, are serious concerns of these who administer semi-pro leagues. However, the caliber of umpiring must not be sacrificed in order to save a few dollars, even though leagues are struggling with their finances.

A three-fold approach to upgrading umpiring quality would be to:

1. Hire more experienced umpires, those who do the college and high school games.

2. Urge umpiring associations to raise their standards by requiring more stringent training and regular seminar sessions.

3. Encourage more young umpires to attend professional training schools, with the goal of moving up the umpiring ladder.

Organized baseball would best be served if more non-pro, high school and college umpires, with the support of umpiring associations, would upgrade their umpiring skills, not necessarily with a professional career in mind but just to improve their skills. The surest way to achieve this goal is to sign up for one of the sanctioned umpire training schools run by former big league umpires. Those umpires who enroll would receive financial assistance through a special Umpiring Development Fund, jointly established by the various leagues who hire the umpires and the umpire associations. Funds should be made available in the form of grants or scholarships for umpires to attend an umpire development school. Such assistance would help pay for the enrollment fee or transportation costs.

This type of approach would constitute a major step in upgrading the quality of umpiring throughout the amateur ranks, in addition to serving as a much needed source for other levels of play, in cooperation with the various umpire associations.

The caliber of umpiring must not be sacrificed in order to save a few dollars.

Profile of a Semi-pro Manager

Bob Alles – Jasper, Indiana Reds
Alles exemplifies the underlying spirit and longtime tradition of semi-pro baseball, although not as successful as those managers who distinguished themselves with championships in the NBC World Series, such as Bauldie Moschetti and Bob Sullivan. Recognition of Alles and the "100th Anniversary of the Jasper Reds" was based on intangibles and achievements other than trips to Wichita. The Reds were invited only once to the NBC classic, in 1993, the year Jasper celebrated their anniversary.

Back in 1974, when Jasper's team was about to fold, Alles, then a young college sophomore, took on what would have been a most difficult task for even the most seasoned manager. And he came through like a true veteran. He led his teams to numerous winning season, then after 21 years as manager, he retired in 1993, only to be asked again to return in 1996.

For nearly a quarter of a century, Alles has served with much distinction as the Reds' field manager, in addition to handling the club's business affairs, the often times frustrating financial deficits, concerns about crowd support, travel problems and fielding a competitive team. Still in his 25 years as a manager, his teams have won over 400 games. In all of his years of managing, he missed just three games. The Reds, by the way, lost all three! He buys the equipment, makes up the schedule, finds the players and orders their uniforms, hires the umpires, and keeps a close eye on the checkbook.

Alles has had to beg for money to pay for uniforms. He has seen his team's treasury dip below $3.00, knowing full well there will not be more than 50 people in the stand when his team plays its next game. Occasionally, he has had to coax players to come out to play or hold off their vacation until the season is over.

On the field, Alles has the responsibility to make decisions of strategy that can advance the runner, shifting the outfield over to right, and executing the double steal. As for team rules, he has only two, "One that the guys can't play softball during the season, and the other, they have to tell me if they can't come to a game. I'm not a strict disciplinarian. My players have had enough coaches getting on them. Sure, we have some beer after the game, but we're very serious while on the field. Come in to our dugout and you'll see fire in guys' eyes."

Alles talked about team spirit and dedication. "We have players who will go to a place like Danville, Illinois in the middle of the week. They know they won't get back until 2 o'clock in the morning and have to go to work the next day. Spirit like that means more to me than winning or losing a game."

As for the formation of the team roster, Alles explained one of the things he always has done. "If someone plays with us one year and is real faithful to the team, I'll write his name down the next year. Sure, there have been times when I could find better players, but I think, there's something to be said for loyalty. When our team went to Wichita, I had people tell me, 'Load up!' But we just don't do it. According to the rules, a team is allowed to pick up players. I don't care if we get beat 50 to nothing, these guys played for me all summer, and I want them to play in the NBC World Series. We had a camaraderie that the other teams did not have. Players on other teams didn't know some of their teammates. One player told me, 'I don't know him. He just joined the team.'"

The Jasper Reds has been Bob Alles' life, with strong support from his wife, Brenda. The team has also been the life of his three brothers, Bill, Tom and Jerry, whose father, Jerome "Chick" Alles, played for the Reds over a distinguished 15-year span. Indeed, this is the kind of dedication and commitment that has made semi-pro and hometown baseball so essential to a community.

Successful Teams

Sullivan's of Grand Rapids, Michigan
Sullivan's was named after their long time sponsor, manager, and players, Bob Sullivan. Appearing in Wichita 30 times, the team won four NBC championships and three second-place finishes. The large majority of the players are from local colleges and those living in the area the year around, including a mixture of ex-pros. The team, having changed its name to Little Caesars, draws between 300 and 500 fans a game.
Sullivan ranks the 1970 teams as among his best. Seven players from that team would go on to play in the major leagues. As many as 280 Sullivan alumni were

signed to professional contracts, including Kirk Gibson, Jim Kaat, Mickey Stanley, Willie Horton, and Phil Regan.

Boulder Collegians of Colorado
The Collegians won four national championships at Wichita under their longtime manager and sponsor, Bauldie Moschetti, including back-to-back crowns in 1966 and 1967. They also won in '75 and '78. From 1964 through 1980, Boulder won 796 games and lost only 198. As many as 113 of the Collegians went on to play pro ball. Moschetti stopped sponsoring the club in 1980. Squabbling over facilities was the main reason he bowed out.

In 1980, a trick play cost Moschetti's Collegians $12,000 and the NBC championship. In his book, "Baseball's Barnum", Bob Broeg wrote, "In a key game with Anchorage, Bobby Meecham lifted what would have been a game-winning homer over the right field fence. Trouble was, with only two umpires working the game, rather than three, the Alaskan right fielder had a trick up his shirtsleeve or, rather, another ball in his hip pocket. As he raced back to the wall, he grabbed the hidden ball, wheeled and threw to the infield."

Outstanding Managers

Bauldie Moschetti, Boulder Collegians
Starting in 1964, Moschetti managed the Collegians to a total of four NBC national championships -- in 1966, 1967, 1975, and 1978. Bauldie recruited heavily from major college programs. As many as 80-90 percent of his players were collegians. Over the years, more than 100 Boulder players went on to professional baseball careers, including Tony Gwynn, Joe Carter, Burt Hooton, Bob Horner, Mark Langston, and Larry Guru.

"Bauldie just wanted do win," recalled Larry Davis of the NBC. "It was an obsession with him. He recruited great talent, and his kids loved to play for him." Bauldie, his wife Sybil and his mother "Grandma" Moschetti, became "family" for his players and popular figures among the fans in Wichita. At home, Sybil fed the team almost every night. Bauldie made a lot of money, in real estate and his liquor store, but he spent it on baseball.

Even when temperatures soared over 100 degrees at L-D Stadium, Moschetti was always attired in this trademark black windbreaker and black dress shoes.

Bob Sullivan of the Sullivan's

This highly successful manager and sponsor's relationship with Grand Rapids began as a player in 1952. After a couple of years, the team lost its sponsor, so Sullivan began sponsoring the team through his carpet business. He continued playing through 1956 when he took over as the team's manager, which he handled for 35 years. Winning four national championships and three second place finished, Sullivan's teams never finished lower than fifth in eight tournament season. "All we do is play like a team -- to win!", said Sullivan.

Sullivan has long been an NBC crowd favorite. He is perhaps best known for his frequent rhubarbs with umpires. Dumont enjoyed Bob's antics so much that he once requested Sullivan to begin an argument to stir up the crowd.

In 1991, Sullivan retired from management of his amateur team. In 1994, he was inducted into the NBC Hall of Fame.

Merl Eberly of the Clarinda A's

Born and raised in Clarinda, Iowa, Eberly has been the central figure for the hometown A's semi-pro team. The program started in 1955 with a 7-9 record against local farm communities, and throughout the 1997 season, Clarinda holds a record of 1,584-642 against many of the nation's best amateurs. Eberly retired in 1997, at age 62, after 30 years in the newspaper business.

Eberly was one of the most feared hitters in the history of Iowa's cornfield baseball. Merl's athletic skills earned him a contract as a 22-year-old catcher with the Chicago White Sox organization. Married to Pat, his high school sweetheart, they have raised six children. The three Eberly boys all played for dad's Clarinda A's and the three girls have been mainstays in the A's auxiliary, a project of their mother for over 20 years.

In over 40 seasons with Clarinda, Eberly has managed two dozen future big league players, including Ozzie Smith, later one of the game's great shortstops with the St. Louis Cardinals. "I can remember getting up to play a game at 8 o'clock in the morning," said Ozzie. "There would still be dew on the grass."

Organizations

National Baseball Congress

Mailing address: P.O. Box 1420, Wichita, KS 67201
Telephone: (316) 267-3372   FAX: (316) 267-3382

President: Robert Rich, Jr.
Vice President: Steve Shaad
General Manager: Lance Deckinger
National Commissioner: Larry Davis

Executive Vice President:
  Melinda Rich
Administration Director:
  Dian Overaker

NBC World Series

Site: Wichita, Kansas   Date: First two weeks in August
Ages: Unlimited (Non-professional and ex-professional)
Purpose: Determines U.S. national championship for non-pro ball
Teams entered: 32 to be determined
Contact: National Baseball Congress
National tournament Director: Larry Davis

Summer College Leagues

National Alliance of Collegiate Summer Baseball
Mailing Address: 6 Indian Trail, South Harwich, MA 02661
Telephone: (508) 432-1774   FAX: (508) 432-9766
Executive Director: Fred Ebbett   Secretary: Buzzy Levin
Assistant Executive Director: Joel Cooney

Men's Senior and Adult Baseball Leagues

Senior- (30 and Over, 40 and Over)   Adult- (18 and Over)
Mailing address: One Huntington Quadrangle, Suite 3N07, Melville, NY 11747
Web site: www.msblnational.com
Telephone: (516) 753-6725   FAX: (516) 753-4031
President: Steve Sigler   Vice President: Gary D'Ambrisi

National Adult Baseball Association

(Age 18-65)
Mailing address: 3900 East Mexico Avenue, Suite 330, Denver, CO 80210
Telephone: (303) 639-9955   FAX: (303) 753-6804
E-Mail address: nabanati@aol.com
President: Brad Coldiron   Vice President/DEO: Shane Fugita

Roy Hobbs Baseball

(Open, 30 and Over, 40 and Over, 48 and Over)
Mailing address: 2224 Akron Peninsula Rd., Akron, OH 44313
Telephone: (888) 484-7422   FAX: (330) 923-1967
E-Mail address: Tom@royhobbs.com   Web site: www.royhobbs.com
President: Tom Giffen   Vice President: Ellen Giffen
Director, Operations: Todd Windhorst

High school baseball is the centerpiece in the development of highly skilled players in America.

For prep baseball to gain much needed visibility and a higher profile, it needs a showcase event.

Japan's high school national championship is the most followed sporting event in Japan, more popular than the World Series.

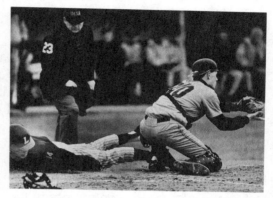

Moving the season back to warmer weather will do much to upgrade high school baseball.

Lack of funding continues to be a serious complaint of high school coaches.

The decline of baseball at the pickup and Sandlot level has hurt the overall quality of play.

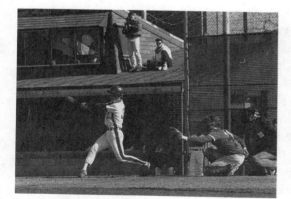

To increase crowds, entertain fans, and put on a show, high school programs need to build themselves a ball park.

For prep baseball to become a revenue-maker, it has to do a better job of promoting the games. Observe fence signs at Jesuit High in Sacramento.

9 High Schools

High school baseball is the key to baseball's career ladder, say big league scouts. They contend it is the most critical level of play in the development of major league talent. Strong prep programs benefit all levels of play. They are crucial to the overall development of professional ball players. They are most essential to improved Jaycee and college baseball, and the youth leagues need their close support more than ever.

Baseball's future, to a large degree, exists in our high schools. Prep baseball, in fact, could well be the centerpiece in the development of highly skilled players in America. For young players, it is their first opportunity to truly learn the game from coaches who have the knowledge to teach them correctly. Prior to that, many of the people coaching youth baseball have little knowledge of baseball and minimal coaching skills.

Despite its vital role in baseball's career ladder and player development, prep baseball has shown a general decline in the execution of basic skills. Coaches who responded to our surveys were unanimous in the belief that the decline of baseball at the pickup and sandlot level has hurt the overall quality of play. Clyde Metcalf, head coach at Sarasota High School in Florida, explained that "Fundamentally, the entry level of players coming into high school has declined. Today's youth rely on adult instruction and use that as their sole avenue. My generation, even youth 10-years ago, learned also through peers and played much more sandlot."

As they have on the other levels of play, aluminum bats have had an overall negative impact on how the prep game is played. Soaring home run totals and serious safety concerns have prompted the high school baseball rules committee to recommend strict bat performance standards and to consider the conversion to wood-composite bats. The National Federation of State H.S. Associations is moving toward regulations on bats. Coaches, as well as parents, have expressed strong concern as to the speed of balls off bats and the increased potential for injuries.

For high school programs to continue to produce highly skilled players for professional baseball and the colleges is strong testimony as to the quality of coaching at the prep level. The ability of coaches to acquire knowledge and information necessary to teach the sport is better than ever. The availability of outstanding videos and the big increase in instructional materials have proven very beneficial. A huge array of camps and clinics has contributed to the improvement and development of players. Videos with their stop-action and playback capability are most effective in teaching basic techniques.

Prep Baseball Needs Higher Profile

If the premise is true that high school baseball is the centerpiece in America's player development system, then a stronger foundation must be developed. High school programs continue to lose athletes to football and basketball because these sports have higher profiles and greater resources. For prep baseball to gain much needed visibility and a higher profile, it needs a showcase event it has always lacked. Patterned after Japan's phenomenal success, a national high school baseball championship would propel the prep game to unprecedented popularity.

Serious problems have prevented high school baseball from building stronger national popularity and achieving a long sought after higher profile. Budgetary cutbacks continue to hurt programs. Prep ball urgently needs financial assistance, not only from the local community but also from professional baseball. Through the many years, the high school game has received very little, if any, financial help from Major League Baseball. Yet the majors are throwing millions of dollars at top prep prospects.

For high school baseball to achieve its goals and reach its potential, it must make a stronger effort to become a revenue maker and be more self-sufficient financially. Otherwise, programs will continue to be under-funded and lack the necessary resources to conduct a quality program. Fully aware that other sports programs have the same objective, coaches must utilize every means of promoting their games, conducting successful fund-raising campaigns, and getting the support of the community.

For High School programs to boost the size of crowds, they need to build a scaled-down "Pro ball park", like Donaldson Park, above, in Grand Forks and Roseburg, Oregon, below

For prep baseball to achieve a higher profile and become a revenue-maker, it needs a show-case event -- a National H.S. Baseball Championship!

The weather in northern regions continues to be a major problem, as has the lack of adequate indoor facilities. A change of season is vitally needed. Teams in the north have always had to suffer through unbearable cold weather until the end of April. Moving the season back to warmer weather would not only help prep baseball become a revenue-maker but would facilitate the staging of a national championship.

High school baseball is the centerpiece in the development of highly skilled players in America.

H.S. Baseball – Status Report

From an overall standpoint, there has been a general decline in the execution of the basic skills as well as the desire to work on them. Many young players today don't see fundamentals as important, so they don't work at them. As a result, they are not learning the game like they should.

There are fewer all-around fundamental players. More kids can hit but not field. Or, they can field but can't throw. The general skill of throwing a ball correctly and strength of the arm has gotten weaker. The power of throwing arms has been diminished by tight, bulky muscles in the shoulder and upper arm areas due to the excessive use of heavy weights. The arms are being damaged by restrictions on pre-season practice time. Pitchers do not have sufficient time to properly condition their arms and are being over-used. Particularly in tournaments when the desire of coaches to win becomes more important than the physical well being of top pitching prospects. Proper base running and bunting technique have been overshadowed by the desire today to hit the long ball.

Power hitting has dominated the high school game. The long ball mania in the majors has come down to the high school level, with many hitters going for the fences. Hitters are swinging hard even on 0 and 2 and 1 and 2 counts, rather than try to make contact. Kids see the pros on TV and want to do the same.

Take for example what Josh Plosker of Somerset High School did on April 24, 1996 in Fall River, Mass. Josh hit three "grand slams" in one game! He finished 3-for-5 with 12 RBI. Ironically, his team lost 21-20.

Despite the financial advantage, metal bats have hurt the development of both pitchers and hitters. Pitchers are having difficulty making the adjustment into professional ball because the aluminum bat forced them to pitch differently to hitters swinging metal bats. Hitters are receiving false impressions of their skills because they are swinging a 34-inch, 29-ounce bat that "forgives improper hitting techniques." Aluminum bats have contributed to a lack of strong pro-type hitters. Bob Williams says, "The metal bat is not baseball and their cost should not be a factor in replacing it."

Fewer Quality Athletes

The number of quality athletes playing prep baseball has diminished. All-around and fundamentally sound players are fewer today. Over 65% of the coaches believe there has been a general decline in the execution of basic fundamental skills. "Competition for the talented athlete from other sports, as well as a need for jobs, are some of the reasons why top-drawer baseball players are getting scarce," said Dale McReynolds, veteran scout of the Los Angeles Dodgers. "Unless they have a good coach and program, kids might think of something else." Because sports are specializing more, high school baseball is losing a lot of good athletes to basketball and other sports. More young athletes are playing one sport the year around.

Over the past two decades, high school baseball has shown a general decline in the execution of basic skills, in large part attributable to the decline of baseball at the pick-up and sandlot level. Players are bigger, stronger, and faster, but they do not know the game better. Fundamentals require repetition, and fewer players and coaches today are willing to put in enough time to develop them.

Many coaches attribute the decline to getting fewer quality players from the youth leagues. They are lacking in bunting skills, double cut-offs, fielding bunts and slow rollers. Base running is neglected. Throwing technique and strength, catching the ball and the development of pitchers are big weaknesses.

Drop-off in Number of Players

Based on a number of surveys, there has been a drop-off in the number of boys playing high school baseball. "The good kids seem to still be coming out to play," wrote Iran Novick in Collegiate Baseball, "but where are the others? The ones you counted on to fill out your squad, provide depth and a base to build upon for the next season. These kids are not out on the diamond like they used to be. They have found other things to do and other sports to participate in.

Kids do not like to sit on the bench. The number of three-sport athletes has declined. There is a tremendous struggle taking place at most schools among the sports. Competition for athletes is at an all-time high. "Parents and kids no longer see the multi-sport athlete as a viable goal," said Novick. "With parents on the lookout for college scholarship dollars, they are pressuring their kids into a system of one-sport stars."

Failure of the Youth Leagues

Young players arrive in high school knowing very little about the fundamentals of the game. "Many kids today, having been told by coaches and their parents how good they are, do not see fundamentals as that important and don't work at them," said Bill Erickson, baseball coach for Beverly Hills High School. An overwhelming number of high school coaches believe most Little League programs are not adequately teaching the basic fundamentals. Even Little League administrators admit that most of their coaches lack a good basic knowledge of the fundamentals.

Little League programs are not teaching proper mechanics. Too much emphasis is on winning and not enough teaching of the basic fundamentals. Relatively few youth coaches are attending clinics and seminars when offered by college and high school coaches, and as a result, they are unable to teach them to the children. The baseball coach at Crestwood High in Ohio, Bob Merritt, has noticed the decline of basic skills among little leaguers. He asked, "Could this be due in part to the decline of baseball at the pick-up and sandlot level?" Most definitely. For the large majority of youth league players, the season is too short, with too many play-off games and all-star teams. As a result, most kids get half the playing time they used to.

Prep Baseball's Decline in Skills Over the last two decades, high school ball has shown a general decline in the execution of basic fundamental skills. Players are getting better instruction because coaches have more knowledge than those in the past. For those players who attend camps, the skills are better, but fewer young players are spending the time necessary to learn the finer points of the game. Players are less prepared as "students of the game." Situational skills are lacking. Some basic skills are down due to specialization, where players are expected to lift weights all summer, and athletes in the basketball program must play in the summer league.

Too often, the decline is due to attitude, with players lacking the desire to work on the skills. They are too lazy or think they know it all. They are selfish and quick to blame others for their shortcomings. In our society today, we tend to accept less than perfection. As Tommy Williams of Lexington, South Carolina said, "We need to start demanding again more than asking."

Many young players spend too much early season time in hitting cages and not enough playing catch and fielding practice. They work on skills only at a scheduled practice or game. Quite often the problem relates to a poor work ethic. There are too many practices with people standing around. Not enough time is spent on fundamental work on the basic techniques.

Maximizing High School Baseball

A number of major problems have prevented prep baseball from maximizing its potential. For the high school game to become more financially stable, upgrade the quality of coaching, and build its popularity, the various problems and needs have to be solved. To attain optimum growth, high school baseball must gain a much higher profile, if only to be a more attractive alternative for athletes competing in football and basketball.

Based on the premise that baseball's future exists in our high schools, strong efforts must be made to maximize their programs. The following steps of action should be taken:

Organize a National Championship

A national tournament each year would do much to kick the prep game in to high gear. Such a showcase event would be similar to the remarkable success of the Japanese and would help the high school game gain much needed visibility. High school baseball is extremely popular in Japan, largely because of the national tournament that draws crowds of 40,000-50,000. In the United States, every level of play has a national championship or World Series event except the high schools.

While working out all the state schedules would be complex, the event would generate a great amount of interest and enthusiasm at the grass root level. A national championship would involve some time constraints because of the way the current season is. The tournament would have to be completed by the end of July.

JAPAN'S SCHOOLBOY TOURNAMENT   First held in 1915, Japan's high school national championship is the most followed sporting event in Japan, more popular than the World Series. Robert Whiting, in his book, "You Gotta Have Wa," wrote, "For two solid weeks, starting with the second Friday in August, the eyes and ears of virtually the entire nation are turned to aging Koshien Stadium, near Osaka, where the top schoolboy teams in the country battle for national supremacy."

This annual extravaganza is the nation's single biggest sporting event, comparable to America's Super Bowl and World Series. "Even people who don't like baseball watch it," says Whiting. "It's the thing to do. Boys who play at Koshien become idols of their towns. More than 50,000 fans fill the stadium every day. The competition is a single-elimination tournament involving 49 teams gathered from nearly four thousand participating schools in regional preliminaries. Every game is carried live on television and radio."

Of much significance, the Koshien tourney has become one of the few remaining ways Japanese have of displaying regional loyalties. Koshien is more than an athletic meet. It is a social event. Whiting wrote, "There is strong evidence of 'regional ties', a large proportion of those who attend are elderly people, with logos and badges showing their school affiliation. The stands are filled with beaming parents, little brothers and sisters cheering their elder siblings."

Lengthen and Move the Season Back

As in the case of the colleges, moving the season back to warmer weather will do much to upgrade high school baseball. While the southern and West Coast schools enjoy ideal weather in March, the large majority of teams suffer through intolerable cold weather well into April. In Ohio, bad weather can delay games until the second week in April, and the league season finishes as early as May 23rd. Jim Panther, whose Libertyville team plays in northern Illinois, said, "In mid-April, we are playing in 40-degree weather."

A change-of-season would also help prep baseball become a revenue-maker. In addition, the season should be lengthened to a minimum of 30 games. Of considerable importance, teams should have more practice time prior to the first game. They need to be allowed to properly condition and develop young arms so pitchers will not suffer career-ending injuries. The pitching arm needs six weeks to get in throwing condition. The Wisconsin State Association, for example, allows practice to start March 15 and games to begin April 1, with no time allowed for pitchers before March 15.

There are some encouraging signs. An increasing number of prep schools have moved the season back. They start later and go into the summer. The state of Iowa plays almost totally in the summer. In Illinois, the State Association has increased the number of games from 20 to 35, and no more than 20 can be doubleheaders. "We're allowed 35 games in the spring and another 25 games in the summer," said Panther.

Become a Revenue-Producer

For high school baseball to upgrade programs, develop a stronger profile, and attract a larger audience, an all-out effort must be made to become a revenue-maker. Lack of funding continues to be a serious complaint of high school coaches. Does the prep level have the capability and potential to do so? Yes. If high school baseball is promoted and marketed effectively, it does have the capability to develop into a good revenue producer, with the full realization that competition for the almighty dollar continues to increase. But it will require a great amount of determination and resolve on the part of coaches, parents, and the community.

The coach, of course, must lead the way with strong support from parents, players, past and present, businesses and clubs. An increasing number of coaches are finding creative ways to attract funding. The formation of a Baseball Boosters Club will do much to draw support from the community.

There is an urgent need for Major League Baseball to support high school programs financially and otherwise. Subsidization of prep baseball by professional baseball is long overdue. As I will point out later, the majors and minors will receive in return more than they will give, in ticket sales as well as much needed good will by the most valuable fans of all—baseball families of America. In the "Multi-Funded Approach", I will explain how the Professional Baseball-High School Agreement would work.

An increasing number of high schools are already doing some of the revenue-producers that colleges have done for years. Increasingly, coaches and their A.D.'s are seeking assistance from corporate firms, commercial enterprises and service organizations in the community. And there are ways to obtain funds for that much needed pitching machine or scoreboard. Many coaches now have a regular pattern of promotions that raise moneys that otherwise would not be available for baseball. They have worked hard in improving their communication skills with prospective donors.

Promote High School Game
For prep baseball to become a revenue-maker, it has to do a better job of promoting the games. While the type of promotions needs not be on the level of the minors and college, still, with creativity, a flair for showmanship, and some direction, high school students will do a good job.

Promotions should appeal not only to students and faculty on campus, but families, young players and their grandparents. Getting local businesses and organizations in the community involved will also enhance the success of the promotion.

The resources and level of professionalism will not likely match the higher levels of organized baseball, but high school programs are more than capable for promoting their games and entertaining those who attend. In the minor league and college sections of this book, I have provided lists on "Successful Promotions" and "Sources of Financial Support."

Take a Multi-Funded Approach

To provide much needed financial stability to high school baseball, the school's annual general athletic fund should be supplemented by:

1. Fund-raising committee – A model plan would include:
   - Formation of Baseball Boosters Club
   - Golf tournament
   - Baseball Annual

   Among the many other creative ways to attract funding sources include: pancake breakfast, spaghetti feed/dinner, pizza and bake sales, sale of Christmas trees, candy sales, bingo, alumni games, Hit-A-Thon and Marathon games, team uniform sales (each player buys his uniform and keeps it at the end of the season).

2. Corporate involvement, including the building of a scaled-down minor league (or college) model baseball stadium. This community-supported construction project includes donated materials, volunteer labor, etc.

3. Assistance from Major League Baseball. In helping to subsidize high school baseball, the majors would contribute money to finance the conversion from metal bats to wood-composition bats, used by a growing number of pro-supported summer leagues. High school programs, in return, would purchase an agreed upon block of tickets to big league games. Players, students, family members and boosters can buy and sell tickets, with a percent of the revenue going to their baseball programs. Hopefully, minor league clubs will be willing to adopt a similar plan of subsidization.

4. Pay-For-Play. Programs lacking sufficient funding have the option to utilize the Pay-For-Play concept, in which each player pays from $50 up to $250, for example, to cover program expenses.

Build a Scaled-down Pro Ball Park

If high school programs really want to increase the size of their crowds, entertain the fans, and put on a show, they need to build themselves a ball park. With creativity, hard work, and strong support from the community, a scaled-down replica of an old-time minor league or even college stadium can be built, eventually one with lights!

As demonstrated so well at minor league and collegiate games, the entertaining and fun aspects of going to the ballpark have to be effectively staged and promoted. Spectators are more comfortable and have pride in a new stadium. And, too, providing ball players with a smooth, level playing field will contribute significantly to a better brand of baseball.

Reinstate Program Cutbacks

In the early 1990s, high schools were squeezed drastically by the economy. The cutbacks in games and practice time were alarming and inflicted serious harm to the game. As a result of declining budgets in school districts, governing officials seriously impeded programs and players development.

"Practice time prior to the first game is not nearly adequate," said Ken Schreiber, retiring baseball coach at LaPorte High in Indiana. "We need to have both of these returned to the original time and number." Ron Tugwell of West Springfield High in Virginia agreed by stating, "We need more practice time and scrimmages. Our state will not allow spring sports to begin practice before March 1." A Kansas coach wrote, "We need to play more games. The 20-game limit in Kansas is not enough." Harvey Krupnick of Holliston High in Massachusetts summed it up by saying, "We need better weather, a longer season, more money and better fields."

The high school game, in its quest for optimum development, would benefit significantly by upgrading programs and improving the quality of play. To achieve this much-needed goal, the cutbacks wrongly inflicted in the early 1990s should be reinstated.

Mandatory Coaching Certification

Over 30 states now require some form of mandatory coaching certification. In 1997, a mandatory course designed to provide better training for new coaches who don't teach and have no contact with students beyond sports was approved by the Massachusetts Interscholastic Athletic Association. Coaches must complete the course within a year of their hiring.

Traditionally, most coaches were trained as physical education teachers and had a basic understanding of coaching fundamentals and training techniques. "Today, massive layoffs have depleted the state's teaching ranks," wrote Carolyn White in USA TODAY. "Only 54% of Massachusetts' 15,000 high school coaches are certified teachers."

MIAA Spokesperson Brian Halloran, a former school superintendent, explained, "We've seen cases where incoming coaches place too much stress on winning rather than on developing the student-athlete, where they're unable to plan practices in a logical way, using improper training methods and don't have the best methods for correcting misbehavior."

The Massachusetts Interscholastic Athletic Association uses a program sponsored by the American Sports Education Program (ASEP) in Champaign, Illinois. ASEP's program is used in many states and endorsed by the National Federation of State H.S. Associations.

Upgrade the Quality of Umpiring

Stronger efforts must be made by local umpiring associations to provide the most qualified umpires possible, with more structured development and recruitment procedures. For these goals to be achieved, the competencies, training and pay of umpires need to be upgraded. Those who umpire on the prep level should also have the opportunity to develop, attend training schools, and move up to a higher level.

"Umpires don't have to be pursuing a professional career to attend umpire schools," said Brent McLaren of the Umpire Development Program. "Many of those who attend will return with more knowledge and skills to their local area and leagues."

Professional umpire schools operate during the winter months. The Jim Evans Academy of Professional Umpiring holds amateur courses in November, while

professional courses are taught in January-February.   The Harry Wendelstedt
Umpire School is also offered in January-February.

Jim Evans Academy of Professional Umpiring
12741 Research Blvd., Suite 401, Austin, TX 78759
Telephone: (512) 335-5959   FAX: (512) 335-5411

Harry Wendelstedt Umpire School
88 South Street, Andrews Drive, Ormand Beach, FL 32174
Telephone: (904) 672-4879

Allow Players to Play Other Sports
There is increasing competition from other sports for the talented athlete. High school basketball has become a year-round game. The season never truly ends any more.   Basketball and soccer camps are a big problem during the baseball season. The high school state championships in California concludes in March, but shortly after, players can be seen running the floor again. Players are told to practice basketball all summer and play nothing else, or they won't be playing next year. Soccer coaches, in particularly, have gone all out to recruit young athletes, from kindergarten on up, and children are being forced to specialize early.

Young athletes should be allowed to participate in other sports. Ken Schreiber of LaPorte High, explained, "Even though we are in an era where players are more specialized, there should be good cooperation between the different sports." Coaches of all sports must be flexible in allowing youth to be multi-sport athletes. They should not insist on year-around participation in their programs. There should be room for compromise on the part of coaches of all sports.

Helping the Youth Leagues
For too many years, youth leagues, in general, have failed to take advantage of those who have the experiences and knowledge, high school, college and jaycee coaches. For some strange reason, Little League coaches, for the most part, unqualified and lacking in basic skills and organizational methods, have given "the cold shoulder" to those who want to help them do a better job. And the league presidents and so-called training coordinators continue to do very little about it. Little League has yet to certify their coaches, and they make no attempt to recruit those who are qualified. For the most part, Little League has continued their longtime policy

dependent on volunteer parents, which from the standpoint of the overall quality of play and level of competition has proven to be detrimental to player development.

Then what can and should be done about a situation that has been ignored for decades? Should high school and college coaches come riding in on their white horses to the rescue of the unqualified and inexperienced youth coaches? Not really. Rather, they need to be asked by the many youth league organizations to help them solve the problem. First, though, the administrators of youth league baseball must be convinced there is a problem and what should be done about it. In greater detail, we will discuss the problem in chapter 10.

By working closely with the youth leagues, high school coaches will not only benefit their programs but their assistance will contribute much to higher levels of play in all youth baseball programs.

Stress Academics to Players

Student-athletes need to be motivated to excel in the classroom, as well as on the playing field. Coaches should encourage their players and praise them when they do well in the classroom. Showing an interest in their players' grades can be a very important motivating factor in their striving for excellence. Above all, young athletes need to be urged to give their best efforts rather than just try to get by. Student-athletes must realize they are a student first and then a baseball player."

Coaches can monitor their players by compiling a list of players in every teacher's class. The list is sent out every three weeks, informing the coach of the players' current grades, their conduct and the number of absences in each class. Immediate feedback is given to each player, informing them as to which classes need improvement and praising them for those they are doing well in.

Education for one's life ahead is far more important than signing a professional contract—with one major exception. "If the boy is a high draft choice and receives a six-figure signing bonus, then grab it and run," advised Lou Pavlovich, publisher of Collegiate Baseball. Jim Kaat, ex-major league pitcher and for many years a popular broadcaster, said, "I would recommend high school players go to a good college program, rather than going straight to the minor leagues. There's too much idle time in the minors and more instruction in college."

Urge Athletes to Make Stronger Commitment

Athletes should be more committed to their goals than they currently are. Ken Schreiber has developed a program over the past 37 years with young athletes willing to make the commitment. "We are not willing to let individuals of modern day thinking tear down or destroy what has been built over the previous years."

Schreiber is very concerned about what is happening to a growing number of the nation's youth in recent years. In his interview with Lou Pavlovich of Collegiate Baseball, Ken stated that "So many kids are embracing drugs, obscene music, violence, a 'don't-care' attitude about education and thus have a shocking lack of preparation of life." Schreiber strongly believes that discipline, dedication and a commitment to educational goals can save the youngsters from a decaying lifestyle that is so widely accepted today.

How did Schreiber compile such a remarkable coaching record at LaPorte? He sums up his success in one word—COMMITMENT. "People should make commitments, but even more important, keep and meet their commitments." But Schreiber says, "We don't get the commitment that we used to get." Schreiber believes society has become too permissive, irresponsible, and unaccountable. He explained, "One of the major culprits is the fall of the traditional home and the values that were so evident in two-parent families who were there for their kids."

Control Super Star Syndrome

Many coaches, particularly those on the youth levels, spend too much time working with the "great talents" and not enough with the others. As Bill Erickson of Beverly Hills High explained, "It takes nine guys to win at this game consistently. Coaches do not realize that by not working harder with the sixth, seventh, eight, and ninth guys, they are hurting their teams. These 'other' players are turning off from baseball and we are losing them. In years gone by, these guys would stick it out and many got better by perseverance and hard work. How many big leaguers weren't all-stars in Little League? How many got cut in high school?"

Develop Good Relations with Faculty and Staff

Coaches should not ignore the faculty and classified staff, and certainly not the administration. All should be kept informed on the baseball program and its events. Involvement of the faculty, in particular, should be invited in as many functions as possible. Study nights should be set up for all the players, and teacher-student contacts should be initiated for the purpose of getting study hints. Coaches must realize that their main purpose is the welfare and education of the student, not just what happened on the playing field.

Establish Better Rapport with Parents

Before the season begins, a coach should strive to establish a common base of understanding with parents. If the coach can earn the parents' respect and confidence, it will be an easier task to have the players follow. A pre-season meeting should be scheduled with the parents, at which time the coach will explain his teaching philosophy and the program as a whole. Both parents and boosters should be kept informed of the team's progress by means of a mailed flyer, as well as information sheets.

Winning at the High School Level

To be successful at the prep level, a team must have talented players, ably supported by a coaching staff that has the ability to teach and inspire, as well as maintain discipline and have the respect of the players.

Good pitching and a tight defense will prove a winning combination for any baseball team. The best pitcher in baseball is still someone who has a little something extra on the fast ball, complemented by an effective assortment of off-speed and breaking pitches. With a staff of pitchers who can throw strikes, a well-drilled, alert defensive team will prove hard to beat. To win a championship, a team has to make the double play. It is the biggest defensive play in the game.

An aggressive attack, capable of exerting continual pressure on the defense, is still the most consistent and dependable offense for high school teams. Using more powerful aluminum bats and a livelier ball, more prep teams have taken a liking for the long ball attack of the pros and collegians and are going for the long ball and big inning. Of course, the type of personnel should be the determining factors. If a team has power and good hitters, it will hit away. If blessed with speed but short on hitting power, the coach will go more to a running game and try to manufacture runs.

The aggressive, positive type of coach who takes the initiative and employs the elements of surprise and deception in his offense can achieve considerable advantage.

Promote the Fundamental Approach The most

successful approach to winning a baseball championship is to make fundamentals the foundation of the program. A major problem in youth baseball is the lack of fundamental instruction. Kids come into high school knowing very little about the fundamentals of the game. Compounding the problem, too many coaches in recent years have been drifting away from the basic fundamental approach. As Joe Potulny, coach of Jesuit High in Sacramento, said, "Coaches are too fond of putting in a dozen pick-off plays, bunt defenses, etc., into their system. The game is still a matter of throwing strikes, playing catch and putting the ball in play. We emphasize to our players that baseball takes time to learn and play."

What can high school coaches do to promote the fundamental approach to baseball play?

- Be a teacher as well as a coach. To be successful, a coach must know how to teach.
- Teach fundamentals daily and insist that skills be done correctly.
- Keep the game simple and basic; break the skills down into steps or parts.
- Emphasize the importance of repetition and details. Repeat-repeat-repeat!
- While drills can often be boring, teams win with drills. Nothing takes the place of doing.
- Teach the basics of catching and throwing from the opening day of practice to the last.
- Demand that young players learn how to "play catch" correctly.
- Conduct organized and disciplined practices. Make them challenging, competitive, even fun to do.
- Put together a detailed plan for every practice. Develop a check list of the basic fundamentals that must be covered.

- Follow a daily practice plan that emphasizes the basic skills.
- Try to simulate game conditions in practice, so players can learn to react to specific game situations.
- Work on your verbal skills, but stress to players the need to listen.
- Read and listen more about the game — books, how-to manuals, articles, big league games on TV and instructional videos.
- Use videotapes often to teach the basics. Study the game to learn the best methods of teaching the basics.
- Attend clinics and seminars and talk to successful coaches. Always work at getting better and learning more.
- Try to make the game FUN — both practice and games.
- Emphasize enjoying and playing the game well, rather than dwelling excessively on wins and losses.

Most Abused Fundamentals
Based on our national survey of high school coaches, the basic skills in most need of improvement are:

1. Proper Throwing Mechanics
2. Proper Hitting Mechanics
3. Bunting Techniques
4. Base Running Techniques
5. Proper Fielding Techniques
6. Pitching Mechanics
7. Outfield Play Skills
8. Catching — The Catcher
9. Cut-offs and Relays
10. Baseball Knowledge
11. Two Hands in Catching Ball
12. Hand and Foot Coordination

What Scouts Look for Most
When major league scouts attend high school games, they are much more interested in instincts and raw, basic skills, rather than statistics. Tools are most important. Rarely will they see a five-tool player. There are at a premium. The one tool many scouts like above the rest is speed. Others like size, skills, and raw power. Can he run and throw? Is he smooth? With high school players, scouts are looking for an athlete.

The reason great high school players are so easily identifiable, in addition to running 6.8-second 60-yard dashes and producing impressive numbers, they understand and have mastered many of the nuances of the game. They possess all-around ability, flexibility, agility, and good hands. Scouts are obsessed with speed and size, and are not overly concerned if players have raw undeveloped skills.

Training Aids
Their Value to Baseball Players

In recent years, countless training aids and equipment, as well as gimmicks, have been available to players and teams. The extent of their individual value varies with the product. In our questionnaire to 1,500 high school coaches, we asked them to rate the following training aids as to their relative value to their team and the improvement of the players.

Rank Order	Training Aid	Rating	Training Value
1.	Batting Tee	4.1	Extremely Valuable
2.	Soft Toss	4.1	Extremely Valuable
3.	Video Tape Recorder	3.9	Very Important
4.	Player Charts	3.1	Very Useful
5.	Vision Training	3.1	Very Useful
6.	Pitching Machines	2.4	Moderately Important
7.	Speed Guns	2.1	Moderately Important

WRITE-IN TRAINING AID: Long Throw - A large number of coaches strongly emphasized the "Extreme Value" of this training aid in strengthening the throwing arm.

Issues and Problems

Aluminum Bats—A Detriment to the Game

Metal bats have changed the game tremendously. The aluminum bat, in particular, has been a detriment to pitching, largely because it is tougher to come in on hitters. Pitchers are then reluctant to pitch inside. Even more significantly is the safety problem that powerful aluminum bats present to the physical well being of the players.

From a financial standpoint, metal bats have saved the amateur game money, but what a price to take. Coaches say, "We can't afford wood", that aluminum has "saved our game", but there has to be a better way. "The aluminum bat has been good for our program because of the financial factor," said Jim Panther. "But what high school baseball needs is a bat that has very similar physical properties as a wooden or wood-composite bat."

Convert to Wood-Composite Bats

Supported by a subsidization agreement with professional baseball, the long overdue conversion from metal to wood-composition bats would give prep baseball the impetus it needs to move into the new century. And, Major League Baseball will have a golden opportunity to help high school programs.

In helping subsidize high school programs, the majors would contribute money to finance the conversion. In turn, high school programs across the country would purchase an agreed-upon block of tickets to major league games. A similar plan would involve minor league clubs.

New Bat Performance Standards

The National Federation of State High School Association is in the process of placing performance limitations on baseball and softball bats. New regulations were expected to be in place for the 2000 season, but the Federation decided to extend its timeline to ensure that it can compile accurate and decisive data before possibly banning some bats.

According to Brad Rumble, Assistant Executive Director of the National Federation, there is strong sentiment among the rules committee to make non-wood bats used in prep contests perform exactly like wood bats. The rules committee continues to monitor the progress being made concerning various bat-testing methodologies before adopting any kind of additional rules governing the bat. The committee feels strongly about non-wood bats having the same performance as wood, that there is additional safety.

Inside Pitching Is Part of the Game

Throwing inside is a pitcher's right and responsibility. Clyde Metcalf explained, "Pitching tight, even getting hit, is part of the game. However, it should not result in retaliation and brawling. 'Head-hunting', of course, is a serious matter which umpires must not allow."

Coaches should suggest to hitters a more positive response to close pitches than injury-inflicting brawls. "When a hitter wants to fight after an inside pitch, it tells me he is afraid of it," said Phil Garner, former manager of the Milwaukee Brewers, "and I will keep doing it until he hits it." When a hitter hits a "rope" back through the box, you never see the pitcher charge the batter.

Hitters need to be taught how to roll or curl away and take the inside pitch. Get the hitters off the plate. Many of those who are hit often are leaning well out over the plate. Ken Schreiber says, "At the high school level, we don't stress standing close to the plate."

Overworked Pitchers

Too many high school pitchers are being over-used. Many young prep hurlers, especially in the colder regions, are not only throwing too many pitches early on but come tournament time, arms are being blown out.

Tony Woods of Grand Prairie, Texas, drafted by the Cubs in the 4th round, was "forced" to be in both ends of a regional doubleheader, throwing a total of 175 pitches. Back in 1983, Jackie Davidson was a sixth round pick by the Cubs. His arm was blown out pitching every hour-on-the-hour in the playoffs. He never made the major leagues. Needless to say, Ed Lynch, general manager of the Cubs, blasted the coach, and he considered a suit if the kid should get hurt.

High school coaches should be restricted from overusing their pitchers, particularly early in the season. A rule should be initiated where prep pitchers can pitch once in 72 hours, or in relief three times a week no more than 10 innings. As Joe McIlvaine once said, "You have to protect coaches from themselves."

Coaches Calling the Pitches

Calling pitches, a practice started by collegiate coaches, has contributed to serious developmental problems for catchers. Professional scouts are most critical of the practice, calling it over-coaching. As one coach said, "Let the kids play the game!" Another coach said, "Young catchers should learn how to call the game, and my job is to teach them the proper way." Coaches responding to our survey were asked, "Do you allow your catcher to give the signals?" 62% responded "Yes", 18% said "No", while 19% replied "Most of the time", depending on the catcher.

"I call some, but I don't call them all," said Jim Panther. "Sometimes we like it when the other coach calls the pitches because we can pick-up what the pitches will be. We played one team and we knew what he was throwing."

Risks of Creatine and Androstendione

High school players have become bigger and stronger than ever before, the result of heavy amounts of weight lifting and performance-enhancing substances and drugs. The most popular supplement is Creatine, taken orally to maximize the benefits of weight training. An article in the Mayo Clinic Health Oasis stated that, "Creatine monohydrate is a compound produced by the body that helps release energy in muscles. It can boost short-term bursts of power. However, there are serious questions concerning long-term use of Creatine."

"Whether the kidneys can process that much Creatine for a number of years is a prime worry," said Dr. Edward Laskowski, co-director of the Sports Medicine Center at Mayo Clinic. "No one knows what a supplemental dose of Creatine will do over a long period of time."

Despite many testimonials, there is no evidence that Creatine, androstendione or any other substance enhances performance over what can be attained by practice, training, and proper nutrition. Androstendione is a precursor hormone in the production of testosterone. Marketers claim that a 100-milligram dose of andro increases the male hormone by up to 300 percent. But few scientific studies have been done on its use. "There's not even an answer to the question: 'What does it do?' says Todd Nippoldt, an endocrinologist at Mayo Clinic.

Team physicians believe androstendione has raised concerns about serious health risks and an "unfair advantage" in competition. The Association of Professional Team Physicians has even recommended that androstendione be banned from all competitive sports. The group said, "Androstendione has a chemical structure like that of an anabolic steroid – a usually synthetic drug that functions like testosterone."

Mandatory Drug Testing
Mandatory drug testing programs can and have saved thousands of lives. Dixon was the first high school in California to require drug testing of its athletes when it began its anti-drug program in 1996. The program has proven highly successful, with strong interest nationwide. Students are tested randomly throughout the season.

Dixon High's program is modeled after a similar program that has operated in Vernonia Unified School District in Oregon since 1989. The U.S. Supreme Court upheld that program in 1995 after a couple challenged the drug testing of their seventh-grade son. The Court held that students give up some of their privacy rights in becoming athletes and can be subjected to more stringent rules than non-athletes.

In her excellent article, "Pushing the Idea of Drug Testing" in the Sacramento Bee, Pamela Martineau described Dixon's program: "All kids trying out for a sport must submit to a Rapid Eye Test, an examination of the pupils of the eye that can make a preliminary determination of drug use. If that test is positive, the prospective athlete must take a urinalysis. If drugs are detected, the student is barred from sports for the rest of the season and must attend counseling."

Smokeless Tobacco on Decline
Baseball is finally losing its taste for smokeless tobacco. One by one, players are quitting the habit for major health reasons—snuff, dipping, and smoking. Major League Baseball banned the use of smokeless tobacco in the minors in 1993, however, 25-30% of minor league players still dip. Many big league players are trying to quit or cut down. What is disturbing are the reports that the prevalence of smokeless tobacco among prep athletes is widespread!

The physical addiction of chewing tobacco can be very crippling. Studies have shown that some brands of snuff can deliver a dose of nicotine four times greater than cigarettes. Nicotine is almost as addicting as cocaine. The withdrawal of nicotine requires major help. One-third of smokeless tobacco users have gum disease. The risk of developing oral cancer, a disfiguring, often deadly disease, is 50 times greater for long term users than non-users.

More and more, players are being pressured to quit, either from family members or total strangers. Anti-tobacco advocates are urging the ban of chewing and smokeless tobacco throughout organized baseball.

Walk-on Coaches

A number of coaches believe the walk-on or rent-a-coach, as they are referred to, has contributed to substandard play. They say the "off-campus" coach is a major reason for the decline in the overall teaching of the game. With no professional standards, the "walk-on" coach is not as committed to the total student-athlete, and at times, has shown a lack of sportsmanship. Phil Swimley, longtime coach of the University of California at Davis, believes "The walk-on coach is detrimental to all athletics. We need to get coaches in the schools who are there all day long, who can talk with the kids in the morning, and encourage them to come out for ball. If the coaches are not there until practice time, who does the recruiting to get kids to come out to play?"

Is the walk-on coach as serious a problem as some people make them out to be? Yes and no. Some of the off-campus coaches have had strong backgrounds in baseball, and they have much to offer the coaching profession. On the minus side, walk-on coaches are only on the campus during practice and games and are not a faculty member who is an integral part of the educational process and atmosphere. I can understand the shortcomings of a walk-on coach, such as not being involved with the educational process earlier in the day, without a commitment to the total student, but I have observed some very competent coaches who come from off the campus to coach.

Still, high schools need to be more cautious in hiring coaches from off the campus. They must make sure they fit into the academic environment. Of considerable importance, they must have the ability to teach. Before they begin work, it is more essential for them to receive a good orientation of the overall school academic goals and objectives. In addition, perhaps give the coach the opportunity to speak at a faculty meeting, acquainting them with his philosophy of coaching and the importance he places on the academic aspects of a high school education.

Increased Mobility of Transfer Students

Once upon a time, public school students were required to attend their neighborhood high school. Today, however, intra-district and inter-district transfers have allowed students increased mobility. The number of parents moving their kids from one school to another because of athletics has hit a new high. The squabbles that have high school principals and coaches calling for investigations are over the issue of transfer students.

In an effort to prevent large numbers of students from changing schools without restriction and to preserve the spirit of fair play, the California Interscholastic Federation has installed a set of stringent guidelines regarding the transfer of high school athletes between schools. In 1996, the CIF voted to revise its by-laws. Under the new rule, open-enrollment transfers will have to be filed by May 15 of the preceding school year instead of within 15 days of the start of the fall semester to maintain athletic eligibility. The date switch should help reduce the influence of summer sports camps, where coaches or boosters club members from other schools often recruit athletes.

The uneasy alliance between public and private high school athletic programs is being tested under a revised open-enrollment policy that has been approved by the California Interscholastic Federation. The State Legislature has passed new laws allowing parents to move their children from one public school to another campus within or outside of a school district, regardless of boundaries. But there was no such requirement for private schools which continued to pick and choose whom they allowed to enroll.

The transfer of student-athletes to private schools is widespread. Athletes have transferred at will, finding loopholes in school regulations. Many Catholic schools have benefited by having feeder grammar school programs throughout a city. Private school coaches are often charged with improper recruiting.

Private schools have had definite advantages in developing athletic programs on the high school level. In addition to larger budgets and superior facilities, private schools in general, have unlimited recruiting capabilities. Many can recruit from distant areas and transfer is easier to do.

Coaching Styles

Billy Bock, Pine Bluff High (Arkansas)
Selected as the "National High School Coach of the Century", Bock has compiled a superlative record. For over 40 years, he has guided his teams to incredible achievements. When asked by Collegiate Baseball to give the secrets of his success, he replied, "My philosophy can best be summed up in the 4 F's: FUNDAMENTALS, FIRM, FAIR, and FUN". Fundamentals must be stressed over and over again, every day. It's the little things that get you beat – not hitting the cut-off man, missing a signal, not laying down a bunt."

Clyde Metcalf, Sarasota High (Florida)
Coach Metcalf also tries to keep the game simple. His teams spend a considerable amount of practice time on fundamentals and game situations. "Our players are very receptive to drill work that they fail to get in youth leagues," he said. "We tell our players that without throwing skills, there is no position to play, and therefore, no team to play for."

"We spend 50 percent of our time on the offensive game, striving for a minimum of 100 swings per day for each player. We spend 20-30 minutes a day on base running fundamentals. All of our sprints are base running oriented. We work on specific real-game situations in our daily workouts". Metcalf is a stickler on conditioning. He conducts a year-round strength program that is required of all players. "We start with our ninth graders," he said. "We taper off during the season, but we hit it strong in the summer and fall."

Ken Schreiber, LaPorte High (Indiana)
Coach Schreiber is a strong believer in running disciplined and organized practices. "We insist that skills be done right," said the legendary coach. "It's up to the coaches to demand that young kids practice repetitions by drilling them. The young people who are subject to Situation Baseball and the Fundamentals of Play are the ones who succeed."

"We drill EVERY DAY with our infield, just like the pro's and colleges. We hit fungos by the 100's each day. We emphasize throwing without any inhibition." Schreiber emphasized, "Don't be afraid to make a mistake! Players today do not throw enough nor do they throw for distance enough to strengthen their arms. Our kids play 'Long Throw' catch three days a week. We make them play catch and properly. Throw with a purpose, and when catching the ball, have them move into the throw."

Bernie Walter, Arundel High (Maryland) "The most effective instruction is REPETITIVE," said Coach Walter, "at a slow rhythmic pace with every movement done precisely. Many coaches do not understand how fundamental fundamentals are. If the foundation is solid, the building will be solid. We consider base stealing a vital part of our offensive package," said Walter. "Regardless of speed, we always attempt to steal bases when the defensive club demonstrates a weakness."

According to Walter, "Arundel players are 100 percent committed to the continued improvement of strength and conditioning. This excellent attitude and work ethic is what sets Arundel apart from the rest. Our players are willing to pay the price in advance."

Bill Erickson, Beverly Hills High (California) Coach Erickson advises coaches to "Select a philosophical game plan, stick to it, and believe in it. Then, sell it to the kids. Consistency and structure are things young players need and want. Try to see how new ideas can supplement your philosophy, not replace it. Go to clinics, talk to the 'old guys' and borrow their ideas. Get involved in coaching organizations."

"Make sure that everybody in your program, especially coaches and players, are aware of what you want done and how you want it done. Set up a checklist for every area you feel needs to be covered in getting your team ready to play. Then write out how and when you want to teach it to the players."

High school baseball is the first opportunity for young players to truly learn
the game from coaches who have the knowledge to teach them correctly.
In suburban Chicago, retired coach Ron Klein (New Trier), above, Jim Panther
(Libertyville),below left, and Bernie Walter (Arundel, Maryland), below right,
exemplify the high quality of coaching on the High School level.

Jim Panther, Libertyville High (Illinois)

"We teach the game the way it should be played," said Panther. "Being an ex-big leaguer helps me understand the game a little better." He teaches the little things that he picked up in the big leagues. "On a gapper to left-center field, I will send my shortstop out to retrieve the cutoff. Meanwhile, the second baseman goes 45 to 60 feet behind the shortstop, while the first baseman follows the runner to second. Many teams will simply send the second baseman to cover second base." As to how Panther organizes his practice schedule, he replied, "My practice plans are so unpredictable because of the weather. I make sure we get the necessary things done and concentrate on pitching early. If the weather is bad, we can always hit indoors."

Mike Cameron, Moeller High (Cincinnati)

The organization and preparation of Moeller's practice program is very goal-oriented. During the off-season, Coach Cameron compiles a list of objectives and goals. Mike makes a calendar for the season with target dates for competition. His practices are drill-oriented. "We give the players numerous repetitions of the basic skills so that they will be ready to handle any game situation. Our players work hard at practice," said Cameron, "but we also have fun doing it. The team that is most relaxed plays best. We try to always be positive, and by doing so, we are able to build self-confidence."

Rich Arbinger, Start High (Toledo, Ohio)

Coach Arbinger stresses hard work on the playing field, as well as in the classroom. He tries to make baseball fun for his players. To achieve these goals, he has developed two creative programs:

- SCHOLAR ATHLETES PROGRAM. To spark interest in the classroom, Arbinger started a program where the team presents a nice, three-button T-shirt to any baseball player attaining a 3.0 or higher grade point average. The shirt has "Start Scholar Athlete" on the front with the player's name and number on the back.

- PRACTICE-CAN-BE-FUN PROGRAM. Arbinger sees to it that practices are spiced up. "The most boring thing in baseball," he said, "is batting practice. But we try many ways to make it fun."

Organizations

NATIONAL FEDERATION OF STATE HIGH SCHOOL ASSOCIATIONS

Office Address: 11724 NW Plaza Circle, Kansas City, MO 64153
Mailing Address: P.O. Box 20626, Kansas City, MO 64195
Telephone: (816) 464-5400   Fax: (816) 464-5571
Web site: www.nfhsa.org
Executive Director: Robert Kanaby

NATIONAL HIGH SCHOOL BASEBALL COACHES ASSOCIATION

Mailing Address: P.O. Box 5128, Bella Vista, AR 72714
Telephone: (501) 876-2591   Fax: (501) 876-2596
Executive Director: Jerry Miles
Administrative Assistant: Elaine Miles
President: Herb Kupfer (Omaha, NE)

NATIONAL HIGH SCHOOL ATHLETIC COACHES ASSOCIATION

Mailing Address: P.O. Box 2569, Gig Harbor, WA 98335
Telephone: 1-800-coach95   Web site: www.hscoaches.org
Executive Director: Gary Brines

AMERICAN BASEBALL COACHES ASSOCIATION

Over 2,500 high school baseball coaches are members of the ABCA, an organization comprised largely of collegiate coaches which promotes open discussions and rapport among the various levels of baseball.

Office Address: 108 South University Avenue, Suite 3,   Mt. Pleasant, MI 48858
Telephone: (517) 775-3300   Fax: (517) 775-3600
Executive Director: Dave Keilitz

For young baseball players today, every-thing is organized and structured. Adults tell them where to be and what to do.

Medical and child psychology authorities have strong concerns about Little League's excessive emphasis on winning.

The excesses of Little League never end, another all-star team, another tournament, and one curve after another.

Little League Baseball®

Little Leaguism has diminished the spontaneous culture of free play and games among American children.

While organized youth leagues continue to grow in numbers, children today are not playing enough on their own.

The large majority of Little Leaguers are not getting enough practice by them-selves.

The need for reform in youth baseball is now greater than ever, highlighted by the return of playground baseball.

10   Youth Baseball

Youth baseball leagues continue to grow in America, providing competitive opportunities to millions of children and youth. Despite the strong growth and unprecedented popularity of Little League and other organized youth leagues, the most serious problems and weaknesses in America's player development system are in youth baseball. The excesses and abuses of Little League Baseball are impeding the growth and development of young players.

While there are more organized leagues than ever, children are not playing enough on their own. Unstructured play has almost disappeared from most parks and school playgrounds. Young players are not practicing and playing by themselves, in sandlot diamonds and around the home, nor are they playing pick-up games like they used to. The only way kids play the game today is with their team, a team practice or game. Baseball play, in large part, has been institutionalized.

"Little Leaguism has diminished the spontaneous culture of free play and games among American children," wrote Edward C. Devereux, developmental psychologist at Cornell University, "and that it is robbing our children not just of their childish fun but also of some of their most valuable learning experiences." Devereux explained, "In Little League ball, the spontaneity is largely killed by schedules, rules and adult supervision, a fixed time and place for each game, a set number of innings, a commitment to a whole season's schedule at the expense of alternative activities."

In greater numbers, kids are quitting organized baseball far too early. Fundamental instruction is lacking at the younger age levels, the large majority of youth coaches are untrained, non-certified, mostly parents. Too much emphasis is placed on winning the game. Many young players are giving up baseball as early as 13 or 14 years of age, burned out and often abused. The basic skills are not being practiced as much as they have in the past. Fewer fundamentally sound players are coming through the youth leagues.

Even more significantly, society and our culture today have had a profound influence on play at the youth levels. Among the many reasons children are not playing enough are the various social and cultural forces such as technology, video games and the computer. Many other sports and recreational pursuits are attracting the attention of young people. Kids sit at home playing Nintendo and other games. Parents have to be more protective about the safety and security of their children.

Excessive Emphasis on Winning

Through the years, many medical and child psychology authorities have expressed strong concerns about Little League's excessive emphasis on winning, competitive pressure, and the resulting anxiety. Highly structured leagues run by hypertensive adults, urged on by over-enthusiastic fathers and mothers have turned off many kids.

Much too often, the Little League season is an emotional summer journey, with excessive emphasis on winning. During the summer of 1998, Peter Jennings and ABC's camera crew were in Hagerstown, Maryland to watch Little League Baseball. Jennings observed that "We watched parents as they anxiously endured the tough calls and eagerly celebrated the good breaks. We also tried to face the disappointments bravely. For all of these teams, the goal of the regular season is to win the league championship."

For young baseball players today, everything is organized and structured. Adults tell them where to be and what to do. The days when the neighborhood kids got together and played baseball from morning until dark , are gone. Only rarely will someone get a game up on their own. John Rosemond, a family psychologist, explained, "Somewhere along the line, someone got the brilliant idea that sports would be a more meaningful experience for children if the games were managed by adults." They organize the leagues, assign children to teams, select team names and uniforms, determine the play schedule, decide who will play what position, and conduct the practices. As for the players, they do what they are told, rather than teaching one another how to play, developing leadership skills, learning how to resolve disputes, and acquiring decision-making skills.

The large majority of little leaguers are not getting enough practice by themselves, not enough swings, fielding opportunities and throwing. The typical little leaguer may get 16 swings a week, then come up twice in a game. Kids practice for one hour, get 5 swings and throw 25 times, then go home, sit down and watch TV. Back in the 1940s and 50s, all we had was a bat, ball and glove, and we played for hours.

The only way kids play baseball today is with their team, a team practice or game. Baseball play, in large part, has been institutionalized.

Little League Baseball

In Little League ball, the spontaneity is largely killed by schedules, rules and adult supervision, a fixed time and place for each game, and a set number of innings.

Unstructured play has disappeared from most parks and school playgrounds. Young players are not practicing and playing by themselves, in sandlot diamonds and around the home.

The scene above of a father pitching to his son at the plate is seldom seen today. If young players would practice and play on their own, with friends or parents, the overall level of play in youth baseball would increase significantly.

Tournaments Dominate the Summer

The excesses of Little League never end, another all-star team, another tournament, and one curve after another. All youth leagues, with the exception of Legion Baseball, are geared toward all-star teams and play-offs. The number of teams competing in the Little League World Series will double to 16 in 2001. The spectacle in Williamsport will now take nine days, and twice as many children age 12 and under will endure the intensive pressure of playing in a worldwide tournament viewed by millions.

Rather than let all the kids play and practice all summer long, all-star team deadlines limit the playing season from April to June. Many times, the Little League season will allow for about one or two weeks of practice before the season begins, then there are few practices once the games begin. And these are about an hour long and unorganized. Only the better players compete, and other players do not have a sufficient opportunity to catch up.

"Competition, reasonably supervised, is essential to the full maturing of the individual," wrote James Michener in Sports in America. "Children should have the widest possible experience of play but heavily organized competition with end-of-season championships should not be initiated before the age of twelve, if then. A sense of competition is natural in children, provides healthy emotional outlets and must not be suppressed, but it should not be exaggerated, either. Adults must not dominate the play of children."

Many people have staunchly advocated the pressure-packed activity as a beneficial preparation for a competitive society. However, the competition can be a nightmare. The agony of having to see on TV little children lose is often unbearable. Countless numbers of viewers switch off their sets after being subjected to the never ending vision of a pitcher burying his face in sorrow after giving up a game-winning hit.

The overriding factor, however, which supersedes all other concerns, is the quality of adult leadership provided by the parents and coaches who guide these programs. The desire to win at all cost by many coaches has undermined the teaching process. The pressure of the Little League World Series is so intense that one has to wonder, why should a program be geared from start to finish to play in the tournament when the problems it produces are so detrimental to young children? Participation should be what Little League is all about.

Has the time come when adults should step aside and give the games back to the kids? As for playground and sandlot programs, yes, children should be allowed to play their own game, with a minimum of adult supervision. Even in organized youth league competition, the adults should back off and let the kids play. However, adults, particularly the parents, have contributed too much to youth baseball for them to sit at home or in the grandstands. Adults are needed to administer and supervise, even coach, providing they meet the standards of leadership. But their roles and responsibilities should be redefined, and they must be better prepared and trained.

The need for reform in youth baseball is now greater than ever, highlighted by the return of playground baseball, unstructured play, a revival of pick-up games and a re-opening of parks and playgrounds to baseball. Kids need to play on their own.

Status Of Youth Baseball

The organized side of youth baseball appears sound. In figures released in its 1998 State of the Industry Report, the Sporting Goods Manufacturers Association said, "The combined enrollment of children who were 18 years or younger in amateur leagues grew from 1.8 million players in 1985 to 4.6 million in 1996, an impressive 156% growth over 12 years." On the playing field, however, the number of quality players coming out of the younger leagues has declined, largely due to a lack of quality instruction and repetitions at the lower levels of play.

Decline in the Basic Fundamentals
Based on our national surveys on youth baseball, 70% of those who responded said there has been an overall decline in the overall quality of play and the execution of the basics. The decline can be attributed in part to the failure of players to learn them at a young age. This has had a major impact, a domino effect, from the high schools and colleges on up to the professional ranks.

High school coaches have told me they are seeing fewer quality players coming out of the youth leagues. Among the reasons are:

- Kids are not practicing on their own
- Many are failing to execute the basics properly
- Youth league coaches are lacking in baseball knowledge
- Youngsters are not playing pick-up games
- Players do not play catch enough, nor can they play a good game

Young players are not being taught proper throwing technique. As a result, the throwing skills of many young players are below average. Arm strength is a major weakness of young players. Furthermore, the desire of young players to work on their skills has declined considerably. The "lost arts" of the game continue to decline, like bunting, base running and sliding techniques. Increasingly, the game is being dominated by the long ball, somewhat similar to the big leagues. The total game and its fundamentals are not equally addressed.

"Compared to 10 years ago, the quality is not there," said Al Anicich, former Legion Commissioner in Sacramento. "It has dropped down quite a bit. Kids are not participating during the off-season, and their motivation is different. Baseball used to be an essential part of their identity, their drive and satisfaction. It is a skill-oriented game that requires time, commitment and practice. Today, kids do not have the same level of instincts, nuances, and not as much knowledge of the game. Many young players are lacking in competitive skills, like hitting the ball hard, running hard, throwing to the right base, etc. Years ago, if a player didn't do these things, he wouldn't be playing."

Young players, from the majors on down, are doing too much heavy lifting of weights, which has caused the biceps of many players to be tight and bulky. This has resulted in a lack of looseness in the muscles and tendons of the throwing arm. There is too much emphasis on the all-mighty home run. Everyone is bulking up muscles of the body to develop a powerful hitting swing. But throwing and fielding skills are being neglected.

Kids Are Dropping Out

By the time they are 13, about 75% of youth league players drop out of baseball. "Many don't find it fun any longer because of the pressure," explained Dr. Jack Llewellyn, a sports psychologist. "Something needs to be done to remove some of the pressure on kids." Bob Malina, director of the Michigan State Institute for the Study of Youth Sports, said, "It's not enough anymore to enjoy the game. Now they have to win. Kids are still learning how to play. They are uncomfortable with it. There is also a fear component, especially if the youngster pitching is a lot bigger than he is."

What should be done to keep the youth playing the game? Perhaps Malina said it best, "Let 'em play and teach them the game. The thing that kids want most out of sports is fun." Llewellyn believes, "The emphasis for young players shouldn't be on hitting the ball, but executing the skill. Coaches should give points for taking a good swing and watching the ball." As he told writer Ray Glier of USA TODAY Baseball Weekly, Llewellyn would like to see more practice than games for youngsters." While stress receives the most blame for kids dropping out of sports, there are many other factors. Among them are loss of interest in the sport; their coach was a poor teacher; too much pressure to excel; or the coach played favorites.

Coaching Quality Has Declined
Youth leagues are having difficulty getting qualified coaching. A large number of parents are coaching Little League, as many as 80 percent. But as one veteran coach pointed out, there is no reason why the coaching parents cannot improve their skills if given the necessary assistance. However, most leagues provide very few coaching clinics, rules and training sessions, and minimal instructional materials. When clinics are conducted, they are poorly attended because they are not made mandatory. And Little League still does not certify their coaches.

The thousands of managers, coaches, umpires, league officers and other adults who volunteer their services in youth programs deserve strong praise. Despite the good leaders, however, Little League has had too many poor ones. Many of them have done serious harm to their players. These are the coaches who represent the greatest threat to youth baseball programs. The large majority of youth league coaches are untrained, just supervising and not instructing. Lacking knowledge in the basic fundamentals, they are failing to properly teach the skills and techniques. Nor are they seeking information as to the correct way to teach the basics.

There is too much emphasis on winning at too early an age. The desire to win at all costs by many youth coaches has undermined the teaching process. Mike Mussina, one of baseball's truly outstanding pitchers, believes "Little League is too often a 'rushed exercise' in which coaches stress winning, not improving. Emphasis must be on improving, not winning."

Overcoaching continues to hinder the development of young players. Among the most common problems are:

- Coaches calling signals for the catcher
- Excessive shifting of positions
- Overemphasis on taking pitches, trying to draw a walk

Decline in Summer Baseball

Many young players are not improving their skills in the summer months. A large majority of youth league players have finished their seasons by July 1, and unless selected on an all-star team, they have few opportunities to play in a league or town team in the community. There is an increasing number of baseball players who are playing other sports in the summer.

If Little League and other youth leagues would reduce emphasis on never-ending tournament play-offs, the regular league season could extend into a good portion of the summer. If this does not happen, however, then public agencies should offer more recreational leagues and sandlot playground programs. Bringing back the community town teams would provide much needed impetus, and a greater number of players could be playing summer baseball.

High school coaches need to provide their leadership, knowledge and expertise in directing these programs, with college and high school players, and physical education majors serving as coaches. As a result, those who play in these recreation leagues would be receiving a type of instruction and training that many of them failed to receive in organized youth leagues.

Need for More Unstructured Play

Most opportunities for incidental learning which occur in spontaneous self-organized and self-governed children's games have somehow been sacrificed in "the altar of safety and competence." In his book, "Joy and Sadness in Children's Sports", Rainer Martens wrote: "The major problem with Little League is that the whole structure of the game is rigidly fixed once and for all. It is all handed to the children ready-made, together with the diamonds, bats and uniforms. It is all so carefully supervised by adults, with almost nothing left for the children to do but play the game."

"The informal, backyard variants have far more learning values for children than the formally organized, adult-supervised version," said Martens. "My most fundamental opposition to Little League Baseball is based not so much on what it does by way of either harm or good to the players, as it is on what Little Leaguism is doing to the whole culture of childhood, to participants and non-participants alike, and to the schools, families, neighborhoods, and communities where Little Leaguism has taken root."

Martens emphasized the need "to stress the important role of spontaneous play and of unsupervised, self-organized games for young children, and the consequences involved when children are pushed into competitive sports too early. Once a game has been taught and children catch on to it, let the kids handle it themselves."

> **"It's not what the boy is doing to the ball,**
> **but what the ball is doing to the boy!"**
> *- Rainer Martens*

Society's Impact on Play

Society and the various forces and conditions in today's culture have had a strong influence on baseball play at the youth levels. In past generations, young and old people alike did not have many options. There were few distractions. Families tended to stay together. There was a middle class ethic involved with participation in baseball. Today however, everyone is coming and going. Kids have so many other things to do. On top of this, we are living in a society of crime violence and drug abuse which continues to effect the security and well being of everyone. A more dangerous environment has forced parents to exert stricter controls on their children.

Strong emphasis on organized play has also contributed to the drastic decrease of children playing baseball, particularly pick-up games, where repetition really occurs. Parental concerns about street crimes have sharply curtailed play at neighborhood schoolyards and park playgrounds. Often, schools and parks have not been able to offer protection against violence and abuse. When public recreation facilities are no longer safe havens, parents are reluctant to allow their children to play there.

Today, very few children can be seen playing alone without their parent or adult leaders. Children are often restricted from going outside to play, sharply limiting normal childhood opportunities. Somehow, this type of restriction has to be changed. The number of kids living in vulnerable situations has increased dramatically. The divorce rate has gone up, and there are many more single parent families. Millions of children are growing up without fathers. USA TODAY reported that "In the early 1960s, less than 10% of children lived in single-parent households. It is now well over one in four!

"Baseball's bedrock is the family, the heritage of passing the game from father to son," said Bob Costas. "However, the growing reality of the single parent family threatens to break that chain. In past decades, the way many children were able to watch baseball was for their fathers to take them to a game. In many homes today, this is missing."

More than ever, society and baseball need more fathers passing the game on to their sons and daughters, its traditions, and the intangibles. In too many homes, though, both parents are working. It takes two incomes to support a family these days, and parents either don't have the time, or are unwilling to take the time in the evening or on weekends to spend with their kids, developing their skills, as parents did in the past.

The age of electronics has had a tremendous impact on society. Nearly 90% of children age 9-13 play video games at home or at a friend's house. They average 1.4 hours of play a day. Is there any way we can get kids away from television and video games and have them play more baseball and other sports? Marian Elliott, commissioner for Babe Ruth's Pacific Southwest Region, believes, "It is attitude, and attitude is developed by parents. Many of the habits and ways of doing things are developed in early years of their life. It extends all the way to the idea of getting away from the TV set, and that can be controlled by the parents, having children go outside and get some healthy exercise."

In recent years, there has been an alarming decline of African Americans playing baseball. African American representation in the major leagues has dipped to its lowest point in nearly forty years. Parents and children of low-income families cannot afford to attend a big league baseball game. The cost of baseball is a big factor in the exodus. Many kids cannot afford gloves, balls, bats, and spikes. Finding fields to play on is another problem. Most black youth and poor families, in general, cannot afford to attend needed summer baseball camps. Black athletes in America's inner-cities, unable to afford the game, develop or compete, have largely quit the game.

A Renaissance Is Needed

Little League is too over-organized and structured. Adults have completely taken charge of what was once the play of children and adolescent youth. A long overdue renaissance of youth baseball is needed in America, sparking a revival of the game involving not only the youth leagues but would re-open parks and playgrounds to baseball. The nationwide reform would be highlighted by a return of sandlot baseball and a revival of pick-up games.

Little League and other youth league programs do not need to be abolished but their excesses must be curtailed. Despite repeated warnings and criticisms for many decades, the refusal of Little League to take remedial action and respond to medical, orthopedic and child development advice is intolerable. A plan of reform is urgently needed. In a comprehensive survey of over 1,000 high school and college coaches, the question was asked: Should action be taken by appropriate agencies and organizations, including the PTA and medical profession, to attempt to persuade Little League to initiate some meaningful changes? 83.65 of the coaches responded "Yes". Respondents of our five-year study were also asked: Should Little League Baseball change its overall philosophy? 56.9% responded "Yes", 22.2% said "no", and 20.8% were uncertain.

Our studies have revealed that a large majority of the coaches recommended philosophical and program changes by Little League and other youth baseball organizations. Excessive emphasis on winning and a pressurized atmosphere is not in the best interests of young children. More than ever, kids are in need of a more skill-based, fun-resulting program, as opposed to high-pressure, result-oriented little leagues.

The development of the game at the youth level can best be achieved by giving kids a choice, an alternative program. Many communities across the country have taken action to provide an alternative program for children who prefer participation and fun. I am referring to a casual, pick-up type of play during the summer months when kids can play on their own, in the mornings without parents present. Such programs would provide the sandlot-type of atmosphere that many of us experienced as kids. The rewards and outcomes as to a child's growth and development would be numerous.

Would quality after-school and summer programs and an opportunity for free play with peers in a safe and attractive environment give children a more positive outlook on life? Most definitely. Would a comprehensive youth sports program, available to boys and girls at all economic levels, help to encourage dialogue between different ethnic groups and serve to deter youth from seeking out gang activity or turning to drugs? Yes. Time after time, sports programs have proven their worth. If public agencies would fund these programs, the crime rate and drug traffic could be reduced significantly.

Public recreation and parks could be the key to a renaissance in youth baseball. There is an urgent need for public recreation to make a comeback. For much of this century, the recreation and parks industry has contributed greatly to the quality of life for all people. Now, more than ever before, those representing park systems throughout the nation need to take preventive action and offer all children positive alternatives and values that can give direction, develop self-esteem, and provide opportunities.

Providing youth with a comprehensive program of organized, supervised activities can be the first step toward addressing this dilemma. Most at-risk kids in inner-cities go to the streets when leaving school each day because they have no alternative. How many problems of juvenile delinquency could have been avoided, or at least diminished, if there had been an active park or drop-in center in more of these neighborhoods?

Reform in Youth Baseball

If Little League truly desires to serve the social, physical and psychological well-being of young children, it must make changes in its organizational structure, in addition to formulating a new philosophy, which would effectively meet the basic needs of youth. The main focus and objectives of Little League and other organized youth leagues should be directed to the children. This can be achieved by de-emphasizing winning, learning the fundamental skills, and giving them a positive experience, a fun time, without undue pressure from the coaches and parents.

Little League must take a real, hard look at their excessive approach to play-offs, all-star teams and national travel. Youth baseball continues to be excessively geared toward the national championships. There is too much pressure to win. The game has always been more for adults, rather than for the kids. The many excesses have had damaging and often unhealthy repercussions on American children. Not only Little League, but all programs need to become more interested in skill development than getting to the World Series.

Little League prides itself that the program instills positive leadership values in children and the healthy development of the "total child". But why does it allow coaches to call the signals for their catchers? Another high priority of Little League is to enhance the safety of children, but then the organization allows young children in their growth and development years to damage their pitching arms with an excessive number of breaking pitches. Still another program objective of Little League is to teach the basic skills and techniques of the game, yet the large majority of volunteer coaches are not given sufficient training and instruction as to coaching a team of inexperienced children.

Over twenty years ago, James Michener, supported by experts from the fields of medicine and child development, called for action and changes, all of which fell on deaf ears. As the program moves past a half century of existence, Little League and other youth baseball programs must be told again, in even stronger terms, to provide solutions to their excesses and abuses and make meaningful changes.

Reform is needed to address the problems of coaching, the lack of quality leadership, the program's excessive emphasis on fathers and mothers, and their lack of baseball knowledge and coaching skills. Making the problem more difficult to remedy is their failure to attend training sessions and the inability of Little League to make available instructional how-to manuals, practice procedures, etc. and require coaches to read them.

Despite their weaknesses, organized baseball leagues are here to stay. Little League, Babe Ruth, Pony, American Legion, and other programs give millions of kids a chance to play on a team, under relatively safe conditions and under adult leaders. There would be no amateur baseball without local organizations and those who administer the programs. These people spend countless hours making schedules, securing coaches, preparing the playing fields and raising funds. Without strong organized youth baseball leagues, many more children and teenagers would be playing other sports, perhaps getting into trouble, and spending more time with video games and the like.

Administered properly, with more qualified coaches, our youth leagues can play a major role in upgrading America's system of player development. A well-organized and conducted Little League program can be a productive experience, athletically, physically, and emotionally. A youth league game can provide many positive aspects: healthy exercise, satisfying relationships between players, parents, and coaches.

No, we must not lose our organized youth leagues, but they need to make meaningful and constructive changes. Society's emphasis on organized play must be supplemented by more unstructured play by children. Kids need to have alternative opportunities in the summertime and after school play in safe supervised areas. Little League should continue to provide a competitive brand of ball but in doing so, it has to control its excesses and abuses.

Top priorities of a reformed Little League program should be:

- Having fun, participation, camaraderie, and team spirit
- Developing basic skills, learning how to play the game
- Learn the importance of good character, discipline, sportsmanship, and teamwork
- Enjoyment of not only the game but practice and training
- Winning, doing your very best

Organize Task Force Study
A special task force committee should be organized to study the need for reform in youth baseball, with the following objectives:

1. Study the overall impact of Little League's short season, excessive emphasis on summer-long play-off tournaments and all-star teams, which for decades have dominated L.L.'s season.

2. Determine how the various youth league programs can provide more skill development, participation, fun and enjoyment, rather than just getting to the World Series.

3. Initiate meaningful and constructive philosophical and program changes and reform to eliminate or lessen excesses and abuses

4. Hold a national forum on youth baseball for the purpose of airing the various viewpoints relative to the overall status of organized youth leagues and the need to give young children more unstructured play opportunities in the form of pick-up games, and playground programs.

In addition to coaches and administrators representing both philosophical viewpoints, forum participants should include authorities in child development, orthopedic and medical doctors, along with officials of recreation and parks, schools, and the P.T.A. Representatives of Little League and other youth baseball organizations would be given opportunities to respond.

At the conclusion of the forum, a report containing conclusions and recommendations should be released to the news media and the appropriate agencies and organizations. A select central planning committee should be formed to implement recommendations of the forum and a Plan of Action.

Philosophical Changes Needed

Little League has always been overly ambitious with overpowering desire for world-wide expansion – making the professional model increasingly identical to Major League Baseball, while making the program bigger and bigger. However, many problems have developed as a result of Little League's philosophical shortcomings.

Youth baseball must finally recognize the need and the responsibility to serve two different interests: organized leagues and unstructured play. Society's emphasis on highly competitive play and winning has to be supplemented by unstructured playground and sandlot programs with emphasis on fun and skill development. A new philosophy is needed. Parents and coaches must stop interfering with the games. It is time for adults to back off and let the kids go out and have fun.

Will Little League be receptive to making meaningful changes? They will if forced to, like giving young children a choice in the form of less competitive and more fun-oriented programs, such as Wildcat Baseball (Fort Wayne, Indiana) and Playground Baseball in America, which I will propose later in the chapter. If Little League chooses not to make philosophical and organizational changes and fails to reduce its excesses and abuses, then cities and towns in America should take action and provide alternative programs. Either Little League must reorganize and reform or communities throughout the country will take the initiative and make program changes.

There have been signs in recent years that Little League is making an attempt to be more flexible, by making some changes and modifications. An increasing number of local leagues have implemented philosophical and structural changes in their programs. Bob Toellifer, president of the Citrus Height Little League, has made a strong effort in giving the league back to the children and away from the adults, because in his words, "That's where it belongs. It doesn't belong to the parents, nor the Board. It belongs with the kids."

"Developing baseball players is not the role of Little League," said Norm Fuller, District 5 administrator in Sacramento. "Primarily, we are there to develop citizens of good character and morality. Teaching the children to be good citizens is very important to Little League. We try not to stress competitiveness within the younger divisions. We do not want coaches who want to relive their youth through their children. We try to steer away from these people." At the Big League level, however, it is competitive.

In Youngstown, Ohio, the local little leagues have undergone a reorganization, from a highly competitive, pressurized atmosphere to one that emphasizes fun and recreational play. The program is dedicated to the development of youngsters as citizens, good sports, and well-skilled players. They want the kids to even have fun in practice.

In the 1970's, following an extensive 6-year experimental study in Canadian Little League Baseball, J. Zarebsky and R. Moriarty recommended the following changes:

- Emphasize fun and socialization
- Conduct coaching clinics focused on social and psychological goals rather than on excellence

- Decrease emphasis on scoring and standings
- Eliminate all-star teams and championships at lower levels
- Increase league competition and decrease tournament play
- Evaluate leagues on the basis of skill improvement and overall participation rather than on competitive success

Modify the Professional Model

The professional model that Little League introduced over fifty years ago has to be modified. In the opinion of numerous authorities, medical, sociological, and educational, this type of organizational structure does not serve the best interests of young children. Highly pressurized competition for young children is not emotionally and psychologically sound.

Kids need a more skill-based, fun-resulting recreational program as opposed to one that is highly pressured and result-oriented. Young children need to see baseball as a fun activity, not something they have to do because of peer or parental pressure. The goals of Little League should be designed to meet the basic needs of children. In survey after survey, children in the elementary grades have ranked "having fun" as the No. 1 reason for being involved. Winning, the most pursued goal in organized sports, has always been a relatively poor motivator for kids. Young players leave the game because they do not have fun and lose interest.

Even in the older teens, having fun is most important. A 1989 study at Michigan State University asked 10,000 junior high and high school students to list their 12 top reasons for participating in sports. At the top: to have fun. The boys ranked winning eighth. Those who conducted the study concluded that "The goal of youth coaches should be to teach the kids the sport and let them have fun."

Child-Centered Model More Appropriate

Since it was founded in 1947, Little League Baseball has applied a miniature model of the big leagues to a development situation. To this day, little leaguers are exposed to the same highly competitive and oftentimes stressful and emotional atmosphere that typifies a major league game. The ladder of success is identical, league play, an extended play-off period which is climaxed with a nationally televised world championship game. And these kids are 12 and under years of age!

The professional model of Little League has always stood in the way of a child-centered model. This must change. In his criticism of the professional model, Dr. Bruce Ogilvie, professor of sports psychology at San Jose State University, has stated that a child-centered model is more appropriate and would be far more beneficial. This model focuses on the intrinsic needs of children to participate and to have fun, rather than a professional focus on achievement and success -- winning!

The professional model for competition has to be replaced or at the very least, significantly modified. Philosophical changes must be made from a professional characterization to a child-centered program. Young children should be provided with alternative opportunities of play. Parallel leagues need to be made available for children who prefer participation and fun and do not want to play in adult-run, highly competitive leagues.

Return of Playground Baseball

Back in the 1950s and 1960s, neighborhood kids across the nation could be seen gathering every morning at local playgrounds for pick-up baseball. Every park had a leader or supervisor. In 1939 when I was growing up in Libertyville, Illinois, Arthur Kruckman, a neighbor, used a county highway department tractor to grade the vacant lot across the street from our family home. Jim Dowden, a longtime buddy of mine, and I then built a ballfield. Our team was the Libertyville Mudhens, and we even had road games, bicycling to near by towns like Grayslake and Half Day.

We were both the coaches and umpires. The players picked the captains who then picked the teams, assigned positions and determined the batting order. We even resolved our own disputes, modified the rules to suit the number of players. We learned how to cooperate, how to be good winners and good losers. Essentially, we ran our own game. No one was excluded. Nobody said, "You can't play." Later, with the growth of parks and recreation facilities, neighborhood children met at the local playground. When enough players arrived, they would have a good ball game, even rotating and playing different positions.

What can be done to get kids back to playground baseball? The key to the return of sandlot baseball is the thousands of public recreation and park agencies across the country. Children today do not play enough playground baseball, and we need to revive the concept and promote a movement. More opportunities to play baseball in parks and playgrounds need to be provided by local park and recreation departments and school districts. City playgrounds should be open longer and the necessary equipment provided.

A major effort should be made to have local recreation and park agencies nationwide spearhead a multiple-sponsorship of Playground Baseball of America, a non-profit organization coordinated by the National Recreation and Park Association and state affiliates. Such a national movement would require the joint cooperation of local and regional recreation agencies and ably supported by a national service organization, school districts, major and minor leagues, law enforcement agencies, the news media and funded by corporate sponsors.

Will city recreation agencies be willing to provide facilities and administrative support for Playground Baseball to become a reality? They will if the number of participants, program funding and volunteer leadership justifies their involvement and sponsorship. If successful, Playground Baseball will force Little League and other youth leagues to make changes. Youth baseball will also benefit by giving kids an alternative to Little League. Even more importantly, the program will contribute immeasurably to the revival of sandlot ball and the pick-up games concept, as it will to baseball itself, helping return the national pastime to America's parks and playgrounds.

Playground Baseball of America

A national organizational structure is now being developed, with the goal of locating playground baseball programs in cities and towns throughout the country. Rather than serve as a youth league, PBA is a playground program, which hopefully will be supported jointly by the National Recreation and Park Association, local recreation agencies, a major corporate sponsor, and perhaps, a service club.

Playground Baseball programs will provide and promote summer sandlot baseball opportunities for youth between the ages of 7 and 14. The program has been designed for those who prefer FUN and PARTICIPATION. With supervisory support from a local recreation agency, young children organize themselves in a playground, sandlot atmosphere, with no league champions, no all-star teams and national championships.

Support Playground Baseball Movement
- - Become a Member of PBA

As a subsidiary of our web site, Baseball Play America, Playground Baseball of America is a membership organization which has been formed to coordinate and assist individuals, groups and public agencies who want to join the movement and organize a Playground Baseball program in their communities.

Baseball Play America, the national headquarters for Playground Baseball, will provide organization materials to those who wish to become a member. Membership will include the following benefits:

- Program organization booklet (sample schedules, how-to-play instruction, checklists, favorite pick-up games, funding, etc.)
- Quarterly newsletter and membership card
- Web site access to information, materials, progress reports, instruction, downloading sequence photographs on basic skills
- Free membership in Baseball Play America
- Official report of "A Plan for Baseball"

Annual dues of $36.00 will provide membership in both Playground Baseball and BPA. This can be paid by check or charged to your credit card.

To receive membership information and how to organize a Playground Baseball program in your city or area, write: Playground Baseball, P.O. Box 4182, El Dorado Hills, CA 95762. Telephone: (916) 933-7459   Fax No. (916) 933-7447.

The E-mail address: plaground@worldnet.att.net or visit our Web site at: www.baseballplayamerica.com.

Proposed Organizational Plan

Playground Baseball of America is a proposed non-profit youth organization, established to provide summer sandlot baseball opportunities for youth between the ages of 7 and 14 who prefer PARTICIPATION and FUN, without a highly-competitive atmosphere. The program motto is "Everybody Makes the Team".

PRIMARY OBJECTIVE is to offer children a much needed and overdue alternative program, in contrast to highly competitive and over-structured youth leagues.

PARTICIPANTS, in addition to playing, will share in the umpiring, even do some coaching on occasion. The captains will pick the team each day. The players, assisted by the captains, will assign positions each day, determine the batting order and resolve disputes.

PROGRAM SUPERVISION will be assumed by playground supervisors who will be provided by the local recreation department. Leaders will provide equipment, give a clipboard to the captains for the day who will assign teams by random.

INSTRUCTION will be provided one day a week by high school and college coaches, with emphasis on the basic fundamental skills.

SUMMER SCHEDULE: Monday, Wednesday, and Friday, 9 a.m. to noon. On Tuesday morning, instruction on the basic fundamentals will be given by high school coaches. Thursday will be an off-day, but the kids will be encouraged to play pick-up games with friends.

LENGTH OF PROGRAM Funding will determine the number of weeks, hopefully a minimum of 4 to 6 weeks. Since many youth leagues are over in June, Playground Baseball, ideally, can begin in mid-June and conclude in late July, or the first week in August.

ORGANIZATION AREAS OF CONCERN: Finance, Funding, Budget, Staff, Facilities, Equipment, Promotion, Publicity, Security, Safety, etc.

MAJOR SPONSOR OF PLAYGROUND BASEBALL: A major national company whose product is enjoyed by young and old Americans alike, such as Hershey, Snickers, Wheaties, etc.

NATIONAL MEMBERS IN SUPPORT OF THE PROGRAM: National Recreation and Park Association, a national service club, like Kiwanis, Lions, Jaycees, Rotary, etc.; National H.S. Baseball Coaches Association; American Baseball Coaches Association; Parents and Teachers Association; Major League Baseball; minor leagues, etc.

LOCAL SPONSORS: The local city recreation or county recreation and parks department; high school and community college coaches; local P.T.A.; a service club; and local outlets of the national corporate sponsor of Playground Baseball of America.

FINANCE AND FUNDING: Playground Baseball need not require a large budget, since equipment and leadership needs are minimal. Ideally, a site director should be at each location. Otherwise, the local recreation department would provide someone to hand out equipment and offer general supervision, with assistance from service club members and occasional security surveillance from law enforcement. Only if necessary, a small fee could be charged each participant.

Funding role of the corporate sponsor would be primarily for:

- Equipment and supplies, like bats and balls, although the children would be encouraged to bring their glove and ball.
- Promotion and publicity, to market, advertise, and promote the program on a national scale.
- Instructional How-to Manual, with full page advertising for the corporate sponsor (front inside and back covers).

ORGANIZATIONAL STRUCTURE : National headquarters (president or chairman; director of program development and media relations; national board of directors; and regional directors).

LOCAL PLANNING COMMITTEE : High school baseball coach; park and recreation director; service club and P.T.A. representatives; the marketing and sales director of the sponsoring company, with the support of the community services and public relations director of Major League Baseball.

OTHER PROGRAM PROVISIONS : No league standings; no national tournaments; no all-star teams; parents will not attend games, etc. Every child will play an equal amount of time regardless of their skills and abilities. No curve balls will be allowed.

PUBLICATIONS : A national newsletter and an instructional training manual will be given to each participant, with emphasis on the basic fundamental skills.

Wildcat Baseball League (Fort Wayne, Indiana)

On a pleasant day in April 1960, 80-year-old Dale W. McMillen Sr. was riding through McMillen Park in Fort Wayne. The founder of Central Soya Company noticed that Little League tryouts were in progress, and he had his chauffeur stop the limousine so he could watch. It was evident to McMillen that there were more boys than places to fill on just four teams. At the end of the try-outs, he could see the disappointment on the faces of those who failed to make a team. The crushed expressions on the faces of a nine and ten year old was too much for "Mr. Mac" to take.

After discussing the problem with the Executive Secretary of the McMillen Foundation, McMillen decided to do something about it. After much consultation, he formed the Wildcat Recreation Association. The major purpose of the association was to give all boys who wanted to play organized baseball a chance to participate regardless of their skill, ability, race, creed or religion.

Two experienced teachers with baseball backgrounds were chosen to help develop the program and carry out the day-to-day details of running a summer baseball league. They would serve as commissioner and league secretary. After forming the initial organization, it was necessary to find locations to play.

Before hiring site directors to conduct the program at the various locations, the following program philosophy was drawn up: "Any boy within the age group of the Wildcat League who wants to play, and whose parents want him to play, shall be assigned to a team and be given the opportunity to play. 'Everybody makes the team' will be the motto of the Wildcat League."

WILDCAT OATH

- I pledge to conduct myself in a true sportsmanlike manner.

- I shall not in any way cause damage to equipment, parks, school property, or any other property of any description.

- I shall regularly attend church and/or Sunday School of my choice.

- I shall do my best - always.

- My conduct shall always be in a manner acceptable to my parents, my friends, school authorities, civil authorities, and to myself.

- I shall show respect for all people regardless of their age, race, religion, or beliefs.

After seeing the disappointment of young children who failed to make a team, Dale W. McMillen, Sr., formed the Wildcat Recreation Association to give all boys and girls a chance to play baseball. Above, two Wildcatters visit with Mr. Mac in 1964.

In the Wildcat Baseball League, the teaching of fundamentals are emphasized over winning championships. Games and practice sessions involve the children in a positive educational experience.

The first week was spent on tryouts that included instructions and practices. The major purpose of testing the skills was to match up abilities and create balanced teams. By the end of the week, the teams were chosen and schedules handed out. Since 1971 the baseball teams have been coed, while the girls softball program began in 1989. The league was divided into three divisions according to age. Today, the Kitty Division consists of children 8, 9 and 10 years of age. In the Kat Division, the players are 11 and 12. The oldest division, the Tigers, is comprised of boys and girls 13, 14 and 15. Each team is composed of 12 to 16 players. Wildcatters pay for their own uniforms, a T-shirt and cap, with the Wildcat insignia emblazoned on the shirts.

Major emphasis of Wildcat Baseball is on participation, with very little pressure put on the child to attend or win. Each team plays two games a week in the eight-week program, in addition to one practice per week. Among the many differences between Wildcat and Little League is that parents are not encouraged to attend games or practices. If they wish, they can attend, but any parent who becomes unruly or puts down his or her child for making a mistake is asked to leave.

Coaches are not assigned to individual teams, and they generally work games and practices in pairs. While one coach remains near the bench, the other assumes a position behind the mound, umpires and assists the base runners and the defense. Nicholas Dawidoff explained in Sports Illustrated, "If a ball trickles through the first baseman's legs, a coach is likely to stop play and briefly explain the proper way to field a grounder."

Carl Erskine, former pitching star of the Brooklyn Dodgers, was the one who advised McMillen to emphasize teaching the fundamentals in his league over winning championships. Staff members of the Wildcat League have never lost sight of Erskine's advice. Each of the practices during the eight-week season is devoted to teaching a single skill, like fielding grounders or laying down bunts.

Fun still takes priority over winning titles or developing stars of the future. "We believe in winning and it is important to win, but we believe there are other things that are just as important, said John S. Grantham, president of Wildcat Baseball since 1965. "Nurturing the child's self-image and developing good, solid citizens is an important part of our philosophy. We create a situation where kids can be successful."

Since the program began in 1961, the McMillen Foundation has provided 100% of the funding for the Wildcat Baseball League, over $5,000,000. The annual budget is now over $250,000, with insurance alone over $17,000. As much as 60% of the budget goes to staff salaries for the eight-week program.

The program's governing body is the Wildcat Recreation Association, whose board of directors approves the overall policies and the budget. But to a large degree, the enduring success of Wildcat Baseball can be attributed to the energy and dedicated leadership of John Grantham. His moral integrity and concern for all people has provided guidance and strong inspiration to both the staff and the youth of Fort Wayne, Indiana. As Grantham pointed out, "The score of the game and the situations involved, all are less important than the player we are helping." Today, following four decades of existence, over 4,500 boys and girls participate each summer. As for the future of Wildcat Baseball, Erskine said, "The community is so aware of what the program has done that the city would support it even if for some reason the trust vanished."

The eight-week instructional baseball program interfaces with the Parks and Recreation Department and School Systems for facilities, giving the league access to 40 baseball diamonds.

The energy and dedication leadership of John Grantham, president of Wildcat Baseball since 1965, has been a major factor in the success of the program.

Revival of Pick-up Games

The best way to get children to play more baseball on their own is to promote a return of pick-up games. The youngsters of America need to be taught how to organize pick-up games on their own. "We don't see kids playing strikeout against a wall, nor do they play scrub," said Jim Panther. "Children don't realize they can play 2 against 2 in baseball or play with five guys and have them hit to the left side of second base, having ghost, imaginary runners."

Many years ago, during the summer, in the afternoons following school and on weekends, youngsters made the neighborhoods reverberate with the sounds of playing games in parks, vacant lots and in the streets. Among the many games were stickball, scrub, over-the-line, wall ball, strikeout, and later on, wiffleball. There were always 3 or 4 of us to play some version of a game. If we couldn't hit to right, we would stack the fielders, so there was enough to go around. If kids didn't have enough players for stickball, they would play "Catch-a-fly and you're up" and Army Ball. Recalling his youthful days in Oakland, Joe Morgan said, "There were numerous home runs when we played. I had 800 one year." How did Joe know? "We all were fanatical record keepers."

Do kids need a partner? No. Actually, all they need is a wall and a tennis ball, preferably a fairly hard rubber ball. Every building has a wall somewhere. They should use a garage to practice pitching against and fielding the return. Throw the ball to a certain spot in the strike zone and see how many times they can hit the spot.

Favorite Pick-up Games

Ever mindful that the large majority of young kids today do not play pick-up games, nor do they and their parents know how, the following low organized games are those that young children used to play. Quite often, they were played from morning hours to the evening. In preparing the directions of these games, I received assistance from a number of people, but special thanks must go to Chuck Davis, recreation and park administrator in Sacramento, California, whose handout on "Lead-up Games" I shared many years with my recreation students and leaders, and Jim Panther in Libertyville, Illinois, who for many years has taught young children how to play pick-up games.

Work Up   Equipment: Baseball and bat. Directions: Work-up is where one player gets to bat until he or she makes an out. When the hitter makes an out, he moves into the field and the fielders move up one position until each has a turn at bat. "Working up" starts from right field position and continues from right to center field; from center to left field; from left field to shortstop; shortstop to third; then to second base, first base, pitcher, catcher, and finally the batter. The batter tries to stay at bat for three successive runs while those in the field try to put the runners out. If there is only one batter, he runs between home and first base and continues as batter until he is put out, or successfully completes three successive runs. If there are two batters, they run from home to first, to third and home again. If there are three or more batters, all the bases are used.

Scrub   Equipment: Baseball and bat. Directions: One player is at bat, with a catcher, pitcher, first base and other fielders. All players are numbered: the batter is scrub; catcher, one; pitcher, two; first base, three; fielders, four and up. The batter hits a ball pitched to him, and runs to first base and back. If he is put out by being tagged at first base or home, striking three times, hitting three fouls or having a fly ball caught, he goes to the field and takes the number of the last fielder. Each player moves over one position and number, first base to pitcher, pitcher to catcher, and catcher to batter (scrub). If the batter gets home safely, he will bat again. Each batter is allowed to make three runs before taking to the field, provided he is not put out.

Wall Ball   Equipment: A wall with a drawn strike zone, rubber or tennis ball, and home plate. Directions: One or more players stand about 20 to 40 feet from the wall, preferably concrete. The game begins by having each player throw a ball against the wall. As a drill, throws can be fielded by the player who made the throw. As a competitive game, a player other than the thrower has to field the ball and the "pitcher" can vary the type, speed and difficulty of throws. Rules can be established as to catching the ball on a fly or a bounce. The players can keep score and the one who has the most points will win. Another game involves a pitcher pitching an imaginary game against the wall. He keeps the count, outs, innings and score. To make this an even more competitive experience, two pitchers can oppose each other, alternating innings and keeping score.

Army Ball   Equipment: Hard rubber ball and bat. Directions: This popular West Coast "stick" and ball game often involves three players, a pitcher, batter and fielder. Of course, more players can play. As to how the game got its name, the field was spread from any makeshift backstop to any tall building, barracks, whatever. This was strictly a pull-hitting game. Batters cannot hit the opposite way. If the batter hit the building above one level, it is a double, another level a triple, and the roof and over, a home run. There are no walks in Army Ball. The batter stays at bat until he hits or strikes out. This serves to make hitters wait for desired pitches.

Catch-A-Fly and You're Up   Equipment: Ball, bat. Directions: One player is at bat and the rest of the players are in the field or down the street. When a fielder catches a fly ball, he gets to hit. Most kids will come up to the plate swinging, trying to hit a home run or a hard line drive. Some will hit a few on the ground so they will stay up longer. So a pitcher may want to throw high pitches to make the batter hit flies. Rather than be close behind the plate, the catcher will position himself safely farther back. If he catches a pop foul, he may be allowed to hit.

Stickball   Equipment: rubber or tennis ball and bat (or a broom or stick). Directions: Best known as the New York city street sport, there are many ways to play stickball. Ground rules depend on the site, which may be a backyard, driveway, or a tennis court wall at a nearby park. If played on a street, the bases can be drawn with a piece of chalk, or cardboard squares can be used. A high-bounce rubber ball is ideal, while the rod part of a mop or broom can be used for a bat. Quite often, there are just two players, a batter and pitcher. The pitcher throws against a wall, which may be decorated with a hand-drawn "strike zone". Balls and strikes can be called, although arguments are frequent. In the street game version, the sides can expand to two players each so that a catcher can serve as backstop. In still another way, there is not pitcher, only a batter and an outfielder. The pitcher can simply throw the ball up and hit it for doubles, triples or home runs.

Play Catch   Equipment: Ball and gloves. Directions: Ever since baseball was invented, Play Catch has been regarded as the game's most valuable drill. Although better known as a warm-up drill, playing catch with another player can also be made a game, one that can be funful and challenging. For example, a player can see how many times out of 10 throws he can hit a designated target, such as a glove, chest area, or around the knees. When Jimmy Key was growing up in Alabama, his father, Ray, taught him a simple lesson about how to play catch. "Always throw to a target," he said. Move the feet when playing catch. Then stretch out the throwing arm by moving farther away from a partner and play Long Toss but keep the throw on a line, not a lollypop toss.

Wiffleball   Equipment: Plastic baseball-size Wiffleball and bat.

Directions: The minimum number of players required to play Wiffleball are two, the pitcher and batter. The maximum number can be ten, five players to a side. Each side can consist of the catcher, pitcher, double area fielder, and home run area fielders. As in baseball, one team is at bat and one in the field. Captains for each team are selected and they can choose their teams alternately. Standing about 40 feet in front of a plate (or a glove), the pitcher throws a ball which the hitter attempts to hit. The two players can keep score: line drive (3 points); fly ball over pitcher's head or ground hit past the pitcher (2 pts.); an easy pop fly or ground ball fielded by pitcher (1 pt.). The players switch roles following a pre-set number of swings. Another version of Wiffleball, between the foul lines, a ball hit in the single area is a single; a ball hit in triple area and not caught is a triple. A ball hit beyond the triple markers and not caught is a home run.

Over the Line   Equipment: Ball and bat. Directions: Referred to also as Line Ball, this is a favorite playground, school yard game. With two teams 30 feet apart and perhaps 6 players on a team, the object is for the batter to drive a ground ball through the other team. Each team has a bat. The first player tosses the ball up and tries to bat it across the other team's goal line. The ball must hit the ground between the two lines. The other team tries to field the ball and then attempts to bat it back across the opponent's goal line. Each member of each team gets a chance to bat. One point is scored for each ball that crosses the other team's goal line. Another variation is for the players to throw rather than bat the ball.

Revitalizing Youth Baseball

Having cited the need for a renaissance in youth baseball and the rationale for youth leagues to reform, now I will recommend what has to be done for a reformation to occur. In answering the following questions, some practical solutions and approaches will be presented as to how youth baseball can be revitalized.

- What changes are needed in the organizational structure of Little League and other organized youth leagues?
- What alternative opportunities do young children need most?
- How can player development be upgraded in America and is there a need for an American system of play?
- Why can't Major League Baseball build some academies in the United States?

The development of baseball players at the youth level can best be achieved by giving kids a choice, an alternative program, such as summer playground programs and parallel leagues. Our society's strong emphasis on organized league play must also be supplemented by unstructured play. Young children, even older youth, need to play low-organized pick-up types of games on their own, and it is most essential that cities and towns, large and small, re-open their parks and playgrounds to baseball.

Alternative Opportunities Needed   Children need an
alternative to the highly-competitive pressure and atmosphere which exists in Little League Baseball and other youth organizations. Today's young people are overorganized. They are not playing enough on their own to fully develop their skills. Fewer children are spending the time to learn to play baseball. They need a summer playground program where they can go to a park or school ball field and play baseball, either pick-up game with their friends or in low-organized and fun-oriented team competition.

An alternative program is just what the name implies – to give young children a choice, an opportunity to play baseball without the highly competitive pressure and atmosphere, which prevails in little league today. Kids play in the mornings without parents present. The rewards and outcomes as to the children's growth and development are numerous. The program is designed to provide the sandlot type of atmosphere that many of us experienced.

"When I was a kid, I played in a league during the day where we picked our own teams," said Jim Panther. "There were no coaches, and we just had games. We had no umpires. We just argued with each other. No parents were involved. But today, somebody has to be there to hand out the equipment. We found balls and took wood bats that the high schools broke. To buy a bat or ball, we would collect bottles and got 2 cents a bottle. We scrounged around and got it. The park district would run the program and when we did not have enough players for a team game, we'd play pick-up games. When we couldn't find a ballfield, we would move home plate close to the tennis courts, so now the fence was like Fenway Park, and we had a ball playing there. That's what is needed today."

For a playground baseball program to be successful nationally, it must have the support and the sponsorship of recreation and park agencies, the schools, and parent-teachers organizations. When asked for his thoughts, Panther responded enthusiastically, "If we can get the help of parks and recreation departments and school districts around the country, where the kids can come to a park or school playground with a supervisor who provides equipment, a limited amount of instruction but lets the kids play, I really believe playground baseball could return."

Stress Skill Development, Not Winning

The goals of youth baseball should be based on the growth and development needs of children. Greater emphasis should be on developing skills, enjoyment, and funful experiences. The fundamental baseball concept and approach has to be practiced and promoted. The lack of pick-up games and sandlot baseball has hurt the development of young players.

A major priority in player development is for coaches and parents to promote the "Play Catch" concept. Like they used to, kids need to play more catch, with their parents, a friend or big brother. Since they are not playing enough catch, the throwing skills of young children have diminished. Try to make games of playing catch. Make them fun and challenging.

Young children are not learning enough of the basic fundamentals in Little League. Youth leagues are not teaching proper mechanics largely because

428

coaches don't put in the time to learn the basics themselves. Baseball is a skill-oriented game, which requires much time commitment and practice. Young players today want the quick-result approach.

The most successful and innovative program to develop the game of baseball is Honda's Hit, Run and Throw contest, which is offered to schools, parks, and after-school programs in many countries. It has created much needed awareness of baseball in schools and park agencies by offering quality lesson plans and free equipment for physical education classes and recreation programs.

The program consists of five age divisions: boys 12-13, girls 12-13, and mixes 10-11, 8-9 and 7 and under. In Canada, the champions from each of the provinces are flown to Toronto's Skydome to compete for the Canadian championship prior to a Toronto Blue Jays' game in September.

Developing An American System of Play
In contrast to the growing number of nations who have developed systems for training baseball players, there has never been a structured system of player development in the United States. In many other countries, young baseball players are benefitting significantly from a definitive system of nationally funded programs.

Baseball in America needs a strong, more efficient development system with all youth baseball programs involved. The lower levels of amateur baseball have experienced a decline. American youth teams have not done well in international competition. A major reason is that the United States does not have a structured system of player development. While the USA does not need Cuba's highly regimented program, a more systematic approach to development would be beneficial not only to our most promising 14-17 year old prospects but every level of play.

While U.S. Soccer has a most impressive game plan in developing their soccer players, baseball has none. Soccer has 9 national coaching coordinators while baseball has none. To develop skills of young baseball players, the entire baseball industry must come together. It should come from a combination of places, the Major Leagues, National High School Federation, NCAA, NAIA, NJCAA, and the many organized youth leagues, coordinated by an expanded USA Baseball in Tucson, Arizona. Major League Baseball, with strong corporate assistance, must counter the U.S. Soccer Federation's huge funding for youth soccer.

The advisory and educational duties of the national coordinator would be directed toward the achievement of such objectives as:

- More qualified and trained coaches
- Distribution and use of instructional materials
- The realization of safer and more secure play facilities
- Ways and means for kids to practice at home
- More affordable clinics and camps for players and coaches

Baseball Academies Needed in U.S.

Major League Baseball continues to spend millions of dollars building and maintaining academies and training facilities in countries outside of the United States. But there are no academies in this country subsidized or sponsored by the majors. Other than USA Baseball's training headquarters in Tucson, only a few privately owned centers for young amateurs exist.

Wouldn't the money be better spent training our own children and youth to be better ball players? Wouldn't more of our players in the majors have greater identity with fans? I have to believe the answers to these questions should be a resounding "Yes". There is an urgent need for player development academies to be built in the United States, created primarily for American athletes.

For decades, Cuba has been very successful in developing highly skilled baseball players, and a big part of their success can be attributed to baseball training academies at each of their 14 provinces. As many as 400 players participate on 14 teams which play a 92-game season. Cuba's top 50 players are then chosen to train near Havana. The number is later narrowed down to 20 for the national team that plays at international events.

There is a great need for a system of training young players in America, similar to the Kansas City Royals Academy established in 1970. Rather than focusing increasingly on foreign prospects and building academies in other countries, Major League Baseball should concentrate on youngsters here at home. The big leagues, in cooperation with the nation's colleges, high schools, and youth programs, should be offering young American prospects the training and instruction they need. Benefits would be enormous, such as better players and a larger fan base.

Coordinated through the commissioner's office, in conjunction with their minor league affiliates, each of the 30 clubs would have player development camps within the territorial areas where they are responsible. Using the academy system, the development camps will produce much better baseball players, and in such large numbers, the majors and minors would not have to be so dependent on players from foreign countries.

Expand RBI Program in Cities

Reviving baseball in the inner-city was the brainchild of founder John Young in 1989. The former major league scout discovered that most inner-city youth stopped playing baseball between the ages of 13 and 16. His hope was to create a program that prepared kids athletically and academically for future success. "Our goal is to get kids educated, to be productive citizens," stated Young. "If they get to the big leagues that's fine." Other RBI goals is to increase participation, provide more opportunities to compete, develop self-esteem, and motivate children to become better students.

As many as 58 percent of Los Angeles kids are high school drop-outs. RBI's goal is to give them a place to look for a dream and to get out of the situation that surrounds them. It represents an outlet of hope, to show inner-city kids that baseball is fun and give them the same opportunities as those in the suburbs.

Major League Baseball is to be commended for expanding their support of the RBI program. In their efforts to reinvest in the nation's inner-cities, they are in the process of applying the program in all major league cities. Each big league team would be responsible for helping disadvantaged youth and promoting the game to a new generation of fans. The potential impact of the RBI program on baseball and the lives of inner-city youth can be enormous. Having started on a small scale and with only a decade of existence, RBI has yet to achieve its potential growth.

Challenges for Little League

Although the basic philosophy and program framework of Little League Baseball has drawn strong criticism, the organization itself has achieved remarkable success, expanding to phenomenal proportions. Unfortunately, the quality and stature of Little League and other youth leagues have been marred by their excesses and abuses, particularly in the younger age divisions.

Most of Little League's problems and needs have largely been the result of excessiveness and abuse, and the victims have been the children for whom the program was created. For Little League and other programs to be more responsible and more effectively serve the best interests of our young ball players, the following recommendations will serve as a challenge:

Limit Post-Season Play

Based on studies involving organized youth leagues, emphasis on post-season tournaments and all-star teams is excessive and must be reduced. Tournament play for Little League begins as early as late June, which means the baseball season for most children is over when summer begins. Only the very few players who make the all-star teams are playing baseball during the summer.

From a positive point of view, tournament play that is limited to local, state and even regional competition provides young people with new experiences of travel and association. But for the 11 and 12-year old kids who play in the Little League World Series, the pressure, nervous anxiety and emotional stress is much too excessive. To make matters worse, the problem was magnified when Little League officials decided to double the number of teams from 8 to 16 teams in 2001. The event will now take nine days.

De-emphasize All-Star Teams

A growing number of administrators, coaches, and parents are saying there is too much emphasis on all-star teams and tournament play. For the best players, being an all-star is an exciting and proud experience. However, for equally deserving players who are left off the team, it is often a shattering experience, for them and their parents. For most players, it limits the season. The baseball season is over in June when summer begins. Only those selected on all-star teams are playing.

In explaining the purpose of post-season play-offs, Norm Fuller stated that "Tournament play involving all-star teams is to be a culmination of a season that highlights the program and provides additional recreation opportunities for the more skilled players."

"I personally agree that we have placed too much emphasis on all-star competition," said Fuller, who has directed numerous tournaments involving all-star teams. "But being in America, everyone wants their child to be an all-star, but when you consider what Little League is all about, it's not about building or developing skills for kids to play high school and college baseball. It is about providing a recreation program for as many children as there are in the community who wants to play, regardless of their abilities and talent."

Because of decreased revenue, administrators, local and national, will not want to cut back, but in doing so, they will continue to hurt the development and overall well-being of growing children.

Ban Curve Balls for Kids 12 and Under
Young pitchers are still throwing too many breaking ball pitches and are doing serious harm to their pitching arms. Yet, Little League officials who have the responsibility for the safety and health of the players continue to ignore the curve ball problem. But a growing number of local little leagues, like Middleboro and Springfield in Massachusetts, are protecting their young pitchers by banning the curve ball: No curve balls for pitchers 9 through 12 years of age.

In our survey of 1,000 veteran college and high school coaches, we asked them, should the curve ball be banned from Little League Division competition? 64.9% answered "Yes". Many of the coaches, in explaining their views, cited the stress on a developing arm and improper throwing mechanics. Dr. Rainer Martens concurred by saying, "Any risk is too much and that throwing curves should be eliminated until bone growth is completed, usually 14 or 15. Al Rosen who wrote the excellent book, Baseball and Your Boy, was more blunt in stating that "I cannot think of a single legitimate excuse for having a Little League pitcher throwing curve balls."

Little League programs throughout the world must do what local leagues in Massachusetts have done: Abolish all breaking pitches until the 13-15 age level, at which time, the number of curves should be limited. Umpires would have the authority to first issue a warning to the coach, and the catcher and pitcher, but if the number of curves continue, he would remove the pitcher from the game similar to how umpires handle beanball/knockdown situations.

If Little League refuses to take action, each individual league should do so by either eliminating the curve altogether or keep the number to an absolute minimum. A growing number of leagues have outlawed the curve by verbal agreement or in writing. They agree not to teach the pitch and try to discourage those who pick it up on the side. As for the slider, it is even more dangerous than the curve ball.

Upgrade the Quality of Coaching

Little League and other youth baseball programs must make a stronger commitment to train their coaches. The level of coaching skills and baseball knowledge continues to be a serious problem in player development in America. A large majority of coaches today are parents, and most have very little knowledge of the basic fundamentals.

The qualifications and training of youth coaches must be strengthened. There has to be some type of standards set. Youth coaches should be required to attend clinics and training sessions. They need a manual containing instructional materials on the basics. In addition, they should receive suggested practice organization plans, lists of drills and their explanations, and checklists on the basic skills and techniques.

The training of youth league coaches can increase significantly the likelihood of a beneficial experience for the players. There is absolutely no reason why parents can't improve their coaching skills. Either better qualified coaches need to be enticed into coaching, or the current volunteers need more training. It has always been a mystery why Little League has not made a stronger effort to develop and provide an effective training program for both coaches and players.

Certify Youth League Coaches

Better trained coaches are urgently needed in Little League and other youth baseball programs. For this to be achieved, Little League must certify its coaches. To coach youth baseball, an individual must go through a certification program instructed by an experienced high school or college coach.

As to how youth leagues can implement a certification process, a very practical way is for the local community college to offer a class in "Youth Baseball Coaching". Students who successfully complete the class will receive a certificate to coach, including an emblematic patch to wear. Training methods should be "hands-on", skill-oriented, where they learn the basic fundamentals, how to organize and conduct a practice session.

Another approach to certification, particularly if the league itself provides the training, coaches would be required to attend a set number of hours of instruction. Similar to the class conducted by the college, participants would be required to take a written and practical exam, and upon completion will wear what hopefully will be regarded as a coveted emblem.

Control Parental Interference
Many parents can not separate themselves from their children's successes and failures. They expect too much too soon. Too often, parents will push their children into Little League even though they are not athletically inclined or sufficiently interested in doing so. When local leagues choose all-star teams, parents are very upset that their son was not selected to the tournament team. They make calls to league officials wanting to know why.

I asked Bob Taillefer, former president of the Citrus Heights, California Little League how he deals with parents? He explained, "Essentially, listening to what the parent has to say, what the coach and manager has to say, evaluate everything, and go from there. Ninety percent of the complaints are that 'My son is not playing enough.' However, Little League does have a rule where every player has to play half the innings per week. We do audit the scorebooks to make sure this is being done. When we do have a problem, I will audit the book and show the parents, 'Your son is playing.' Maybe he's not playing as much as you feel he should, but I can't step in and interfere with the coach. That's an issue that you have to take up with the coach."

Uphold Respect and Integrity of Umpires
Disrespect toward umpires seems to be increasing, especially in amateur baseball. More umpires are being taunted or even threatened with physical abuse. Such actions on the part of those at the ballpark – coaches, players, parents, and fans, should not be tolerated. Considering that those who umpire in

the younger youth leagues are volunteers trying to do their best makes such actions even more intolerable.

Umpires are hired or recruited to be arbiters of the game to oversee the contest and make appropriate rulings, and they must be allowed to carry out their duties. Respect for officials must be maintained, and they deserve the support of league officials. Those who administer organized youth leagues have a responsibility to provide as high a level of competency and skills as possible. To achieve this goal, umpires, including those who volunteer must be qualified and trained and participate regularly in rules meetings with other association umpires. The need for certifying umpires is just as essential as for coaches.

Keep Kids From Quitting
A study conducted in 1988 by Michigan State University revealed that "Children are quitting youth sports in droves". According to the results, one-half of them will drop out by age 12 and three-fourths by age 15. The largest single age dropout comes at 14, about the time kids encounter larger fields, bigger opponents and curve balls.

Among the reasons behind the drop-out rate:

- "The coach picked on me too much"
- Parents were overzealous and expected too much
- Overemphasis on winning; the demand was too great
- Lack of success; "I never got any better"
- Lack of fun
- Baseball loses young athletes to sports easier to play
- Having a fear of failure
- Players simply lose interest

Provide Safe Play Areas
Safety and security is a great concern of parents of children. Young children need to feel safe to go down to a park or playground and play ball. The cities and towns of America should provide them with safe play areas where kids can go without fear and play among themselves. In many communities, it is not safe to leave children alone to play.

The time is long overdue to make play areas safe enough for parents to feel comfortable enough to allow their children to go there. While park agencies cannot afford to assign leaders at all facilities, as many playgrounds as possible should have someone in charge, supervising and monitoring the area. Law enforcement agencies working closely with public and private institutions must make a greater effort to provide safer and more secure play areas for children, as well as young and old people alike. To support such action, however, families must get together to take charge of their neighborhood.

Make Youth Baseball Safer

The American Academy of Pediatrics in 1996 published a study of more than 2,800 Little Leaguers ages 7-18. The study concluded that Little League Baseball is safe and has a low injury rate. Still, the overall safety and health of young children deserve more scrutiny and concern. Those responsible for the physical well-being of those who compete, the administrators and Board of Trustees, continue to ignore that countless numbers of young pitchers have ruined their arms and shortened careers by throwing an excessive number of curve balls. The pitching elbow and the vulnerable shoulder area can and has been permanently damaged.

The use of powerful, menacing aluminum bats represent a serious danger to young pitchers and infielders. Numerous injuries have been caused by line drive smashes, since a ball comes off metal bats much quicker than wooden bats. Livelier baseballs constitute still another safety danger to the children. In addition to closely checking the performance levels of bats, officials should do the same with balls because they are livelier than ever. The use of a softer ball at younger levels, at least during early training, will minimize the anxiety of young children when at bat and in the field. The fear factor contributes to injuries because many young players just freeze up. While a softer ball should be used on the T-Ball level, studies conclude that the older leagues should not change.

Strengthen Throwing Arms

Throwing arm strength is the biggest shortcoming among most youth league players today. Kids coming up don't seem to have the arm strength they used to. Arm strength has diminished considerably because young players are not throwing enough. Nor do they throw for distance enough to strengthen their arms. Many are spending too much time in hitting cages and weight rooms, which for many has contributed to tight, bulky throwing arms.

The most effective way to develop a strong arm is to throw over and over. Kids should be encouraged to play catch often. The basic throw-catch routine has to become a habit, something players must do every day. Few Little Leaguers can actually play a good game of catch, and this is a major reason why arm strength is not as strong as it used to be. As a boy, Mike Mussina spent hours in his basement throwing a rubber ball against a wall.

Few coaches are emphasizing the development of strong throwing arms. Long throw should be taught to kids at a young age. The throwing arms of most young players have not been sufficiently extended. Their throwing muscles and tendons are tight, rather than loose, supple, and elastic. Long throw will stretch them out.

Give Kids More Physical Exercise
The lack of physical exercise among the youth of America, including those who play baseball, has contributed to a serious health problem. As the life styles of both children and teenage youth become increasingly sedentary, watching television, working with computers, searching the Internet, and playing video games, the fitness level of children has reached unprecedented low levels.

"Children need physical activity to build flexibility, cardiovascular and muscle fitness," said professor Charles B. Corbin of Arizona State University. "By establishing the 'physical-activity habit' in childhood reduces the odds of becoming totally sedentary, which, sadly, describes about 25% of American adults."

The National Association for Sport and Physical Education has issued guide-lines advising that children age 6 to 11 be physically active for at least one hour and up to several hours each day. Dr. Michael O'Shea, chairman of the Sports Training Institute, emphasized the need for parents to be actively involved with their children. "Plan walks after dinner," he said. "Play catch and ride a bike, or go on a nature walk. Shoot a few baskets or go for a swim."

Parents and their children can establish a "physical-activity habit" early in life:

- Encourage your children to practice skills and to share what they learned in physical education classes.
- Contact other parents, school board, and PTA for assistance in improving the school's physical education program.
- Encourage your children to participate in physical activities outside of school, especially activities that can be done throughout life.

Make Camps and Schools Affordable   Summer baseball camps are better today than ever before, but most of them are too expensive. Most families, particularly the middle class and lower, can't afford to send their children to camps and schools. The children of low-income African-American families and other minorities are unable to pay for not only camp fees but even play in organized leagues.

Back in the 1950s and 60s, baseball clinics, sometimes a school, were sponsored by public recreation agencies or a group of former professional ball players and scouts who would team up together to conduct them free of charge. Or, a youth league would arrange for area coaches or an ex-pro to put on an early season clinic. I can recall those I co-directed with Bobby Bragan and players on his Spokane Indians team, in which our Spokane Park Department would have 2000 kids bussed in from various neighborhoods.

Today, however, baseball camps and schools have developed into a highly lucrative industry. Most operate under private ownership, but now coaches have recognized the fund-raising benefits and the personal income. Some schools have been moderately priced, but others have priced themselves far beyond what most families can afford to pay. Five-day camps run from $150 to $400 per player, while 3-day camps are priced from $75-$125. The Dusty Baker School of Baseball in his hometown Sacramento is one of the nation's finest camps for children 8-12 and 13-18 years of age. Dusty always finds the time to spend a day with the kids and invites them to the Giants' ballpark in San Francisco.

Youth League Organizations

ALL AMERICAN AMATEUR BASEBALL ASSOCIATION
331 Parkway Drive, Zanesville, OH 43701)
Tel: (614) 453-8531   Fax: (614) 453-3978   Year Founded: 1944
President: James McElroy   Executive Director: Bob Wolfe

AMERICAN AMATEUR BASEBALL CONGRESS
118-119 Redfield Plaza, P.O. Box 467, Marshall, MI 49068
Tel: (616) 781-2002   Fax: (616) 781-2060   Year Founded: 1935
President: Joe Cooper

AMATEUR ATHLETIC UNION OF THE UNITED STATES (AAU)
P.O. Box 1000, Lake Buena Vista, FL 32803
Tel: (407) 828-3459   Fax: (407) 934-7242   Year Founded: 1982
Sport Manager/Baseball: Sheldon Walker

AMERICAN LEGION BASEBALL
P.O. Box 1055, Indianapolis, IN 46206
Tel: (317) 630-1213   Fax: (317) 630-1369   Year Founded: 1925
Program Coordinator: Jim Quinlan

BABE RUTH BASEBALL LEAGUE, INC.
1770 Brunswick Pike, P.O. Box 5000, Trenton, NJ 08638
Tel: (609) 695-1434   Fax: (609) 695-2505)   Year Founded: 1951
President/Chief Executive Officer: Ron Tellefsen

CONTINENTAL AMATEUR BASEBALL ASSOCIATION
82 University St., Westerville, OH 43081
Tel/Fax: (614) 899-2103   Year Founded: 1984
President: Carl Williams   Executive Director: Roger Tremaine

DIXIE BASEBALL, INC.
P.O. Box 231536, Montgomery, AL 36123
Tel: (334) 242-8395   Fax: (334) 242-0198   Year Founded: 1962
Executive Director: P.L. Corley

HAP DUMONT YOUTH BASEBALL
P.O. Box 17455, Wichita, KS 67217
Tel: (316) 721-1779   Fax: (316) 721-8054   Year Founded: 1974
National Chairman: Jerry Crowell

LITTLE LEAGUE BASEBALL, INC.
P.O. Box 3485, Williamsport, PA 17701
Tel: (717) 326-1921   Fax: (717) 326-1074   Year Founded: 1939
President/Chief Executive Officer: Steve Keener

NATIONAL AMATEUR BASEBALL FEDERATION
P.O. Box 705, Bowie, MD 20715
Tel/Fax: (301) 262-5005   Year Founded: 1914
Executive Director: Charles Blackburn

NATIONAL ASSOCIATION OF POLICE ATHLETIC LEAGUES
618 N. US Highway 1, Suite 201, North Palm Beach FL 33408
Tel: (561) 844-1823   Fax: (561) 863-6120   Year Founded: 1944
Executive Director: Joseph Wilson

PONY BASEBALL, INC.
P.O. Box 225, Washington, PA 15301
Tel: (724) 225-1000   Fax: (724) 225-9852   Year Founded: 1951
President: Abraham Key   Director, Operations: Don Clawson

REVIVING BASEBALL IN INNER-CITIES (RBI)
350 Park Avenue, New York, NY 10022   Founder: John Young
Tel: (212) 339-7800   Fax: (212) 888-8632   Year Founded: 1989
Executive Director: Kathleen Francis   National Manager: Tom Brasuell

U.S. AMATEUR BASEBALL ASSOCIATION
7101 Lake Ballinger Way, Edmonds, WA 98026
Tel/Fax: (425) 776-7130   Year Founded: 1969
Executive Director: Al Rutledge

U.S. AMATEUR BASEBALL FEDERATION
7355 Peter Pan Ave., San Diego, CA 92114
Tel/Fax: (619) 527-9205   Year Founded: 1995
Commissioner: Tim Halbig

Epilogue

For nearly a century, baseball has changed right along with society, adjusting to meet technical advancements, which prompted Bruce Jenkins' reaction that "The game has a brand of conscience changing right along with American Society. That's why so many people feel it's the greatest game of all. You don't have to touch it. But, even after all the changes, it has retained the rich, pastoral feel of a family picnic."

"With a single exception – opening its doors to all races – baseball never needed to do anything. If it had stayed exactly the same since the early 1920s, it would be just as wonderful today. In fact, it could be argued that nearly all of the so-called improvements have been detrimental to baseball's essence."

Baseball must be more than just the home run. While fans will always love the long ball, there is much more to love about the game - a quickly turned double play, a surprise bunt single and a stolen base can win games, too. Baseball has to emphasize much more of the game than only slow trots around the bases. As Tim Keown wrote, "The home run now that it has done its main job, needs to take a well-deserved rest. Give us subtlety, a double in the right field corner scoring a slow runner from first – just barely – to win a crucial September game between teams locked in a pennant race. We don't need another 70-homer season. The home run needs a return to its roots, brought out only for special occasions."

Yes, baseball needs the beautiful arc of the long-hit ball, the suspense of where it will land. But, it also needs the graceful diving catch, the picture-perfect swing, the rally-killing double play, the flawless execution of the hit-and-run, a well-pitched ball game, the high-hard one that makes a loud sound in the catcher's glove, followed by the roar of the crowd, a father and son playing catch, the umpire calls, "Play ball!" and the crowd roars.

While it would be most harmful to the game, C.W. Nevius wrote, "This could be only the beginning of an era of power hitting the game has never seen. For the third year in a row, at least two players have hit more than 50 home runs. No fewer than eight players had a shot at 50 in the last month of this season." In his explanation of the power surge, Tony LaRussa believes the home run surge is because "Home run hitters are mastering the science of getting elevation on the ball. They know how to hit the ball in the air. That top-hand-off-the-bat extension-type swing generates a lot of power." While it was criticized by some as making singles hitters out of everyone, LaRussa says it helped players who had power increase it."

For baseball to capture the imagination of the public as it once did, major league players need to raise the caliber of play to the level of their exceptional talents. They have a responsibility to learn to play the game more thoroughly, including fielding and base running. As Tim McCarver pointed out, "They owe it to the fans, to themselves, and they owe it to baseball. Fundamentals have to be learned through restatement by managers, coaches, and instructors. Unfortunately, some superstars don't pay much attention to the basics. They think it is more important to have flair and style."

Baseball must stop tinkering with the ball and designing juiced-ball eras, a century-long practice, which has left records almost meaningless. Yet, those who are responsible do it in such a secretive, covert manner. Such acts are surely not in the best interests of the game. And Major League Baseball must finally implement a drug policy, ban performance-enhancing substances and steroids, and enforce it with mandatory drug testing.

Baseball is a big, often brutal business, but as John Feinstein wrote, "It is worth saving and it is worth caring about, even with its myriad of problems." The cherished old game, once and always America's pastime, is too good to go under, despite the assaults of greed, infighting, financial problems, and sheer gall and arrogance among those who think they own it. If anyone owns it, it is the fans, those who pay for the tickets and much more.

Still, baseball is on the verge of a popularity explosion that it has never experienced before. McCarver wrote, "If you think interleague play was a boon to attendance, wait until international play." Indeed, a World Cup of Baseball has the potential to provide the game with unprecedented appeal and popularity.

"People will always come back to baseball," stated Joe Buck in Fox Sports' presentation following the 1999 MLB All-Star Game. "They think baseball is our pastime, but the game of baseball means so much more. For the better part of the 20th Century, baseball has marvelously marked our time. The faces may change but the game remains constant and perfect. And with the millennium setting summer sun, baseball is ready to take its place into the 21st century and beyond."

"A hundred years from now, the ball will still be thrown from 60 feet, 6 inches, and daylight will always remain 90 feet away. Millions of fans will still be in awe of a wooden bat sending a small leather ball disappearing into the night. And when every summer baseball's greatest stars will come out and shine ever so bright, July will always make shining stars align in perfect symmetry."

"Baseball will always be the great American game," said Buck, "because in baseball, when one king fades in history, another king will rise as history will always repeat. When an iron horse loses his steam, another man of iron will be there to carry on. And when we wonder who will dominate like this lefty once did, another will walk to the top of the hill."

"Baseball will live on well beyond the next century," concluded Buck. "Why? Because baseball is about rebirth and every summer in July we're reminded of our youth as we marvel this year's model called the "Boys of Summer".

The Game will be just fine - - -
if those in baseball will only leave it alone.

Bibliography

Books

Alston, Walter and Don Weiskopf, The Complete Baseball Handbook. Boston: Allyn and Bacon, Inc., 1984.

Alvarez, Mark, The Old Ball Game. Redifinition Press, 1990.

Broeg, Bob, Baseball's Barnum.   Wichita State University: Center for Entrepreneurship, 1989.

Chadwick, Bruce, Baseball's Hometown Teams. New York: Abbeville Press, 1994.

Colgan, Michael, Optimum Sports Nutrition. New York: Advanced Research Press, 1993.

Dickson, Paul, The Dickson Baseball Dictionary. New York: Facts on File, 1989.

Edelman, Rob, Baseball on the Web. New York: MIS:Press, 1998.

Feinstein, John, Play Ball. New York: Villard Books, 1993.

Geist, Bill, Little League Confidential. New York: Del Publishing, 1992.

Helyar, John, Lords of the Realm. New York: Ballantine Books, 1994.

Holtzman, Jerome, The Commissioners. New York: Total Sports, 1998.

Martens, Rainer, Joy and Sadness in Children's Sports. Champaign: Human Kinetics Publishers, 1878.

McCarver, Tim, with Danny Peary, Tim McCarver's Baseball For Brain Surgeons and Other Fans. New York: Villard, 1998.

McIntosh, Ned, Managing Little League Baseball.   Chicago: Contemporary Books, Inc., 1985.

Michener, James, Sport in America. New York: Random House, 1976.

Miller, Jon, Confessions of a Baseball Purist. New York: Simon & Schuster, 1998.

Miller, Marvin, A Whole Different Ball Game. New York: Simon & Schuster, 1991.

Nemec, David, etc., Players of Cooperstown – Baseball's Hall of Fame. Lincolnwood, IL: Publications International, LTD., 1994.

Thorn, John, Baseball: Our Game. New York: Penguin Books, 1995.

Thorn, John and Palmer, Pete, Editors, TOTAL BASEBALL. New York: Harper Collins Publishers, 1993.

Turkin, Hy and Thompson, S.C., The Official Encyclopedia of Baseball. New York: A.S. Barnes and Company, 1951.

Ward, Geoffrey C. and Burns, Ken, Baseball: Who Invented the Game. Alfred A. Knopf, New York, 1994.

Photo Credits:

Associated Press
Central Michigan University
Dickson Baseball Dictionary
Fresno State University
Jasper Herald, Indiana
Illinois, University of (Chicago)
Lake Elsinore Storm
LaPorte High School, Indiana
Liberty University
Libertyville, IL High School
Library of Congress

Major League Baseball
Men's Senior Baseball League
Merriam, Douglas
National Baseball Congress
National Baseball Library (Cooperstown, N.Y.)
Pioneer Press, Suburban Chicago
Pittsburg, CA H.S. (Herc Pardi)
Profile Products, Buffalo Grove, IL
Radford University
San Francisco Giants

Photo Credits, cont.:

Smithsonian Magazine
Sporting News, The
Sports Illustrated
Stallings, John
Thornton, Jerry

Toledo Mudhens
Turface Pro League
United Press International
Wide World
Wildcat Baseball League
(Ft. Wayne, IN)

Magazines/Periodicals:

Baseball America
Baseball Digest
Collegiate Baseball
Fortune
International Rundown
Newsweek

Smithsonian
Sport
Sports Illustrated
Sporting News, The
Time
USA TODAY Baseball Weekly

Newspapers:

Associated Press
Baltimore Sun
Boston Globe
Chicago Sun Times
Chicago Tribune
Christian Science Monitor
Cleveland Plain-Dealer
Denver Post
Detroit Free Press
Evansville Press (Ind.)
Houston Free Press
Jasper Herald (Ind.)
Kansas City Star

Lakeland (Grayslake, IL)
Los Angeles Times
Milwaukee Journal
Morris News Service
New York Daily News
New York Times
Oakland Tribune
Sacramento Bee
San Francisco Chronicle
San Francisco Examiner
St. Louis Post-Dispatch
USA TODAY
Washington Post

Television/Radio:

Brando, Tim (CBS)
Buck, Joe (Fox)
Burns, Ken (PBS)
Costas, Bob (NBC)
Cuoma, Mario (PBS)
Gammons, Peter (ESPN)
Harwell, Ernie (Detroit Tigers)
Jennings, Peter (ABC)
Keown, Tim (ESPN Magazine)

King, Larry (CNN)
McAdam, Sean (ESPN Sports)
McCarver, Tim (Fox)
McDonough, Sean (CBS Sports)
Miller, Jon (ESPN/Giants)
Morgan, Joe (ESPN/NBC)
Scully, Vin (Dodgers)
Simon, Bob (60 Minutes)
Wallace, Mike (60 Minutes)

Index

450

452

www.baseballplayamerica.com

Established to promote and protect the best interests of baseball and to help implement and support the goals and objectives of A PLAN FOR BASEBALL. The primary mission of Baseball Play America is to upgrade the quality of play on all levels of organized baseball.

Baseball Play America

-- Featuring BPA's philosophical concept, the book, and the nation-wide movement.

A Plan for Baseball

-- Represents a game plan for the entire sport, with recommendations and solutions.

Baseball Fans

-- Baseball fans must unite to receive a stronger voice.

Playground Baseball

-- Children today need a safe and secure place to play sandlot baseball again.

Memberships

-- Join our memberships described on next page.

Levels of Play

Major emphasis will be given to:

Major League
Minor League
USA/International
College/University
Non-Pro/Adult
High School
Youth Baseball

<   Making fans part of baseball's equation
<   Stopping the exodus of small-town teams
<   Developing a stronger player development
<   Narrow competitive disparities between teams
<   Revive and expand non/semi-pro baseball
<   Help prep game achieve a higher profile
<   Reform youth leagues; return playground ball

P.O. Box 4182, El Dorado Hills, CA 95762 Tel: 916/933-7459 Fax: 916/933-7447
E-mail: donweiskopf@worldnet.att.net

Visit Our Web Site:
www.baseballplayamerica.com

Membership Benefits

Baseball Play America
Members will receive:

- Quarterly newsletter consisting of BPA concerns
- Official report of A Plan for Baseball
- Membership card
- Access to BPA's web site (news releases, surveys, photos from author's photo gallery, downloading or requesting prints, etc.)
- Discounts, such as books, memorabilia, tapes, etc.

Annual dues of $36.00 will provide membership in both BPA and its subsidiary, Playground Baseball America.

Playground Baseball America
Members will receive:

- Program organization booklet (sample schedules, how-to instruction, favorite pick-up games, check lists, funding sources, etc.)
- Web site access to PBA information, progress reports, downloading sequence photos of basic fundamental skills, etc.
- Free membership in Baseball Play America

Baseball Play America To order, send check or moneyorder payable to: Weiskopf Enterprises, P.O. Box 4182, El Dorado Hills, CA 95762-0014

Cost: $36.00/year

Name _____

Address _____

City _____ State _____ Zip _____

Charge to: _____Visa _____MC _____American Express

Card #:_____ Exp: _____ Phone #:_____

Signature: _____